SERIES
IN
HUMAN
RESOURCE
DEVELOPMENT

SERIES
IN
HUMAN
RESOURCE
DEVELOPMENT

THE 1984 ANNUAL: DEVELOPING HUMAN RESOURCES

(The Thirteenth Annual)

Editors

J. WILLIAM PFEIFFER, Ph.D.

and

LEONARD D. GOODSTEIN, Ph.D.

UNIVERSITY ASSOCIATES, INC.
8517 Production Avenue
San Diego, California 92121

Looseleaf ISBN: 0-88390-009-2
Paperbound ISBN: 0-88390-010-6

Library of Congress Catalog Card Number 73-92841

Printed in the United States of America

Published by
University Associates, Inc.
8517 Production Avenue
San Diego, California 92121
619-578-5900

University Associates of Canada
4190 Fairview Street
Burlington, Ontario L7L 4Y8
Canada

University Associates International, Ltd.
Challenge House
45/47 Victoria Street
Mansfield, Notts NG18 5SU
England

University Associates

PREFACE

Readers will note several major changes in this volume of the *Annual*. First and most obvious is the change in the title, the third change in its thirteen-year history. The *Annual* began in 1972 as a volume for group facilitators, reflecting both the nomenclature and the culture of that time. In 1982, the title was changed to include trainers and consultants, reflecting the changes in focus (and titles) in the field, from human relations to human resources. Within the last four years, however, there has been an incredibly rapid expansion and integration of the human resources field—a trend that we believe will continue. (Our article elsewhere in this volume describes and comments on these developments.) Given this integration, we made the decision to again change the title of the *Annual* to reflect the newly expanded arena of human resource development.

From the beginning, one of the central aims of the *Annual* has been to keep our readers abreast of the current developments in the field. To achieve this, the contents of the *Annuals* have been selected and edited to reflect these shifting trends. We now perceive an integration of human resource functions in most organizations and a heightened awareness of the importance of these resources in assessing the long-term strategy of organizations. If our editorial decisions can help to advance the progress of this trend, we will have no regrets.

Faithful readers of the *Annual* series also will recognize another important change, the elimination of the Lecturette, Theory and Practice, and Resources sections as separate entities. Through the years, the distinction between these categories has become blurred, so these three sections are now integrated into one Professional Development Section. This allows us greater flexibility in selection and permits us to better track what we see occurring in the field. There is no reduction in the total size of the *Annual*.

From now on, Lecturettes (conceptual materials for human resource professionals to present to clients or participants in either verbal or written form) will include clear indications of the context and settings in which they have been or can be used. Similarly, those articles previously included in the Resources section—bibliographies, research reviews, lists of potential resources, and so on—will state the importance and potential use of these materials.

In the Instrumentation Section, we intend to continue to publish useful measurement devices of practical utility for trainers and consultants; however, we will now include both the theoretical background and practical suggestions for application for each instrument. This should make the Instrumentation Section of even greater value to our readers. Those persons who intend to submit instruments or other materials for consideration for future editions of the *Annual* should take these new standards into account.

There are several aspects of the *Annual* series that will not change. One is our bias that the *Annual* be user oriented. Everything in the *Annual* is designed to be potentially useful to our readers. We believe that our readers are the professional cadre of the human resources field— trainers, consultants, and facilitators. Thus, the content of the *Annual* will continue to focus on increasing the professional competence of our readers and, therefore, their impact on the organizational world. To further this objective, we continue to allow users to duplicate and modify materials from the *Annuals* for educational and training purposes, so long as the credit statement found on the copyright page of the volume is used. However, if University Associates materials are to be reproduced in publications for sale or are intended for large-scale distribution (more than one hundred copies in twelve months), *prior written permission* is required. Also, if a footnote indicates that material is copyrighted by some source other than University Associates, no reproduction is allowed without written permission of the actual copyright holder.

We continue to solicit materials from our readers, especially material with a clear organizational focus. The success of the *Annual* as a clearing house for human resource professionals depends on the continual flow of materials from our readers. We encourage the submission of structured experiences, instruments, and articles, including both innovative methods and tried-and-true procedures. The continued sharing of these materials is one important aspect of our professional development.

We want to express our heartfelt appreciation to the several people who have worked with us to bring this *Annual* into creation: Rebecca Taff, managing editor; Arlette C. Ballew, senior editor; Carol Nolde, staff editor; and Lori Barbano, staff artist. As always, we express our deep gratitude to our authors—our peers and colleagues—for sharing with all of us their ideas, materials, and techniques.

J. William Pfeiffer

Leonard D. Goodstein

San Diego, California
December, 1983

About University Associates

University Associates is engaged in publishing, training, and consulting in the broad field of human resource development. UA has earned an international reputation as the source of practical publications that are immediately useful to today's facilitators, trainers, and consultants. A distinct advantage of these publications is that they are designed by practicing professionals who are continually experimenting with new techniques. Thus, UA readers benefit from the fresh but thoughtful approach that underlies UA's experientially based materials, resources, books, workbooks, instruments, and tape-assisted learning programs. These materials are designed for the HRD practitioner who wants access to a broad range of training and intervention technologies as well as background in the field.

UA's practical, applied, theory-based approach is evident in its training and consulting activities as well. Its experienced trainers and consultants conduct training programs in both the public and private sectors, train trainers, and consult with organizations and communities to solve human and organizational problems. Activities include workshops on fundamental and current topics in human resource development and organization development, as well as workshops that are customized to meet specific client needs. In addition, professional certification is offered by the UA Graduate School through its intern program in laboratory education and its master's degree in human resource development.

The wide audience that UA serves includes training and development professionals, internal and external consultants, managers and supervisors, and those in the helping professions. For its clients and customers, University Associates offers a practical approach aimed at increasing people's effectiveness on an individual, group, and organizational basis.

TABLE OF CONTENTS

Preface   v

General Introduction to the 1984 *Annual*   1

STRUCTURED EXPERIENCES

Introduction to the Structured Experiences Section   3

Structured Experience Categories   5

*365. Inquiries and Discoveries: Managing Interviewing Situations   9

366. The Seven Pieces: Identifying Group Roles   16

367. MACE: Demonstrating Factors that Affect Performance   22

368. Role Power: Understanding Influence   26

369. Follow the Leader: An Introduction to Situational Leadership™   38

370. QC Agenda: Collaborative Problem Identification   44

371. Constructive Discipline: Following Organizational Guidelines   49

372. The Shoe-Distribution Company: Exploring the Impact
      of Organizational Roles   55

373. Threats to the Project: A Team-Building Activity   62

374. Trouble in Manufacturing: Managing Interpersonal Conflict   67

375. Datatrak: Dealing with Organizational Conflict   74

376. Group Savings Bank: An Introductory Experience   92

INSTRUMENTATION

Introduction to the Instrumentation Section   97

The Concept of Learning Style: *Ronne Toker Jacobs* and
Barbara Schneider Fuhrmann   99

Exploring Supportive and Defensive Communication Climates:
James I. Costigan and *Martha A. Schmeidler*   112

Interpersonal Styles: The SPIRO Instrument: *Udai Pareek*   119

Quality of Work Life-Conditions/Feelings (QWL-C/F):
Marshall Sashkin and *Joseph J. Lengermann*   131

A Bibliography of Applications of the Myers-Briggs Type Indicator (MBTI)
to Management and Organizational Behavior: *John A. Sample*   145

PROFESSIONAL DEVELOPMENT

Introduction to the Professional Development Section   153

Human Resource Development: Current Status and Future Directions:
Leonard D. Goodstein and *J. William Pfeiffer*   155

---

*See Structured Experience Categories, p. 5, for an explanation of numbering.

Line Managers and Human Resource Development: *Udai Pareek*
and *T. Venkateswara Rao*   161

OD with a Management Perspective: *John C. Lewis*   168

Organizational Use of the Behavioral Sciences: The Improbable Task:
Warren Bennis   176

Organization Development and Power: *Willem F.G. Mastenbroek*   188

Needs Assessment: Avoiding the "Hammer" Approach: *Joe Thomas*   195

An Organization Development (OD) Primer: *Leonard D. Goodstein*
and *Phyliss Cooke*   207

Sociotechnical Systems Thinking in Management Consulting:
A Holistic Concept for Organization Development: *Arthur Zobrist*
and *Robert E. Enggist*   216

A Guide to Participative Management: *Marshall Sashkin*   227

The Transformational Manager: Facilitating the Flow State:
Linda S. Ackerman   242

The Expectancy Theory of Motivation: Implications for Training
and Development: *John A. Sample*   257

Interpersonal Feedback: Problems and Reconceptualization:
Raymond V. Rasmussen   262

Neurolinguistic Programming: A Resource Guide and Review
of the Research: *Donald William McCormick*   267

Encouraging Managers To Deal with Marginal Employees:
J. William Pfeiffer   282

Contributors   289

GENERAL INTRODUCTION TO THE 1984 ANNUAL

The 1984 Annual: Developing Human Resources, a collection of practical and useful materials for human resource development professionals, is the thirteenth in the series. Not only does this volume have a different title than its predecessors, but its format is different as well. There are now only three rather than five sections: Structured Experiences, Instruments, and Professional Development. The new Professional Development section combines the Lecturettes, Theory and Practice, and Resources sections that appeared in the first twelve volumes in this series. Over the years, some of the distinction among these three categories has become blurred, and it seemed that some of the materials would be of more use elsewhere. Therefore, readers will now find a lecturette that is related to a particular structured experience incorporated within that structured experience. Similarly, a resource piece related to a particular instrument is now found within the Instrumentation section. We hope that this new arrangement will both relate the published pieces more logically and also allow us more flexibility in meeting our readers' needs and interests.

One aspect of the series has not changed in this thirteenth volume of the *Annual*: quality of content. As always, materials have been chosen for their quality of conceptualization, applicability to real-world concerns, relevance to today's practitioners, clarity of writing, and ability to provide readers with assistance in being a more effective professional.

This year, among the twelve structured experiences, readers will find a greater focus on internal organizational issues. With the growing number of organizational HRD practitioners and trainers among the readers of the *Annual*, it seemed appropriate to include more structured experiences with direct organizational relevance, ones that could be used with ongoing work groups. The first structured experience builds skill in managing interviewing situations; the next three deal with various group characteristics such as roles, motivation, and leadership; the fifth examines group task behavior; and the next three provide experience in awareness/diagnosis within organizations by focusing on specific organizational issues such as discipline, roles, and the use of power and influence. The ninth, tenth, and eleventh structured experiences also deal with organizational concerns: team building and conflict management. The final selection is a "getting acquainted" experience designed to facilitate the learning program that follows it. Whereas the introductory structured experiences—"ice breakers," "getting acquainted," etc.—used to be found at the beginning of the Structured Experiences section (to indicate their simplicity of presentation and processing), they—as all structured experiences— now will be found in the order dictated by the categorization scheme of our *Structured Experience Kit* and *The Reference Guide to Handbooks and Annuals*. Again, we believe that this will ultimately prove to be more logical and easier for our readers, especially those who use the structured experiences in their work.

The Instrumentation section contains four new paper-and-pencil instruments and one comprehensive bibliography on a popular, commercially published instrument. The four new instruments will enable the reader to measure the learning styles of trainers and trainees and compare them for adequacy of fit, measure the defensiveness-supportiveness of the interpersonal climate in an organization, assess the interpersonal styles used by persons in supervisory and managerial roles, and tap the attitudes of employees concerning the work-life conditions in an organization. As always, these instruments are intended for training, consulting, and practical use rather than for research or clinical application. Finally, the comprehensive bibliography brings together the wide-ranging literature on the Myers-Briggs Type Indicator, an instrument that is widely used in training and development. Readers who use the Myers-Briggs will find this up-to-date listing useful in identifying important references; those readers who have not used the instrument will find some applications that might arouse their interest in learning more about this approach to understanding human behavior.

The Professional Development section is intended to assist readers of the *Annual* in their own professional development. The fourteen articles cover a broad range of issues that confront the human resource development field, including the current status of and future developments in the field, the role of line managers in human resource development, the necessity for having a management perspective in organization development, the difficulties in applying the behavioral sciences in organizational life, how to carry out an effective training-and-development needs assessment, how to explain organization development to managers, the importance of power issues in organization development, the importance of applying sociotechnical concepts in organization development, an in-depth analysis of participative management, the need to manage energy and transformation in organizational life, the expectancy theory of motivation, a reconceptualization of interpersonal feedback, a research overview and bibliography of neurolinguistic programming, and how consultants can help managers to deal with marginal employees. This is indeed a rich mix.

The observant reader will note several concurrent and interrelated themes running through this year's Professional Development section. These include a strong tendency toward a total-systems overview, toward seeing the training and development function as one system within the organization and the organization as a system within the environmental system. Furthermore, the interrelatedness of systems implies that the organization must manage human as well as physical resources in an integrated fashion and that change and transitions are a natural part of the organizational system and all other systems. This perspective puts increased pressure on training and development professionals to fully enter into the management culture of the organization and to become full stakeholders in the management function. The systems orientation also requires a new kind of management, one that is more strategic in its approach and more proactive than reactive.

Many of these changes have come about because of the growing awareness of the problems in American productivity and the perceived superiority of the Japanese managerial system. Serious questions have been raised about traditional organizational practices, especially the management of people, as a result of this awareness. Managers are now much more willing to see the importance of organizational culture, of the formal and informal socioemotional and cultural influences on how work is done, and the impact that these influences have on motivation, morale, and productivity in an organization. As a consequence, human resource development must involve an integration of training, personnel, and organization development with a concern for strategic planning and productivity. The human resource system must link performance with the organization's reward and control systems. Reading these articles makes it clear that a new kind of *accountable humanism* has become the watchword of the 1980s.

The editors continue to be pleased with the quality of the materials submitted to the *Annual* for publication. But, just as the *Annual* cannot accept every piece that is submitted, readers may not find every published piece to be equally useful. We actively seek feedback from our readers in order to do a better job of selecting pieces that meet their needs.

INTRODUCTION TO THE
STRUCTURED EXPERIENCES SECTION

It is our impression that experiential learning, most notably the use of structured experiences, has gained wider acceptance in organizations in recent years. To encourage that trend, and also to balance the contents of the thirteen *Annuals*, we have selected several structured experiences this year that deal with organizational issues and concerns. The first selection, "Inquiries and Discoveries," offers managers and other participants an opportunity to learn effective ways of handling difficult respondents in an interview situation and introduces the concept of "behavioral" interviewing. Following this trend toward using a structured experience to illustrate a basic theory or technique, "Follow the Leader" presents an introduction to Paul Hersey's theory of Situational Leadership™ and points out the different types of leadership style that may be employed. This activity allows participants to explore the effects of four distinct leadership styles on the motivation of group members as they complete assigned tasks.

"QC Agenda" introduces the process by which quality circles identify and select work-related problems to be solved. It also allows participants to practice this process and to experience the advantages and disadvantages of collaborative efforts. Another activity, "Threats to the Project," offers members of intact work groups an opportunity to work together to analyze and resolve sample problems and thereby enhance their effectiveness as team members. "Constructive Discipline" addresses a subject of concern to all managerial and nonmanagerial personnel: the administration of disciplinary measures in response to employee misconduct. This activity provides an opportunity for the participants to apply disciplinary guidelines in order to analyze several sample situations of misconduct. By completing the analysis, the participants become aware of the complexity of disciplinary issues.

Two structured experiences, "The Shoe-Distribution Company" and "Role Power," explore group power dynamics and deal with the impact and interplay of organizational roles. Two others, "Trouble in Manufacturing" and "Datatrak," address the complex issue of conflict and its management or resolution within an organization. "MACE" not only demonstrates but also allows participants to experience the factors that affect individual performance within a group: motivation, ability, conditions, and expectations. "The Seven Pieces" builds participants' awareness of the roles assumed by group members as they complete tasks.

Finally, "Group Savings Bank" offers participants an opportunity to become acquainted with one another and to experiment with abandoning characteristic qualities and behaviors and adopting new ones. This is an example of an introductory activity that may provide a worthwhile experience but is primarily intended to facilitate the learning process by building norms of openness, encouraging interaction, increasing trust, or clarifying expectations for the participant group.

Readers of past *Annuals*, and those familiar with other University Associates publications, will note that the structured experiences are presented in an order that reflects their classification into categories, according to their focus and intent. A listing of these classifications can be found immediately following this introduction, and an explanation of the categorization scheme can be found in the "User's Guide" to the *Structured Experience Kit*, in the discussion beginning on page 37 of the *Reference Guide to Handbooks and Annuals* (1983 Edition), and in the "Introduction to the Structured Experiences Section" of the 1981 *Annual*.

Similarly, it would be redundant to print here a caveat for the use of structured experiences, but practitioners who are not experienced in using this training technology are strongly urged to read the "Introduction to the Structured Experiences Section" in the 1980 *Annual* or the "Introduction" to the *Reference Guide to Handbooks and Annuals* (1983 Edition). Both of these articles present the theory behind the experiential learning cycle and explain the necessity of adequately completing each phase of the cycle in order to permit effective learning to occur.

STRUCTURED EXPERIENCE CATEGORIES

Numbers of Structured Experiences		Numbers of Structured Experiences	
1-24	Volume I, Handbook	197-220	Volume VI, Handbook
25-48	Volume II, Handbook	221-232	1978 Annual
49-74	Volume III, Handbook	233-244	1979 Annual
75-86	1972 Annual	245-268	Volume VII, Handbook
87-100	1973 Annual	269-280	1980 Annual
101-124	Volume IV, Handbook	281-292	1981 Annual
125-136	1974 Annual	293-316	Volume VIII, Handbook
137-148	1975 Annual	317-328	1982 Annual
149-172	Volume V, Handbook	329-340	1983 Annual
173-184	1976 Annual	341-364	Volume IX, Handbook
185-196	1977 Annual	365-376	1984 Annual

PERSONAL   *Vol.-Page*

Self-Disclosure
Fantasies (16)   I-75
Graphics (20)   I-88

Sensory
Awareness Expansion (19)   I-86
Lemons (71)   III-94
Relaxation & Perceptual
  Awareness (136)   '74-84
T'ai Chi Chuan (199)   VI-10

Feelings Awareness
Feelings & Defenses (56)   III-31
Think-Feel (65)   III-70
Frustrations &
  Tensions (75)   '72-5
Group Exploration (119)   IV-92
Expressing Anger (122)   IV-104
Projections (300)   VIII-30
Feelings (330)   '83-14

Feedback
Johari Window (13)   I-65
Analyzing & Increasing
  Open Behavior (99)   '73-38
Coins (23)   I-104
Peer Perceptions (58)   III-41
Puzzlement (97)   '73-30
The Portrait Game (107)   IV-24
Stretching (123)   IV-107
Payday (146)   '75-54
Adjectives (168)   V-114
Person Perception (170)   V-131
Choose an Object (198)   VI-7
Introspection (209)   VI-57
Affirmation of Trust (216)   VI-110
Cards (225)   '78-34
Developing Trust (303)   VIII-45
Giving and Receiving
  Feedback (315)   VIII-125

Assumptions
Sherlock (213)   VI-92
Young/Old Woman (227)   '78-40
Pygmalion (229)   '78-51
Prejudice (247)   VII-15
Managerial
  Characteristics (273)   '80-31
Data Survey (292)   '81-57
Sexism in
  Advertisements (305)   VIII-58
Manager's Dilemma (331)   '83-19

Values Clarification
Ideal Cards (143)   '75-43
Wants Bombardment (261)   VII-105
Banners (233)   '79-9
Louisa's Problem (283)   '81-13
Lifeline (298)   VIII-21
Introjection (321)   '82-29

Life/Career Planning
Life Planning (46)   II-101

                                                          Vol.-Page
What Do You See? (137)   '75-7
Career Renewal (332)   '83-27

COMMUNICATION

**Communication Awareness Experiments
(Oral)**
One-Way, Two-Way (4)   I-13
Rumor Clinic (28)   II-12
Ball Game (108)   IV-27
Dominoes (202)   VI-21
Blivet (241)   '79-46
Meanings Are in
  People (250)   VII-28
Mixed Messages (251)   VII-34
Re-Owning (128)   '74-18
Maze (307)   VIII-64
Resistance (309)   VIII-75
Organizational TA (310)   VIII-83

**Communication Awareness Experiments
(Nonverbal)**
Nonverbal
  Communication I (22)   I-101
Nonverbal
  Communication II (44)   II-94
Nonverbal
  Communication III (72)   III-97
Behavior Description
  Triads (50)   III-6
Gestures (286)   '81-28

**Communication Awareness Experiments
(Oral/Nonverbal)**
Babel (153)   V-16
Blindfolds (175)   '76-13

Developing Interpersonal Trust in Dyads
Dyadic Encounter (21)   I-90
Intimacy Program (70)   III-89
Dialog (116)   IV-66
Dyadic Renewal (169)   V-116
Disclosing &
  Predicting (180)   '76-46
Letter Exchange (190)   '77-28
Dyadic Risk Taking (220)   VI-130
Conflict Management (242)   '79-54
Physical
  Characteristics (262)   VII-108
Party Conversations:
  FIRO (138)   '75-10

Sexual Awareness
Sexual Assessment (226)   '78-36
Sexual Values (249)   VII-24
Sexual Attraction (272)   '80-26

Listening
Listening Triads (8)   I-31
Not Listening (52)   III-10
Helping Relationships (152)   V-13
Defensive & Supportive
  Communication (238)   '79-28
Active Listening (252)   VII-39
Sunglow (257)   VII-73

                                                          Vol.-Page
Interviewing
Live Case (142)   '75-40
Assistant Wanted (333)   '83-31
Inquiries and Discoveries (365)   '84-9

Assertion
Conflict Fantasy (130)   '74-22
Boasting (181)   '76-49
Submission/
  Aggression/Assertion (206)   VI-36
Escalation (219)   VI-127
Praise (306)   VIII-61

GROUP CHARACTERISTICS

Process Observation/Awareness
Group Tasks (29)   II-16
Cog's Ladder (126)   '74-8
Group-on-Group (6)   I-22
Process Observation (10)   I-45
Self-Interaction-Task (37)   II-68
Group Development (39)   II-76
What to Look for
  in Groups (79)   '72-19
The In-Group (124)   IV-112
Slogans (276)   '80-51
Committee Meeting (9)   I-36
Baseball Game (270)   '80-14
Team Development:
  TORI (208)   VI-54
Stones, Bands,
  & Circle (254)   VII-53
Group Identity (299)   VIII-25
The Seven Pieces (366)   '84-16
MACE (367)   '84-22

Leadership-Membership/Power
Line-Up & Power
  Inversion (59)   III-46
Toothpicks (121)   IV-99
Cups (167)   V-111
Power Personalities (266)   VII-127
Power & Affiliation (277)   '80-54
Role Power (368)   '84-26

Leadership-Membership/Styles
T-P Leadership
  Questionnaire (3)   I-7
Styles of Leadership (154)   V-19
Pins & Straws (162)   V-78
Staff Meeting (207)   VI-39
Choosing an
  Apartment (274)   '80-37
Boss Wanted (296)   VIII-15
Follow the Leader (369)   '84-38

Leadership-Membership/Motivation
Dividing the Loot (60)   III-49
Motivation: A
  Feedback Exercise (100)   '73-43
Fork-Labyrinth (159)   V-53

Vol.-Page

Motivation: A
Supervisory-Skill Activity (204) VI-28
Penny Pitch (253) VII-46
Leadership-Membership/Effect on Groups
Auction (35) II-58
Status-Interaction
Study (41) II-85
Package Tour (192) '77-35
Executive Pie (195) '77-54
Race from
Outer Space (239) '79-38
Project Colossus (288) '81-43
Dynasell (290) '81-50

Communication

Organization Structures (110) IV-34
Faculty Meeting (139) '75-15

Values Clarification/Stereotyping

Traditional American
Values (94) '73-23
Growth Group Values (113) IV-45
Kidney Machine (135) '74-78
Who Gets Hired? (215) VI-106
Sex-Role Attitudes (258) VII-85
Polarization (62) III-57
Discrimination (63) III-62
Sex-Role Stereotyping (95) '73-26
Sex-Role Attributes (184) '76-63
Leadership
Characteristics (127) '74-13
Headbands (203) VI-25
Who Killed John Doe? (235) '79-15
Alpha II (248) VII-19
Four Cultures (338) '83-72

GROUP TASK BEHAVIOR
Problem Solving/Awareness

System Problems (111) VI-38
Broken Squares (7) I-25
Numbers (221) '78-9
Shoe Store (102) IV-5
Joe Doodlebug (103) IV-8
Hung Jury (134) '74-64
Word-Letter (200) VI-15
Puzzle Cards (240) '79-41
Island Commission (260) VII-99
Analytical or Creative? (285) '81-24
Four-Letter Words (287) '81-34
Vacation Schedule (312) VIII-100
Tangram (313) VIII-108
Pebbles (335) '83-45
The Lawn (337) '83-65

Generating Alternatives

Brainstorming (53) III-14
Quaker Meeting (76) '72-11
Nominal Group
Technique (141) '75-35
Poems (185) '77-13
QC Agenda (370) '84-44

Group Feedback

Team-Building (66) III-73
Twenty-Five
Questions (118) IV-88
Leveling (17) I-79
Dependency-Intimacy (18) I-82
Role Nominations (38) II-72
Nominations (57) III-33
Psychomat (84) '72-58
The Gift of Happiness (104) IV-15
I Hear That You . . . (291) '81-54
Group Sociogram (316) VIII-131
The Car (326) '82-55

Competition (Win-Lose)

Model-Building (32) II-29

Vol.-Page

Towers (54) III-17
Intergroup
Model-Building (81) '72-36
Wooden Blocks (105) IV-8
Riddles (150) V-5
LEGO Bridge (161) V-73
Darts (210) VI-61
Spy (218) VI-117
Slingshots (256) VII-69
Structures (308) VIII-69
Risk Game (311) VIII-93

Competition and Collaboration
(Win-Lose/Win-Win)

Win as Much as
You Can (36) II-62
Prisoners' Dilemma (61) III-52
Unequal Resources (78) '72-17
Decisions (83) '72-51
World Bank (147) '75-56
Testing (164) V-91
Marbles (165) V-98
X-Y (179) '76-41
Blue/Green (189) '77-24
Circle in the Square (205) VI-32
Balance of Power (231) '78-63
Line of Four (237) '79-21
Al Kohbari (178) '76-26
Murder One (212) VI-75
Monetary Investment (265) VII-124
Paper Box (243) '79-60
Trading Cards (263) VII-112
War Gaming (264) VII-117
Move to Newtown (278) '80-60
Creative Products (279) '80-69
High Iron (280) '80-78
Territory (314) VIII-120

Collaboration (Win-Win)

Lutts & Mipps (31) II-24
Energy International (80) '72-25
Pine County (117) IV-75
Farm E-Z (133) '74-44
Sales Puzzle (155) V-34
Room 703 (156) V-39
Farmers (284) '81-16
Cross-Group Negotiation
and Cooperation (302) VIII-41
Intertwine (319) '82-20
Block Buster (320) '82-24

Conflict Resolution/Values Polarization

Conflict Resolution (14) I-70
Absentee (158) V-49
Negotiating Differences (217) VI-114
Controversial Issues (224) '78-28
Whom to Choose (267) VII-141
Budget Cutting (323) '82-35

Consensus/Synergy

Top Problems (11) I-49
Choosing a Color (12) I-56
Residence Halls (15) I-72
NORC (30) II-18
Kerner Report (64) III-64
Supervisory Behavior/
Aims of Education (69) III-84
Team Identity (77) '72-13
Consensus-Seeking (115) IV-51
Lost at Sea (140) '75-28
Cash Register (151) V-10
Letter Occurrence/
Health Professions
Prestige (157) V-44
Wilderness Survival (177) '76-19
Pyramids (187) '77-20
Admissions Committee (223) '78-15
Alphabet Names (236) '79-19
Lists (255) VII-57
Values for the 1980s (271) '80-20

Vol.-Page

ORGANIZATIONS
Awareness/Diagnosis

Force-Field Analysis (40) II-79
Organizational Mirror (67) III-78
Wahoo City (73) III-100
Strategies of Changing (98) '73-32
Roxboro Electric Co. (131) '74-24
Tug O'War (188) '77-22
Tri-State (193) '77-39
Greeting Cards (82) '72-44
Coloring Book (163) V-85
Top Secret Contract (194) '77-47
Homesell (228) '78-46
Meetings Audit (325) '83-49
Constructive Discipline (371) '84-49
The Shoe-Distribution
Company (372) '84-55

Team Building

Hollow Square (33) II-32
Intergroup Meeting (68) III-81
Tinkertoy Bridge (160) V-60
MANDOERS (232) '78-71
Agenda Setting (166) V-108
Role Clarification (171) V-136
Intergroup Clearing (289) '81-48
Group Effectiveness (297) VIII-18
Chips (322) '82-31
Work-Group Review (327) '82-60
Threats to the Project (373) '84-62

Decision Making/Action Planning

Planning Recommen-
dations or Action (132) '74-32
What's Important on
My Job? (244) '79-71
Dhabi Fehru: MBO (259) VII-91
Missiles (275) '80-43
When to Delegate (304) VIII-52
Reviewing Objectives
and Strategies (328) '82-65
Robbery (334) '83-40
Vice President's
In-Basket (336) '83-49

Conflict Resolution/Values

Lindell-Billings
Corporation (144) '75-46
Conflict Styles (186) '77-15
Sexual Values in
Organizations (268) VII-146
Organizational
Blasphemies (339) '83-77
Conflict Role Play (340) '83-80
Trouble in Manufacturing (374) '84-67
Datatrak (375) '84-74

Consultation Skills

Hampshire In-Basket (34) II-41
Consulting Triads (183) '76-53
HELPCO (211) VI-66
Willington (230) '78-55

FACILITATING LEARNING
Getting Acquainted

Listening & Inferring (1) I-3
Who Am I? (5) I-19
"Who Am I?" Variations (49) III-3
Getting Acquainted (101) IV-3
Tea Party (245) VII-5
Autographs (269) '80-11
Alliterative Names (281) '81-9
Birth Signs (282) '81-11
Name Tags (293) VIII-5
Learning Exchange (294) VIII-7
People on the Job (295) VIII-10
Rebus Names (317) '82-9
Just the Facts (329) '83-11
Group Savings Bank (376) '84-92

Vol.-Page

Forming Subgroups
Two-Four-Eight (2)   I-5
Jigsaw (27)   II-10
Hum-Dinger (125)   '74-7
Limericks (173)   '76-7
Empty Chair (51)   III-8

Expectations of Learners/Facilitators
Participant-Staff
  Expectations (96)   '73-29
Perception of Task (91)   '73-15
Needs, Expectations,
  and Resources (324)   '82-46

Dealing with Blocks to Learnings
First Names, First
  Impressions (42)   II-88
Peter-Paul (87)   '73-7
The "T" Test (112)   IV-41
Sculpturing (106)   IV-21
Gunnysack (89)   '73-11
Verbal Activities
  Within Groups (43)   II-91
Communication
  Analysis (191)   '77-32
Win What, Lose What? (145)   '75-51
Resistance to Learning (301)   VIII-37

Building Trust
Helping Pairs (45)   II-97
Make Your Own Bag (90)   '73-13
Current Status (196)   '77-57
Dimensions of Trust (120)   IV-96

Building Norms of Openness
Group Conversation (25)   II-3
"Cold" Introductions (88)   '73-9
Labeling (174)   '76-10
Best Friend (197)   VI-3
Building Open &
  Closed Relationships (93)   '73-20
Growth Cards (109)   IV-30
Forced-Choice
  Identity (129)   '74-20
Personal Identity (246)   VII-11

Energizers
Energizers (149)   V-3

Evaluating Learning-Group Process
Personal Journal (74)   III-109
Buttermilk (234)   '79-13
Growth & Name
  Fantasy (85)   '72-59
The Other You (182)   '76-51
Roles Impact Feelings (214)   VI-102
Assumptions About
  Human Relations
  Training (24)   I-107
Group Self-Evaluations (55)   III-22
Medial Feedback (92)   '73-17

Developing Group Facilitator Skills
Miniversity (26)   II-7
Microlab (47)   II-113
Process Intervention (48)   II-115
Group Leadership
  Functions (148)   '75-63
Group Composition (172)   V-139

Closure
Symbolic Closing
  Exercise (86)   '72-61
Closure (114)   IV-49
Symbolic Toast (176)   '76-17
Bread Making (201)   VI-19
Golden Awards (222)   '78-12
Kia Ora (318)   '82-12

365. INQUIRIES AND DISCOVERIES: MANAGING INTERVIEWING SITUATIONS

Goals

    I. To identify effective and ineffective interviewing techniques.

    II. To help the participants to develop skills in conducting interviews with different types of respondents.

Group Size

    Five groups of three or four participants each.

Time Required

    One and one-half to two hours.

Materials

    I. A pencil for each participant.

    II. A clipboard or other portable writing surface for each participant.

    III. Blank paper for each interviewer and each observer.

    IV. A copy of the Inquiries and Discoveries Interviewer Sheet for each interviewer.

    V. One set of Inquiries and Discoveries Role Sheets for the respondents and one set for each observer. (Each respondent receives a different role sheet, but each observer receives all five sheets.)

    VI. A copy of the Inquiries and Discoveries Observer Sheet for each observer.

Physical Setting

    A room in which the groups can conduct separate interviews without disturbing one another. Movable chairs should be provided for the participants.

Process

    I. The activity is introduced as one that involves conducting interviews. The facilitator selects five participants to be interviewers, five to be respondents, and those remaining to be observers. It is explained that after the activity the respondents and the observers will be asked to give feedback to each interviewer on his or her interviewing style and effectiveness.

    II. Each interviewer is given a copy of the interviewer sheet, blank paper, a pencil, and a clipboard or other portable writing surface. Then the interviewers are asked to leave the room for fifteen minutes to read the handout and to consult with one another about how to approach the interviewing process, how to keep the interviews flowing smoothly, and how to cope with any problems that might arise.

III. Pencils and clipboards or other portable writing surfaces are distributed to all remaining participants. The facilitator gives each respondent the appropriate role sheet and each observer a copy of each of the five role sheets. The respondents are asked to read their handouts and to discuss their roles with one another, developing specific behaviors that they might want to use during the interviews. The facilitator clarifies that the respondents may draw from their own work experience in responding to the interviewers, but that they may do so only when such responses do not conflict with their role descriptions.

IV. While the respondents are discussing their roles, the facilitator distributes blank paper and copies of the observer sheet to the observers and asks them to read the handout. Questions are elicited, and the task is clarified as necessary. Then the observers are invited to listen to the respondents' discussion, but not to take part.

V. At the end of the fifteen-minute period allotted to the interviewers, they are asked to return to the room. The facilitator assembles the participants into five groups, each of which consists of one interviewer, one respondent, and one or two observers. Then the interviewers are instructed to begin.

VI. After three minutes the facilitator stops the interviews, instructs each respondent to join a different group, and asks the interviewers to begin again. This process is repeated until each interviewer has interviewed all five respondents. (Twenty minutes.)

VII. The interview process is concluded. The facilitator asks the interviewers and the observers to remain in their groups and instructs the respondents to form a separate group. The observers are asked to share and discuss their observations with the interviewers, and the respondents are asked to discuss the positive and negative aspects of the various interviewing styles that they encountered. (Fifteen minutes.)

VIII. The total group is reconvened. Feedback is elicited from the observers, and the respondents and interviewers are invited to comment on the feedback and to share their perceptions of the activity. (Twenty minutes.)

IX. The facilitator leads a final discussion, eliciting comments on how to manage difficult respondents in a variety of interview situations, such as employment interviews, performance-appraisal sessions, and surveys.

Variations

I. To accommodate more than twenty participants, the facilitator may add extra groups. In this case additional respondent roles should be created.

II. The facilitator may present a lecturette on effective interviewing techniques.

III. The interviewers may be given roles to demonstrate effective and ineffective interviewing approaches.

Similar Structured Experiences: *'75 Annual:* Structured Experience **142**; *'79 Annual:* **238**; *'83 Annual:* **333**; *Volume IX:* **358**.

Lecturette Sources: *'73 Annual:* "Conditions Which Hinder Effective Communication"; *'74 Annual:* "Five Components Contributing to Effective Interpersonal Communications"; *'80 Annual:* "The Four-Communication-Styles Approach"; *'81 Annual:* "Defensive and Supportive Communication."

Submitted by Elizabeth Solender.

Elizabeth Solender *is a manager of human resources with Sun Exploration and Production Company in Dallas, Texas. She holds a master's degree in communication from Purdue University in Lafayette, Indiana, and is presently a lecturer in the Management and Administration School at the University of Texas at Dallas. Her areas of expertise are employee relations, organization development, training, equal employment opportunity, benefits administration, and compensation.*

INQUIRIES AND DISCOVERIES INTERVIEWER SHEET

During this activity you are to conduct five three-minute interviews, each with a different respondent. These interviews will be observed, and at the end of the entire process you will receive feedback regarding your effectiveness as an interviewer.

The following probes[1] should form the basis of each interview. Try to obtain as much information as possible from each respondent and remember to make notes.

1. What were the major obstacles that you had to overcome in your last job? How did you deal with them?

2. Describe how you scheduled your time on an unusually hectic day in your last job. Give a specific example.

3. What would you say is your most creative accomplishment in your last position? Be specific.

4. Almost all work situations require us to interact with some people we dislike. Describe such a situation that you have encountered and explain how you handled it.

5. Give me an example of a time when you had high morale on the job. What caused it?

---

[1]From P.C. Green and D.D. Horgan, *Behavioral Interviewing Leader's Guide*, copyright © 1982, Paul C. Green. Used with permission.

INQUIRIES AND DISCOVERIES ROLE SHEET 1

The Reticent One

During the interview you may make gestures, but say as little as possible. Try to appear confused.

Do not reveal these instructions to any interviewer.

INQUIRIES AND DISCOVERIES ROLE SHEET 2

The Rambler

When responding to an interviewer's questions, try to talk as long as possible. Discuss subjects other than the ones about which you are being questioned. Try to keep the interviewer from interrupting you.

Do not reveal these instructions to any interviewer.

INQUIRIES AND DISCOVERIES ROLE SHEET 3

The Role Reverser

Try to establish control of the interview. Start asking your own questions as soon as possible. (Before the interviews begin, you may want to spend a few minutes thinking of questions that you might ask.)

Do not reveal these instructions to any interviewer.

INQUIRIES AND DISCOVERIES ROLE SHEET 4

The Suspicious One

Act as if you are suspicious of the interviewer's questions and intentions. Question him or her closely concerning who will have access to the information you are providing, the real purpose of the interview, and so forth. Be very negative and untrusting.

Do not reveal these instructions to any interviewer.

INQUIRIES AND DISCOVERIES ROLE SHEET 5

The Amiable One

Be positive throughout the interview; do not say anything negative. Attempt to please the interviewer by being excessively nice and cooperative.

Do not reveal these instructions to any interviewer.

INQUIRIES AND DISCOVERIES OBSERVER SHEET

During this activity you will be assigned to one interviewer. For *each* of the five interviews conducted, you are to observe the interviewer's behavior and make notes on answers to the following questions.

1. How did the interviewer react to the respondent?
2. What did he or she do to try to overcome the problems that arose during the interview?
3. Which of the interviewer's specific comments and gestures were particularly effective?
4. Which comments and gestures were ineffective?

366. THE SEVEN PIECES: IDENTIFYING GROUP ROLES

Goals

    I. To introduce the participants to the roles that emerge in a group.

    II. To provide the participants with an opportunity to experience and assume some of these roles and to observe their impact on the group process.

Group Size

    Three or four groups of five to seven participants each.

Time Required

    Approximately one hour.

Materials

    I. One large, sealed envelope for each group. Inside each envelope are the pieces of a puzzle constructed by the facilitator prior to conducting the activity (see The Seven Pieces Puzzle Directions).

    II. One copy of The Seven Pieces Lecturette on Group Roles for each participant.

Physical Setting

    A room with a table and chairs for each group.

Process

    I. The participants are assembled into three or four groups of five to seven participants each. Each group is seated at a table.

    II. Without discussion or instruction, the facilitator places a large envelope containing puzzle pieces on each group's table. If asked any questions, the facilitator responds, "It's up to your group."

    III. The facilitator observes the groups as they decide what to do with the envelopes and their contents.

    IV. After each group has completed the puzzle, the facilitator distributes copies of the lecturette on group roles and asks the participants to read this handout. Then the members of each group are instructed to identify the roles that emerged as they worked together and the specific members who assumed these roles. The members are further instructed to discuss the impact of these roles on the way in which they approached and completed the task. (Twenty minutes.)

    V. The total group is reconvened for a concluding discussion during which the facilitator asks the following questions:

1. How did you feel when the envelope was placed on your group's table without comment? What thoughts entered your mind?
2. How did your group begin its work? What roles were important at the beginning?
3. What procedure did your group use to complete the puzzle? What roles contributed to this procedure?
4. Which roles were not assumed by any of the members of your group? How did the absence of these roles affect the group process? What might have happened if these roles had been assumed?
5. In your back-home group affiliations, which roles do you fulfill? How do these roles contribute to your feelings about the groups to which you belong?
6. What roles are missing in your back-home groups? How does the absence of these roles affect your feelings about these groups?
7. What new group roles would you like to assume in the future? How might you accomplish this?

Variations

I. The facilitator may announce the goals of the activity and have the groups compete on the basis of time.

II. The facilitator may follow this activity with another that stipulates the roles that the participants are to assume (see Similar Structured Experiences).

Similar Structured Experiences: *Volume I:* Structured Experience 12; *Vol. II:* **38**; *Vol. VI:* **200**; *'80 Annual:* **270**; *'81 Annual:* **287**; *'82 Annual:* **326**.

Suggested Instrument: *Volume I:* "Process Observation Report Form."

Lecturette Sources: *'72 Annual:* "What to Look for in Groups"; *'76 Annual:* "Role Functions in a Group."

Submitted by Nadine J. (Hoffman) Carpenter.

Nadine J. (Hoffman) Carpenter *received a master's degree in social work from the University of Chicago and now resides in Concord, New Hampshire. She specializes in clinical work with individuals, families, and groups in such areas as child abuse and spouse abuse.*

THE SEVEN PIECES PUZZLE DIRECTIONS

Materials Needed

  I. One piece of cardboard for each puzzle, each piece to be 8½ inches by 11 inches.

  II. A pair of scissors.

  III. A felt-tipped marker.

Directions for Constructing Each Puzzle

  I. Cut the cardboard into strips as follows:

    1. Four strips, each 1 inch wide by 7 inches long;

    2. One strip 1 inch wide by 5 inches long;

    3. One strip 1 inch wide by 9 inches long; and

    4. One strip 1 inch wide by 10 inches long.

  II. Using a felt-tipped marker, write words on the strips as illustrated below (one letter or space per square inch, omitting letters as indicated):

    1. 1-inch-by-7-inch strip: A L G E B   A

    2. 1-inch-by-7-inch strip: H   S T O R Y

    3. 1-inch-by-7-inch strip: E N G L I H (vertical)

    4. 1-inch-by-7-inch strip: B I O L O Y (vertical)

    5. 1-inch-by-5-inch strip: M U S I C

    6. 1-inch-by-9-inch strip: C H E M I T R Y (vertical)

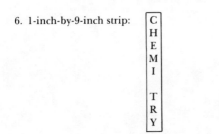

7. 1-inch-by-10-inch strip: P S Y C   O L O G Y

Solution to the Puzzle

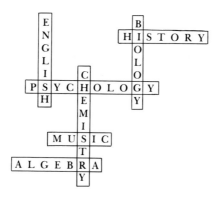

THE SEVEN PIECES LECTURETTE ON GROUP ROLES

Within any group the members assume different roles, several of which have been determined to be necessary for a smoothly functioning, effective group. These roles may be assumed by separate members or shared by various members at different points, and in many cases one or more of the individual members may fulfill more than one role.

Because every group has both *task* and *maintenance* functions, some of the essential roles are task related in that they help a group to accomplish things, and some are maintenance related in that they facilitate the participation of the members.

Task roles include:

- *Initiator:* Proposes tasks, goals, or actions; defines group problems; suggests procedures.
- *Information seeker:* Asks for factual clarification; requests facts pertinent to the discussion.
- *Opinion seeker:* Asks for clarification of the values pertinent to the topic under discussion; questions values involved in the alternative suggestions.
- *Informer:* Offers facts; gives expression of feelings; gives opinions.
- *Clarifier:* Interprets ideas or suggestions; defines terms; clarifies issues before the group; clears up confusion.
- *Summarizer:* Pulls together related ideas; restates suggestions; offers decisions or conclusions for the group to consider.
- *Reality tester:* Makes critical analyses of ideas; tests ideas against data to see if the ideas would work.
- *Orienter:* Defines the position of the group with respect to its goals; points to departures from agreed-on directions or goals; raises questions about the directions pursued in group discussions.
- *Follower:* Goes along with the movement of the group; passively accepts the ideas of others; serves as an audience in group discussion and decision making.

Maintenance roles include:

- *Harmonizer:* Attempts to reconcile disagreements; reduces tension; gets people to explore differences.
- *Gatekeeper:* Helps to keep communication channels open; facilitates the participation of others; suggests procedures that permit sharing remarks.
- *Consensus taker:* Asks to see whether the group is nearing a decision; "sends up trial balloons" to test possible solutions.
- *Encourager:* Is friendly, warm, and responsive to others; indicates by facial expressions or remarks the acceptance of others' contributions.
- *Compromiser:* Offers compromises that yield status when his or her own ideas are involved in conflicts; modifies in the interest of group cohesion or growth.
- *Standard setter:* Expresses standards for the group to attempt to achieve; applies standards in evaluating the quality of group processes.

This lecturette has been adapted from E. Guthrie and W.S. Miller, *Process Politics: A Guide for Group Leaders*, University Associates, 1981. The descriptions of task and maintenance roles originated with and have been adapted with special permission from "What to Observe in a Group," by Edgar H. Schein, from *Reading Book* by Cyril R. Mill and Lawrence C. Porter, Editors, pp. 28-30, copyright 1976 NTL Institute for Applied Behavioral Science.

It can be useful for a group to determine which roles are fulfilled by which members. If certain roles appear to be missing, the members can plan to incorporate the associated behaviors into their group activities. In addition, determining roles allows the members to form a clear perception of their value to the group, and they can consciously build on the behaviors that they naturally exhibit and that are comfortable to them, thereby helping the group to realize its potential.

367. MACE: DEMONSTRATING FACTORS THAT AFFECT PERFORMANCE

Goal

To demonstrate that individual performance within a group is influenced by four major factors: *motivation, ability, conditions,* and *expectations* (MACE).

Group Size

Ten to fifteen dyads.

Time Required

One to one and one-half hours.

Materials

I. Blank paper and a pencil for each participant.

II. A one-dollar bill.

III. A five-dollar bill.

IV. A chalkboard and chalk or a newsprint flip chart and a felt-tipped marker.

Physical Setting

A room with a chair and a writing surface for each participant.

Process

I. The facilitator introduces the activity and begins the first phase:

"To illustrate the main factors that influence performance, we are going to conduct some experiments. During the first of these experiments, do exactly as I say, but do not ask any questions or compare notes with other people."

Each participant is given blank paper and a pencil.

II. To show the effects of unclear *expectations* on performance, the facilitator gives the following instructions:

"I want you to perform a simple clerical task. Listen to the instructions, but do not start until I tell you to do so. Write the letters of the alphabet. For each letter that has a fully enclosed component, place a dot inside that component. For each letter that does not have a fully enclosed component, draw a circle around the entire letter. For example, 'a' and 'e' have fully enclosed components, and you should place a dot inside each of these components."

The facilitator demonstrates by writing the letters on a chalkboard or a newsprint flip chart:

a   e

"On the other hand, 'f' and 'z' do not have fully enclosed components and should, therefore, be circled."

As before, the facilitator demonstrates:

"Your objective in completing this task is to dot and circle as many letters as you can in the allotted time of thirty seconds. When I say 'go,' start working and continue until I tell you to stop. Ready, 'go.' "

III. At the end of the allotted time, the participants are told to stop working. Each participant is asked to exchange papers with the person seated next to him or her. Then the facilitator gives directions for scoring:

"Now score your partner's work. Give one point for each *lower-case* letter that is correctly dotted or circled."

It is explained that those who used upper-case letters are disqualified and that this requirement should have been evident from the examples given. The facilitator asks each participant to state his or her partner's score. As these results are announced, they are recorded on a chalkboard or a newsprint flip chart.

IV. The facilitator leads a discussion to explore various ways in which the instructions were and might have been interpreted. It is emphasized that performance can be influenced dramatically by failure to agree on expectations. The discussion should include the following questions:

1. How did you feel about the instructions that you were given?
2. How did these feelings affect your performance?

(Ten minutes.)

V. To show the effects of *ability* on performance, the facilitator begins the second experiment:

"Let's consider the experiment we just completed to be a practice session. We'll try the same task again. Does everyone now know what is expected?"

After answering any questions that the participants have, the facilitator starts the experiment in the manner indicated in Step II.

VI. After the participants have worked for thirty seconds, the facilitator stops the experiment, asks the participants to trade and score their papers as they did previously, and records the results next to those of the first experiment.

VII. The facilitator leads a discussion of the results, emphasizing the following points:

1. Performance is affected by ability; some people are better than others at specific tasks.
2. There is a range of ability in many groups in both work and nonwork settings.

The following questions should be included in this discussion:

1. How was this experience different from the first one?
2. How do you explain the effect of ability on performance?

(Ten minutes.)

VIII. To show the effects of *motivation* on performance, the facilitator conducts the third experiment:

"Now let's repeat the same task, but change the goal. This time your objective is to exceed your last score. In addition, the person who exceeds his or her previous score by the greatest number of points will win one dollar."

A one-dollar bill is displayed prominently, and the facilitator starts the experiment in the same manner as before.

IX. Step VI is repeated.

X. After awarding the one-dollar prize to the winner, the facilitator leads a discussion. It is emphasized that performance is improved by motivation and that there are many different ways to motivate, such as those used in Step VIII. Questions to be included in this discussion are as follows:

1. How did this experience differ from the previous one?

2. What can you conclude about the effect of motivation on performance?

(Ten minutes.)

XI. To show the effects of changed conditions on performance, the facilitator begins the last experiment:

"Let's try the task once more. This time the person who can most improve his or her performance over the last trial will win five dollars. However, you must complete the task this time with your *nonpreferred hand*."

A five-dollar bill is displayed, and the facilitator starts the experiment.

XII. Step VI is repeated.

XIII. If there is a winner, the facilitator awards the five-dollar prize. Then the following points are emphasized in discussion:

1. Performance depends on the conditions under which a task is performed. With many tasks, the conditions may have a more dramatic effect on people than motivation, ability, or expectations.

2. Factors that may affect performance negatively include rules or regulations as well as the anticipation of failure, which leads to lowered motivation.

The discussion questions should include the following:

1. How did this last experience differ from the previous three?

2. How do you explain the impact of conditions on performance?

XIV. In conclusion, the facilitator elicits answers to the following questions:

1. How can you relate what you have learned about performance to your back-home work group?

2. What can be done to maximize the positive effects of expectations, ability, motivation, and conditions on performance?

3. What can be done to minimize the negative effects?

Variations

I. The facilitator may prefer to conduct all four experiments before leading a discussion on the determinants of performance.

II. The participants may be asked to work in teams rather than individually.

Similar Structured Experiences: *Volume VI:* Structured Experience **204**; *Vol. IX:* **354**.

Suggested Instruments: *'73 Annual:* "Motivation Feedback Opinionnaire"; *'81 Annual:* "Supervisory Behavior Questionnaire."

Lecturette Sources: *'75 Annual:* "Skill Climate and Organizational Blockages"; *'80 Annual:* "Dimensions of Role Efficacy"; *'84 Annual:* "The Expectancy Theory of Motivation."

Submitted by Stephen Dakin and Russell Robb.

Stephen Dakin, Ph.D., *teaches organizational behavior and personnel management in the Department of Business Administration at the University of Canterbury in Christchurch, New Zealand. He specializes in the development of appraisal and assessment systems, and his research interests lie in the area of managerial and supervisory selection.*

Russell Robb *is a management trainer who works with four hospital boards from a base at North Canterbury Hospital Board in Christchurch, New Zealand. His background is in the areas of education and personnel management, and his special interest is organization development.*

368. ROLE POWER:
UNDERSTANDING INFLUENCE

Goals

I. To explore the types of power inherent in different roles in group settings.

II. To acquaint the participants with various power strategies that can be used in a decision-making process.

III. To help the participants to develop an understanding of effective and ineffective uses of power *influence.*

Group Size

Three to five groups of six or seven participants each.

Time Required

Approximately two hours.

Materials

I. A copy of the Role Power Situation Sheet for each participant.

II. A set of Role Power Description Sheets for each group: Each set includes one copy of the role description for each of the following roles:

1. Controller;
2. Director of merchandising;
3. Personnel director;
4. Promotion director; and
5. Operations director.

III. A copy of the Role Power Public-Knowledge Sheet for each participant.

IV. A copy of the Role Power Political-Base Sheet for each participant.

V. A copy of the Role Power Observer Sheet for each observer.

VI. A pencil for each observer.

VII. A clipboard or other portable writing surface for each observer.

Physical Setting

A room that is large enough to allow the groups to work without disturbing one another.

Process

I. The facilitator informs the participants that they are to be involved in a role play and explains the goals of the activity.

II. Each participant is given a copy of the Role Power Situation Sheet and is asked to read this handout. (Five minutes.)

III. The participants are assembled into three or four groups of six or seven each. Within each group the facilitator assigns the following roles and distributes the corresponding role sheets:

1. Controller;
2. Director of merchandising;
3. Personnel director;
4. Promotion director; and
5. Operations director.

Each of the remaining members of each group is designated an observer and is given a copy of the Role Power Observer Sheet, a pencil, and a clipboard or other portable writing surface. The observers are asked to read this sheet and to become familiar with their task while the role players study their roles. (Ten minutes.)

IV. The facilitator distributes copies of the Role Power Public-Knowledge Sheet to all participants and asks them to read this sheet. (Five minutes.)

V. It is explained that the individual groups are to complete the task described in the situation sheet. The facilitator elicits and answers questions about this task, advises the role players that they must maintain their roles during the role play, and then instructs the groups to begin their meetings.

VI. After thirty minutes the facilitator interrupts the groups and gives each participant a copy of the Role Power Political-Base Sheet. The participants are told to read this sheet and then to continue their meetings.

VII. After twenty minutes the participants are told to stop their role plays. It is explained that in each group the observer is to report observations and the other members are to share their reactions to these observations. (Twenty minutes.)

VIII. The facilitator leads a concluding discussion by asking the following questions:

1. How did exercising the power of your role affect your feelings about yourself and the other members of your group? How did it affect your perspective on the situation and your problem-solving behavior?
2. How did the various power roles and strategies affect the outcome in each group?
3. What could you have done differently to use your power more effectively?
4. What can be generalized about the use of power in an organization?
5. How can you use power or your understanding of power more effectively back home?

Variations

I. The political-base sheet may be eliminated.

II. A role sheet may be created for the owner, who either may be present for the entire meeting or may return while the meeting is in progress. If this variation is selected, the situation sheet may need to be altered.

Similar Structured Experiences: *Volume I:* Structured Experience 9; *'77 Annual:* **195**; *Vol. VII:* **266**; *'80 Annual:* **278**; *'82 Annual:* **323**; *Vol. IX:* **346**.

Suggested Instrument: *'79 Annual:* "Power and OD Intervention Analysis (PODIA)."

Lecturette Sources: *'73 Annual:* "Win/Lose Situations"; *'74 Annual:* "Hidden Agendas"; *'76 Annual:* "Power"; *'80 Annual:* "Dealing with Organizational Crises"; *'84 Annual:* "Organization Development and Power."

Submitted by Patrick E. Doyle.

Patrick E. Doyle is a teaching master at St. Lawrence College in Kingston, Ontario, Canada. He is active in the field of human resource development in both the retail and the public administrative sectors of the economy.

ROLE POWER SITUATION SHEET

You are employed by a large chain of retail clothing stores in your city. The company is privately owned, and the owner takes an active part in its management. The most appropriate description of his management style would be that of a benevolent autocrat. It is clearly understood by all employees that he makes the final judgment on any major decision.

In addition, the owner is paternalistic in his approach to dealing with the employees of the organization. This approach seems to have worked thus far; his competitors have been unionized, but his own operation remains without a union.

However, in recent months the performance of the various stores has deteriorated, primarily due to the poor economic condition of the marketplace. A meeting has been called to address this problem, and you have been asked to attend. The owner plans to discuss the areas in which significant cutbacks could be made in the organization.

As the meeting begins, the owner is called away on a personal emergency. He tells the group, "You know why you are here. I won't be back today, but I want you to proceed without me. I'll expect your recommendations on my desk by tomorrow morning."

ROLE POWER DESCRIPTION SHEET: CONTROLLER

The following information is supplied so that you can fulfill your role in the role play. You may use any of this information in any way you wish.

Public Knowledge

You are the individual who is ultimately responsible for controlling and safeguarding the company's financial assets. Although you are not the owner of this large retail operation, it is commonly accepted within the company that you have the final judgment on the acceptance or rejection of any budget or major financial decision.

Private Knowledge

1. You are not convinced that the stores are operating as efficiently as they could. You believe that they still have buffer zones in their budgets, but you are unable to prove this belief.

2. You feel that the current economic environment is going to cause a decrease in sales and an increase in inventory surplus if the organization's original merchandise plans are adhered to. You want to implement a program to cut the inventory allotment.

Your Political Base

Although you have the owner's confidence as well as the authority to legislate changes, you realize that traditionally the merchandising arm of the organization has had significant power to influence the decision-making process. Because of the implied power of the merchandising arm, you are concerned about and want to avoid a direct confrontation during the meeting.

ROLE POWER DESCRIPTION SHEET: DIRECTOR OF MERCHANDISING

The following information is supplied so that you can fulfill your role in the role play. You may use any of this information in any way you wish.

Public Knowledge

As the director of merchandising, you are ultimately responsible for all buying and selling in the organization. You are under constant pressure from your subordinates to increase inventory allotments as well as the wage dollars available to hire salespeople.

Private Knowledge

1. You are beginning to accept the idea that perhaps your subordinates are right. Despite the economic situation, you may have cut back too far on inventory allotments. Even you have noticed that the salespeople in the various stores are becoming discouraged because there is insufficient depth in the merchandise. They complain that when they finally have convinced customers to buy, they cannot find the right sizes or colors of merchandise.
2. The service department is receiving increasing numbers of complaints from customers who have not been able to find salespeople to wait on them.

Your Political Base

Although you are fully aware of the fact that the controller ultimately has power over you, you do not readily accept the situation. You know that the owner has confidence in you and you feel that if it came to a final showdown, he might support you. However, you are not totally sure of this.

You are convinced that in a retail organization the merchandising arm should be the most powerful because merchandising is "where the action is" and where profits are made or lost.

ROLE POWER DESCRIPTION SHEET: PERSONNEL DIRECTOR

The following information is supplied so that you can fulfill your role in the role play. You may use any of this information in any way you wish.

Public Knowledge

You are responsible for the recruitment, employment, and training of all employees. In addition, you are in charge of training future managers of the organization and evaluating their career development. It is also your responsibility to keep the company competitive in wages. Your organization does not have a union, and you do not wish one to gain a foothold.

Private Knowledge

1. You feel that the adverse economic conditions are having negative effects on company morale. For example, several employees have just completed the management-training program and are now ready for supervisory positions, but no positions are available. A new group of trainees is about to begin the program.
2. From your point of view, the real problem lies in the fact that the director of merchandising is not forcing his department managers to practice close enough supervision of their operations. Each of these managers is responsible for the merchandising in one department of one of the stores. Too frequently these managers are away from the sales floors; either they are out of the stores during peak business hours, or they choose to run their departments from their offices.
3. Recently you have put a lot of effort into developing new training packages and evaluation procedures. Just when you were ready to institute these programs, you heard about the possibility of financial cutbacks. To you this means staff cutbacks, and if these occur, you feel that your new programs might never be implemented because you would no longer have the personnel to run them.

Your Political Base

You feel that you have less power than the director of merchandising and the controller. Although the owner listens to you and has confidence in you, you are convinced that in a direct confrontation with the director of merchandising, in particular, you would lose.

Cancellation of your new programs would further erode whatever power you have.

ROLE POWER DESCRIPTION SHEET: PROMOTION DIRECTOR

The following information is supplied so that you can fulfill your role in the role play. You may use any of this information in any way you wish.

Public Knowledge

As the promotion director, you are responsible for advertising, visual merchandising, and the total image that the stores project. The image you are attempting to build for your organization is one of current fashion, with some conservatism; you do not see the organization as a fashion leader, but as a fairly close follower of current trends. You are attempting to attract upper-income individuals as customers.

Private Knowledge

Although the image of a local retailer is determined by many factors, such as the selection of merchandise, it is built primarily on "institutional" advertising (emphasizing the advantages of the facility and its location) as opposed to special promotions of merchandise.

However, institutional advertisements do not generate the immediate sales that special promotions do. As a result you are under constant pressure from the department managers in the individual stores (who are judged on the basis of sales) to direct more and more of your advertising dollars to special promotions.

You remain convinced of the importance of the long-run benefits of institutional advertising. You know that it takes years to build an appropriate image, but very little time to destroy one. However, you also know that when cutbacks come, the pressure will increase to generate sales and to lower inventory levels through a series of "specials." You feel that this approach could seriously damage the company's image and make it look like a massive "bargain basement."

Your Political Base

The owner has confidence in you, and you feel that he is pleased with the company's present image and with your efforts to continue it. But you have very limited access to him and realize that he does not consider you to be on the same level as the controller or the director of merchandising.

You are aware that the employees who work for you are frequently treated as "outsiders" because of the creative nature of their work. It is also obvious that your subordinates are seen as lacking in discipline.

ROLE POWER DESCRIPTION SHEET: OPERATIONS DIRECTOR

The following information is supplied so that you can fulfill your role in the role play. You may use any of this information in any way you wish.

Public Knowledge

You are responsible for all functions not directly related to finance, personnel, and merchandising. This includes such things as store maintenance, workroom maintenance, security, and warehousing.

The most pressing problems you have are the following:

1. *Store Maintenance.* Not only do you have the problems of day-to-day maintenance and emergencies (such as breakdowns of elevators and escalators), but two other sources of difficulty are also bothering you.

- The department managers in the individual stores are moving display units whenever they desire; and
- You are constantly receiving requests either to put up temporary walls to isolate boutiques or to tear down walls to create more space.

2. *Security.* With the onset of adverse economic conditions, shoplifting on the part of both the public and the employees is rapidly increasing. You seem unable to control the situation.

Private Knowledge

Although inflation is running at approximately 11 percent, the inflation rate for equipment and supplies in your area (such as oil) is running closer to 22 percent. You personally believe that unless budget increases are forthcoming, you will not be able to maintain the company trucks and other equipment properly.

Your Political Base

You have a low profile in the organization, but your power base is strong. For one thing, the owner has confidence in you. In addition, some of your power is supplied by external sources, such as safety legislation and fire-prevention regulations. The employees in general are less well acquainted with your area than with others and, therefore, tend to accept your statements as valid. However, your power is restricted in one sense: People in the company accept your word as fact when it pertains to operations, but would be surprised if you ventured opinions on matters outside your area. The power of the others attending the meeting is not restricted in this way; for example, they would feel free to comment on issues involving operations.

ROLE POWER PUBLIC-KNOWLEDGE SHEET

The following information is public knowledge about the people attending this meeting.

Controller

This individual is ultimately responsible for controlling and safeguarding the company's financial assets. Although this person is not the owner of this large retail operation, it is commonly accepted within the company that the controller has the final judgment on the acceptance or rejection of any budget or major financial decision.

Director of Merchandising

The director of merchandising is ultimately responsible for all buying and selling in the organization. This person is under constant pressure from subordinates to increase stock allotments as well as the wage dollars available to hire salespeople.

Personnel Director

This individual is responsible for the recruitment, employment, and training of all employees. In addition, this person is in charge of training future managers of the organization and evaluating their career development. It is also the responsibility of the personnel director to keep the company competitive in wages. The company does not have a union, and this director does not want one to gain a foothold.

Promotion Director

The promotion director is responsible for advertising, visual merchandising, and the total image that the stores project. The image that this person is attempting to build for the organization is one of current fashion, with some conservatism; the promotion director does not see the organization as a fashion leader, but as a fairly close follower of current trends. This individual is attempting to attract upper-income individuals as customers.

Operations Director

This person is responsible for all functions not directly related to finance, personnel, and merchandising. This includes such things as store maintenance, workroom maintenance, security, and warehousing.

The most pressing problems facing the operations director are the following:

1. *Store Maintenance.* Daily maintenance and emergencies are a concern, and two situations are particularly bothersome.

- The department managers in the individual stores are moving display units whenever they desire; and
- The director constantly receives requests either to put up temporary walls to isolate boutiques or to tear down walls to create more space.

2. *Security.* With the onset of adverse economic conditions, shoplifting on the part of both the public and the employees is rapidly increasing. The director seems unable to control the situation.

ROLE POWER POLITICAL-BASE SHEET

The following is information about the political base of each person attending the meeting. The owner of the company has confidence in all of these people.

Controller

The controller has the authority to legislate changes, but realizes that traditionally the merchandising arm of the organization has had significant power to influence the decision-making process. Because of the implied power of the merchandising arm, the controller is concerned about and wants to avoid a direct confrontation during the meeting.

Director of Merchandising

The director of merchandising is fully aware of the fact that the controller ultimately has greater power, but does not readily accept this situation. If it came to a showdown, the director feels (but is not certain) that the owner might side against the controller.

The director is convinced that in a retail organization the merchandising arm should be the most powerful because merchandising is "where the action is" and where profits are made or lost.

Personnel Director

The personnel director feels that both the controller and the director of merchandising have greater power and that in a direct confrontation with the director of merchandising, in particular, the personnel director would definitely lose.

This individual has recently put a lot of effort into developing new training packages and evaluation procedures. Cancellation of these programs would further erode whatever power the personnel director has.

Promotion Director

The promotion director feels that the owner is pleased with the company's present image and with the director's efforts to continue it. However, this person has very limited access to the owner and realizes that the owner does not consider the promotion director to be on the same level as the controller or the director of merchandising.

This individual is aware that the employees who work in the area of promotion are frequently treated as "outsiders" because of the creative nature of their work. It is also obvious to this person that these employees are seen as lacking in discipline.

Operations Director

The operations director has a low profile but a strong power base. Some of this power is supplied by external sources, such as safety legislation and fire-prevention regulations. The employees are less well acquainted with the area of operations than with others and, therefore, tend to accept the director's statements as valid. However, this power is restricted in one sense: People in the company accept the director's word as fact when it pertains to operations, but would be surprised if this person ventured opinions on matters outside this area. The power of the others attending the meeting is not restricted in this way; for example, they would feel free to comment on issues involving operations.

ROLE POWER OBSERVER SHEET

As the role play progresses, watch and listen closely and answer the following questions. Afterward you will be asked to share your answers with your group.

1. How was power demonstrated during the role play?

put influence & persuasion

2. Who seemed to be the most powerful member of the group? What did this person say or do to gain and maintain power?

3. What strategies did each member use to act out his or her power?

4. How effectively was power used to complete the task assigned to the group? How did it hinder the completion of the task?

369. FOLLOW THE LEADER: AN INTRODUCTION TO SITUATIONAL LEADERSHIP™

Goals

I. To allow the participants to experience each of the four leadership styles that constitute the basis of Situational Leadership™ theory.

II. To explore the ways in which leadership styles, tasks, and work groups affect one another.

Group Size

Four groups of four to six participants each.

Time Required

Approximately two and one-half hours.

Materials

I. One copy each of Follow the Leader Task Sheets 1 through 4.

II. Four copies of the Follow the Leader Observer Sheet.

III. One copy of the Follow the Leader Theory Sheet for each participant.

IV. Two complex jigsaw puzzles of at least five hundred pieces each.

V. Two world-map jigsaw puzzles of approximately eighty-five pieces each.

VI. Four dice.

VII. Blank paper and a pencil for each observer.

VIII. A clipboard or other portable writing surface for each observer.

Physical Setting

A room large enough to accommodate five tables with chairs for the participants.

Process

I. After announcing that the participants are to be involved in an activity that deals with leadership, the facilitator assembles the participants into four groups. Each group is given one die and is seated at a table. Within each group each member rolls the die; the member with the high roll becomes the leader, and the member with the low roll becomes the observer.

It is recommended that the facilitator become familiar with Situational Leadership™ theory before conducting this activity. A summary handout and numerous other theory pieces as well as instruments may be obtained from University Associates, Inc., 8517 Production Avenue, San Diego, California 92121, phone 619-578-5900.

II. The four leaders are asked to join the facilitator at a separate table. Materials are distributed in the following manner: Two of the leaders receive Task Sheets 1 and 2, respectively, and one of the complex puzzles; the other two leaders receive Task Sheets 3 and 4, respectively, and one of the world-map puzzles. The facilitator asks the leaders to read their sheets and to discuss their responsibilities quietly until the facilitator returns.

III. The remaining participants within each group are asked to spend the next few minutes discussing various leadership characteristics and behaviors that they admire.

IV. The facilitator returns to the leaders to clarify their responsibilities as necessary. (Ten minutes.)

V. The leaders are asked to return to their groups. Each group's observer is given a copy of the observer sheet, a pencil, and a clipboard or other portable writing surface and is asked to read the sheet and to follow the directions. Then each group leader is instructed to begin the activity.

VI. After twenty-five minutes the facilitator requests that each group stop its work, disassemble its puzzle, and replace the puzzle pieces in the box. The leaders who have Task Sheets 1 and 2 are instructed to exchange puzzles with the leaders who have Task Sheets 3 and 4.

VII. Each observer is given a new copy of the observer sheet, and each leader is asked to begin the activity again, following the same instructions.

VIII. After twenty-five minutes the groups are told to stop their work. Each group is asked to complete the following procedure:

1. The observer reports his or her observations on both phases of the activity;
2. The leader shares the content of his or her task sheet; and
3. All group members discuss the reported observations and their own reactions to both phases of the activity.

(Twenty minutes.)

IX. The total group is reconvened, and each leader is asked to read his or her task sheet aloud.

X. The facilitator leads a discussion of the experience by asking the following questions:

1. As you worked on each puzzle, how confident did you feel about completing the task in the specified time frame?
2. How did you feel about your leader while you worked on the first puzzle? What changes in your feelings did you experience when you switched to the second puzzle?
3. While you worked on each of the two puzzles, did you receive the appropriate amount of direction from your leader?
4. How might the leader have done a better job of helping you to complete each of the two tasks? How does your answer relate to the leader characteristics that you admire?

(Fifteen minutes.)

XI. Copies of the Follow the Leader Theory Sheet are distributed, and the participants are asked to read this handout. (Five minutes.)

XII. The facilitator leads a concluding discussion, relating the activity to the theory sheet and eliciting back-home applications. The following questions may be asked during this discussion:

1. Which leadership style did your leader employ? How did your leader's behavior coincide with the description of this style?

2. Under what circumstances might a subordinate's capacity to complete a task decrease or increase from one occasion to the next? Given Situational Leadership™ theory, how should a leader respond to such decreases and increases?

3. How does Situational Leadership™ compare to the management style used to lead your back-home work group?

4. How might you use Situational Leadership™ theory to improve your own leadership behavior?

Variation

In Step IX the facilitator may substitute copies of the Situational Leadership™ summary handout for the copies of the theory sheet. (See the footnote on the first page of this structured experience for information about purchasing these handouts.)

Similar Structured Experiences: *Volume I:* Structured Experience 3; *Vol. V:* **154**, **162**; *Vol. VI:* **207**.

Suggested Instrument: *'76 Annual:* "Leader Effectiveness and Adaptability Description."

Lecturette Source: *'72 Annual:* "The Maslow Need Hierarchy."

_____

Submitted by Kaaren S. Brown and Donald M. Loppnow.

Kaaren S. Brown *is an assistant professor in the Department of Social Work at Eastern Michigan University in Ypsilanti. She has collaborated on a number of special projects providing technical assistance to child-welfare agencies and to the supervisory staff in various organizations. Her professional background is in mental health, social work in medical settings, and child-welfare services. Supervision is her special area of interest.*

Donald M. Loppnow *is a professor and head of the Department of Social Work at Eastern Michigan University. He is also the director of the University's gerontology program. He has published several articles relating to the foster parenting of teenagers and has directed numerous research and program-development grants, including technical assistance for supervisory-staff projects. Leadership administration is his special professional interest.*

FOLLOW THE LEADER TASK SHEET 1

Each member of your group is to complete the task of assembling a puzzle section of *at least ten pieces*. The individual sections need not be put together.

It is up to you to decide how this task might best be accomplished. After you have determined an approach, you will have twenty-five minutes to explain the task to the members; present your plan; and then supervise the work to completion, using your plan and the picture of the puzzle as a guide. You are the custodian of this picture; although you may show it to individual members, you may not give it to them.

Be sure to clarify the time limit and to remind the members of the remaining time at intervals. If the members suggest alternative approaches, explain that the time constraint makes it impossible to use their input.

FOLLOW THE LEADER TASK SHEET 2

Each member of your group is to complete the task of assembling a puzzle section of *at least ten pieces*. The individual sections need not be put together.

You are to explain this task to the members and to involve all of them in a discussion of how the task might best be accomplished in the allotted time. Once a plan has been developed, it is your responsibility to see that it is carried out by your group. You are to direct the members' work, using the agreed-on plan and the picture of the puzzle as a guide. You are the custodian of this picture; although you may show it to individual members, you may not give it to them.

The type of puzzle you have been given can be quite frustrating to work on. Do your best to make the members feel involved and comfortable.

You and your group have a total of twenty-five minutes to develop and execute the plan. Be sure to clarify this time limit and to remind the members of the remaining time at intervals.

FOLLOW THE LEADER TASK SHEET 3

The members of your group are to spend twenty-five minutes completing the puzzle that you have been given. When you present this task to them, suggest that they plan and organize their efforts. Your job is to facilitate this process by encouraging the members, making them feel involved and comfortable, and praising them as they develop and execute their plan. However, you are not to be directive.

You are the custodian of the picture of the completed puzzle. Although you may not give this picture to the group, you may show it to individual members when they inquire about it.

FOLLOW THE LEADER TASK SHEET 4

The members of your group are to complete the puzzle in the allotted twenty-five-minute period. Be nondirective and allow them to formulate their own approach to this task; do not get in their way. Your sole responsibility is to explain the task and the time parameters clearly. Once the members understand what has to be done, give them the puzzle, find something else to do, and make yourself inaccessible to them.

FOLLOW THE LEADER OBSERVER SHEET

As your group works on its assigned task, observe the process and make notes about answers to the following questions. Later you will be asked to report your answers to your own group and then to the total group.

1. Which of the following leadership behaviors did the leader demonstrate and to what degree?
   - *Directive behaviors* (instructing the members as to how to complete the task, monitoring their progress, and making suggestions)

   - *Supportive behaviors* (encouraging the members, making them feel comfortable, and praising them)

2. How effective were these behaviors in terms of facilitating task accomplishment?

3. How did the leader and the group go about accomplishing the task? How effectively was it accomplished?

4. How did the group members interact among themselves?

5. How did they interact with the leader?

FOLLOW THE LEADER THEORY SHEET

Situational Leadership™ theory offers a method for managing people whereby a supervisor can adjust his or her leadership style according to what an individual subordinate needs in order to complete a specific task at a specific time. This adjustment is made in response to the subordinate's demonstrated levels of capacity as well as confidence and willingness with regard to performing the task at the time that it must be performed. The leadership alternatives consist of four basic styles.

Style 1. If a subordinate is lacking the capacity to complete a task on a particular occasion, the supervisor must be directive and provide explicit, detailed instructions about how the task is to be performed.

Style 2. On another occasion during which the task is to be performed, it is possible that the supervisor may need to be directive again, repeating the detailed instructions. At this point, too, if the subordinate is lacking the confidence or the willingness to complete the task, the supervisor must be supportive by providing the kind of encouragement that will build confidence and an appropriate attitude.

Style 3. As the subordinate develops and demonstrates the capacity to complete the same task, the supervisor provides increasingly little in terms of instructions, although high levels of emotional support may be necessary during this growth period.

Style 4. Ultimately, the subordinate develops to the point that very little is required of the supervisor in terms of fostering either capacity or confidence and willingness with regard to the specific task.

An example can help to explain how Situational Leadership™ works. For instance, a student who is attending the first session of an introductory typing course must be taught the essentials of typing. In this case the teacher as leader employs Style 1 and provides the student with detailed instructions about these essentials, such as how to place the fingers on the keys.

After the instructions have been given, the teacher may need to follow through step by step with the student by providing demonstrations as necessary and repeating the instructions from time to time. It is possible that this procedure may need to be followed for several sessions. In addition, because the student has not yet succeeded by demonstrating the capacity to type, he or she may lack confidence or willingness and may require emotional support from the teacher to help to build the appropriate attitude (Style 2).

Soon the student reaches a point at which he or she demonstrates the capacity to type, but too slowly to meet certain standards. At such a time, the teacher no longer needs to provide detailed information about how to type. However, because of the speed factor, the student still may feel far from confident or willing with regard to typing; thus, the teacher's job is to use Style 3 and provide further emotional support so that the student does not become frustrated.

Eventually, the student demonstrates self-confidence and willingness as well as the capacity to type and needs little guidance or encouragement from the teacher (Style 4).

When a supervisor applies Situational Leadership™, not only is each subordinate managed as an individual, but also each subordinate is managed differently according to the task involved. When geared according to a subordinate's demonstrated behavior, this approach allows a supervisor to be fair with all subordinates and still flexible enough to deal with a variety of circumstances.

More detailed information about this theory of leadership is presented in the Situational Leadership™ summary handout, copies of which may be purchased from University Associates, Inc., 8517 Production Avenue, San Diego, California 92121, phone 619-578-5900.

370. QC AGENDA: COLLABORATIVE PROBLEM IDENTIFICATION

Goals

I. To introduce the process by which quality circles identify and select work-related problems as projects.

II. To allow the participants to practice behaviors that are associated with effective circle membership: participating collaboratively in circle efforts, listening to other members, and withholding judgment while considering issues that are before the circle.

Group Size

Two to four intact work groups.

Time Required

Approximately one and one-half hours.

Materials

I. A copy of the QC Agenda Work Sheet for each participant.

II. A copy of the QC Agenda Procedure Sheet for each participant.

III. A pencil for each participant.

IV. A newsprint flip chart and a felt-tipped marker for each group.

Physical Setting

A room that is large enough to allow each group to work without disturbing the other groups. A writing surface should be provided for each participant.

Process

I. The facilitator introduces the activity as one that deals with the procedure used by quality circles to identify and select work-related problems as projects.

II. Each participant is given a copy of the QC Agenda Work Sheet and a pencil and is instructed to complete the sheet. (Ten minutes.)

III. The participants are assembled into their own work groups. The members of each group are asked to share their work sheets and to select the one problem of those listed that they would most like to solve as a group project. (Fifteen minutes.)

IV. After all groups have completed the task, the facilitator reassembles the total group and distributes copies of the QC Agenda Procedure Sheet and asks the participants to read this sheet. (Five minutes.)

V. The facilitator briefly discusses the content of the procedure sheet and elicits and answers any questions that the participants may have. The participants are told that although it will not be possible within the course of the activity to complete the entire QC procedure, the remaining time will be spent on the first two steps described in the handout. (Ten minutes.)

VI. The individual work groups are reassembled, and each is given a newsprint flip chart and a felt-tipped marker. It is explained that each group is to repeat the process of selecting one work-related problem as a project, but that this time the members are to take a different approach and follow Steps 1 and 2 of the procedure used by quality circles. The facilitator emphasizes that the members should practice the behaviors cited in the procedure sheet: collaborative participation, careful and thoughtful listening, and withholding judgment until it is time to make a final decision. (Twenty minutes.)

VII. After all groups have chosen problems as projects, the total group is reconvened. The entire activity is discussed, and the facilitator asks the following questions:

1. What were the differences in the two procedures used to complete the task?
2. Which of these two procedures proved to be more satisfying to you?
3. Did the second procedure change the chosen problem? If so, how?
4. What appear to be the advantages of the procedure used by quality circles? What are the disadvantages?
5. What additional behaviors besides those listed in the procedure sheet might be useful to members of quality circles?
6. In your experience, how and by whom are work-related problems usually solved? What is your general level of satisfaction with the outcome?
7. Which steps of the quality-circle procedure might be used by any group? What is it about these steps that can be generalized?

Variations

I. During Step IV the facilitator may lead a discussion by eliciting the participants' feelings about and satisfaction with the first procedure chosen to complete the task.

II. The activity may be continued by asking each individual work group to complete additional steps of the QC procedure.

III. The facilitator may use the activity with new groups by instructing the participants to phrase their back-home problems in general terms (for example, absenteeism, unsafe working conditions, conflict, and high scrap rate).

Similar Structured Experiences: *Volume III:* Structured Experience 53; *Vol. IV:* 111; *'82 Annual:* **327.**

Suggested Instruments: *'75 Annual:* "Problem-Analysis Questionnaire"; *'80 Annual:* "Organizational Diagnosis Questionnaire"; *'81 Annual:* "Work-Group-Effectiveness Inventory"; *'83 Annual:* "The Team Orientation and Behavior Inventory (TOBI)."

Lecturette Source: *'83 Annual:* "A Look at Quality Circles."

Submitted by Michael J. Miller.

Michael J. Miller, Ph.D., *is the chair of the Department of Supervision at Indiana-Purdue University at Fort Wayne. His teaching, research, and consulting activities are in the areas of organizational behavior and organization development. Dr. Miller is active in a variety of professional organizations and has published numerous articles on subjects related to the field of human resource development.*

QC AGENDA WORK SHEET

In the spaces provided below, list the *work-related problems* that are currently plaguing your immediate work group. Think of a problem as a situation or condition for which you can identify a difference between how things are and how you would like them to be. Be *as specific as possible* in stating each problem.

1.

2.

3.

4.

5.

QC AGENDA PROCEDURE SHEET

A quality circle consists of three to twelve employees who constitute a single work unit. These employees may or may not perform the same work, but generally they do share the same work area, belong to the same department, and work for the same supervisor. They meet regularly, generally once a week on company time, for the purpose of identifying, analyzing, and solving problems related to their work and work area. They develop recommendations for solving these problems, present their recommendations to management (if necessary), implement solutions, and then evaluate the impact of the implemented solutions.

In order to function effectively, the members of a quality circle must develop certain behaviors that allow them to complete the problem-solving procedure. These behaviors include not only participating collaboratively in circle efforts, but also listening carefully to fellow members and withholding judgment about various ideas and suggestions until it is time to select a final solution.

The problem-solving procedure that calls for the use of these behaviors includes the following steps:

1. *Identifying Problems.* To identify work-related problems, the members use a technique called brainstorming in which they take turns making contributions of problems that might make worthwhile projects. When used effectively, brainstorming works in the following way:

- As ideas are contributed, they are listed on newsprint or a chalkboard.
- Each member offers only one idea per turn. If a member does not have a contribution to make on any particular turn, he or she simply says "pass."
- No opinions about ideas, either positive or negative, may be stated. The withholding of judgment at this point is important so that creativity is not stifled.
- The process continues until all contributions have been exhausted.

2. *Selecting a Problem.* A circle works on solving only one problem at a time. The members discuss all problems identified in Step 1 and then choose one. The process used to arrive at this choice is governed by the following principles:

- No voting, bargaining, or lobbying is permissible.
- Each member must be offered an opportunity to express his or her opinion and the reasons for holding this opinion.
- No member may say that the opinions of another member are "wrong."
- All members must care about the problem that is finally chosen; they must be willing to commit themselves to its resolution.
- The members must be able to do something about the chosen problem. Problems that the circle cannot possibly solve either on its own or with help provided by management constitute inappropriate projects.

3. *Analyzing the Problem.* After a problem has been selected, it must be defined in writing in precise, detailed terms. Defining includes specifying why the situation or condition is a problem; where and when the problem exists; and the impact of the problem on productivity, morale, and so forth. Another task to be completed is determining the causes of the problem, which may necessitate obtaining data from experts.

4. *Generating and Evaluating Possible Solutions.* During this step the members think as creatively as possible to come up with a wide range of alternative solutions. Brainstorming is the

Adapted from R.G. James and A.J. Elkins, *How to Train and Lead a Quality Circle,* copyright © 1983, University Associates, and from L. Fitzgerald and J. Murphy, *Installing Quality Circles: A Strategic Approach,* copyright © 1982, University Associates.

technique that is generally used for this process. Subsequently, the benefits, costs, and possible ramifications of each alternative are considered.

5. *Selecting a Solution.* After each alternative has been analyzed, the members choose the one that seems most appropriate.

6. *Implementing the Solution.* A detailed plan to guide the implementation is essential. When developing this plan, the members outline what should be done, when the work should begin, and who should do it. They also consider potential problems and ways to deal with these problems. Finally, they develop a plan for evaluating the solution by determining what they will accept as evidence that the solution has worked, how they will collect this evidence, who will collect it, and when it will be collected.

371. CONSTRUCTIVE DISCIPLINE: FOLLOWING ORGANIZATIONAL GUIDELINES

Goals

    I. To help the participants to develop an understanding of the importance and complexity of discipline problems within an organization.

    II. To develop the participants' awareness of the guidelines that can be used to handle discipline problems.

Group Size

    Any number of triads.

Time Required

    Approximately two hours.

Materials

    I. A copy of the Constructive Discipline Lecturette for each participant.

    II. A copy of the Constructive Discipline Data Sheet for each participant.

    III. Blank paper and a pencil for each arbitrator.

    IV. A clipboard or other portable writing surface for each arbitrator.

Physical Setting

    A room that is large enough to allow the triads to work without disturbing one another.

Process

    I. The facilitator announces that the participants are to be involved in an activity that deals with constructive discipline within an organization. Each participant is given a copy of the Constructive Discipline Lecturette and is asked to read this handout. (Ten minutes.)

    II. Questions about the content of the handout are elicited and answered. (Ten minutes.)

    III. The facilitator assembles the participants into triads, distributes copies of the Constructive Discipline Data Sheet, and asks the participants to read this sheet. (Five minutes.)

    IV. Within each triad the following roles are assigned: *proponent, opponent,* and *arbitrator.* Each arbitrator is given blank paper, a pencil, and a clipboard or other portable writing surface. It is explained that each triad is to use the following procedure to analyze each of the five problems on the data sheet:

        1. The proponent and opponent discuss the situation, the proponent supporting the position that the disciplinary action taken was appropriate and the opponent supporting the position that it was inappropriate.

        2. The arbitrator listens carefully to this discussion, decides whether the disciplinary action was appropriate or inappropriate, and explains his or her rationale.

3. If the arbitrator determines that the action taken was inappropriate, all three members work to establish a better way to handle the situation. The arbitrator makes notes about the new disciplinary approach that is established.

V. The facilitator elicits and answers questions about the task, announces that each triad has forty-five minutes to complete its work, and instructs the participants to begin.

VI. After forty-five minutes the facilitator asks the triads to stop their work. The total group is reconvened, and the arbitrators are asked to report their decisions and any new disciplinary approaches that were established. (Fifteen minutes.)

VII. The facilitator leads a concluding discussion by asking the following questions:

1. For those of you who served as proponents and opponents, how were you affected when you had to defend positions with which you disagreed?
2. For those of you who served as arbitrators, how were you affected by having to choose between the two sides?
3. How did the proponents and opponents react to the arbitrators' decisions?
4. How often did disagreement result in your triad because the parties in a particular case problem had not followed the guidelines presented in the lecturette?
5. What can be concluded about the disciplinary process in organizations?
6. How does your experience with this activity relate to your back-home situation? How can you improve your back-home situation as a result of this experience?

Variations

I. Within each triad the roles of proponent, opponent, and arbitrator may be switched for each case problem considered.

II. The participants may be asked to use their own disciplinary problems as cases to be considered.

III. The participants may be asked to use their own disciplinary problems for the purpose of contracting back-home efforts after Step VII.

IV. Copies of the lecturette may be distributed after the triads have completed their task rather than before. Subsequently, the triads may be instructed to evaluate their decisions according to the guidelines presented in the lecturette.

Similar Structured Experience: *Volume V:* Structured Experience 158.

Suggested Instrument: *'82 Annual:* "Managerial Attitude Questionnaire."

Lecturette Source: *'76 Annual:* "Making Judgments Descriptive."

Submitted by Allen J. Schuh.

Allen J. Schuh, Ph.D., *is a professor of management sciences in the School of Business and Economics at California State University, Hayward. He is active in community, professional, and university activities and consults with public and private organizations on individual, group, and organizational practices. Dr. Schuh's major areas of expertise are effectiveness evaluation and training of individuals, groups, and organizations.*

CONSTRUCTIVE DISCIPLINE LECTURETTE

Discipline within an organization involves the administration of negative motivational techniques in response to rule infraction or other misconduct on the part of an employee. Infraction of a rule occurs when an employee has been informed of a specific rule, knows that there are consequences for the inappropriate behavior in question, and then violates the rule by omission or commission.

It is generally accepted as reasonable, then, that employees know in advance what they are expected to do and what they are expected not to do. Forewarning tends to promote the desired behavior, and the burden of such forewarning generally rests with an employee's supervisor. When disciplinary action becomes necessary, this action should be constructive in that it should attempt to guide future behavior.

Certain types of misconduct that are not governed by written rules can also necessitate disciplinary action. An organization cannot and should not be expected to generate rules governing matters that are dictated by common sense or by some higher authority than that of the organization, such as state or Federal law. For example, no employee should require forewarning that he or she is not to burn down the company facility or physically assault a fellow employee.

Practical Guidelines for the Supervisor

1. The supervisor should build good relations before there are problems by being firm but fair and by ensuring that subordinates understand the rules of the organization.

2. If disciplinary action is called for, the employee's immediate supervisor should administer the action.

3. Disciplinary action should be administered as promptly as possible. However, the supervisor should take time to calm down if he or she is angry or emotionally upset so that the disciplinary action will be objective and fair. Also, extra time may be needed to obtain the facts about what happened. The supervisor must listen to the offender's side of the story.

4. The burden of proof is on the supervisor to show that a subordinate is guilty of an alleged offense. An employee should be presumed innocent until proven guilty. The amount or degree of evidence required varies with the seriousness of the charge; the more severe the charge, the more evidence is needed to establish the guilt of the subordinate. If there is doubt as to an employee's guilt or innocence, arbitrators may be called in.

5. One of the main criteria used in administering disciplinary action is the concept of "just cause." In determining whether there is just cause for disciplining a subordinate, the supervisor must answer three questions:

   - Can it be proven that the employee did, in fact, commit the improper act?

   - Should the employee be punished for the behavior? The fact that the employee committed an infraction does not mean that he or she should be punished automatically. If industry custom, company tradition, past practice, or some other rationale can be given to explain or justify a specific behavior, it may be appropriate to waive the penalty for the infraction.

   - Does the contemplated punishment fit the nature of the offense? When a violation occurs and does warrant punishment, the penalty assigned must be appropriate. This requirement prevents the exacting of severe penalties for minor infractions, such as the firing of an employee for coming to work late on one occasion. This provision is sometimes referred to as a "reasonableness criterion."

6. For moral as well as legal reasons, penalties must be exacted in a nondiscriminatory manner. In general, two employees should receive the same penalty for the same offense,

although there are exceptions. To introduce flexibility into a disciplinary system, a range of penalties may be established for the same offense. Flexibility is both needed and justifiable. For example, if two employees arrive late for work, one may be verbally reprimanded and the other may be fired. This discrepancy in punishment could be justifiable if the verbally reprimanded employee had never been late for work before, whereas the fired employee had been formally warned repeatedly and had even been suspended recently for the same offense.

7. Strict consistency may not be entirely fair. Court judges and public administrators, who must strive for consistency in administering laws, use the term "strategic leniency" in circumstances in which some bending of the rules is wise. Such considerations as intent, provocation, inexperience, and temporary disability may justify more favorable treatment of one person than another. Of course, once an exception is made, the door is open to further appeals and to abuse. At this point it is important to recall the purpose of disciplining. If the subsequent behavior of the employees who know of the case will be improved by making an exception, then consistency should be sacrificed. However, the supervisor who elects to sacrifice consistency should be prepared to make an exception for any subordinate in similar circumstances, and he or she should let the reasons for the exception be known so that it will not appear to be arbitrary favoritism. When handled in a way that is generally regarded as fair, adjusting disciplinary measures to individual circumstances actually can improve the effect that the discipline has on future behavior.

8. Rule infractions are generally grouped into two broad categories: minor or major offenses. No such classification could apply to all organizations and all situations, but examples of representative minor and major offenses are as follows:

Minor Offenses	Major Offenses
Loafing	Maliciously destroying company property
Sleeping on the job	Deliberately falsifying company records
Being absent without an excuse	Physically fighting with a supervisor
Gambling	Carrying a concealed weapon
Engaging in horseplay	Stealing money or equipment
Being habitually tardy	Conducting oneself in a grossly immoral, indecent, or disgraceful manner
Producing defective work	
Selling or canvassing on company property	Failing to obey safety rules
Failing to report an accidental injury	Engaging in drug or alcohol abuse
Leaving the work area without authorization	
Generating excessive scrap and waste	
Punching another employee's time card	

9. The main forms of organizational penalties, in the general order of their severity from mild to harsh, are as follows:

- Verbal reprimand
- Written warning
- Loss of privileges
- Fines
- Temporary suspension
- Demotion
- Permanent discharge

Violations of a minor offense are usually subject to a progressive penalty system; the second incident carries a stronger penalty than the first, and the third incident warrants an even stronger penalty. However, the first offense of a major infraction can bring immediate suspension or discharge. Loss of privileges, fines, and demotions are not commonly used within private business.

10. As a general rule, disciplinary action should be administered privately, but there may be exceptions.

11. After disciplinary action has been taken, the supervisor should attempt to assume and re-establish a normal attitude toward the disciplined subordinate. It is important that the supervisor express confidence in the subordinate's ability to improve.

12. An infraction should be erased from the offender's personnel record after one or two years. There is no justification for holding against an employee, in perpetuity, indiscretions of past years if the employee has reformed.

13. Sometimes there is a question as to whether an employee has actually committed an infraction of the rules. Consequently, an accused employee should always have the right to appeal to an authority higher than the immediate supervisor. A full hearing before higher authorities may be desirable to demonstrate to all parties that the accused person has been treated justly. The appeal system is also needed for situations in which the supervisor has not properly judged the merits or severity of a case. Still another possibility in serious cases may be the intervention of a union arbitrator or of a legal agency.

CONSTRUCTIVE DISCIPLINE DATA SHEET

Problem One

Stacy, the senior sales representative for the company, comes to work drunk one day. The sales manager sends Stacy home. The next morning Stacy comes in drunk, picks up a stapler, and throws it at the manager, who must be sent to the hospital for stitches and x-rays. The company discharges Stacy for insubordination, assault with a deadly weapon, and intoxication on the job.

Problem Two

The company has struggled to make it clear that absenteeism will not be tolerated. Within the past year, Terry, a highly skilled maintenance technician, has been absent without notice once or twice each month. Terry has worked for the company for six years and has a reputation for doing high-quality work, accepting almost any assignment unquestioningly, and working overtime when necessary. When confronted with the problem of the absences, Terry always promises to do better; however, the continuation of the problem led to a disciplinary layoff, and since then there still has been no improvement. Although quiet and uncommunicative, Terry is known to have family problems. There are six children, one of whom is always ill, and the home is run in a disorganized manner. The company reluctantly decides to discharge Terry because other employees are complaining.

Problem Three

The senior editor, Sandy, was assigned to a complicated project a year ago. Original estimates indicated that the project could be accomplished in six months. Sandy has been working diligently to complete the project and is deeply concerned that it is so far off schedule. For the past three months, the managing editor has noticed that Sandy has begun falsifying written reports about the progress that has been made. After the first incident, the managing editor discussed the situation with Sandy, emphasizing that the falsification must not take place again. After the second incident, the managing editor again discussed the situation with Sandy and wrote a formal reprimand to be placed in Sandy's personnel file. Finally, there is a third incident, after which the managing editor decides to remove Sandy from the project and to demote Sandy to the position of staff editor.

Problem Four

The general manager goes to the washroom and finds Dale, a machine operator, asleep on a bench. Without awakening Dale, the manager stuffs a dismissal notice in Dale's pocket. The manager returns from the washroom and discovers that the maintenance crew is repairing Dale's machine. The maintenance supervisor told Dale to "get lost" for a couple of hours.

Problem Five

The purchasing manager hears from a sales representative that Kim, the secretary in the purchasing department, is "selling" the manager's appointment time to sales representatives for gifts of liquor, theater tickets, and so forth. The informant, who says that the fee has been increasing recently, states, "We have to pay it because we can't afford to lose your account." The purchasing manager telephones the personnel department and asks that Kim be transferred to a new job "for personal reasons."

372. THE SHOE-DISTRIBUTION COMPANY: EXPLORING THE IMPACT OF ORGANIZATIONAL ROLES

Goals

    I. To explore organizational dynamics.

    II. To help the participants to identify motivating forces within different organizational roles.

    III. To provide an opportunity for the participants to observe competition and/or collaboration as a result of organizational dynamics and roles.

Group Size

    Thirteen to twenty-five participants.

Time Required

    Approximately two and one-half hours.

Materials

    I. A copy of The Shoe-Distribution Company Task Sheet 1 for the participant who plays the role of the retired board chairperson.

    II. A copy of The Shoe-Distribution Company Task Sheet 2 for each member of the top-management group.

    III. A copy of The Shoe-Distribution Company Task Sheet 3 for each member of the middle-management group.

    IV. A copy of The Shoe-Distribution Company Task Sheet 4 for each member of the worker group.

    V. A copy of The Shoe-Distribution Company Task Sheet 5 for each observer.

    VI. A pencil for each observer.

    VII. A clipboard or other portable writing surface for each observer.

    VIII. Name tags as follows:

        1. One that reads "Retired Board Chairperson";

        2. Three to seven that read "Top Manager";

        3. One that reads "Top-Management Observer";

        4. Three to seven that read "Middle Manager";

        5. One that reads "Middle-Management Observer";

        6. Three to seven that read "Worker"; and

        7. One that reads "Worker-Group Observer."

    IX. A copy of The Shoe-Distribution Company Discussion Sheet for each participant.

X. A newsprint flip chart and a felt-tipped marker or a chalkboard and chalk.

Physical Setting

A room that is large enough to accommodate interaction among the three groups.

Process

I. The facilitator explains the goals of the activity.

II. All participants are instructed to remove their shoes and to put them in a pile in a designated place in the room.

III. The facilitator announces that the participants all work for The Shoe-Distribution Company and that the purpose of the company is to distribute the participants' shoes efficiently and in a manner that is consistent with the company's structure and methods of operation.

IV. One participant is selected to be the retired board chairperson and is introduced to the others as fulfilling this role. This individual is given a copy of the appropriate task sheet and is asked to read the sheet.

V. The remaining participants are divided into three groups of approximately equal size. These groups are publicly designated as the top-management group, the middle-management group, and the worker group. Each member of each group is given a copy of the appropriate task sheet and is asked to read it.

VI. Each group is instructed to select an observer. The chosen participant from each group is given a copy of the observer sheet, a pencil, and a clipboard or other portable writing surface. The observers are told to read their sheets and to comply with the instructions.

VII. Each participant is given the appropriate name tag and is asked to put it on.

VIII. The participants are told that they have forty-five minutes to accomplish the distribution of the shoes, but that they must adhere to the guidelines set forth in their individual task sheets. Then they are instructed to begin.

IX. While the groups work, the facilitator monitors their activities, announcing the remaining time at intervals.

X. At the end of the forty-five-minute period, the activity is stopped. The facilitator asks the participants to reclaim any undistributed shoes and then return to their groups. The participant who played the role of the retired board chairperson is invited to join one of the groups and to participate actively in the upcoming discussion.

XI. Copies of The Shoe-Distribution Company Discussion Sheet are distributed to all participants. Each group is asked to follow the guidelines on this sheet and to select one member to record the group's answers to the questions listed in Item 3. (Forty-five minutes.)

XII. The facilitator reconvenes the total group and asks the recorders to share the answers recorded in the previous step. (Fifteen minutes.)

XIII. The facilitator leads a concluding discussion on the following topics, listing major points on newsprint or a chalkboard:

1. The ways in which each group's task, rules, and restrictions affected its perceptions and behavior;

2. The dynamics and patterns that developed within The Shoe-Distribution Company;

3. The ways in which the company as a whole functioned well and the ways in which it functioned poorly;

4. Generalizations about positions in an organization and resulting attitudes and behaviors; and

5. Possible applications to the participants' back-home situations.

Variations

I. The task sheet for the retired board chairperson may be altered so that this individual serves as a helpful consultant. Another option is to eliminate the chairperson and substitute a government official or a union representative, in which case a new role sheet must be written and the observer and discussion sheets must be altered.

II. The task sheet for the middle-management group may be changed to stipulate that the middle managers may not decide on a method of distribution; instead, they may only implement a method determined by the top managers.

III. The task sheet for the worker group may be altered to stipulate that the workers may speak only to the middle managers. Another alternative is to carry this stipulation one step further by allowing the workers to speak to the middle managers only if the managers initiate the conversation.

IV. The role of the observer may be eliminated.

Similar Structured Experiences: *Volume II:* Structured Experiences **33, 41**; *'77 Annual:* **194**; *'80 Annual:* **274**.

Suggested Instruments: *'80 Annual:* "Role Efficacy Scale," "Increasing Employee Self-Control (IESC)"; *'81 Annual:* "Organizational-Process Survey"; *'83 Annual:* "Organizational Role Stress Scale"; *'84 Annual:* "Quality of Work Life-Conditions/Feelings."

Lecturette Sources: *'77 Annual:* "The Organizational Gestalt"; *'80 Annual:* "Dimensions of Role Efficacy."

Submitted by Marc A. Silverman.

Marc A. Silverman is the director of organization consulting service for Silverman and Associates, Inc., in Plaistow, New Hampshire, as well as the director of Growth Education Service, for which he runs a training program in group dynamics and human relations skills. In his work in organization development, he specializes in power dynamics and organizational structure. He is a member of the Association for Specialists in Group Work, the American Society for Training and Development, and the Organization Development Network.

THE SHOE-DISTRIBUTION COMPANY TASK SHEET 1:
RETIRED BOARD CHAIRPERSON

Instructions: While the three groups are involved in their activities, you are to visit each group at least once. During each visit you are to behave as follows:

- Suggest that *only you* know what is best in this situation and for the company in general;
- Offer approaches to resolving the situation that require difficult negotiations with the other groups; and
- Make cynical, pessimistic comments about the group's plight.

THE SHOE-DISTRIBUTION COMPANY TASK SHEET 2: TOP-MANAGEMENT GROUP

Your Task

As a group, determine three ways to distribute the shoes, select the most efficient one, and then implement it through the middle managers.

Rules and Restrictions

1. The members of your group and the middle-management group may not do any manual labor.
2. Only your group may make decisions on policy matters (such as compensation for employees).
3. You and the other members of your group may not initiate conversation with the workers; however, you may reply if they speak to you.

THE SHOE-DISTRIBUTION COMPANY TASK SHEET 3: MIDDLE-MANAGEMENT GROUP

Your Task

As a group, decide on the most efficient way in which the shoes can be distributed, but take no action until your decision is approved by top management.

Rules and Restrictions

1. The members of your group may not do any manual labor.
2. Only the top-management group may make decisions on policy matters (such as compensation for employees), but you may offer suggestions to this group.
3. You may talk freely with the members of the worker group as well as the top managers.

THE SHOE-DISTRIBUTION COMPANY TASK SHEET 4: WORKER GROUP

Your Task

As a group, decide what compensation you require in order to distribute the shoes. Be creative in making your decision.

Rules and Restrictions

1. You may not work without compensation.
2. You have no decision-making power regarding how the shoes are to be distributed, but you may offer suggestions.

THE SHOE-DISTRIBUTION COMPANY TASK SHEET 5: OBSERVER

You are an observer rather than an active member of your group. Therefore, you are not to speak until you are instructed to do so, which will be at the completion of the activity. Announce this to your group.

During the activity watch and listen closely as your group works on its task. Make notes on answers to the following questions:

1. Who participated most? Who participated least?

2. Was there a group leader? If so, how did this person become the leader?

3. How did the group make decisions?

4. How would you describe the energy level of the group? Did it change at different times?

5. What was the attitude of the group? Did it change during the course of the activity? If so, how?

6. What norms were established in the group? Did these norms enhance or inhibit the group's effectiveness?

7. How well did the group react to unforeseen changes?

8. How did the behavior of the retired board chairperson affect the group?

9. What stance did this group take toward the other groups?

THE SHOE-DISTRIBUTION COMPANY DISCUSSION SHEET

1. The observer begins the discussion by sharing answers to the questions on his or her task sheet.
2. The other members share their reactions to the observer's comments.
3. The members discuss and answer the following questions:

   - How did being a member of your particular group affect your feelings and your behavior during the activity?

   - How did you feel toward the other groups? How did you feel toward the retired board chairperson?

   - Did your group collaborate or compete with the other groups? How was this behavior expressed?

   - How well did your group utilize its power? How could you have utilized this power more effectively?

373. THREATS TO THE PROJECT: A TEAM-BUILDING ACTIVITY

Goals

I. To increase the participants' understanding of group dynamics.

II. To enhance the participants' effectiveness as team members.

Group Size

Two to four intact work groups.

Time Required

Approximately one hour and forty-five minutes.

Materials

I. A copy of the Threats to the Project Situation Sheet for each participant.

II. A copy of the Threats to the Project Work Sheet for each participant.

III. A copy of the Threats to the Project Discussion Sheet for each participant.

IV. A pencil for each participant.

V. A newsprint flip chart and a felt-tipped marker for each group.

Physical Setting

A room large enough so that the individual groups can work without disturbing one another. A writing surface should be provided for each participant.

Process

I. The facilitator introduces the goals of the activity.

II. Each participant is given a copy of the Threats to the Project Situation Sheet and is asked to read this handout. (Five minutes.)

III. The facilitator distributes copies of the Threats to the Project Work Sheet and pencils and instructs the participants to complete the work sheet individually. (Fifteen minutes.)

IV. The participants are asked to assemble into their own work groups. The members of each group are instructed to share the notes that they made on their work sheets and to work together to develop a step-by-step action plan for resolving the nine problems. Each group is provided with a newsprint flip chart and a felt-tipped marker so that the details of the action plan can be recorded.

V. After thirty minutes the groups are asked to stop their work. The facilitator gives each participant a copy of the Threats to the Project Discussion Sheet and states that each group is to use the sheet as a guide in a discussion of the activity. (Thirty minutes.)

VI. The total group is reconvened, and the facilitator invites the participants to share their answers to the questions on the discussion sheet. (Twenty minutes.)

Variations

I. The facilitator may use this structured experience with one intact work group by omitting Step VI.

II. In Step IV each group may be given a tape recorder so that the members can record their discussion and then play the recording in Step V when they assess their teamwork.

III. Process observers may be asked to assess each group's teamwork and then provide the members with feedback.

IV. After Step VI the participants may be instructed to resume the activity of Step IV. Subsequently, after another thirty minutes they should be asked to compare their behavior to that manifested during their previous completion of Step IV.

Similar Structured Experiences: *Volume VIII:* Structured Experience **297**; *'82 Annual:* **327**.

Suggested Instruments: *Volume III:* "Team Building: Sensing Interview Guide"; *'81 Annual:* "Work-Group-Effectiveness Inventory"; *'83 Annual:* "The Team Orientation and Behavior Inventory (TOBI)."

Lecturette Source: *'80 Annual:* "Team Building from a Gestalt Perspective."

Submitted by Donald T. Simpson.

Donald T. Simpson *is a personnel and organizational consultant in the Rochester, New York, area. His background is in military logistics management, industrial engineering, adult education and educational design, and management-development programs. Currently, his professional efforts focus on process consulting in problem solving, decision making, and planning.*

THREATS TO THE PROJECT SITUATION SHEET

A month ago you became a first-line manager in a large industrial firm. This is your first managerial position and, like all other new first-line managers, you are required to attend a management-training program conducted by the company's training department. You started the program two months ago, just after you learned that you were to be promoted. At first you were excited at the prospect of learning how to be an effective manager, but as the training has progressed, your enthusiasm has waned. You and the other trainees are frankly perplexed about the program, which seems to be poorly planned, prepared, and executed.

One of the problems is that the trainers are not credible; they know the program content, but cannot relate to the experience of the first-line manager. You and your fellow trainees see them as "ivory-tower types." In addition, the trainers lecture too much, apparently because they are pressed to cover a lot of material in little time. Consequently, the trainees do not have the chance to voice their opinions and share the experience.

You also have a quarrel with the content of the program. The trainers deal in generalities and use examples that seem irrelevant and outdated. What you and the other trainees want and need is training in specific skills and "how-to" information. Often you cannot determine how to use the training you receive.

Not all of the problems lie with the trainers and the program content, though. The middle managers, such as your supervisor and those who supervise the other trainees, do not support the training program. They are uninformed about the program content; they often ask their subordinates to leave training sessions to take care of minor problems; and they do not arrange to cover for their subordinates during training.

Because of the climate within some departments of the company, you and some of the other trainees are not allowed to apply what is learned. Even when on-the-job application is possible, the middle managers do not actively support the reinforcement of the training. The trainers wish they could help, but they have no authority or accountability in the trainees' individual departments. In short, the training seems to be an isolated effort; the trainees are not encouraged to view and experience the program as part of their career planning.

At this point the trainees seem to be the only ones who are truly concerned about these problems. In the past the only effort that has been made to evaluate the program is the administration of an end-of-course participant-reaction form. You are not certain who receives the data from these forms and what, if anything, is done with the information. The upper and middle managers never seem to know whether the benefits from the training are worth the investment in trainer and trainee salaries, time, materials, and so forth.

The program is scheduled to continue for another two months, and you do not want it to be a total waste. Consequently, you and your fellow trainees have decided to hold a meeting to discuss the problems involved and to determine what can be done to salvage the training experience.

University Associates

THREATS TO THE PROJECT WORK SHEET

To organize your thoughts before the meeting, list your suggestions about ways to solve the various problems involved in the situation. When you meet with your group, you will be sharing these suggestions and helping to construct a step-by-step action plan for salvaging the training program.

Problem	Suggestions
1. Trainers not credible	
2. Too much lecture	
3. Too much theory, not enough application	
4. Irrelevant material	
5. No middle-management support	
6. Application of learning not allowed	
7. No on-the-job reinforcement	
8. Training not integrated into career development	
9. Inadequate evaluation and follow-up of program	

THREATS TO THE PROJECT DISCUSSION SHEET

1. How satisfied are you with the final action plan?
2. Does the plan reflect the ideas and viewpoints of all of the members? What process did you use to arrive at the plan and to determine which ideas to incorporate and which to exclude?
3. How satisfied are you with this process? What elements of the process pleased you? Which displeased you?
4. How did the process fit with your definition of a team?
5. Did everyone participate in the discussion? If so, how did the group achieve total participation? If not, what inhibited the participation of some members?
6. What member behaviors helped to support teamwork?
7. What behaviors hindered teamwork?
8. As you worked together, did some members' opinions conflict? If so, how were the conflicts handled?
9. How did this activity reflect the way in which you typically work together? What atypical behaviors arose? How can you use this information in your work together in the future?
10. What are the benefits of working together as a team to solve problems? What can you do to ensure that these benefits are experienced in future team efforts at problem solving?
11. What are the drawbacks to team efforts? How can you help to overcome some of these drawbacks?

374. TROUBLE IN MANUFACTURING: MANAGING INTERPERSONAL CONFLICT

Goals

    I. To examine ways of managing interpersonal conflict in an organizational setting.

    II. To provide the participants with an opportunity to practice conflict management.

Group Size

    Three groups of five or six participants each.

Time Required

    Approximately one and one-half hours.

Materials

    I. A copy of the Trouble in Manufacturing Primer on Conflict for each participant.

    II. A copy of the Trouble in Manufacturing Case-History Sheet for each participant.

    III. A set of role sheets for each group. Each set consists of one copy each of Trouble in Manufacturing Role Sheets 1 through 4.

    IV. A copy of the Trouble in Manufacturing Observer Sheet for each observer.

    V. A pencil for each observer.

Physical Setting

    A room with a table and chairs for each group. The three tables should be positioned in such a way that the groups do not disturb one another while they work.

Process

    I. The facilitator announces the goals of the activity.

    II. Each participant is given a copy of the Trouble in Manufacturing Primer on Conflict and is asked to read this handout. (Five minutes.)

    III. The facilitator elicits questions about the handout, explaining the various methods of conflict management as necessary. (Ten minutes.)

    IV. The participants are assembled into three groups of five or six each. The facilitator distributes copies of the Trouble in Manufacturing Case-History Sheet and asks the participants to read the sheet. (Ten minutes.)

    V. After eliciting and answering questions to ensure that the participants understand the task, the facilitator distributes role sheets and observer sheets; within each group four of the members receive different role sheets, and the remaining member or members receive observer sheets. The facilitator does not answer questions about the roles and does not provide any further information. (Ten minutes.)

VI. The facilitator reminds the groups of their time limit and instructs them to begin the activity.

VII. At the end of the twenty-minute period, the facilitator stops the role plays and reassembles the total group.

VIII. The facilitator debriefs the activity, asking the observers to report their observations and allowing the participants to realize that no group achieved a consensus. To illuminate the situation further, role descriptions are shared. (Fifteen minutes.)

IX. The experience concludes with a discussion of the following questions:

1. How did you feel as the discussion progressed?
2. How would you evaluate your behavior during the activity?
3. What steps were taken to manage the conflicts that arose among the members of your group?
4. How does what happened reflect the information provided in the primer on conflict?
5. During this activity what measures could have been taken to manage conflict more effectively?
6. How can you apply these measures in your back-home environment?

Variations

I. In Step II the facilitator may deliver a lecturette on conflict. In this case the primer on conflict may be eliminated as a handout.

II. The case-history sheet may be altered so that it focuses on interpersonal conflicts between the supervisor and one or both subordinates (that is, between Pat and Lee and/or Pat and Chris).

III. The facilitator may wish to emphasize *inner* conflict (individual stress) and *intergroup* conflict and competition as well as interpersonal conflict. If this is the case, the following changes should be made:

1. A separate room should be provided for each group.
2. The Trouble in Manufacturing Primer on Conflict should be altered to include information about inner conflict and intergroup conflict and competition.
3. The groups should be told that they are in competition with one another during the activity and that the group whose course of action is judged to be the "best" will be the winner. A system should be developed for judging the results, rewarding the winner (if any), and processing the feelings generated by the competition.
4. The following steps should be added between Steps VI and VII:
   a. After five minutes the facilitator visits each group and says that the other groups are progressing so well that the time limit is being cut to a total of fifteen minutes.
   b. After five more minutes, each group is again visited and told that the other groups have completed the task and are waiting and that only five more minutes can be allowed.

   Subsequently, in Step VII, the participants should be asked to return to the main assembly room.
5. Appropriate questions should be added to Step IX.

Similar Structured Experiences: *Volume V:* Structured Experience 158; *'77 Annual:* **186;** *Vol. VI:* **217;** *'83 Annual:* **340;** *'84 Annual:* **375.**

Suggested Instruments: *'81 Annual:* "Conflict-Management Climate Index"; *'82 Annual:* "Conflict-Management Style Survey."

Lecturette Sources: *'73 Annual:* "Confrontation: Types, Conditions, and Outcomes"; *'74 Annual:* "Conflict-Resolution Strategies"; *'77 Annual:* "Constructive Conflict in Discussions: Learning to Manage Disagreements Effectively," "Handling Group and Organizational Conflict"; *'82 Annual:* "Coping with Conflict"; *'83 Annual:* "Preventing and Resolving Conflict."

Submitted by John E. Oliver.

John E. Oliver, Ph.D., *is an associate professor of management and information systems at Valdosta State College in Valdosta, Georgia. His specialties include organizational behavior, personnel management, organization development, and management consulting. He is the author of articles in the* Academy of Management Journal, Exchange: The Organizational Behavior Teaching Journal, *and other periodicals.*

TROUBLE IN MANUFACTURING PRIMER ON CONFLICT

Much organizational activity creates interpersonal conflict. Because such conflict can be either destructive or useful, the organizational climate must be managed to ensure that destructive conflict is resolved and that useful and creative conflict is encouraged.

Interpersonal conflict occurs between or among individuals and is usually the result of differing goals, competition for resources or rewards, or personal differences. There are several ways to react to interpersonal conflict. With *avoidance,* a conflict can be ignored or smoothed over, but it usually resurfaces at a later date. Another tactic is *defusion,* which consists of postponing dealing with the conflict, primarily to alleviate the anger or frustration of those involved. As is the case with avoidance, defusion rarely results in a satisfactory resolution of the problem. Still another approach is to handle the situation through formal *power* or an *appeal* to people who are higher in the organizational hierarchy than those involved in the conflict. Although this short-term solution may allow those involved to work around the issue for a short period of time, the conflict still exists and continues to affect other transactions in the relationship.

The more effective methods for dealing with conflict usually involve some sort of *confrontation* between the parties involved so that both (or all) sides can express their feelings, perceptions, and frustrations. This allows *collaboration* to take place, which results in negotiation and compromise. If appropriate methods of managing conflict are used, it is possible to achieve a "win-win" situation in which everyone receives at least part of what he or she wants. This outcome is the opposite of the traditional "win-lose" situation in which one of the parties achieves personal goals at the expense of the others who are involved.

TROUBLE IN MANUFACTURING CASE-HISTORY SHEET

Background

Pat, the manager of a small garment-manufacturing plant, has identified a problem: Two employees, Lee and Chris, have an interpersonal conflict that hampers their work. Lee, the plant superintendent, is fifty-one years old and has been with the company for thirty-four years, having quit high school to start working at the plant as a maintenance helper. For a number of years, Lee has scheduled production through the plant using a method based on sophisticated guessing. During the last three years, however, this method has not worked well, largely because the volume of production and the variety of products being manufactured in the plant have increased.

In an effort to address the scheduling difficulties, Pat recently hired Chris, who is twenty-five years old and just received a master of science in industrial engineering from an Ivy-League college. Pat met with Lee and Chris to explain that Chris was to assume full responsibility for scheduling. Since then, Chris has impressed Pat by setting up a computerized system for scheduling production and controlling inventory. Because of this system, Pat has saved money for the company by carrying less inventory, purchasing in larger lots, and reducing setup time for plant equipment by increasing the length of production runs. The warehouse has reported fewer instances of stock depletion, and Pat has been able to give the company superiors more accurate information regarding dates when out-of-stock items will be available. For the first time in the history of the plant, there is a three-month production schedule that is not only fairly accurate, but also flexible enough that it can be updated as necessary.

Pat's satisfaction with these improvements is marred by the fact that Lee and Chris just cannot get along. They fight about almost everything concerning the scheduling system and its benefits to the plant. At first Pat tried to ignore this problem, hoping that it would go away, and then tried to act as a go-between in order to keep Lee and Chris from sniping at each other. Now no decisions are being made unless Pat assumes the responsibility for them. In addition, Sandy, one of the plant foremen, has come to Pat and complained about being in the middle of a disagreement between Lee and Chris.

It is obvious that both Lee and Chris could do a better job if each would cooperate with the other. For instance, Chris needs feedback on how the production schedule is working in order to make adjustments, and Lee could gain some valuable insight into more efficient plant operation by learning the theory behind Chris's plans. Pat wants to learn why the conflict is occurring so that an effective method for dealing with it can be selected.

Instructions

The task assigned to your group is to *decide what Pat should do* to resolve the conflict between Lee and Chris. The group members must be in *total agreement* about the course of action that Pat should take. You have twenty minutes in which to complete this task.

Do not begin working until you are instructed to do so.

TROUBLE IN MANUFACTURING ROLE SHEET 1

Your primary goal in completing this task is to help the members to reach total agreement about what Pat should do. This goal takes precedence over any other concerns that you may have during the course of the activity, such as promoting a course of action that you personally prefer.

Do not share this information with anyone until you are instructed to do so.

TROUBLE IN MANUFACTURING ROLE SHEET 2

During this activity you are to function as a "devil's advocate." No matter what ideas are proposed, you are to think of every possible disadvantage of these ideas and voice them to your fellow members. If, after thorough discussion, you decide that a particular course of action is worthy of your support, you may agree to it.

Do not share this information with anyone until you are instructed to do so.

TROUBLE IN MANUFACTURING ROLE SHEET 3

Your objective during this activity is to block consensus. You may participate actively in the discussion, but do not agree to any particular course of action under any circumstances.

Do not share this information with anyone until you are instructed to do so.

TROUBLE IN MANUFACTURING ROLE SHEET 4

During this activity you are to generate as many ideas as possible about what Pat should do. Encourage the other members to join you in a discussion of each idea. When the time comes to choose one course of action, use your best judgment.

Do not share this information with anyone until you are instructed to do so.

University Associates

TROUBLE IN MANUFACTURING OBSERVER SHEET

During this activity you are to observe your group as the members attempt to reach agreement regarding what Pat should do. Be sure to make notes about answers to the following questions; later you will be asked to share these answers with the total group.

1. What occurred in the group? Were the members able to complete their task?

2. Which of the following approaches to conflict were used? In each case how effective were they?
   - *Avoidance*

   - *Defusion*

   - *Collaboration*

   - *Confrontation*

   - *Power*

375. DATATRAK: DEALING WITH ORGANIZATIONAL CONFLICT

Goals

I. To illustrate the types of conflict that can arise within a work group.

II. To provide the participants with an opportunity to experience and deal with organizational conflict.

III. To help the participants to identify effective and ineffective methods of resolving conflict.

Group Size

Twenty-six to thirty participants.

Time Required

Two to two and one-half hours.

Materials

I. One copy of the Datatrak Background Sheet for each participant.

II. Seven or eight copies of the Datatrak Accounting Department Sheet (one for each of the six department members and one for each of the department's observers).

III. Six or seven copies of the Datatrak Purchasing Department Sheet (one for each of the five department members and one for each of the department's observers).

IV. Six or seven copies of the Datatrak Operations Department Sheet (one for each of the five department members and one for each of the department's observers).

V. Seven or eight copies of the Datatrak Marketing Department Sheet (one for each of the six department members and one for each of the department's observers).

VI. One copy each of the following role sheets (a different sheet for each of the twenty-two participants who are designated as department members):

   1. Datatrak Accounting Role Sheets 1 through 6;

   2. Datatrak Purchasing Role Sheets 1 through 5;

   3. Datatrak Operations Role Sheets 1 through 5; and

   4. Datatrak Marketing Role Sheets 1 through 6.

VII. One copy of the Datatrak Observer Sheet for each observer.

VIII. A pencil for each observer.

IX. A clipboard or other portable writing surface for each observer.

The authors would like to extend special thanks to John Anderson, Gary Fleming, Greg Harrison, Jan Hognett, and John Knott for their help in developing this structured experience.

X. A name tag for each participant. Prior to conducting the activity, the facilitator completes twenty-two of these tags with the job titles appearing on the role sheets and each of the four to eight remaining tags with the word "Observer."

Physical Setting

A room with movable chairs and plenty of space to accommodate four separate groups as well as a group-on-group configuration (see Process, Step VIII).

Process

I. After announcing that the participants are to be involved in an activity that deals with organizational conflict, the facilitator forms four groups and designates them as follows:

1. The Accounting Department (seven or eight participants);
2. The Purchasing Department (six or seven participants);
3. The Operations Department (six or seven participants); and
4. The Marketing Department (seven or eight participants).

Each group is seated at a separate table.

II. Each participant is given a copy of the background sheet and a copy of the appropriate department sheet. The participants are instructed to read these handouts, beginning with the background sheet. (Ten minutes.)

III. Within each department the facilitator distributes the appropriate role sheets and gives each remaining member a copy of the observer sheet, a pencil, and a clipboard or other portable writing surface. All participants are asked to read their sheets, but are cautioned not to share the contents. (Ten minutes.)

IV. Each participant is given a name tag that identifies his or her role. The facilitator instructs the participants to put on their tags.

V. The facilitator emphasizes the importance of maintaining roles during the role play and then elicits and answers questions about the task. After telling the department managers that they have thirty minutes in which to conduct their meetings and make their decisions, the facilitator instructs them to begin.

VI. At the end of the thirty-minute period, the facilitator stops the group meetings and asks the managers to spend five minutes announcing their decisions to their subordinates and explaining their rationales.

VII. The role plays are concluded. The observers are asked to provide their groups with feedback, and the remaining members within each group are asked to share their reactions to the feedback. (Fifteen minutes.)

VIII. The four managers are instructed to form a circle in the center of the room, and the remaining participants are asked to form a circle around the managers. The facilitator leads a discussion with the managers, requesting that the remaining participants listen but not participate. The following questions form the basis of the discussion:

1. How did the details of your role affect the way in which you directed the department meeting? How did these details affect your decision?
2. How might your decision have been different if you had not been required to play a role?
3. How did you deal with the conflicts that arose?
4. How effective were your methods for managing conflict?

(Twenty minutes.)

IX. After the managers have completed their discussion, the facilitator leads a total-group discussion by eliciting answers to the following questions:

1. What were the consequences of your role behavior during this activity?
2. How did you feel about the constraints that your role placed on you?
3. How did the roles in your group affect the interaction of the members?
4. How might you have behaved in the same situation if you had not been required to play a role?
5. In your back-home work group, what methods does your supervisor use to manage conflict? How effective are these methods?
6. What steps can you take in the future to help to manage conflict in your own work group?

Variations

I. Instead of requiring each manager to come to an individual decision regarding which employee to lay off, the facilitator may instruct the four managers to meet to help one another to determine which employee should be terminated from each department.

II. The facilitator may change the requirement that each department must lay off one employee; instead, it may be stipulated that the entire organization must lay off two or three employees. In this case appropriate changes must be made to the handouts and the process.

Similar Structured Experiences: *'80 Annual:* Structured Experiences **278**, **279**; *'82 Annual:* **323**.

Suggested Instrument: *'82 Annual:* "Conflict-Management Style Survey."

Lecturette Sources: *'73 Annual:* "Win/Lose Situations"; *'74 Annual:* "Conflict-Resolution Strategies"; *'77 Annual:* "Constructive Conflict in Discussions: Learning to Manage Disagreements Effectively," "Handling Group and Organizational Conflict"; *'82 Annual:* "Coping with Conflict"; *'83 Annual:* "Preventing and Resolving Conflict."

Submitted by David J. Foscue and Kenneth L. Murrell.

David J. Foscue *is a graduate student in industrial and organizational psychology at the University of West Florida in Pensacola. His training and special interests are in the area of organization development, with an emphasis on the assessment of managerial skills.*

Kenneth L. Murrell, D.B.A., *is an associate professor of management at the University of West Florida. He has been a visiting professor at the American University in Cairo and has served as the executive director of the Egyptian and Middle Eastern operations of the Organizational Renewal, Inc., Consulting Group. Dr. Murrell has extensive international experience in organization development and management development.*

DATATRAK BACKGROUND SHEET

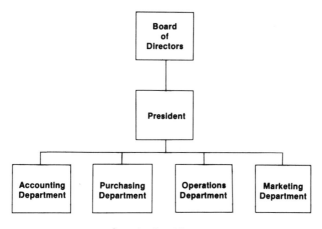

Organizational Structure

Products

Datatrak manufactures computer hardware and software designed to meet the specific needs of individual customers.

Organizational Objectives

The company's objectives are as follows:

- To manufacture computers designed to meet the specific needs of individual customers.
- To accomplish manufacturing in a manner that is cost effective to customers and that generates substantial revenue for the company and its stockholders.

Present Situation

The country is currently in the worst recession that it has ever experienced. Unemployment has reached 30 percent and is rising. The stock market has closed each day for the past several months in a downward trend that, some economists fear, may lead to a stock-market crash.

Datatrak, your employer, is feeling the effects of the recession and is presently trying to cope with a reduction in sales and profits. An outside auditing firm has audited the company's books and determined that if the company is to survive the recession, it must reduce expenses. Consequently, the board of directors has just announced that, as a cost-reducing measure, each department must lay off one employee. Each department manager has been asked to meet with his or her subordinates in order to elicit input and opinions regarding which position should be terminated; then the manager is to make the ultimate decision. The department meetings are to take place in a few minutes.

DATATRAK ACCOUNTING DEPARTMENT SHEET

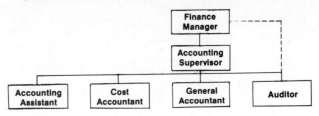

Job Descriptions

Finance Manager

Responsible for managing the Accounting Department and for presenting pertinent financial data to the president and the board of directors to facilitate timely and sound business decisions.

Accounting Supervisor

Responsible for directly supervising the accounting personnel and establishing and monitoring departmental budgets. Also responsible for other duties as assigned by management. Reports to the finance manager.

Accounting Assistant

Responsible for typing reports, providing assistance to the accountants and the auditor when necessary, and helping to put together the monthly operating report. Also performs a monthly bank reconciliation.

Cost Accountant

Responsible for accurately recording and classifying the cost of materials and properly accounting for work in progress, finished goods, and the cost of goods sold. Also responsible for providing the general accountant with this information for the preparation of the monthly operating report.

General Accountant

Responsible for preparing the balance sheet, the statement of income and retained earnings, the statement of changes in the financial position, and the monthly operating report.

Auditor

Responsible for ensuring that all departments comply with company financial policies and procedures. Also responsible for conducting periodic audits of inventories as necessary. Reports to the accounting supervisor for routine matters, but has the authority to consult the finance manager or to report directly to the president regarding significant matters.

Rumors About the Department

1. The accounting supervisor has no real work other than to report weekly to the finance manager and then to communicate the manager's wishes to others.
2. The accounting assistant habitually arrives late, frequently socializes in other departments, and often calls in sick.
3. The cost accountant is rumored to be interviewing for positions with several competing companies.

DATATRAK PURCHASING DEPARTMENT SHEET

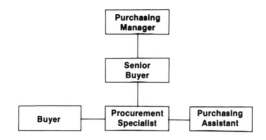

Job Descriptions

Purchasing Manager

Responsible for planning and supervising the effective procurement of materials and supplies requested by all departments within the company. Also responsible for ensuring that such items are bought after firm but fair negotiations and are delivered on a timely basis at the requested place and in excellent condition.

Senior Buyer

Responsible for planning and supervising the procurement of materials and supplies requested by all departments within the company. Also responsible for ensuring that such items are bought after fair negotiations and are delivered promptly and without damage.

Buyer

Responsible for procuring materials, equipment, and services at the lowest possible cost consistent with the requirements of sound company operation. Also responsible for selecting vendors through an evaluation of price, availability, specifications, and other factors.

Procurement Specialist

Responsibilities are the same as those of the buyer.

Purchasing Assistant

Responsible for providing stenographical and other services necessary to maintain and support the functions of the Purchasing Department. Duties include transcribing material from handwritten or typed copy to final form through the use of word-processing equipment and operating terminal equipment to transmit and store textual and statistical information.

Rumors About the Department

1. The buyer is receiving kickbacks from vendors.
2. The senior buyer is eligible for early retirement, but wants to work a few more years to build a larger retirement fund. This person frequently arrives late and leaves early, apparently without regard for the consequences.
3. Although the company has a policy against nepotism, the procurement specialist has a close relative in upper management.

DATATRAK OPERATIONS DEPARTMENT SHEET

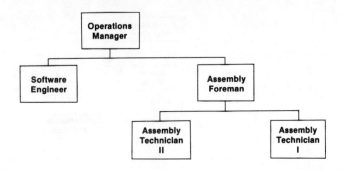

Job Descriptions

Operations Manager

Responsible for the final design, assembly, and packaging of all computer hardware and software. Also responsible for keeping assembly costs to a minimum while maintaining maximum quality and ensuring that all orders are completed on time. Supervises two people, a software engineer and an assembly foreman.

Software Engineer

Responsible for providing the software to meet each customer's needs. Also responsible for providing customers with manuals and training sessions on computer use and user language. Designs software diagnostic programs for troubleshooting the software packages. By virtue of experience and training, is the software expert in the company.

Assembly Foreman

Responsible for ensuring that computer parts are stored and assembled properly. Also responsible for checking each computer after assembly to ensure that it is operational, properly packaged, and sent to the warehouse. Makes sure that the proper tools and equipment are available to assemble each machine. Supervises assembly technicians I and II.

Assembly Technicians (I and II)

Responsible for assembling and packaging new computers and any spare parts required for existing computers, performing maintenance on tools and equipment necessary for assembling, and delivering packaged computers to the warehouse for shipping. Strong background in electronics required for both positions.

Rumors About the Department

1. The assembly foreman is given to back stabbing and to frequent verbal outbursts that upset people throughout the organization.
2. The assembly technician II is a free spirit who is often late to work and frequently calls in sick.
3. The operations manager, who was the software engineer before being promoted, spends a lot of time helping the present software engineer.

DATATRAK MARKETING DEPARTMENT SHEET

Job Descriptions

Marketing Manager

Responsible for effectively coordinating the delicate balance between the national coverage of advertising and sales. Exercises control over both the advertising supervisor and the sales supervisor in order to maintain this balance. Tasks include implementing budgets passed on by superiors, effectively reporting department sales to superiors, and informing superiors of advertising needed to maintain proper market coverage.

Advertising Supervisor

Responsible for managing all company advertising, maintaining a close relationship with the Operations Department in order to promote product lines, and advertising as effectively as possible within the limits of the budget. Works directly with the marketing manager.

Advertising Assistant

Responsible for preparing all advertising layouts and coordinating all advertising efforts with various media. Good art background required.

Marketing Secretary

Responsible for processing all paperwork for the department; answering all phone calls; and effectively managing all office equipment, such as copiers, typewriters, teletypewriter devices, and so forth.

Sales Supervisor

Responsible for setting all sales quotas, covering major accounts, and solving any and all major sales problems. Must be sensitive to market needs and must maintain a close working relationship with the Operations Department so that each sale can meet the customer's time requirements.

Senior Salesperson

Responsible for covering existing accounts in an assigned territory and acquiring enough new accounts to meet a quota.

Rumors About the Department

1. Although the company has a policy against nepotism, the sales supervisor is related to the president. Also, sales have been deteriorating since the sales supervisor has held this position.
2. The marketing manager spends many work days playing tennis.
3. The marketing manager shows favoritism toward the marketing secretary.

DATATRAK ACCOUNTING ROLE SHEET 1: FINANCE MANAGER

You have been with the company for fifteen years and have worked up through the ranks. The president will soon become the chairperson of the board of directors. Because you have been with the company longer than any of the other managers, you feel that you are the natural successor to the presidency, a position that is extremely important to you.

You are a very task-oriented person and believe that the task must be performed above all else. As far as you are concerned, this belief has enabled you to become a manager and has increased your qualifications for the presidency.

The accounting supervisor reports to you on the status of activities within the Accounting Department. The accounting assistant, cost accountant, general accountant, and auditor report to the supervisor. However, when matters of significant importance are concerned, the auditor has the authority to consult you or to report directly to the president.

The accounting assistant often complains to the supervisor about the work load, frequently calls in sick or asks for vacation, and is often found socializing with friends on the phone or in other areas of the company. As a result, department work is often late.

The cost accountant, who has a degree in accounting, is very ambitious and often seems bored with the job. This person is frequently late at turning in work and becomes defensive when asked about its status. You have heard that the cost accountant is searching for another job.

The general accountant is very punctual at completing assigned tasks. This person is working toward a degree in night school, but is always receptive to your special requests.

The auditor, who also has an accounting degree, is very proficient, but tends to go over your head to the president with information that you feel is routine in nature.

DATATRAK ACCOUNTING ROLE SHEET 2: ACCOUNTING SUPERVISOR

You report to the finance manager. When the president becomes the board chairperson, you hope to be promoted to manager. For this reason, you are anxious to keep the present manager happy. For instance, the manager does not tolerate late reports from the department. However, you have to prod your subordinates to complete these reports on time. You are not interested in their excuses; you simply want them to perform their duties.

The cost accountant is the worst in this respect. The fact that this person is frequently late with work assignments angers the manager and makes you look bad as a supervisor. With any task, you must check on the cost accountant's work repeatedly if it is to be completed on time. These checks normally result in extremely defensive behavior on the part of the cost accountant.

The promotion to manager is extremely important to you. You have a son who is a senior in high school, and the increase in salary would enable you to send him to a prestigious college, as you have always wanted.

DATATRAK ACCOUNTING ROLE SHEET 3: ACCOUNTING ASSISTANT

The accounting supervisor does not seem to appreciate you and, in your opinion, assigns you an excessive work load. You have a lot of friends in other departments, and phoning them and seeing them during the day is one of the things you enjoy most about your job. You visit them on breaks, at lunch, and whenever you do not have work to do. However, your supervisor constantly reprimands you for socializing.

In most respects, you and the others in your department get along well. However, you think that the cost accountant, who always assigns you menial tasks such as filing and typing, is a little arrogant. This person seldom finishes work on time and frequently talks back to the supervisor in front of others. You feel that this is wrong and that the cost accountant should either appreciate the job more or find another one.

Two years ago you had open-heart surgery, which left you with large medical bills that were not entirely covered by your insurance. You have no income other than the salary from this job. It is essential for you to keep the job if you are to pay these bills.

DATATRAK ACCOUNTING ROLE SHEET 4: COST ACCOUNTANT

Your supervisor is constantly on your back about completing work on time. You can only prepare your reports when you have received all of the necessary information from others, but the supervisor does not seem to understand this. You would like more challenging work, but your supervisor always gives the special assignments to the general accountant, who, unlike you, does not even have a degree. Although the general accountant's job requires less time to perform, your supervisor seems to be more impressed with this person than with you. You could perform this job as well as your own in the required amount of time, and yet the general accountant makes almost as much money as you. Although you are less than satisfied with your job, you have no intention of searching for a position with another company. Familial obligations necessitate your keeping this job at all costs. The economy is such that opportunities are very limited.

You are also aware that your immediate supervisor may be promoted soon, and either you or the auditor would then become the new supervisor. This position would open unlimited doors to you; you must have it if you are to be the least bit satisfied working at Datatrak. Because you and the auditor are equally qualified for the position, you are constantly looking for opportunities to discredit this person in front of your superiors.

DATATRAK ACCOUNTING ROLE SHEET 5: GENERAL ACCOUNTANT

The accounting supervisor gives you a great deal of support and is impressed not only with your work, but also with your seeking a degree through night school.

The cost accountant appears to be envious of your good working relationship with your boss. This person always gives the supervisor a lot of flak and is constantly reminding you that you do not have a degree.

Although you and the accounting assistant get along well, this individual frequently seems to be preoccupied and spends a lot of time socializing with friends on the phone as well as in other areas of the building. This often requires you to do your own filing as well as other menial tasks while you could be performing more important duties.

You and the auditor are good friends. However, this person is often out of the office performing reviews of other departments, and you wonder how much of this time is spent on company business.

Acquiring an accounting degree would open a lot of doors for you in the company. Therefore, it is extremely important that you retain your job in order to finance this degree. If the economy ever improves, you might be able to go into business for yourself as an accountant.

DATATRAK ACCOUNTING ROLE SHEET 6: AUDITOR

You report to the accounting supervisor on matters of routine importance. Regarding matters that are considered significant, you are authorized to consult the finance manager or to report directly to the president.

You get along well with the others in the department, but the audits that you must perform require you to be out of the office much of the time. Your supervisor frequently inquires about the status of these audits and pushes you to perform them in less time. You are a perfectionist and feel that this pushing will result in audits of lower quality.

If the present supervisor is ever promoted to finance manager, either you or the cost accountant will become the new supervisor. The fact that the cost accountant could be promoted worries you because you know that this person makes no attempt to get along with others in the department and is entirely motivated by self-interest.

You are engaged to be married in a few months. In these poor economic times, if you were to lose your job you would have to postpone the wedding.

DATATRAK PURCHASING ROLE SHEET 1: PURCHASING MANAGER

You have been with the company for ten years. You have an M.B.A. and several professional licenses. You reached your present position within the company very quickly and are the youngest company manager. During your three years in this position, you have initiated innovative improvements that have saved the company thousands of dollars. Your progress has not gone unnoticed; the president of the company and one of the vice presidents on the board of directors have both commended you on your management style and ideas, and it is rumored that you will probably replace this vice president when she retires.

In addition, you are very pleased with the people who work for you. You realize their worth as individuals as well as the importance of each of their jobs. Although some personality conflicts have arisen among several of your employees, you feel that these problems have been straightened out and will not occur again. You are happy with the progress your department has made in the past and expect that it will continue to operate in a very professional manner.

DATATRAK PURCHASING ROLE SHEET 2: SENIOR BUYER

You are the oldest person in the Purchasing Department. You came up through the ranks and have gained valuable experience in many areas of the company. Having worked for the company for thirty years, you are eligible for early retirement. You want to work for two more years in order to receive your full retirement benefits.

Because you have been with the company for such a long time, you feel that you are entitled to take certain liberties, and on several occasions you have done so without regard for the consequences. This practice has caused some resentment between you and other company employees. You have seen the company go through good times and bad, but its present financial situation is the worst to date.

DATATRAK PURCHASING ROLE SHEET 3: BUYER

You are the youngest person in the Purchasing Department. You joined the company three years ago, immediately after graduating from college. Although you have less seniority than anyone else in your department, you have worked hard and achieved a level of expertise at what you do. You are even going to school at night in order to obtain an M.B.A.

However, something happened recently that may jeopardize your job: The procurement specialist intimated that you were receiving kickbacks from vendors. Because your personal integrity is as important to you as succeeding in your work, you are hurt and outraged by this intimation. You are also wondering how to broach this subject with the purchasing manager.

DATATRAK PURCHASING ROLE SHEET 4: PROCUREMENT SPECIALIST

You have been with the company for over twenty-five years. Although you do not have a college degree, you perform the same duties as a buyer (a job that requires a degree). You are resentful of the fact that you and the buyer make approximately the same salary in view of the fact that the buyer has only been with the company for three years. You have also heard a rumor that the buyer is receiving kickbacks from vendors.

Another situation is causing you anxiety, too. You were hired before the company initiated its policy against nepotism. You have a close relative in upper management, and in the past this gave you a feeling of job security. However, in light of the company's present financial situation as well as the policy against nepotism, you have begun to have reservations about the security of your relative's job as well as your own. If you were to lose your job, you could not enter the labor market and expect to make your current salary.

DATATRAK PURCHASING ROLE SHEET 5: PURCHASING ASSISTANT

For ten years you have performed the same job. You have a high school education and are currently attending night school at a local community college. You have always worked hard and done a good job, and you are well liked by everyone in your department. In addition, you have always taken on added responsibilities without being told to, but you tend to feel that the others in your department take you for granted. The only requirement for your job is a high school diploma, but because you have worked for the company for ten years you make considerably more money than someone who could be hired to fill your job.

On your salary you support yourself and your elderly parents; losing your job would be disastrous.

University Associates

DATATRAK OPERATIONS ROLE SHEET 1: OPERATIONS MANAGER

You are forty years old. You graduated from Georgia Tech. with a degree in electrical engineering and immediately went to work with IBM. Your training at IBM was in the design of software systems. In addition, you completed your M.B.A. while working there. After ten years with IBM, you left to become a software engineer for Datatrak because the pay and promotional opportunities were better.

Based on your strong performance as a software engineer, you were promoted to operations manager two years ago. You are conservative, neat, and a stickler for detail. You get along well with everyone because of your noncontroversial style. You do not "rock the boat"; you carry out all of your tasks in a timely fashion; and you are, in every sense of the term, a "company person." You are well respected throughout the company and you feel that you are the likely successor to the president.

Your department consists of a software engineer, an assembly foreman, and two assembly technicians (I and II).

The software engineer, who was hired two years ago to replace you when you were promoted, is quiet and hard working. However, this person's software packages are often very complex and difficult for the user to apply. Therefore, you frequently become involved in the software design. Also, you keep reminding the software engineer of the need for programs that are simpler to use.

The assembly foreman was promoted from assembly technician II seven years ago when the previous foreman retired. The promotion was extremely unpopular because this person publicly criticizes employees in all departments and, consequently, is disliked by many people. On the positive side, the foreman does have extensive knowledge and experience in assembly operations and does obtain acceptable results from subordinates. You would like this person to improve relations with others in the company so that the conflicts and problems that are currently being experienced with other departments will decrease.

The assembly technician II formerly was a computer technician in the Air Force and was hired seven years ago to replace the technician who was promoted to assembly foreman. Although an outstanding technician and a whiz at electronics, this person is immature, and you attribute this immaturity to being unmarried. The technician frequently calls in sick or requests one day's vacation at the last minute, and this easygoing, carefree attitude bothers you.

The assembly technician I was hired three years ago when the sales volume was increasing. After a divorce, this person went to vocational school to become a computer technician and, although not great at the job, is dependable and conscientious.

DATATRAK OPERATIONS ROLE SHEET 2: SOFTWARE ENGINEER

You have degrees in electrical engineering and computer science and you have been with the company for two years. You are quiet and hard working. You consider your software packages to be very sophisticated and "state of the art." Although you wish you could be left alone to do your work, your boss is constantly interfering and making you change your software programs.

DATATRAK OPERATIONS ROLE SHEET 3: ASSEMBLY FOREMAN

Seven years ago you were promoted to this position from that of assembly technician II. You have been with the company since its inception. You consider yourself a valuable employee; your knowledge of and experience in assembly operations make you perfect for this job.

You are an extrovert and enjoy conversing with anybody about anything. Often you point out deficiencies in your department as well as other departments so that they can be corrected and result in a more efficient operation.

DATATRAK OPERATIONS ROLE SHEET 4: ASSEMBLY TECHNICIAN II

You are a computer technician who learned this skill in the Air Force. Electronics and computers have always fascinated you, and you know you are an expert on the subject. You are thirty-five and have never married because you like an easygoing, carefree life style without responsibilities.

You like your work, and the money it pays you lets you lead the kind of life you enjoy. You would rather work for someone less abrasive than the assembly foreman, but you do admire this person's expertise in assembly operations.

DATATRAK OPERATIONS ROLE SHEET 5: ASSEMBLY TECHNICIAN I

You were married right out of high school and had two children shortly thereafter. One day your spouse walked out on you and the children and subsequently divorced you. Although you had your house, a clerical job, and some money in the bank, you were concerned about being able to provide adequately for your children. Consequently, you went to vocational school at night to become a computer technician.

You started work at this company three years ago. You consider yourself dependable and hard working. You have learned much about life the hard way and do not want your children to have to do the same. You worry about how you are going to put them through college.

DATATRAK MARKETING ROLE SHEET 1: MARKETING MANAGER

You hold an M.B.A. from a prestigious eastern school. You came up through the ranks and became a manager through the sales division of the Marketing Department. From the time you took over as manager until just recently, the company's sales have been the highest ever. Only since the economy took a downturn and competition became more intense have sales decreased.

The decrease in sales has been a constant source of worry to you in recent months. To relieve the pressure, you have been taking a half-day of vacation twice a month to play tennis. However, in spite of the gloomy economic situation, you are convinced that sales can become what they once were with a more aggressive advertising campaign and with a sales force that is as large as or larger than the current sales force. Therefore, you cannot afford to lose any salespeople.

You have assessed your department to determine where you might be able to cut back, and the only area in which you could justify a cut is the advertising division. However, you have a lot of confidence in the advertising supervisor, who can do the job more than adequately.

On the other hand, the sales supervisor, who is related to the president, is not quite as capable or aggressive as you would like. Although you like the sales supervisor, this person lacks the desire to excel.

The present marketing secretary is the best that the department has ever had and consistently gives 110 percent. Consequently, you give this person more liberties than you have given any former secretaries. Lately, however, you have been wondering whether you should discontinue some of these liberties. It has been hinted in your presence that you show favoritism toward the secretary.

The advertising assistant is well liked in the department. This person is very talented, has turned out some excellent advertising campaigns, and works well with the advertising supervisor.

DATATRAK MARKETING ROLE SHEET 2: ADVERTISING SUPERVISOR

You have been with the company longer than anyone else in the Marketing Department. Under your watchful eyes, the advertising branch of the department has become extremely valuable and has even won some awards. Although your peers consider you to be very capable, you feel that the marketing manager, who favors the sales division of the department, fails to recognize your worth. You fear for your job because of this fact. In addition, you believe that any upward movement in your department will be made by the sales supervisor, who is related to the president of the company.

DATATRAK MARKETING ROLE SHEET 3: ADVERTISING ASSISTANT

You are the first advertising assistant that this company has ever had. You are excellent at advertising layout and were highly recruited when you graduated from college. In addition, you enjoy your work very much. However, because you have been with the company for a shorter time than anyone else in your department, you feel that during this period of economic instability you will be the first to be laid off.

DATATRAK MARKETING ROLE SHEET 4: MARKETING SECRETARY

You have been with the company for three years. Doing a good job has always been your primary concern at work; you are very dependable and conscientious. In addition, you like and are liked by almost everyone in the Marketing Department. You particularly respect the marketing manager because this person is extremely generous and allows you special privileges as a reward for your loyalty and your excellent work. The sales supervisor, who acts like a prima donna, is your least favorite co-worker.

Because you have a retarded child who requires expensive institutional care, it is imperative that you keep your job.

DATATRAK MARKETING ROLE SHEET 5: SALES SUPERVISOR

You are related to the president of the company. After you were hired, the company instituted a policy against nepotism. However, because the president has assured you that the policy does not apply in your case, you have always felt secure in your job. Your primary concern is performing well so that you will be noticed for your work rather than your relationship to the president. You have risen from the ranks and you believe that you have done an adequate job. Although you are rather young to be a supervisor, you feel that your position is well deserved because you were educated at one of the best colleges in the country and you received an M.B.A. at an early age.

At this time you are not happy with your position, but you know that you must "pay your dues." You do not actually like marketing, and, because of poor economic conditions, overall sales have been low since you have been the supervisor. You have tried hard to do your best, but your heart is not in your job. Occasionally you have become frustrated because of the lack of cooperation you have received from your subordinates. The marketing secretary, in particular, places little importance on whatever work you request; no matter how urgent, your work receives less attention than everyone else's. However, you are willing to withstand this hardship because the economy is so bad and a move might be costly.

DATATRAK MARKETING ROLE SHEET 6: SENIOR SALESPERSON

You have been with the company longer than any other salesperson. You attended college for two years and then quit to join the service, where you were trained as a computer programmer. After leaving the service, you worked for a succession of computer companies and finally landed a job with this firm.

Your territory and quota are the largest in the company's history, and you are doing extremely well. You would like to be promoted to a supervisory position, but you feel that a promotion is unlikely because you are such a good salesperson. This feeling is reinforced by the fact that you have more experience than the sales supervisor and should have been named to that position. Even though there is a policy against nepotism, you feel that this supervisor achieved the position by virtue of being related to the company president.

DATATRAK OBSERVER SHEET

During the department meeting, you are to listen and observe carefully and make notes regarding answers to the following questions. After the role play has been concluded, you will be asked to share these answers with the members of your department.

1. What types of conflicts arose?

2. What methods did the manager use to manage these conflicts?

3. How did the other department members respond to these methods?

4. How did the manager gather information from the subordinates?

5. How did he or she use that information to make the ultimate decision?

6. How would you describe the mood of the department at the beginning of the meeting? How did this mood change as the meeting progressed?

376. GROUP SAVINGS BANK: AN INTRODUCTORY EXPERIENCE

Goals

   I. To help the participants to become acquainted with one another.

   II. To develop the participants' readiness for involvement at the beginning of a group session.

   III. To provide the participants with an opportunity to experiment with abandoning old behaviors and/or adopting new behaviors.

Group Size

   A maximum of ten triads.

Time Required

   Approximately forty-five minutes.

Materials

   I. Three large signs designated as Sign 1, Sign 2, and Sign 3, respectively, and printed with copy as follows:

   1. *Sign 1:* Welcome. You are to work on your own to complete the first phase of this group session. Start now with Sign 2.

   2. *Sign 2:* Think for a moment about two services offered by banks: the use of a safe-deposit box and the provision of loans.

   3. *Sign 3:* This is the newly formed Group Savings Bank, which offers unique safe-deposit and loan services that will be of use to you. Pick up a copy of the handout entitled "Group Savings Bank Procedures" and follow the instructions provided.

   II. A copy of the Group Savings Bank Procedures for each participant.

   III. Masking tape with which to hang the signs.

   IV. A pencil for each participant.

   V. An envelope for each participant.

   VI. A number of index cards equivalent to approximately ten times the number of participants.

   VII. A shoe box.

Physical Setting

   A room large enough to accommodate all participants as they complete their individual banking activities. Movable chairs should be provided for the participants. Sign 1 should be placed at the entrance to the room, Sign 2 farther into the room, and Sign 3 on the wall above a table holding the pencils, envelopes, index cards, and shoe box.

Process

I. As each participant arrives, he or she follows the written directions on the three signs and the procedures handout. The facilitator monitors and observes this process and answers questions as necessary. (Fifteen minutes.)

II. After all of the participants have arrived and completed the introductory banking activities, the facilitator assembles the participants into triads and instructs the members of each triad to share the contents of their deposits, loans, and grants. (Ten minutes.)

III. New triads are formed, and the members of each triad again share the results of their banking transactions. (Ten minutes.)

IV. New triads are formed again, and Step III is repeated. (Ten minutes.)

V. The facilitator directs the participants' attention to the content of the rest of the session.

Variations

I. Between Steps IV and V, the facilitator may ask the participants to form groups on the basis of similar desired qualities or behaviors. Within these groups the participants contract for new behaviors.

II. This activity may be used at the beginning of an extended workshop. In this case the procedures handout should be altered to include the following paragraph:

> The bank will remain open during the entire workshop. If, at any time, you find it necessary either to make a withdrawal from your safe-deposit box or to take out a loan or grant in order to use a specific quality or behavior, you are welcome to return to the bank to do so. Similarly, you may make a deposit whenever you wish.

The facilitator may also want to lead a total-group discussion between Steps IV and V by asking the following questions:

1. How did you feel when you deposited some of your characteristic qualities and behaviors? How did you feel when you assumed loans or grants?

2. From what you have heard about the qualities and behaviors deposited and assumed, what is your sense of the members of this group?

3. How can you help yourself to retain the qualities and behaviors that you desire for this workshop? How can you obtain help from the other members in this regard?

Intermittently throughout the workshop and at the closing, the participants share feedback with one another regarding their success at abandoning and adopting specific behaviors.

Similar Structured Experiences: *Volume I:* Structured Experience 5; *Vol. III:* **49**; *Vol. IV:* **101**; *Vol. VII:* **245**; *'80 Annual:* **269**; *'81 Annual:* **281, 282**; *Vol. VIII:* **293, 294**; *'83 Annual:* **329**.

Suggested Instrument: *'74 Annual:* "Self-Disclosure Questionnaire."

Submitted by Debera Libkind and Dennis M. Dennis.

Debera Libkind, Ph.D., *develops and implements training programs for managers at all levels within the Anheuser-Busch Companies, St. Louis, Missouri. She has consulted to financial service, health care, and educational organizations. Her specialties include small-group behavior in an organizational context, consulting to groups concerned with the ways in which women's and minority issues are played out within organizations, and the training of trainers and consultants.*

Dennis M. Dennis, Ph.D., *R.N., is the day-treatment program coordinator at the Seattle Veterans' Administration Medical Center and an assistant clinical professor of psychosocial nursing at the University of Washington in Seattle. Previously, he was an assistant professor of nursing and psychological sciences at Purdue University, where he developed and taught courses in applied organizational behavior for prospective health care managers. His current consulting practice centers on organization development with health care and service organizations.*

GROUP SAVINGS BANK PROCEDURES

The bank materials on this table include pencils, envelopes, index cards, and a shoe box. Write your name on the outside of one of the envelopes, which will serve as your safe-deposit box. It is to be stored at the bank in the shoe box.

Next think of several different qualities or behaviors that you see as characteristic of yourself. If you would like to abandon one of these qualities or behaviors from time to time, write it on an index card and place it in your safe-deposit box. Use as many cards as you need for this purpose.

In addition, the bank will provide qualities or behaviors that you desire but do not already possess. Such a provision can be either a short-term loan or a permanent grant. To make use of this service, designate on an index card whether you want a loan or a grant and write the quality or behavior that you wish to assume; then keep the card. Again, use as many cards as you need for this purpose.

If you have any questions regarding bank services, direct them to your facilitator. After you have completed the tasks described in this handout, wait until the facilitator instructs you further.

INTRODUCTION TO THE
INSTRUMENTATION SECTION

The four instruments included in this section are offered for training and development purposes. That is, they are not intended for in-depth personal growth or therapeutic work, but for use in group settings, in training programs, in organization development intervention sessions, and the like, to generate data that the group can use with the assistance of the trainer, consultant, or facilitator to move the work of the group along.

One of the central dilemmas of adult humans is that we do not ordinarily have a nonpejorative vocabulary for describing human behavior. The ordinary person can describe the physical world with great precision, but we quickly run out of descriptors when we try to describe the behavior of people, especially when we have an adverse emotional reaction to that behavior. One of the principal benefits of using instruments in human resource development is that of providing a neutral vocabulary to describe human behavior. With such a vocabulary, one can describe a person's behavior as "coming from a high need to control" or "a parental ego state" rather than in more subjective or emotionally laden terms. The comparison of scores from an instrument provides a group with a convenient and neutral way of exchanging interpersonal feedback. Thus, there are strong reasons to justify the use of instruments in training and development activities. The important caveat is that the trainer or consultant should recognize that the scores obtained by individuals on an instrument are the result of their answers to a series of questions at one point in time, and that these scores should not be regarded with reverence. Human resource professionals are encouraged to use instruments as one means of obtaining data about individuals, with all of the dangers and potential payoffs that any other data source would yield.

There are four instruments in this *Annual*. The first generates profiles of learning styles, from "independent" to "collaborative" to "dependent," as well as combinations of the three. Both trainer and trainees complete the instrument, and the rightness of "fit" between the two is important to the success of the training program, as is the mix of training-learning styles among the participants.

The second instrument, based on Jack Gibb's (1961) theory of defensive and supportive communication, enables an HRD professional to measure the communication climate in an organization or group. Such information is critical in planning any intervention in a group, especially one that purports to address communication issues.

The third instrument is based on transactional analysis and provides a way of examining influencing behavior such as that used in supervision and management. Identification of such patterns clearly is necessary before any strategy can be developed for changing them.

The final instrument provides the HRD worker with a means of tapping quality-of-work-life attitudes, both those related to objective job conditions and those that reflect the respondent's sense of alienation or separation from the job. Both of these are critical aspects of work satisfaction and affect those job-performance behaviors that are directly a function of satisfaction—turnover, productivity, and quality of work.

Readers of earlier *Annuals* will note that the theory necessary for understanding, presenting, and utilizing each instrument is now included with the instrument. All scoring forms and interpretative materials are also provided. This combination of all related materials should make the instruments even more usable.

The final article in the Instrumentation section is a comprehensive bibliography on the Myers-Briggs Type Indicator, a commercially available instrument that measures personality type according to the personality theory developed by the noted psychoanalyst, Carl Jung. This up-to-date list of references, categorized by area of application, should be helpful to users of the Myers-Briggs instrument in identifying current work. It also will provide potential areas of application for prospective users.

REFERENCE

Gibb, J.R. Defensive communication. *Journal of Communication*, 1961, *11*, 141-148.

THE CONCEPT OF LEARNING STYLE

Ronne Toker Jacobs and Barbara Schneider Fuhrmann

Literature pertaining to teaching and training often emphasizes that learners are not homogenous in the ways in which they learn and that trainers, therefore, need to account for the unique ways in which people acquire knowledge and skills. However, the extensive psychological research on learning styles has, to date, had little impact on training practice. The assumption often seems to be that all the learners in a given situation will learn best in a single way—listening to a lecture, discussing in small groups, or exploring independently. This assumption is often valid; there does seem to be a relationship between the type of learning (content, topic, skills, process) and the appropriate style. However, it is sometimes possible and even valuable for learners to obtain the same learning objective in distinctly different ways.

STUDIES OF LEARNING STYLES

A thorough search of the literature indicates the significance of learning style and reveals that little has been accomplished in providing teachers or trainers with information that could impact practice and achievement.

Various teaching styles have been studied. Joseph Axelrod (1973), in an extremely general overview, classifies teachers as those who rely primarily on didactic modes—that is, they pass information on to students—and those who use evocative modes—they draw information and meaning from students. Joseph Adelson (1961) analogously describes the teacher as either *shaman*, who keeps the focus on himself; *priest*, who focuses on the discipline and sees himself as a representative of it; or *mystic healer*, who focuses on the student. A more discriminating and useful taxonomy was developed by Richard Mann (1970), who describes individual teachers as various combinations of six primary styles. The *expert* defines the role primarily as giving information; the *formal authority* defines it as directing and controlling; the *socializing agent* as preparing new members of a profession or discipline; the *facilitator* as enabling students to develop in ways they select; the *ego ideal* as being an inspiring model; and the *person* as being an interested and caring co-learner.

Less attention appears to have been paid to style of instructional content, with the styles noted by Bergquist and Phillips (1975) apparently most widely accepted. They identify three types of content: (a) *cognitive*, to add to or reorganize existing information; (b) *skill*, to improve performance on specific tasks; and (c) *affective*, to increase self-understanding and self-control. Bergquist and Phillips also describe styles of educational environment as *teacher oriented* (lectures, presentations); *automated* (language and mathematics labs); *interaction oriented* (discussion experiences, simulations, workshops); and *experience oriented* (field practicums and internships).

The unique modes of learner response also have been studied. Richard Mann and his colleagues (1970) analyzed interviews, questionnaires, and tape recordings of class interviews, and distinguished eight "clusters" of student behavior: *compliant* students are well socialized in the system and accept its values; *anxious-dependent* students generally feel incompetent and rely on teachers for support; *discouraged workers* are dissatisfied with themselves; *independents* are competent and not threatened; *heroes* feel superior and look for admiration; *snipers* display a low level of investment and much hostility; *attention seekers* need acceptance and look for social approval; *silent* students do not participate and usually feel helpless and vulnerable.

Another taxonomy was developed by Sheryl Riechmann and Tony Grasha (1974), whose learning-style categories are based on students' reactions to classroom events as well as their attitudes toward learning, their teachers, and their peers. They identified six learning styles: *competitive* students who learn in order to outperform classmates; *collaborative*, who believe they can learn best through sharing; *avoidant*, who are not interested in learning content in traditional ways; *participant*, who want to learn and enjoy the class; *dependent*, who lack curiosity and want to be told what to do; and *independent*, who enjoy thinking for themselves.

K. Patricia Cross (1976) details research that discriminates field-dependent students—those who perceive the world as a whole and emphasize relationships—from field-independent students—those who tend to separate elements and approach the world in an analytical mode. Cross repeatedly emphasizes that "People will probably be...more productive if they are studying...via a method compatible with their style.... No one method should be regarded as a panacea for all students in all subjects.... Educators need to be aware of the cognitive styles of students in order to provide the appropriate kinds of reinforcement.... The learning program [should not be] biased in favor of a particular cognitive style...."

Extensive work in cognitive style has been done by Joseph Hill (1971) and his associates, who have developed a process for learning how an individual prefers to gather information (from associates, family, or individually) and to reason (deductively or inductively), to help individuals better understand their cognitive learning processes.

Stanford Erickson (1974) states that one of the most important factors in instruction is to provide learners with the opportunity to make full use of their talents and interests.

THE MODEL

A simple, practical model is needed to help teachers and trainers account for individual preferences in learning. Glenn Johnson (1976) notes that some students are "dependent prone" and need highly structured settings in which to function, while others are "independent prone" and require greater flexibility and freedom. These categories are similar to the field-dependent/field-independent dimension. We have added a third category to this: the "collaborative prone."

Through our study of the works cited, and based on our experiences with various models of learning styles, we have found a logical model that discriminates three learning styles: the *dependent* style, the *collaborative* style, and the *independent* style. Any one person will learn in all three styles, but may use a particular style in a particular situation, based on personal preferences and the unique characteristics of the subject to be learned or the activity to be engaged in. No one style in this model is better than the others, although one may be more appropriate for a given individual or in a given situation.

Learning-Style Descriptions

The Learning-Style Inventory elicits for each individual a combination of three scores that indicate the relative importance of each style in the positive experiences recalled by the individual.

The D score, indicating *dependence* in the learning situation, refers to the learner's expectation that it is the teacher or trainer who is primarily responsible for the learning that occurs. The learner with a high D score has had positive previous experiences in which the teacher or trainer assumed total responsibility for content, objectives, materials, learning experiences, and evaluation. The learner perceived the teacher or trainer to be the expert and authority.

The C score, indicating *collaboration*, refers to the learner's expectation that the responsibility for learning should be shared by the teacher/trainer and learners. The learner with a high C score has had positive experiences in which the teacher/trainer shared responsibility and encouraged participation in all aspects of the learning design. Such learners enjoy interaction and perceive their peers as well as the teacher/trainer as possessing expertise or input worthy of consideration.

The I score, indicating *independence*, refers to the learner's expectation that he or she will be encouraged to set and attain personal goals. The learner with a high I score has had positive experiences in which the teacher/trainer is perceived as one expert who may be asked to share expertise, but who helps learners to develop their own expertise and authority and frequently acts as a resource to the learners.

No individual style is implicitly better or worse than the others. In fact, each of us has used all three and each has a current preference. The key to effective training is to be able to use the style that is most appropriate. Appropriateness depends on a number of factors, including the individual's ability and willingness to learn the content and the match between the learner's learning-style preference and the teacher/trainer's teaching-style preference. The dependent learner responds best to a directive teacher/trainer, the collaborative learner to a collaborative teacher/trainer, and the independent learner to a delegative teacher/trainer.

A very high score in any one mode may mean only that the learner has been particularly successful with that mode in the past or that he or she tends to overemphasize that mode, thus limiting opportunities to develop other styles. A very low score may mean only that the learner has not been successfully exposed to the particular style, although it also may mean that he or she has avoided learning in that way.

Maturity Level and Learning Styles

Research with the inventory instrument indicates that less mature students (frequently freshman or older adult students) are more dependent in their learning styles. As they grow in maturity, they become more collaborative and then more independent in these preferences. Maturity, as defined by Paul Hersey and Kenneth H. Blanchard (1982) in their Situational Leadership™ model, is assessed in reference to the person's ability and willingness to assume responsibility for directing his or her own behavior. Hersey and Blanchard view *ability* as a person's skill, knowledge, or experience to perform a particular task. They equate willingness with motivation. Therefore, when students are willing or motivated to learn in a particular area or subject, they think that subject is important. They are committed to accomplishing the necessary tasks and feel or become confident in their ability to perform the tasks. Consequently, as students move from lower levels of maturity to higher levels, their competence and confidence to accomplish the learning and to be in command of their learning increases (see Figure 1).

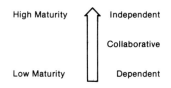

High Maturity   Independent

Collaborative

Low Maturity   Dependent

Figure 1. Maturity Levels and Learning Styles

If we were to superimpose the student learning styles on the Situational Leadership™ *maturity* scale, it would look like Figure 2.

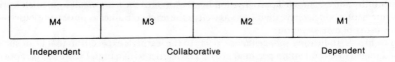

Figure 2. Situational Leadership™ Maturity Levels and Learning Styles

Combining the concept of learning style with the Situational Leadership™ concept of maturity allows us to describe the expected characteristics of an individual with each of the Learning-Styles Profiles used with the instrument. In each profile, a capital letter refers to a dominant style (score of 7 or higher on the instrument) and a lower-case letter refers to a nondominant style.

Profile	Description
Dci	A person with this profile has had highly satisfying traditional learning experiences in which the teacher/trainer assumed major, if not full, responsibility for the learning experience. This learner may be very willing to learn, but is likely to assume a low personal competence base; is most productive in a structured learning environment; and is likely to need a great deal of support to venture into collaborative and/or independent learning experiences.
DCi	A person with this profile accepts the teacher's/trainer's authority and expertise but also enjoys individual participation and values the contributions and potential expertise and experiences of colleagues. This learner probably is quite willing to learn and feels at least somewhat confident, but probably needs encouragement to work independently.
DCI	A person with this profile has had satisfying experiences in all three modes. This versatility makes him or her willing to learn in any style. The person is likely to feel highly competent as a learner, regardless of the style of the teacher/trainer.
DcI	A person with this profile has had success both in the traditional learning environment and on independent projects but may lack interpersonal skills or the ability to function effectively in a group. This learner needs support to work with others and to develop interpersonal competence and may be willing and feel competent only when the learning does not require interaction.
dcI	A person with this profile has had particularly satisfying independent training experiences, working on projects independently and using the teacher or trainer as a resource. This person is comfortable working alone and with infrequent contact with others.
dCi	A person with this profile particularly enjoys participation, interaction, and collaboration. Working in groups and actively contributing to the learning process are valued, and both willingness and perceived competence are high in collaborative situations. This learner may have difficulty in recognizing appropriate teacher/trainer expertise, in taking a back seat, and in designing and executing independent projects.

Profile	Description
dCI	A person with this profile has had particularly satisfying learning experiences working collaboratively and independently. It is likely that this person has had successful dependent experiences as well but has selected the more recent collaborative and independent experiences as highlights. This person probably feels both willing and competent in most learning situations.
dci	This person either has had no really positive learning experiences or has resisted or misread the inventory. If he or she has had no positive learning experiences, this learner is likely to be both unwilling and lacking in self-confidence, regardless of the learning experience offered.

IDENTIFYING LEARNER/TRAINER STYLES

In designing learning experiences, teachers/trainers need to account not only for learner preferences but also for their own experience and preferences. Table 1 details the relationships between learner styles and teacher/trainer roles.

Table 1. Learner-Teacher/Trainer Descriptors

Learner Style	Learner Needs	Teacher/Trainer Role	Teacher/Trainer Behavior
DEPENDENT (May occur in introductory courses, new work situations, languages, and some sciences when the learner has little or no information on entering the course.)	Structure Direction External reinforcement Encouragement Esteem from authority	Director Expert Authority	Lecturing Demonstrating Assigning Checking Encouraging Testing Reinforcing Transmitting content Grading Designing materials
COLLABORATIVE (May occur when the learner has some knowledge, information, or ideas and would like to share them or try them out.)	Interaction Practice Probe of self and others Observation Participation Peer challenge Peer esteem Experimentation	Collaborator Co-learner Environment setter	Interacting Questioning Providing resources Modeling Providing feedback Coordinating Evaluating Managing Observing process Grading
INDEPENDENT (May occur when the learner has much knowledge or skill on entering the course and wants to continue to search on his or her own or has had successful experiences in working through new situations alone. The learner may feel that the instructor cannot offer as much as he or she would like.)	Internal awareness Experimentation Time Nonjudgmental support	Delegator Facilitator	Allowing Providing requested feedback Providing resources Consulting Listening Negotiating Evaluating Delegating

The Learning-Style Inventory contains one form to provide trainers with information about their trainees' perceived learning-style preferences and another form to provide trainers with information about their own perceived preferences of training style. Each version of the instrument contains thirty-six statements, with twelve statements reflecting dependent or directive learning preference, twelve statements reflecting collaborative learning preference, and twelve statements reflecting independent or delegative learning preference. Respondents are asked to identify *two* critical learning or teaching incidents (a learning highlight or peak experience constitutes a critical incident) and to place a check mark in the box by each statement if that statement is descriptive of the learning or teaching experience. If more than ten checks appear in a column for a peak experience, the respondent is asked to circle the ten most significant. After scoring the instrument, respondents are able to obtain a measure of the relative strength of each preference and of the possible preferred conditions.

USES OF THE LEARNING-STYLE INVENTORY

The Learning-Style Inventory can be used to gather data in any learning environment. The resulting information can be used (a) to modify a course or training design, (b) as a pre- and post test if one of the objectives is to increase flexibility in learning styles, and (c) to gauge teacher or trainer effectiveness or potential difficulties if teaching/training style preferences are at odds with student preferences. Other uses include: (d) identification of the need to clarify expectations if, for example, the learners are seeking collaborative work and the instructor intends to lecture; (e) incorporation of mini designs when the majority of the course is one preferred style but the learner preferences indicate a solid mix; (f) discussion of the scores with the learners as a group and/or counseling with them individually regarding the interpretation of their scores. The instrument also can be used in academic advising and professional development work. Teachers or trainers who show a solid preference in one style might choose to seek additional training or experience in one or more of the other styles.

REFERENCES

Adelson, J. The teacher as model. *The American Scholar*, 1961, *30*, 395-398, 400-401.

Axelrod, J. *The university teacher as artist*. San Francisco: Jossey-Bass, 1973.

Bergquist, W. H., & Phillips, S. R. *A handbook for faculty development*. Washington, DC: Council for the Advancement of Small Colleges, 1975.

Cross, K. P. *Accent on learning*. San Francisco: Jossey-Bass, 1976.

Erickson, S. *Motivation for learning*. Ann Arbor, MI: The University of Michigan Press, 1974.

Hersey, P., & Blanchard, K. H. *Management of organizational behavior: Utilizing human resources* (4th ed.). Englewood Cliffs, NJ: Prentice-Hall, 1982.

Hill, J. *The educational sciences*. Bloomfield Hills, MI: Oakland Community College Press, 1971.

Johnson, G. R. *Analyzing college teaching*. Manchaca, TX: Sterling Swift, 1976.

Mann, R. D., Arnold, S. M., Binder, J., Cytrunbaum, S., Newman, B. M., Ringwald, J., & Rosenwein, R. *The college classroom: Conflict, change, and learning*. New York: John Wiley, 1970.

Riechmann, S., & Grasha, T. A rational approach to developing and assessing the construct validity of a student learning style scale instrument. *The Journal of Psychology*, 1974, *87*, 213-223.

Ronne Toker Jacobs *is the president of Ronne Jacobs Associates, Richmond, Virginia. She also is an assistant professor of organization development at the Institute for Business and Community Development, University of Richmond. Ms. Jacobs is an organization development practitioner and consults in the areas of communication (interpersonal, group, and effective presentations), trainer development, leadership development, and team development. She received her M.H.R.D. degree from University Associates in 1983.*

Barbara Schneider Fuhrmann, Ed.D., *is an associate professor in the School of Education, Virginia Commonwealth University, Richmond, Virginia. She also has been an advisor to the university's Center for Improving Teaching Effectiveness. Her book on teaching has been cited by a national survey as one of the most influential books for teachers.*

LEARNING-STYLE INVENTORY
(Trainee)
Ronne Toker Jacobs and Barbara Schneider Fuhrmann

Instructions: In order to determine your preferences in training events, think of two previous training (learning) experiences in which you were involved and which you regard as positive. Then read each statement below and decide if it applies to the first experience. If so, place a check (✓) next to the number in the first space provided. Leave the space *blank* if the statement does *not* apply. After responding to the thirty-six statements, go back and count the checks. If there are more than ten, circle those *ten* checks that are *most* significant. Then repeat this procedure with the second training (learning) experience in mind, again circling your ten most significant checks for that experience.

1st	2nd	
____	____	1. The trainer's frequent monitoring encouraged me to keep up with the workshop.
____	____	2. I appreciated the trainer's presenting most of the material in the course.
____	____	3. I achieved the goals I set.
____	____	4. I cooperated with other participants on the work.
____	____	5. I shared my ideas with other participants.
____	____	6. I appreciated the trainer's having designed all the learning experiences for the workshop.
____	____	7. I criticized others' ideas and pointed out areas they may not have discovered.
____	____	8. Being able to try out new ideas was important to me.
____	____	9. New ideas stimulated my curiosity, and I worked to satisfy myself.
____	____	10. I used available resources for my own purposes.
____	____	11. I frequently encouraged other participants to continue working, looking for alternatives and moving toward goals.
____	____	12. I felt good about the trainer's well-detailed plan and organization of the workshop.
____	____	13. I created ways to accomplish my goals.
____	____	14. I liked having the trainer assign all the materials we used.
____	____	15. I offered ideas and thoughts that were accepted.
____	____	16. I worked on my own.
____	____	17. I developed the work I wanted to do.
____	____	18. I listened to what others had to say.
____	____	19. I evaluated my own learning.
____	____	20. I worked patiently with others.
____	____	21. I worked and talked with other participants.
____	____	22. I went beyond workshop expectations to satisfy my own curiosity.
____	____	23. The other participants and I challenged one another's ideas.
____	____	24. I learned from the trainer's well-executed demonstration.
____	____	25. I appreciated the opportunity to direct my own learning.

_____ _____ 26. I liked the trainer's thorough coordination of the workshop and out-of-class activities.

_____ _____ 27. I did exactly what was expected of me.

_____ _____ 28. I am glad that the trainer directed our discussions.

_____ _____ 29. I like the trainer's assuming full responsibility for assignments and learning tasks.

_____ _____ 30. I was warm and open to the people with whom I worked.

_____ _____ 31. I relied on the trainer's expert knowledge of the material.

_____ _____ 32. I am glad that the trainer alone decided how our work was to be evaluated.

_____ _____ 33. I designed my own experience.

_____ _____ 34. Workshop participants co-designed part of the workshop.

_____ _____ 35. I created a new approach or idea.

_____ _____ 36. I liked having time to work with the other participants.

LEARNING-STYLE INVENTORY
(Trainer)
Ronne Toker Jacobs and Barbara Schneider Fuhrmann

Instructions: In order to determine your preferences in training, think of two previous training experiences in which you were involved and which you regard as positive. Then read each statement below and decide if it applies to the first experience. If so, place a check (✔) next to the number in the first space provided. Leave the space *blank* if the statement does *not* apply. After responding to the thirty-six statements, go back and count the checks. If there are more than ten, circle those *ten* checks that are *most* significant. Then repeat this procedure with the second training experience in mind, again circling your ten most significant checks for that experience.

1st   2nd

_____   _____   1. I employed frequent quizzes to keep the participants on course.

_____   _____   2. I presented most of the material in the workshop.

_____   _____   3. I had participants set their own goals.

_____   _____   4. I worked with participants.

_____   _____   5. I enjoyed having participants share their ideas with one another.

_____   _____   6. I designed all the learning experiences for the workshop.

_____   _____   7. I had participants critique one another.

_____   _____   8. I allowed participants to experiment with new ideas.

_____   _____   9. I encouraged participants to explore their curiosity and to work to satisfy themselves.

_____   _____   10. I suggested that participants use available resources for their own purposes.

_____   _____   11. I frequently encouraged participants to continue working together, exploring alternatives and moving toward goals.

_____   _____   12. I felt good about telling the participants of the well-detailed plan and organization of the workshop.

_____   _____   13. I encouraged participants to create ways in which to accomplish their goals.

_____   _____   14. I liked selecting all the materials we used.

_____   _____   15. I accepted the participants' ideas and thoughts.

_____   _____   16. I developed participants so that they could work on their own.

_____   _____   17. I encouraged participants to adapt the workshop to meet their needs.

_____   _____   18. I listened to what others had to say.

_____   _____   19. I encouraged the participants to evaluate their progress.

_____   _____   20. I worked patiently with others.

_____   _____   21. I worked and talked with participants.

_____   _____   22. I encouraged the participants to explore ideas beyond the workshop.

_____   _____   23. The participants and I challenged one another's ideas.

_____   _____   24. The participants learned from my well-executed demonstrations.

_____   _____   25. I appreciated the participants' directing their own learning.

_____ _____ 26. I enjoyed thoroughly coordinating workshop and post-workshop activities.

_____ _____ 27. I told the participants precisely what to expect.

_____ _____ 28. I controlled the participants' discussions.

_____ _____ 29. I assumed full responsibility for the learning activities.

_____ _____ 30. I was warm and open to the people with whom I worked.

_____ _____ 31. The participants relied on my expert knowledge of the material.

_____ _____ 32. I alone decided how the participants would be evaluated.

_____ _____ 33. I encouraged the participants to design their own experience.

_____ _____ 34. The participants co-designed part of the workshop.

_____ _____ 35. I asked participants to develop new approaches or ideas.

_____ _____ 36. I liked having the opportunity to work with the participants.

LEARNING-STYLE INVENTORY SCORING SHEET
(Trainee)

Instructions: Check to see that you have circled no more than ten items in each column on the inventory. Total your responses (circles) for each item and transfer the total (0, 1, or 2) to the key below. Then total all your responses that fall in column D and write this number at the bottom of the column. Repeat this step for columns I and C.

D	I	C
1. _____	3. _____	4. _____
2. _____	8. _____	5. _____
6. _____	9. _____	7. _____
12. _____	10. _____	11. _____
14. _____	13. _____	15. _____
24. _____	16. _____	18. _____
26. _____	17. _____	20. _____
27. _____	19. _____	21. _____
28. _____	22. _____	23. _____
29. _____	25. _____	30. _____
31. _____	33. _____	34. _____
32. _____	35. _____	36. _____

TOTALS:

D _____	I _____	C _____
(Dependence)	(Independence)	(Collaboration)

Your scores in these three columns indicate the relative importance of each of three learning styles in the positive learning experiences that you have recalled. Most people have a preference for one or two styles but are able to learn in all three styles, depending on the situation.

Your learning-style profile can be drawn by determining your primary and secondary styles. If you scored 7 or higher in the D column, write a capital "D" in the space below. If you scored 6 or lower in the D column, write a lower-case "d" in the space. Do the same for the next two columns, writing a capital "C" or "I" if you scored 7 or higher in either of those columns and a lower-case "c" or "i" if you scored 6 or lower in either of those columns.

There are eight possible profiles, or combinations of learning styles: Dci, DCi, DCI, DcI, dci, dCi, dCI, and dci. The administrator of the Learning-Style Inventory instrument will explain these various combinations to you.

Learning-Style	D _____	I _____	C _____
Profile	D or d	C or c	I or i

LEARNING-STYLE INVENTORY SCORING SHEET
(Trainer)

Instructions: Check to see that you have circled no more than ten items in each column on the inventory. Total your responses (circles) for each item and transfer the total (0, 1, or 2) to the key below. Then total all your responses that fall in column D and write this number at the bottom of the column. Repeat this step for columns I and C.

D	I	C
1. _____	3. _____	4. _____
2. _____	8. _____	5. _____
6. _____	9. _____	7. _____
12. _____	10. _____	11. _____
14. _____	13. _____	15. _____
24. _____	16. _____	18. _____
26. _____	17. _____	20. _____
27. _____	19. _____	21. _____
28. _____	22. _____	23. _____
29. _____	25. _____	30. _____
31. _____	33. _____	34. _____
32. _____	35. _____	36. _____

TOTALS:

D _____	I _____	C _____
(Dependence)	(Independence)	(Collaboration)

Your scores in these three columns indicate the relative importance of each of the three training-learning styles in the positive training experiences that you have recalled.

To determine your profile, write a capital "D" in the space below if you scored 7 or higher in the D column. If you scored 6 or lower in the D column, write a lower-case "d" in the space. Do the same for the next two columns, writing a capital "C" or "I" if you scored 7 or higher in either of those columns and a lower-case "c" or "i" if you scored 6 or lower in either of those columns.

Training-Style Profile	D _____	I _____	C _____
	D or d	C or c	I or i

EXPLORING SUPPORTIVE AND DEFENSIVE COMMUNICATION CLIMATES

James I. Costigan and Martha A. Schmeidler

The communication climate in any organization is a key determinant of its effectiveness. Organizations with supportive environments encourage worker participation, free and open exchange of information, and constructive conflict resolution. In organizations with defensive climates, employees keep things to themselves, make only guarded statements, and suffer from reduced morale.

Gibb (1961) identified six characteristics of a "supportive environment" and six characteristics of a "defensive one." Gibb affirmed that employees are influenced by the communication climate in the organization. He characterized a supportive climate as one having provisionalism, empathy, equality, spontaneity, problem orientation, and description and a defensive climate as having evaluation, control, strategy, neutrality, superiority, and certainty. These items are paired opposites. Capsule definitions of the terms follow:

EXPLORING

Characteristics of a Defensive Climate

Evaluation—The supervisor is critical and judgmental and will not accept explanations from subordinates.

Control—The supervisor consistently directs in an authoritarian manner and attempts to change other people.

Strategy—The supervisor manipulates subordinates and often misinterprets or twists and distorts what is said.

Neutrality—The supervisor offers minimal personal support for and remains aloof from employees' personal problems and conflicts.

Superiority—The supervisor reminds employees who is in charge, closely oversees the work, and makes employees feel inadequate.

Certainty—The supervisor is dogmatic and unwilling to admit mistakes.

Characteristics of a Supportive Climate

Provisionalism—The supervisor allows flexibility, experimentation, and creativity.

Empathy—The supervisor attempts to understand and listen to employee problems and respects employee feelings and values.

Equality—The supervisor does not try to make employees feel inferior, does not use status to control situations, and respects the positions of others.

Spontaneity—The supervisor's communications are free of hidden motives and honest. Ideas can be expressed freely.

Problem Orientation—The supervisor defines problems rather than giving solutions, is open to discussion about mutual problems, and does not insist on employee agreement.

Descriptive—The supervisor's communications are clear, describe situations fairly, and present his or her perceptions without implying the need for change.

DESCRIPTION OF THE INSTRUMENT

The Communication Climate Inventory uses the twelve factors described above as a means of assessing the communication climate within work groups in an organization. Thirty-six questions are presented in a Likert response format. The odd-numbered questions describe a defensive atmosphere, and the even-numbered questions describe a supportive environment. The following chart shows which questions are linked to which characteristic.

Defensive Climate	Supportive Climate
Questions 1, 3, 5—Evaluation	Questions 2, 4, 6—Provisionalism
Questions 7, 9, 11—Control	Questions 8, 10, 12—Empathy
Questions 13, 15, 17—Strategy	Questions 14, 16, 18—Equality
Questions 19, 21, 23—Neutrality	Questions 20, 22, 24—Spontaneity
Questions 25, 27, 29—Superiority	Questions 26, 28, 30—Problem Orientation
Questions 31, 33, 35—Certainty	Questions 32, 34, 36—Description

GUIDELINES FOR INTERPRETATION

The Communication Climate Inventory is designed so that the lower the score the greater the extent to which either climate exists in an organization. However, low defensive scores will probably be an indication that supportive scores are high and vice versa, simply because both climates would not exist together in an organization, although scores will vary according to the supervisor being evaluated.

If the communication climate of an organization appears to be supportive and nondefensive, then probably no changes need to be made. However, if the communication climate is defensive and nonsupportive, an intervention is called for to improve the climate. Structured experiences that develop interpersonal communication skills are useful for this purpose. Overall ratings can be gleaned by having each department plot its scores on the scale at the bottom of the scoring sheet and then looking at any trouble spots.

Scoring the Instrument

If a person agrees or strongly agrees (a score of 1 or 2) with the statements measuring a specific characteristic, that factor is important in the person's work environment. If the person scores the statement as a 4 or 5 (disagree or strongly disagree), it indicates that the characteristic being measured is not part of the person's work environment. A score of 3 indicates uncertainty or that the characteristic occurs infrequently in the environment.

The total of the scores from the odd-numbered questions indicates the degree to which the work environment is defensive, and the total of the scores from the even-numbered questions indicates the degree to which the work environment is supportive. For each individual characteristic, then, a total score of 3 to 6 indicates agreement or strong agreement on either the defensive or supportive scales, a total of 12 to 15 indicates disagreement or strong disagreement, and a total of 7 to 11 indicates a neutral or uncertain attitude.

The lowest possible overall climate score is 18 on either the defensive or supportive scales, which means that the respondent strongly agreed with all questions. The highest possible overall score is 90, which means that the respondent strongly disagreed with all questions. Both extremes are highly improbable.

If more than one person fills out the questionnaire, obtaining the mean score for each item is the most convenient method of scoring the inventory. Summing the means for the questions in each category provides the overall score for the type of climate (defensive or supportive), and comparing those two scores provides a rough estimate of the general organizational climate. The following scales can be used to provide a way of checking the communication climate.

Defensive Scale	Supportive Scale
Defensive, 18-40	Supportive, 18-40
Defensive to Neutral, 41-55	Supportive to Neutral, 41-55
Neutral to Supportive, 56-69	Neutral to Defensive, 56-69
Supportive, 70-90	Defensive, 70-90

In administering the inventory, it is important to be specific about which communication climate (which supervisor's communication) is being surveyed.

USES OF THE INSTRUMENT

The Communication Climate Inventory can be used to measure the organization's total communication environment or the climate of individual work areas. The scores from this inventory can be used to plan needed changes in the communication environment or to indicate which practices should be encouraged.

Organizational consultants can use the inventory to determine whether the communication environment is causing problems. Educators can use it to help students understand the characteristics of supportive and defensive climates. Supervisors can use it to assess how their subordinates feel about their handling of communications in the work environments.

REFERENCES

Combs, G. W. Defensive and supportive communication. In J. E. Jones & J. W. Pfeiffer (Eds.), *The 1981 annual handbook for group facilitators*. San Diego, CA: University Associates, 1981.

Gibb, J. R. Defensive and supportive communication. *Journal of communications*, 1961, *11*, 141-148.

James I. Costigan, Ph.D., *is a professor of communication and the chairman of the Department of Communication at Fort Hays State University, Hays, Kansas. He is a co-author of* Developing Communication Skills: Influences and Alternatives *and is actively engaged in teaching, research, and consulting. Dr. Costigan's background is in the areas of organizational communication, interpersonal communication, and communication theory.*

Martha A. Schmeidler *is the director of religious education for St. Joseph's Parish in Hays, Kansas. She formerly held the position of youth minister in Pasco, Washington. Her background and training are in the areas of interpersonal and organizational communication and religious education, and she has directed numerous workshops and programs for youth.*

COMMUNICATION CLIMATE INVENTORY

James I. Costigan and Martha A. Schmeidler

Instructions: The statements below relate to how your supervisor and you communicate on the job. There are no right or wrong answers. Respond honestly to the statements, using the following scale:

1 - Strongly Agree
2 - Agree
3 - Uncertain
4 - Disagree
5 - Strongly Disagree

	Strongly Agree	Agree	Uncertain	Disagree	Strongly Disagree
1. My supervisor criticizes my work without allowing me to explain.	1	2	3	4	5
2. My supervisor allows me as much creativity as possible in my job.	1	2	3	4	5
3. My supervisor always judges the actions of his or her subordinates.	1	2	3	4	5
4. My supervisor allows flexibility on the job.	1	2	3	4	5
5. My supervisor criticizes my work in the presence of others.	1	2	3	4	5
6. My supervisor is willing to try new ideas and to accept other points of view.	1	2	3	4	5
7. My supervisor believes that he or she must control how I do my work.	1	2	3	4	5
8. My supervisor understands the problems that I encounter in my job.	1	2	3	4	5
9. My supervisor is always trying to change other people's attitudes and behaviors to suit his or her own.	1	2	3	4	5
10. My supervisor respects my feelings and values.	1	2	3	4	5
11. My supervisor always needs to be in charge of the situation.	1	2	3	4	5
12. My supervisor listens to my problems with interest.	1	2	3	4	5
13. My supervisor tries to manipulate subordinates to get what he or she wants or to make himself or herself look good.	1	2	3	4	5
14. My supervisor does not try to make me feel inferior.	1	2	3	4	5
15. I have to be careful when talking to my supervisor so that I will not be misinterpreted.	1	2	3	4	5
16. My supervisor participates in meetings with employees without projecting his or her higher status or power.	1	2	3	4	5

	Strongly Agree	Agree	Uncertain	Disagree	Strongly Disagree
17. I seldom say what really is on my mind, because it might be twisted and distorted by my supervisor.	1	2	3	4	5
18. My supervisor treats me with respect.	1	2	3	4	5
19. My supervisor seldom becomes involved in employee conflicts.	1	2	3	4	5
20. My supervisor does not have hidden motives in dealing with me.	1	2	3	4	5
21. My supervisor is not interested in employee problems.	1	2	3	4	5
22. I feel that I can be honest and straightforward with my supervisor.	1	2	3	4	5
23. My supervisor rarely offers moral support during a personal crisis.	1	2	3	4	5
24. I feel that I can express my opinions and ideas honestly to my supervisor.	1	2	3	4	5
25. My supervisor tries to make me feel inadequate.	1	2	3	4	5
26. My supervisor defines problems so that they can be understood but does not insist that his or her subordinates agree.	1	2	3	4	5
27. My supervisor makes it clear that he or she is in charge.	1	2	3	4	5
28. I feel free to talk to my supervisor.	1	2	3	4	5
29. My supervisor believes that if a job is to be done right, he or she must oversee it or do it.	1	2	3	4	5
30. My supervisor defines problems and makes his or her subordinates aware of them.	1	2	3	4	5
31. My supervisor cannot admit that he or she makes mistakes.	1	2	3	4	5
32. My supervisor tries to describe situations fairly without labeling them as good or bad.	1	2	3	4	5
33. My supervisor is dogmatic; it is useless for me to voice an opposing point of view.	1	2	3	4	5
34. My supervisor presents his or her feelings and perceptions without implying that a similar response is expected from me.	1	2	3	4	5
35. My supervisor thinks that he or she is always right.	1	2	3	4	5
36. My supervisor attempts to explain situations clearly and without personal bias.	1	2	3	4	5

COMMUNICATION CLIMATE INVENTORY
SCORING AND INTERPRETATION SHEET

Instructions: Place the numbers that you assigned to each statement in the appropriate blanks. Now add them together to determine a subtotal for each climate descriptor. Place the subtotals in the proper blanks and add your scores. Place an X on the graph to indicate what your perception is of your organization or department's communication climate. Some descriptions of the terms follow. You may wish to discuss with others their own perceptions and interpretations.

Part I: Defensive Scores

Evaluation	**Neutrality**
Question 1 _____	Question 19 _____
Question 3 _____	Question 21 _____
Question 5 _____	Question 23 _____
Subtotal _____	**Subtotal** _____

Control	**Superiority**
Question 7 _____	Question 25 _____
Question 9 _____	Question 27 _____
Question 11 _____	Question 29 _____
Subtotal _____	**Subtotal** _____

Strategy	**Certainty**
Question 13 _____	Question 31 _____
Question 15 _____	Question 33 _____
Question 17 _____	Question 35 _____
Subtotal _____	**Subtotal** _____

Subtotals for Defensive Scores

Evaluation _____

Control _____

Strategy _____

Neutrality _____

Superiority _____

Certainty _____

Total _____

| 18 | 25 | 30 | 35 | 40 | 45 | 50 | 55 | 60 | 65 | 70 | 75 | 80 | 85 | 90 |

Defensive   Defensive to Neutral   Neutral to Supportive   Supportive

Part II: Supportive Scores

Provisionalism
Question 2 _____
Question 4 _____
Question 6 _____
Subtotal _____

Spontaneity
Question 20 _____
Question 22 _____
Question 24 _____
Subtotal _____

Empathy
Question 8 _____
Question 10 _____
Question 12 _____
Subtotal _____

Problem Orientation
Question 26 _____
Question 28 _____
Question 30 _____
Subtotal _____

Equality
Question 14 _____
Question 16 _____
Question 18 _____
Subtotal _____

Description
Question 32 _____
Question 34 _____
Question 36 _____
Subtotal _____

Subtotals for Supportive Scores

Provisionalism _____

Empathy _____

Equality _____

Spontaneity _____

Problem Orientation _____

Description _____

Total _____

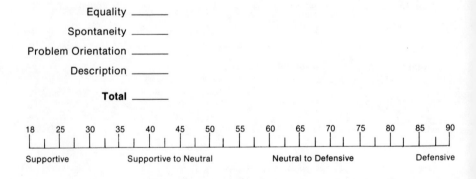

18 25 30 35 40 45 50 55 60 65 70 75 80 85 90

Supportive   Supportive to Neutral   Neutral to Defensive   Defensive

INTERPERSONAL STYLES: THE SPIRO INSTRUMENT

Udai Pareek

A person influences (or at least attempts to influence) other persons with whom he or she interacts. In some roles, e.g., managerial and helping roles, influence is a central function. One of the main functions of a manager is to influence others for the achievement of work objectives. Another managerial function is to help one's subordinates to develop. Even more directly involved in influencing others are teachers, trainers, consultants, and counselors. The process of helping someone to learn and change is essentially the process of influencing the individual's ideas, values, attitudes, and behavior.

Those in influencing roles not only solve problems and help others but they also have an impact on others' ability to solve future problems. They can develop others or they can make them dependent, limiting their autonomy. Their habitual ways of interacting with their employees, participants, trainees, or clients can be called their interpersonal *styles*.

THE FRAMEWORK FOR UNDERSTANDING STYLES

A useful conceptual framework to describe an individual's style is transactional analysis (TA). Transactional analysis concepts are quite popular, and two basic concepts can be used to understand influence styles: the ego states and the existential positions.

Each person involved in transactions with others has three ego states:

1. *The Parent* regulates behavior (through prescriptions and sanctions) and nurtures (by providing support).
2. *The Adult* collects information and processes it.
3. *The Child* has several functions primarily concerned with (a) creativity, curiosity, and fun; (b) reactions to others (including rebellion); and (c) adjusting to others' demands or sulking.

Each ego state is important. However, the functional or dysfunctional roles of these ego states depend on the general existential or life position a person takes. Harris (1969) has conceptualized four primary existential or life positions: I'm OK, you're OK; I'm not OK, you're OK; I'm OK, you're not OK; and I'm not OK, you're not OK.

James (1975) has suggested that, in general, the concepts of OK and not OK can be used to understand how bosses behave. Avary (1980) has similarly proposed OK and not-OK dimensions of the six ego states. Savorgnan (1979) has discussed the OK and not-OK dimensions of the two Parent ego states. Figure 1 shows the four life positions in terms of interaction styles.

The four general interaction styles can be elaborated by combining them with the ego states. Two dimensions of the Parent ego state (critical or regulating and nurturing), three of the Child ego state (adaptive, reactive, and free or creative), and the Adult ego state are used. All three ego states and the subego states are important and perform distinct functions. Each ego state meets a basic need. Avary (1980) has proposed that six basic needs are met by the six ego states, which can be OK or not OK. These are:

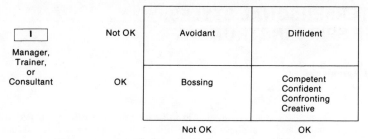

Figure 1. General Interaction Styles in Four Life Positions

1. The need to express love and care, manifesting as Nurturing Parent (OK) or Rescuing Parent (not OK);
2. The need for power, faith, and self-confidence as Firm Parent (OK) or Critical Parent (not OK);
3. The need to think and evaluate information as an Adult (OK) or any not-OK ego state;
4. The biological needs and the need to feel and experience stimulation as a Natural Child (OK) or a Persona (not OK);
5. The need to be creative or intuitive as a "Little Professor" (OK) or a Rebellious or Defensive Child (not OK);
6. The need for approval and safety as an OK-Adapted Child (OK) or a Helpless Child (not OK).

The interpersonal style of an individual depends on the person's combination of the six ego states with the life positions. Combining the six ego states with the four life positions, we obtain twenty-four influence styles, as shown in Table 1.

Table 1. Elaborated Interpersonal Styles

Ego States		Basic Need	Life Positions			
			I'm Not OK You're Not OK	I'm OK You're Not OK	I'm OK You're OK	I'm Not OK You're OK
Parent	Regulating	Love, Care	Traditional	Prescriptive	Normative	Indifferent
	Nurturing	Power	Over-indulgent	Rescuing	Supportive	Ingratiating
Adult		Ration-ality	Cynical	Task obsessive	Problem Solving	Overwhelm-ing
Child	Adaptive	Approval, Safety	Sulking	Complain-ing	Resilient	Dependent
	Reactive	Aggres-sion	Withdrawn	Aggressive	Confronting	Intropuni-tive
	Creative	Crea-tivity	Humorous	Bohemian	Innovative	Satirical

University Associates

STYLES PROFILE

The twenty-four styles shown in Table 1 may be too extensive for some situations. As James (1975) and Avary (1980) have suggested, two dimensions (OK and not OK) can be combined with the various life positions. Combining the six ego states (two Parent, one Adult, and three Child) with the two life positions (OK and not OK), we obtain twelve styles. These are shown in Table 2.

Table 2. Twelve Influence Styles

Ego States	Styles in Two Life Positions	
	Not OK	OK
Nurturing Parent	Rescuing	Supportive
Regulating Parent	Prescriptive	Normative
Adult	Task Obsessive	Problem Solving
Creative Child	Bohemian	Innovative
Reactive Child	Aggressive	Confronting
Adaptive Child	Sulking	Resilient

Rescuing Style: Such a style indicates a dependency relationship in which the manager, trainer, or consultant perceives his or her main role as that of rescuing the subordinate, participant, trainee, or client, who is seen as being incapable of taking care of himself or herself. Another characteristic of this style is that support is provided conditionally, contingent on deference to the provider. The general attitude is one of superiority; the person's support constantly reminds others of their dependence. Obviously, this style does not help other people to become independent and to act by themselves.

Supportive Style: In this style, support is provided when needed. James (1975) uses the term "supportive coaches" for managers with this style. They encourage their subordinates and provide the necessary conditions for continuous improvement. Consultants in this style show patience in learning about the problems of their clients and have empathy with them.

Prescriptive Style: People with this style are critical of the behavior of others and develop rules and regulations and impose them on others. Managers using this style make quick judgments and insist that certain norms be followed by all their subordinates. A consultant may give advice and prescribe solutions for clients rather than helping the clients to work out alternative solutions for their problems.

Normative Style: These managers are interested in developing proper norms of behavior for their subordinates but also in helping the subordinates to understand why some norms are more important than others. A consultant with this style not only helps clients to solve a specific problem but also helps them to develop ways of approaching a problem and raises questions about relevant values. Such a consultant emphasizes the development of a general approach to the problem. Trainers with this style influence the participants through modeling behavior. They also raise questions about the appropriateness of some aspects of behavior and work.

Task-Obsessive Style: People with this style are most concerned with the task. Matters not directly related to the task are ignored. They are not concerned with feelings and, in fact, fail to recognize them, since they do not perceive them as related to the task. They attempt to function like computers. A task-obsessive trainer is insensitive to the emotional needs, personal problems, and apprehensions of the participants.

Problem-Solving Style: In this style, a manager is concerned with solving problems but does not see the problems as being merely confined to the task. For such persons, the problems have various dimensions. The focus of the manager, consultant, or trainer is on dealing with and finding out solutions to problems. In this process they solicit the help of and involve subordinates, clients, trainees, and participants.

Bohemian Style: The creative child is active in this style. The person has lots of ideas and is impatient with current practices. The person is less concerned with how the new ideas work than with the ideas themselves. Such people are noncomformists and enjoy experimenting with new approaches, primarily for fun. They rarely allow one idea or practice to stabilize before going on to another.

Innovative Style: People with this style have enthusiasm about new ideas and new approaches and take others along with them. However, they pay enough attention to nurturing an idea so that it results in concrete action and becomes internalized in the system. Such people are innovators.

Aggressive Style: People with this style are fighters. They show their aggression toward others. They may fight for their subordinates, clients, or participants, or for their ideas and suggestions, hoping that this will help them to achieve their desired results. Their aggressiveness, however, makes people avoid them and not take them seriously.

Confronting Style: In this style, the person is concerned with the exploration of a problem. Perseverance is a main characteristic. They confront the organization to get things done for their subordinates or clients. They are more concerned with confronting problems than with confronting other persons for the sake of confrontation. A consultant with this style may also confront the client in order to help the client to openly explore various dimensions. Such people are frank and open but are equally perceptive and sensitive. They respect the feelings of others.

Sulking Style: People with this style keep their negative feelings to themselves, find it difficult to share them, and avoid meeting people if they have not been able to fulfill their part of the contract. Instead of confronting problems, a person in this style avoids them and feels bad about the situation but does not express these feelings openly.

Resilient Style: In this style, persons show creative adaptability—learning from others, accepting others' ideas, and changing their approaches when change is needed.

Persons in influence roles (managers, consultants, counselors, or trainers) may show several of the behaviors described in this article. Each person, however, uses one style more frequently than others.

THE SPIRO INSTRUMENT

A manager, trainer, or consultant develops a consistent way of interacting with people and situations—a style. There are several dimensions of human and situational interactions, thus, a range of interactional dimensions or styles. The Styles Profile of Interaction Roles in Organizations (SPIRO) has been designed to obtain a profile of managerial (or trainer or consultant) styles—low or high frequency or intensity along specific dimensions.

The SPIRO instrument is based on the use of six transactional analysis ego states (two Parent states, one Adult state, and three Child states) along two dimensions (OK and Not OK). These produce twelve total dimensions or styles.

The SPIRO Instrument contains thirty-six statements for self-rating on a five-point scale.

Administration

Although the instrument is self-administered, the trainer should read the instructions with the participants to make certain that they have no questions. The scoring sheet should not be distributed to the respondents until after the instrument is completed. People can score their own instruments or the trainer can collect the materials and score the items for them. Individual scores should be plotted on the summary and profile sheets, and a group profile should be constructed by averaging the group scores on each of the scales.

For best use of the SPIRO, the trainer should use the following procedure:

1. Administer the instrument;
2. Present the underlying theory to the group;
3. Help participants to understand the instrument and to predict their scores;
4. Score the instrument;
5. Discuss the results;
6. Post the results, openly or anonymously; and
7. Interpret the results and discuss the implications of these results.

Scoring

The responses to the questionnaire are transcribed onto the scoring sheet, and the rows are totaled as indicated. The remaining portions of the scoring sheet are then completed. Underdeveloped OK ego states are those that are two or more standard deviation units below the mean of the standardization sample. According to the available norms, any score lower than those that follow for the various styles would qualify as underdeveloped OK ego states. Underdeveloped OK ego states are then checked in the appropriate boxes on the scoring sheet. These indicate that the respondent should consider working on increasing these behaviors.

Style	Cutoff points for underdeveloped ego state
Supportive	9
Normative	8
Problem Solving	8
Innovative	5
Confronting	6
Resilient	9

The operating effectiveness index shows how effectively the OK dimension of a particular ego state is being used by the respondent. The Operating Effectiveness Quotient (OEQ) can be determined by referring to Table 3.

Table 3. Operating Effectiveness Quotient

Not OK Scores	OK Scores												
	3	4	5	6	7	8	9	10	11	12	13	14	15
3	0	100	100	100	100	100	100	100	100	100	100	100	100
4	0	50	67	75	80	83	85	87	89	90	91	92	92
5	0	33	50	60	67	71	75	78	80	82	83	85	86
6	0	25	40	50	57	62	67	70	73	75	77	78	80
7	0	20	33	43	50	55	60	64	67	69	71	73	75
8	0	17	28	37	44	50	54	58	61	64	67	69	70
9	0	14	25	33	40	45	50	54	57	60	62	65	67
10	0	12	22	30	36	42	46	50	53	56	59	61	63
11	0	11	20	27	33	38	43	47	50	53	55	58	60
12	0	10	18	25	31	36	40	44	47	50	53	55	57
13	0	9	17	23	28	33	37	41	44	47	50	52	54
14	0	8	15	21	27	31	35	39	42	45	48	50	52
15	0	8	14	20	25	29	33	37	40	43	45	48	50

For each ego-state style, the OE scores are given at the intersection of the OK score (in the columns) and the Not OK score (in the rows). These scores are to be noted on the summary sheet. The table indicates the percentage of potential being used effectively in a particular style. Using the table, one can see how reduction in Not OK scores improves OEQ. A respondent can thus strive to obtain the highest score (100) by reducing his or her Not-OK behavior to maximize the use of his or her potential for the present level of an ego state.

If one's scores are on the right side in the row of one's OEQ (i.e., increases OK behavior), one also can add to the OEQ. As Table 3 shows, OEQ cannot be maximized by this approach (but can be by reducing one's Not-OK scores). In other words, *reduction of Not-OK* behavior is more important for increasing one's effectiveness.

Respondents can note their dominant and backup styles by examining their twelve style scores. The styles with the maximum scores qualify as the dominant styles. These are to be noted in the respective column. The styles having the next-to-highest scores are to be noted as the backup styles. While the dominant style is the characteristic style of a person, the backup style is operative under emergency situations, pressure, or stress and is, therefore, as important as the dominant style.

Reliability and Validity

Retest reliability coefficients (with an interval of four weeks) with several groups have been found to range between .51 and .74 for the different styles. All of these were significant at the .01 level. The validity of the instrument was tested by correlating SPIRO scores with egogram scores. Predictions were made for the correlations of the five ego state scores on the egogram with the styles scores. Four correlations were in the predicted direction. However, the Nurturing Parent ego state was found to be correlated not with the supportive style but with the prescriptive style. The "little professor" style was found to correlate with the rescuing style. On the whole, the correlation data provides evidence of the validity of the instrument for training purposes.

Some Uses of the Instrument

This instrument is intended primarily for training purposes. A manager can examine the operating effectiveness scores for each of his or her ego states and, if concerned about the low scores, can prepare a plan for behavioral change based on the related items—by reducing Not-OK behavior and by increasing OK behavior.

The instrument also can be used as an OD intervention. The patterns in a group can be discussed, examining what organizational factors contribute to low OE scores. Managers can discuss in small groups the implications of the scores and develop action plans to improve the operating effectiveness of some ego states.

The instrument also can be used with groups of management students. The students would complete the instrument by answering how they would prefer to behave as managers. They would then learn the underlying concepts and explore what styles they would like to develop and how.

REFERENCES

Avary, B. Ego states: Manifestation of psychic organs. *Transactional Analysis Journal*, 1980, *10*(4), 291-294.

Harris, T.A. *I'm OK-You're OK*. New York: Harper & Row, 1969.

James, M. *The OK boss*. Reading, MA: Addison-Wesley, 1975.

Savorgnan, J.A. Social design of the parental ego state. *Transactional Analysis Journal*, 1979, *9*(2), 147.

Udai Pareek, Ph.D., *holds the Larsen & Toubro Chair in Organizational Behavior at the Indian Institute of Management, Ahmedabad, India. Currently on leave, he is serving as US-AID provincial human-resource-system development consultant to the Government of Indonesia. His specialties are organization development, human resource development, and organizational design. The author of a number of books, instruments, and papers, Dr. Pareek is on the editorial board of several professional journals.*

STYLES PROFILE OF INTERACTION ROLES IN ORGANIZATIONS (SPIRO)
Udai Pareek

Instructions: Completing this instrument will help you to learn more about how you interact with others, an important part of your role in the organization. There are no right or wrong answers. You will learn more about yourself if you respond to each item as candidly as possible. Circle one of the numbers next to each statement to indicate the frequency with which you behave in this manner. Do not spend too much time deciding on any answer; use your first reaction.

	Rarely or never behave this way	Occasionally behave this way	Sometimes behave this way	Often behave this way	Almost always behave this way
1. I assure my subordinates of my availability to them.	1	2	3	4	5
2. I delay doing things that I do not like.	1	2	3	4	5
3. I encourage my subordinates to question me about what should or should not be done.	1	2	3	4	5
4. I communicate strong feelings and resentment to my bosses without caring whether this will affect my relationships with them.	1	2	3	4	5
5. I collect all the information that is needed to solve various problems.	1	2	3	4	5
6. I discuss new ideas with my subordinates without working out the details of these ideas.	1	2	3	4	5
7. I respect and follow organizational traditions that seem to give the organization its identity.	1	2	3	4	5
8. I provide my subordinates with the solutions to their problems.	1	2	3	4	5
9. I take up my subordinates' causes and fight for them.	1	2	3	4	5
10. I admonish my subordinates for not acting according to my instructions.	1	2	3	4	5
11. I think of new and creative solutions.	1	2	3	4	5
12. I collect information and data, even when these are not immediately needed or used.	1	2	3	4	5
13. I help my subordinates to become aware of some of their own strengths.	1	2	3	4	5
14. I avoid meeting my bosses and subordinates if I have not been able to fulfill their expectations.	1	2	3	4	5

15. I help my subordinates to see the ethical dimensions of some of their actions. 1 2 3 4 5

16. I champion my subordinates' causes, even at the cost of organizational effectiveness. 1 2 3 4 5

17. I think out many alternative solutions to problems before adopting one for action. 1 2 3 4 5

18. I overwhelm my subordinates with new ideas. 1 2 3 4 5

19. I accept only those bosses' and subordinates' suggestions that appeal to me. 1 2 3 4 5

20. I instruct my subordinates in detail about work problems and their solutions. 1 2 3 4 5

21. I zealously argue my point of view in organizational meetings. 1 2 3 4 5

22. I give clear instructions to my subordinates about what should or should not be done. 1 2 3 4 5

23. I try out new things. 1 2 3 4 5

24. I spend my time on specific work to be performed. 1 2 3 4 5

25. I reassure my subordinates of my continued help. 1 2 3 4 5

26. I do not express my negative feelings during unpleasant meetings but continue to be bothered by them. 1 2 3 4 5

27. I help my subordinates to examine the appropriateness of proposed actions. 1 2 3 4 5

28. I express resentment to the authorities concerned about things that have not been done as promised. 1 2 3 4 5

29. I continuously search for various resources from which needed information can be obtained in order to work out solutions to problems. 1 2 3 4 5

30. I try out new ideas or methods without waiting to consolidate the previous ones. 1 2 3 4 5

31. I accept help from others and appreciate it. 1 2 3 4 5

32. I encourage my subordinates to come to me frequently to seek my advice and help. 1 2 3 4 5

	Rarely or never behave this way	Occasionally behave this way	Sometimes behave this way	Often behave this way	Almost always behave this way

33. I express my feelings and reactions frankly in meetings with my own bosses.   1   2   3   4   5

34. I clearly prescribe standards of behavior to be followed in my work unit.   1   2   3   4   5

35. I enjoy trying out new ways and see a problem as a challenge.   1   2   3   4   5

36. I work primarily on organizational tasks, sometimes at the cost of sensitivity and attention to the feelings of people.   1   2   3   4   5

SPIRO SCORING SHEET

Name _____ Date_____

Instructions: Transfer your scores from the SPIRO questionnaire directly onto this scoring sheet.

OK Ego State

	Item	Score		Item	Score		Item	Score		Raw Total	Type
Parent	(1)	_____	+	(13)	_____	+	(25)	_____	=	_____	Supportive
	(3)	_____	+	(15)	_____	+	(27)	_____	=	_____	Normative
Adult	(5)	_____	+	(17)	_____	+	(29)	_____	=	_____	Problem Solving
Child	(11)	_____	+	(23)	_____	+	(35)	_____	=	_____	Innovative
	(9)	_____	+	(21)	_____	+	(33)	_____	=	_____	Confronting
	(7)	_____	+	(19)	_____	+	(31)	_____	=	_____	Resilient

Not-OK Ego State

	Item	Score		Item	Score		Item	Score		Raw Total	Type
Parent	(8)	_____	+	(20)	_____	+	(32)	_____	=	_____	Rescuing
	(10)	_____	+	(22)	_____	+	(34)	_____	=	_____	Prescriptive
Adult	(12)	_____	+	(24)	_____	+	(36)	_____	=	_____	Task Obsessive
Child	(6)	_____	+	(18)	_____	+	(30)	_____	=	_____	Bohemian
	(4)	_____	+	(16)	_____	+	(28)	_____	=	_____	Aggressive
	(2)	_____	+	(14)	_____	+	(26)	_____	=	_____	Sulking

SPIRO SUMMARY SHEET

Instructions: Enter your scores in the appropriate boxes below.

EGO STATES

	PARENT		ADULT		CHILD	
	Nurturing	*Regulating*		*Creative*	*Reactive*	*Adaptive*
OK Styles	Supportive	Normative	Problem Solving	Innovative	Confronting	Resilient
	☐	☐	☐	☐	☐	☐
Not-OK Styles	Rescuing	Prescriptive	Task Obsessive	Bohemian	Aggressive	Sulking
	☐	☐	☐	☐	☐	☐
Under-developed OK Ego States	☐	☐	☐	☐	☐	☐
Operating Effectiveness Quotient	☐	☐	☐	☐	☐	☐
Dominant Style	☐	☐	☐	☐	☐	☐
Backup Style	☐	☐	☐	☐	☐	☐

QUALITY OF WORK LIFE-CONDITIONS/FEELINGS (QWL-C/F)

Marshall Sashkin and Joseph J. Lengermann

INTRODUCTION

Since the studies of worker motivation done by Herzberg and his associates (Herzberg, Mausner, & Snyderman, 1959), an awareness slowly has developed of the effects of job design on workers. This has been accompanied by some practical knowledge of how to modify or alter pertinent job conditions. The Quality of Work Life-Conditions/Feelings (QWL-C/F) instrument is an effort to provide a sound basis for designing or redesigning work settings. The basic viewpoint differs from that of Herzberg or Hackman and Oldham (1980), who studied individual psychological work needs and motivation to work.

The QWL-C/F is the result of a ten-year research program that is based on classical sociological analyses of the relation between work and workers in society. These approaches suggest that workers become alienated from their work when the work has little inherent meaning—such as repetition of the same minute set of actions over and over—or denies the worker control, or power, over his or her own actions. These conditions lead to subjective feelings of alienation that sociologists call "self-estrangement"—feelings of being cut off from one's own true working self (Blauner, 1964).

In 1970, several research projects were initiated to empirically examine the relations between alienating job conditions—which we now refer to as "quality of work life conditions"—and workers' self-estrangement, which we call "quality of work life feelings." The striking results led to a series of studies involving computer operators, clerical workers, machine operators, and medical technologists (Kirsch & Lengermann, 1971; Maurer, 1972). This work continues in order to explore effects over time; however, the instrument that was developed during the process of research now has enough evidence of validity to be generally useful (Wilmoth, 1983).

The QWL-C/F consists of two short instruments: the first measures how well three, basic, human work needs are met by objective job conditions; the second provides one score representing the respondent's overall feeling of separation or alienation from his or her own work self. The three, basic, human work needs—need for autonomy or control, need for a "whole" meaningful job, and need for interpersonal contact in the context of doing the job—are described in detail by Sashkin and Morris (1984) and derive from both classic and recent social science research (Marx, 1961; Durkheim, 1893/1947; Mayo, 1933).

FACTORS

A series of factor analyses successfully identified several sets of items on the QWL-C from a larger initial group of questions. These five sets are autonomy, personal growth opportunity, work speed and routine, work complexity, and task-related interaction. Each of these represents a group of five questionnaire items that "hang together" empirically, with each group of items being independent of every other group. In other words, the five sets of items legitimately can be considered as five independent dimensions of work conditions. We may note, however, that two dimensions seem to deal with *power* or control over one's work life (autonomy and work speed and routine) and that two of the remaining three relate to the *meaning* of work (personal growth opportunity and work complexity).

Autonomy (AUT)

Four of the items that form the autonomy index relate to the degree to which the respondent is free to take independent action on work-related issues, rather than having his or her actions approved by a supervisor. These are items 1, 6, 11, and 21. Item 16 refers to the influence that an individual has with his or her supervisor. The autonomy index clearly was the most important of all those identified. (A factor analysis showed that the autonomy index accounted for almost 50 percent of the response variance for a sample of 150 medical technologists.)

Work Speed and Routine (WSR)

The more the work is structured and routine, the less personal control an individual has over the work. Being required to produce a set quantity of work (item 3), working at a constant rate of speed that cannot be self-controlled (item 8), and being required to work rapidly (item 13) are three of the elements in this index. A factor analysis showed that the work speed and routine factor accounted for over 13 percent of the response variation for the medical technologist sample mentioned previously, indicating that it is an important, but not a major, dimension.

Task-Related Interaction (TRI)

One of the basic human work needs identified by Katz and Kahn (1966) and discussed in detail by Sashkin and Morris (1984) is the need for interpersonal contact in the context of doing work. It is important that such contact be part of the task activity, not just friendliness or purely social contact. The items that make up the TRI dimension (5, 10, 15, 20, and 25) were added to the current version of the QWL-C to measure the degree to which a job provides such interpersonal contact as part of the work activity. The TRI dimension was not part of previous versions of the instrument.

Personal Growth Opportunity (PGO)

This factor is a distant second, accounting for about 15 percent of the response variation of the medical technologist sample. Items 17 and 22 refer to trying out new methods of work and learning about other jobs in other areas of the organization. This index seems to relate to the degree of meaning inherent in the job.

Work Complexity (WCO)

Although this dimension accounted for only 10 percent of the response variation in the medical technologist sample, it is most directly related to the sociological concept of "meaningfulness of work." Items 4, 9, 14, 19, and 24 refer to repetitive tasks, undesired procedures, simple jobs, and "the same series of tasks all day." Medical technologists who reported high work simplicity were significantly more likely to say that they planned to quit soon than were persons who reported that their work was more meaningful (less simple).

The five factors, and the questionnaire items that make up each factor, are summarized in Figure 1.

AUTONOMY (Control over one's own work activities):
- worker makes decisions about work (1)
- worker has a great deal of control (6)
- worker solves problems independently (11)
- supervisor acts on worker's suggestions (16)
- worker can make decisions independently (21)

PERSONAL GROWTH OPPORTUNITY (A chance to learn new things and develop one's abilities fully):
- worker has chance of moving to a better job (2)
- worker has opportunity to learn new skills (7)
- worker learns new work methods (12)
- worker tries out own methods on the job (17)
- worker has opportunity to learn about other departments (22)

WORK SPEED AND ROUTINE (Repetition of brief work cycles quickly and indefinitely):
- worker must produce a set amount of work (3)
- worker must work at a constant pace (8)
- worker must work quickly (13)
- worker has no control over work pace (18)
- worker must work to a set schedule (23)

WORK COMPLEXITY (The extent to which the job is meaningful and interesting):
- work is repetitive (4)
- worker must follow set procedures he or she would prefer not to use (9)
- work produces no whole, complete product (14)
- job is simple, does not require worker's full abilities (19)
- worker does same series of tasks all day (24)

TASK-RELATED INTERACTION (The interpersonal interaction required to do the job):
- worker must coordinate with co-workers (5)
- worker works alone with no interpersonal contact (10)
- worker cannot help other workers (15)
- worker must interact to accomplish the job (20)
- work requires contact with others (25)

Figure 1. The Five Dimensions of the QWL-C

DESCRIPTION OF THE INSTRUMENT

The Quality of Work Life-Conditions/Feelings instrument has two parts: the *Conditions* section and the *Feelings* section. The first consists of twenty-five items that ask the respondent to try to describe his or her actual work conditions objectively. These items comprise the five dimensions (or factors) described previously. The second part contains ten strongly interrelated items that measure the respondent's subjective feelings about his or her personal relation to work. This second part yields one score.

The QWL-C/F has several possible uses. The QWL-F score confirms the QWL-C index scores; that is, poor (alienating) work conditions should be associated with negative feelings, while good (involving or nonalienating) conditions should be found along with positive feelings. Repeated research shows these relations to be generally true, so it is a safe prediction that the QWL-F score will confirm the QWL-C index scores. Such confirmation can help respondents to understand and accept how their work conditions affect their feelings about work and the source of their feelings.

The QWL-C/F also can be used to diagnose specific work conditions, as a precursor to change or OD efforts. When workers can see the quantitative effects of negative work conditions, their commitment to change may be obtained more easily and acted on more strenuously.

QWL-C scores can be used to determine whether there is substantial agreement on the quality of work life conditions. If only a few workers report very poor conditions, they may be perceiving the work setting in an idiosyncratic manner or there may be a need for only minor changes centered on these few workers, saving the organization the substantial costs of major organization development/change efforts. Further, the QWL-C is quite specific in pinpointing aspects of the work setting that may or may not need modification. The indices and items involve very clear and detailed guidelines for designing particular changes in work conditions.

Finally, the QWL-C/F can be used as a follow-up assessment tool, since the items refer to specific, existing conditions and affective states and are therefore not likely to be affected severely by the fact that individuals have used the QWL-C/F before.

Psychometric Characteristics

The items used in the QWL-C were developed on the basis of earlier research—by Robert Blauner (1964), Michael Aiken and Jerald Hage (1966), and Barbara Kirsch and Joseph Lengermann (1971). Further research by Freda Lengel (1976) led to a modified version of the QWL-C, which was shown to consist of at least five reasonably independent factors by means of a standard varimax factor analysis (orthogonal rotation, eigenvalues greater than one).

The QWL-F items derive from several sources, including earlier work by George A. Miller (1967), Nancy Morse and Richard S. Weiss (1955), and Melvin Seeman (1959). Two of the items were composed by Kirsch and Lengermann specifically for the study cited above. The scale was shown to possess very high reliability, with Cronbach's (1961) alpha equal to .925 and item-to-scale correlations ranging from .64 to .85 (mean = .78).

HOW TO USE THE QWL-C/F

The QWL-C/F can be used for organizational (or unit) assessment or in a training context. In the former case, if the focus is on changing specific conditions, QWL-F data usually will be of tangential or incidental relevance (unless the workers and supervisors involved in the change effort must be made to see how work conditions affect their personal feelings, in which case QWL-F data may be explored in depth, much as in a training context). When used in OD/change efforts, QWL-C data may be summarized and dealt with in a typical survey-feedback session (Bowers & Franklin, 1977; Hausser, Pecorella, & Wissler, 1977; Nadler, 1977). Alternatively, the "raw" QWL-C data can be examined, much as in a training design (except that QWL-F data would not be examined in depth), and then used to develop action-change plans.

When training is the primary focus, it is very important that trainees have the opportunity to correlate their own QWL-C and QWL-F scores, as well as to examine the relationship between the C and F scores. Although the QWL-C/F data will be easier to interpret when training is conducted with intact or "family" work groups, one must be aware that the result may be increased awareness of commonly perceived negative work conditions and that this could lead to expectations that changes will be made. If no changes actually occur (or are intended), it would be better not to use the instrument, because raising expectations, followed by failure to fulfill those expectations, typically leads to a decline in QWL-F scores and in other, more direct, measures of effectiveness.

The effective use of any instrument in a training setting depends on the trainer's skill in carrying out seven basic steps: (a) administering the instrument; (b) making the theoretical presentation to trainees; (c) helping the trainees to relate to the instrument by examining their own expectations with respect to their scores; (d) scoring the instrument; (e) posting the results and sharing them openly or anonymously; (f) interpreting the results with the trainees in terms of the entire group's results, their own expectations, and norms obtained from other, similar, populations; and (g) providing the trainees with the opportunity to discuss the implications of their scores.

Administering the QWL-C/F

The items on the QWL-C/F are written clearly and should be easy to respond to; there are no hidden meanings or implications. As with any such instrument, honest and accurate expression of perceptions and feelings must be emphasized. In some cases it may be appropriate to assure those taking the instrument that their responses will be confidential. The process of filling out the form is extremely simple: the letters indicating responses are circled and the letters are then transferred to a scoring grid that shows a numerical value for each response. These numbers are in five columns, corresponding to the five dimensions of the QWL-C, so the score for each dimension is obtained by summing the column.

The instrument can be completed easily in ten to fifteen minutes.

The instructions for the QWL-C/F emphasize—and it is useful to remind respondents explicitly of this—the need to respond to the QWL-C items as *objectively* as possible, irrespective of personal likes, dislikes, or reactions, and the need when answering QWL-F items to express honestly and in accurate degree one's *feelings* about work conditions.

Theory Presentation

Respondents should be told of the three basic categories of work conditions that have been found to have strong effects on people's feelings about work. The first is power or control in regard to one's own work activities. The second is the meaning experienced in one's work. The third is the need for task-relevant interaction in the course of performing the work. The five dimensions that have been described in detail—autonomy (AUT), work speed and routine (WSR), task-related interaction (TRI), personal growth opportunity (PGO), and work complexity (WCO)—should be presented and discussed. Participants may, for example, be asked to give examples of positive and negative conditions for each dimension.

Respondents should then be asked what feelings about work they would expect of people exposed to such positive or negative conditions. This should lead to a discussion of the nature of affective (emotional) alienation from work.

Finally, respondents may be told that the QWL-C measures the five quality of work life *conditions*, while the QWL-F measures one's quality of work life *feelings*. By measuring the quality of work life conditions, one can gain insight about what changes are desirable or needed. The QWL-F data can be used to validate these needs, as well as to reinforce the effects of poor work-life conditions.

Examining Expectations

Next, the trainer, or change facilitators using the QWL-C/F with a work group, should ask the respondents to estimate their own scores (and the group scores if respondents are part of an "intact" work group). A simple chart, as shown in Table 1, can be posted for this purpose. The chart also may be used to show "predicted" and "actual" scores. For intact work groups, the trainer may ask each person to hand in an anonymous copy of his or her prediction chart, so that an anonymous group prediction chart can be posted.

Table 1. Chart of Predictions of QWL-C/F Scores

	(AUT) Autonomy		(WSR) Work Speed and Routine		(TRI) Task-Related Interaction		(PGO) Personal Growth Opportunity		(WCO) Work Complexity		(QWL-F) Feelings	
	Personal	Group	Personal	Group	Personal	Group	Personal	Group	Personal	Group	Personal	Group
Very good												
Good												
Average												
Poor												
Very poor												

The distributions shown here are not based on research norms; they are intended to provide general guidelines rather than specific interpretations.

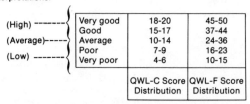

(High)	Very good	18-20	45-50
	Good	15-17	37-44
(Average)	Average	10-14	24-36
	Poor	7-9	16-23
(Low)	Very poor	4-6	10-15
		QWL-C Score Distribution	QWL-F Score Distribution

Scoring the QWL-C/F

Scoring sheets follow the QWL-C and QWL-F forms. After the respondents have circled all the response letters on the instrument forms, they transfer their responses to the scoring sheets, on which corresponding numbers for each response are printed. The scoring sheet shows how the numerical item scores are to be added to obtain scores for each of the five QWL-C dimensions.

For QWL-F scores, the same transfer process yields ten numbers, which are simply added to generate a score.

Posting Results

In general, it is best to collect copies of the respondents' five QWL-C scores and of their QWL-F scores, rather than calling for a show of hands. The responses can be tallied on a chart as shown in Table 1 or respondents may submit forms such as the one that follows:

AUT	High
WSR	Average
TRI	Low
PGO	Low
WCO	Average
QWL-F	Average

Each respondent would merely list the five QWL-C dimensions and the QWL-F, indicating the *range* in which he or she scored for each dimension. This allows the posting process to be completed in considerably less time.

Interpretation and Dyadic Processing

This is likely to be the most important step in the effective use of any instrument. The public posting of scores, even if done anonymously, serves to reduce some of the fears and concerns that respondents have about their own scores being "bad," undesirable, or unusual. Respondents are then able to see that their scores are not strange or out of the ordinary. In groups of more than ten, it is unlikely that any one person will have a unique set of scores. If the group is composed of trainees from a variety of work settings, it is very likely that the results will show a range of scores, so everyone can see that there are others in much the same range, at least with respect to some of the QWL-C dimensions.

If the group is composed of members of an intact work unit, it is almost certain that there will be considerable similarity of QWL-C scores, and many people are likely to be close on QWL-F scores. It is unlikely that anyone will have deviant scores, whether the group is composed of trainees from different jobs or an intact work team. It is, however, quite important that the trainer or consultant explicitly point out the similarities in QWL-C/F scores.

The next task of the trainer is to give a model for dyadic processing. It is usually helpful for the trainer/consultant to first post his or her own scores and to comment on how each score relates to the trainer's pre-test expectations (by explicitly and publicly reviewing the chart from Table 1, which should have been prepared in advance). This also is a good time to review briefly the nature of each QWL-C dimension and the meaning of the QWL-F score.

The trainer or consultant should then review these scores with another member of the training staff, if at all possible. Trainees can listen to this discussion, which should focus on the two sets of scores, their similarities and differences, and what the personal implications of the scores are. The effects or implications for the trainer's own work behavior should be explored. While this should be an open and honest discussion, it should not be psychologically deep or *intensely* personal. About ten minutes of such discussion is sufficient.

After this behavior modeling by the teaching staff, the participants are asked to form pairs and to carry on similar discussions. The pairs should be self-selected, so trainees can pick friends *or* strangers to share with, depending on their preferences. When working with an intact work unit, it also is wise to allow self-selection because there still will be some preferences (e.g., people will feel more positively about certain co-workers and less positively about others).

The dyadic discussions should last for about twenty minutes—ten minutes for each person. The trainer should give a ten-minute time signal so that no one is short changed in speaking time.

Group Processing

The final step can be conducted in small groups of from five to ten persons each or, in the case of an intact work unit, in one large group. The purpose is to integrate personal scores with the concepts behind the QWL-C/F and to relate the scores to behavioral implications. The trainer may wish to begin this step with a lecturette on quality of work life conditions and how they relate to feelings and behaviors, based on the introductory material and the interpretive guide.

Some obvious questions for discussion are:

1. Did the QWL-C dimension scores actually relate to QWL-F scores?
2. How "real" are the QWL-C scores? What evidence is there that these are not just based on individual perceptions?

3. Are high or low scores on any one QWL-C dimension especially important? Which and why?
4. What kinds of *work behaviors* (e.g., work quality, work quantity, tardiness, absenteeism, turnover) are associated with good QWL-C scores? With poor QWL-C scores? With positive QWL-F scores? With poor QWL-F scores?
5. What can be done to change quality of work life conditions for the better?

It is likely that any negative self-perceptions from QWL-C/F scores will be eliminated in this final processing discussion, because it should become clear that the QWL-C taps actual work conditions as seen by various people. However, it is especially important that neither trainees nor intact group members receive the impression that changing work life conditions is quick or easy to do. This is especially true for intact work units; when people expect changes and their expectations are unfulfilled, their QWL-F scores are likely to drop even lower and their work behaviors are likely to be affected negatively. When effectively conducted, however, this final processing can be an initial step toward significant change.

INTERPRETIVE GUIDELINES

The QWL-C/F was developed empirically from a long series of theory-based research studies and is supported by a substantial data base. Because each of the research studies took advantage of prior results and involved revised instruments, no broad set of normative data has yet been developed. Some broad guidelines are shown in Table 1, based on prior experience and assuming an essentially normal response distribution for the QWL-C/F. Because one may have greater confidence in the conceptual basis of the dimensions of the QWL-C/F than in the meaning of specific scores, it is best to interpret the results as a *pattern* of responses of an individual across the five dimensions, rather than focusing on any one score for one dimension. The consistency of QWL-F scores with QWL-C scoring patterns, as discussed above, is also important.

REFERENCES

Aiken, M., & Hage, J. Organizational alienation: A comparative analysis. *American Sociological Review*, 1966, *31*, 497-507.

Blauner, R. *Alienation and freedom*. Chicago: University of Chicago Press, 1964.

Bowers, D.G., & Franklin, J.L. *Survey guided development I: Data-based organizational change*. San Diego, CA: University Associates, 1977.

Cronbach, L.J. Coefficient alpha and the internal structure of tests. *Psychometrika*, 1961, *16*, 297-334.

Durkheim, E. *De la division du travail social [The division of labor in society]* (G. Simpson, trans.). New York: Free Press, 1947. (Originally published 1893.)

Hackman, J.R., & Oldham, G.R. *Work redesign*. Reading, MA: Addison-Wesley, 1980.

Hausser, D.L., Pecorella, P.A., & Wissler, A.L. *Survey guided development II: A manual for consultants*. San Diego, CA: University Associates, 1977.

Herzberg, F., Mausner, B., & Snyderman, B. *The motivation to work* (2nd ed.). New York: John Wiley, 1959.

Katz, D., & Kahn, R.L. *The social psychology of organizations*. New York: John Wiley, 1966.

Kirsch, B.A., & Lengermann, J.J. An empirical test of Robert Blauner's ideas on alienation in work as applied to different type jobs in a white-collar setting. *Sociology and Social Research*, 1971, *56*, 180-194.

Lengel, F. The existence and impact of alienating job conditions in the hospital medical laboratory. Unpublished master's project report, Wayne State University, 1976.

Marx, K. *Economic and philosophical manuscripts of 1844*. Moscow: Foreign Languages Publishing House, 1961.

Maurer, J.G. *The relationship of perceived task attributes and opportunity to contribute to the meaning of work*. Paper presented at the 19th international meeting of The Institute of Management Sciences, Houston, Texas, April 7, 1972.

Mayo, E. *The human problems of an industrial civilization*. New York: Macmillan, 1933.

Miller, G.A. Professionals in bureaucracy: Alienation among industrial scientists and engineers. *American Sociological Review*, 1967, *32*, 755-768.

Morse, N.C., & Weiss, R.S. The function and meaning of work and the job. *American Sociological Review*, 1955, 22, 191-198.

Nadler, D.A. *Feedback and organization development*. Reading, MA: Addison-Wesley, 1977.

Sashkin, M., & Morris, W.C. *Organizational behavior and management: Concepts and experiences*. Reston, VA: Reston Publishing, 1984.

Seeman, M. On the meaning of alienation. *American Sociological Review*, 1959, 24, 783-791.

Wilmoth, G.A. A test of the discriminant validity of two measures of work conditions and two measures of affective responses to work. Paper presented at the annual meeting of the Southeastern Psychological Association, Atlanta, GA, March 1983.

Marshall Sashkin, Ph.D., is a professor of industrial and organizational psychology at the University of Maryland University College. He has conducted training seminars on managerial topics and has published numerous books and professional articles on organizational behavior and change, performance appraisal, leadership, and participative management. Dr. Sashkin's latest UA book, co-edited with William R. Lassey, is Leadership and Social Change (Third Edition, Revised and Updated).

Joseph J. Lengermann, Ph.D., is an associate professor in the Department of Sociology at the University of Maryland, College Park, Maryland, where he teaches courses in industrial sociology, sociology of occupations and professions, formal organizations, and health service organizations. He currently is involved in a synthesis of organizational research performed in hospitals during the 1970s. His other interests are in the areas of professionalization/deprofessionalization and work alienation/satisfaction.

QUALITY OF WORK LIFE-CONDITIONS/FEELINGS

General Instructions:

The Quality of Work Life-Conditions/Feelings (QWL-C/F) instrument measures the objective conditions of one's work setting and one's personal reactions to those conditions. It is then possible to look at how your work conditions compare with those of other people. This can be helpful in identifying possible areas for change and improvement. It is also possible to examine in a quantitative way just how one feels about one's personal relation to the job. This may validate the need for change, because certain feelings have been shown to result from certain objective job conditions.

For the QWL-C/F to be useful to you, it is very important that you respond honestly to each question. It is also important to separate the two parts clearly—Conditions and Feelings. Your answers to the QWL-C items should be descriptive of actual work *conditions* and should *not* reflect how you personally feel about the work or work conditions. The QWL-F items ask for your personal *feelings* about your work and work setting.

QUALITY OF WORK LIFE-CONDITIONS
Marshall Sashkin and Joseph J. Lengermann

Instructions: The following statements describe the objective characteristics of your job as well as the activities of your co-workers and supervisor. Try *not* to respond in terms of how much you like or dislike your job; just be as factually correct as possible. Imagine how an outside observer would rate these statements. Circle the appropriate letter (frequency rating) for each statement.

	All the time	Most of the time	Part of the time	Never
1. People in my position are allowed to make some decisions, but most of the decisions about their work must be referred to their supervisor.	A	M	P	N
2. People who do my job do not normally move on to better jobs as a direct result of the opportunities the job offers.	A	M	P	N
3. People in my position are required to produce a specified amount of work each day.	A	M	P	N
4. People in my position perform tasks that are repetitive in nature.	A	M	P	N
5. My work requires regular coordination with co-workers.	A	M	P	N
6. People in my position have a great deal of control over their work activities.	A	M	P	N
7. People who do my job have the opportunity to learn new skills in the course of their work.	A	M	P	N

The column headers (slanted) read: All the time / Most of the time / Part of the time / Never, corresponding to columns A M P N.

8. People in my position must work at a constant rate of speed; it is not possible to let the work go for a half-hour or so and then catch up later.   A   M   P   N

9. People at my level are required to follow certain procedures to do the work—procedures that they would not choose if it were up to them.   A   M   P   N

10. People in my position work alone, on their own tasks, with little or no interpersonal contact.   A   M   P   N

11. When they encounter problems in their work, people in my position must refer these problems to their supervisor; they cannot take any actions on their own.   A   M   P   N

12. People in my position must learn new methods in order to keep up with changes and new developments.   A   M   P   N

13. People in my position must work very rapidly.   A   M   P   N

14. My work does not involve completing a "whole" task.   A   M   P   N

15. People in my position are not allowed to help one another.   A   M   P   N

16. Our supervisor acts on some of the suggestions of the people in my section.   A   M   P   N

17. People in my position are permitted to try out methods of their own when performing the job.   A   M   P   N

18. People in my position have no control over the pace of work.   A   M   P   N

19. Jobs at my level fail to bring out the best abilities of the employees because they are very simple.   A   M   P   N

20. People in my position must interact with co-workers in order to accomplish their tasks.   A   M   P   N

21. People at my level can make their own decisions without checking with anyone else.   A   M   P   N

22. People at my level have the opportunity to learn about the other departments in the organization while performing their jobs.   A   M   P   N

23. My work must be completed on a set schedule.   A   M   P   N

24. People in my position perform the same series of tasks all day.   A   M   P   N

25. My work requires a great deal of contact with other people.   A   M   P   N

QUALITY OF WORK LIFE-FEELINGS
Marshall Sashkin and Joseph J. Lengermann

Instructions: The following statements describe your own personal feelings about your job. Try to be as honest as possible; do not tone down your feelings and do not exaggerate. Circle the appropriate letter (frequency rating) for each statement.

	Strongly disagree	Disagree	Uncertain	Agree	Strongly agree
1. I like the sort of work that I am doing.	SD	D	U	A	SA
2. My job gives me a chance to do the things that I do best.	SD	D	U	A	SA
3. My job gives me a feeling of pride or accomplishment.	SD	D	U	A	SA
4. My job is an important job.	SD	D	U	A	SA
5. My job is a rewarding experience.	SD	D	U	A	SA
6. If I inherited enough money to live comfortably without working, I still would continue to work at my present job.	SD	D	U	A	SA
7. If I had the opportunity to retire right now, I would prefer to do that rather than to go on working at my present job.	SD	D	U	A	SA
8. The only meaning that I find in my work is my paycheck.	SD	D	U	A	SA
9. I work to earn a living; my more important activities and interests are found outside my job.	SD	D	U	A	SA
10. My work is one of the most important things in my life.	SD	D	U	A	SA

QWL-C SCORING SHEET

Instructions: Transfer your responses to the statements on the QWL-C instrument to the scoring grid below and circle the number below the letter you have selected for each statement. When you have transferred all the letters and circled all the appropriate numbers, add up all the numbers circled in each of the vertical columns and enter the total in the empty box at the bottom of the column. Each of these totals refers to one of the scales of the QWL-C.

1.				2.				3.				4.				5.			
A	M	P	N	A	M	P	N	A	M	P	N	A	M	P	N	A	M	P	N
1	2	3	4	1	2	3	4	1	2	3	4	1	2	3	4	1	2	3	4
6.				7.				8.				9.				10.			
A	M	P	N	A	M	P	N	A	M	P	N	A	M	P	N	A	M	P	N
4	3	2	1	4	3	2	1	1	2	3	4	1	2	3	4	1	2	3	4
11.				12.				13.				14.				15.			
A	M	P	N	A	M	P	N	A	M	P	N	A	M	P	N	A	M	P	N
1	2	3	4	4	3	2	1	1	2	3	4	1	2	3	4	1	2	3	4
16.				17.				18.				19.				20.			
A	M	P	N	A	M	P	N	A	M	P	N	A	M	P	N	A	M	P	N
4	3	2	1	4	3	2	1	1	2	3	4	1	2	3	4	1	2	3	4
21.				22.				23.				24.				25.			
A	M	P	N	A	M	P	N	A	M	P	N	A	M	P	N	A	M	P	N
4	3	2	1	4	3	2	1	1	2	3	4	1	2	3	4	1	2	3	4
Autonomy (AUT)				Personal Growth Opportunity (PGO)				Work Speed and Routine (WSR)				Work Complexity (WCO)				Task-Related Interaction (TRI)			

QWL-F SCORING SHEET

Instructions: Transfer your responses to the ten QWL-F statements to the scoring columns below by circling the numbers corresponding to your letter answers. Add the numbers in each vertical column, then add the five column totals to result in a total QWL-F score. Then enter this score in the box provided.

	SD	D	U	UA	SA
1.	1	2	3	4	5
2.	1	2	3	4	5
3.	1	2	3	4	5
4.	1	2	3	4	5
5.	1	2	3	4	5
6.	1	2	3	4	5
7.	5	4	3	2	1
8.	5	4	3	2	1
9.	5	4	3	2	1
10.	1	2	3	4	5

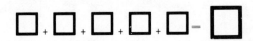

QWL-F Total:

A BIBLIOGRAPHY OF APPLICATIONS OF THE MYERS-BRIGGS TYPE INDICATOR (MBTI) TO MANAGEMENT AND ORGANIZATIONAL BEHAVIOR

John A. Sample

INTRODUCTION

Managers confronted with "personality clashes" between two employees who just cannot seem to get along often attribute such interpersonal confrontations to misunderstandings about roles and goals. However, the importance of individual differences and personality types should not be discounted in the management of human resources.

The Swiss psychiatrist Carl Gustav Jung developed a theory of personality types that says that what appears to be very random variation in human behavior is actually orderly, consistent, and predictable. Basic processes used by everyone are not equally developed in each person, and people have certain natural *preferences* for the ways in which they approach life. In other words, an individual uses all of the four processes identified by typology, but each person's personality type is distinguished by that person's relative preference for each of the processes. The Myers-Briggs Type Indicator (MBTI) is a self-inventory that classifies an individual into one of sixteen personality types, using the following four combinations:

1. Two *Orientations* to life: *Extraverted* (E) types prefer to direct their attention to the outer world of objects, people, and action; *Introverted* (I) types are inwardly attuned to the world of ideas, contemplation, and reflection. Extraverted managers are sociable, action oriented, and generally communicate well with colleagues and visitors. They are sometimes impatient with tedious and drawn-out tasks. The introverted manager will need quiet for concentration and must work without interruptions. Such people may have problems communicating with colleagues and usually work best alone. It is important to remember that although these are opposing orientations, each person has both, with one being dominant (or preferred).

2. Two ways of *Perceiving* (information gathering): *Sensing* (S) types prefer to look at the immediate and tangible facts of experience; *Intuitive* (N) types prefer to search out the future possibilities and to visualize conceptual and theoretical relationships. Sensing types appreciate structure and certainty; they are good bureaucrats because of their comfort with details, rules, and procedures. However, they may become stressed and anxious when ambiguity and uncertainty are introduced into the system. Intuitive people can holistically visualize new and creative possibilities. They are uncomfortable with stability and will become bored if not allowed or encouraged to be innovative and creative. They thrive on opportunities for problem-solving, but may make factual mistakes or jump to hasty conclusions.

3. Two ways of *Judging* (decision making): *Thinking* (T) types prefer to make decisions objectively, impersonally, and analytically in an orderly fashion; *Feeling* (F) types prefer to decide by a valuing process that weighs the importance of alternatives for self and others. Both the thinking and feeling approaches to decision making are rational processes. The manager who prefers the thinking mode is dependent on intellectual processes and has a tendency to fit problems and their solutions into standardized formulas. Although extremely fair in their approaches to personnel problems, such managers may be perceived as hardhearted because they are able to discipline employees or fire them when necessary. In contrast, feeling-type managers are uncomfortable when they have to discipline, suspend, or fire employees. Their decision processes emphasize affective and personal valuing of alternatives. Their need for friendly relations may interfere with results and outcome-oriented decisions. Although feeling-type managers tend to be conformists and accommodators, their empathetic and merciful presence is often needed to balance the impersonal nature of thinking managers.

4. Two *Attitudes* in respect to the outer world: *Judging* (J) types prefer an orderly, planned, and controlled life; *Perceptive* (P) types prefer to be flexible, spontaneous, and adaptable. Managers who prefer to be orderly and controlled will rely primarily on thinking or feeling. Managers who prefer the more flexible and adaptable approach will rely on either sensing or intuition. People who are prone to judging often will make impulsive decisions, while perceptive types may have problems in achieving closure.

As an example, the ESTJ (extraverted, sensing, thinking, judging) personality types have a natural affinity for business, industry, and production. These people like to work where they can achieve immediate, visible, and tangible results. They enjoy the executive role and they have little patience with confusion, inefficiency, or insufficiently thought-out solutions to critical problems. Because they are sensing, rather than intuitive, they are matter-of-fact, practical, and concerned with the here and now. There is great potential for a personality clash if an ESTJ manager attempts to supervise an INFP subordinate, who keeps to himself or herself and judges everything by personal values. Openmindedness and flexibility are the hallmark of the INFP person, who deeply values work that results in something other than a paycheck. The INFP's empathic understanding, insight, and long-range vision could understandably frustrate the practical, here-and-now needs of the ESTJ manager.

It is important to understand that each of the sixteen combinations of preferences has its excellent qualities as well as its problematic excesses. ESTJ's are necessary for the orderly and efficient use of organizational resources. However, they may not contemplate their futures (Intuition) and they may not attend to the affective side of their enterprises (Feeling). On occasion, they probably ought to postpone closure and be more adaptable and spontaneous (Perceptive).

The situational nature of management requires good "type development." The MBTI (Myers-Briggs Type Indicator) is the best method for determining an individual's dominant and auxiliary personality types. Both managers and employees should learn to value and trust the qualities inherent in each personality type. Each of the sixteen combinations can offer something to other people, to work, and to society. However, in the modern world, it behooves managers and employees alike to develop auxiliary strengths. Introverts can learn the skills for socializing comfortably with extroverts, and the intuitive dreamer can learn to be more realistic. The objective thinker who prizes fairness can learn to be more merciful and empathetic, and the orderly, controlled world of judgment can be tempered with spontaneous and open-ended perception. The person who explores his or her own personality type and who becomes sensitive to individual differences enters a dynamic learning environment.

BIBLIOGRAPHY

Use of the MBTI has increased in the past few years, with significant, growing interest from business, industry, and government. This bibliography is in response to that interest. In addition to the specialized references in this bibliography, the reader is encouraged to consult the following general references:

Briggs Myers, I. *Introduction to type.* Palo Alto, CA: Consulting Psychologists Press, 1981.

Briggs Myers, I. *Gifts differing.* Palo Alto, CA: Consulting Psychologists Press, 1980.

Keirsey, D., & Bates, M. *Please understand me.* Del Mar, CA: Prometheus Books, 1978.

Those readers interested in information and training should contact the Center for Applications of Psychological Type, Suite A, 2720 N. W. 6th Street, Gainesville, Florida 32601.

Career Specialization

Keen, P. G. Cognitive style and career specialization. *New perspectives on careers.* New York: John Wiley, 1977. (Chapter 4, pp. 89-104)

Laney, A. R. *Occupational implications of the Jungian personality function-type as identified by the Myers-Briggs Type Indicator.* Unpublished master's thesis, George Washington University, 1949.

Ohsawa, T. *MBTI experiences in Japan: Career choice, selection, placement and counseling for individual development.* Paper presented at the first national conference on the Myers-Briggs Type Indicator, Gainesville, Florida, October 1975.

Accountants

Jacoby, P. F. *An empirical descriptive study of selected personality characteristics of professional accountants based on Jungian typology.* Unpublished doctoral dissertation, George Washington University, 1980.

Jacoby, P. F. Psychological types and career success in the accounting profession. *Research in Psychological Type,* 1981, *4*, 24-37.

Architects

Hall, W. B., & MacKinnon, D. W. Personality inventory correlates of creativity among architects. *Journal of Applied Psychology,* 1969, *53*, 322-326.

Attorneys

Natter, F. The human factor: Psychological type in legal education. *Research in Psychological Type,* 1981, *3*, 55-67.

Health Care/Hospital Administration

Hai, D. M. *Are hospital administrators more humanitarian than their business counterparts: A look at personality type.* Paper presented at the meeting of the American Public Health Association, Miami Beach, Florida, October 1976.

Hai, D. M. Comparisons of personality dimensions in managers: Is there a management aptitude? *Akron Business and Economic Review,* 1983, *14*(1), 31-36.

Williams, M. R. The relationship between the MBTI and job satisfaction: A preliminary report. *American Journal of Medical Technology,* 1975, *41*(2), 56-60.

Williams, M. R. The relationships among the personality types, job satisfactions, and job specialties of a selected group of medical technologists (Doctoral dissertation, Florida State

University, 1976). *Dissertation Abstracts International*, 1977, *37*, 3342B. (University Microfilms No. 76-29, 495)

Engineers

Hay, J. E. The relationship of certain personality variables to managerial level and job performance among engineering managers (Doctoral dissertation, Temple University, 1964). *Dissertation Abstracts International*, 1964, *25*, 3973. (University Microfilms No. 64-13)

Hay, J. E. Self-ideal congruence among engineering managers. *Personnel and Guidance Journal*, 1966, *44*, 1084-1088.

Police

Hanewicz, W. Police personality: A Jungian perspective. *Crime & Delinquency*, 1978, *24*(2), 152-172.

Shealy, A. E. Police corruption: Screening out high-risk applicants. In C. D. Spielberger (Ed.), *Police selection and evaluation*. Washington, DC: Hemisphere Publishing, 1979.

Communication Style

Bledsoe, J. L. Your four communication styles. *Training*, 1976, *13*(3), 18-21.

Yeakley, F. R., Jr. Communication style preferences and adjustments as an approach to studying effects of similarity in psychological type. *Research in Psychological Type*, 1982, *5*, 30-48.

General

Hartzler, G. J., & Hartzler, M. T. Management uses of the Myers-Briggs Type Indicator. *Research in Psychological Type*, 1982, *5*, 20-29.

Lewis, R., & Margerison, C. J. *Personal mapping: Understanding personal preferences*. Cranfield, Bedford, England: Management and Organization Development Research Centre, Cranfield School of Management, 1979.

Pollitt, I. Managing differences in industry. *Research in Psychological Type*, 1982, *5*, 4-19.

Zmud, R. W. On the validity of the analytic-heuristic instrument utilized in the "Minnesota Experiments." *Management Science*, 1978, *24*(10), 1088-1090.

Group Dynamics and Process

Bouchard, T. J., Jr. Personality, problem solving procedure, and performance in small groups (Doctoral dissertation, University of California, 1966). *Dissertation Abstracts International*, 1967, *27*, 3685B. (University Microfilms No. 67-5007)

Bouchard, T. J., Jr. Personality, problem-solving procedure, and performance in small groups. *Journal of Applied Psychology*, 1969, *53*(1, Pt. 2), 1-29.

Gatti, G. M. *A comparison of self-perception between facilitated and leaderless developmental groups*. Unpublished masters thesis, Western Kentucky University, 1975.

Gilliard, W. The analysis of personality types and their relationship to perceived group behavior in a training group session (Doctoral dissertation, Kent State University, 1973). *Dissertation Abstracts International*, 1974, *34*, 3868A-3869A. (University Microfilms No. 73-32, 343)

Haber, R. A. Different strokes for different folks: Jung's typology and structured experiences. *Group & Organization Studies*, 1980, *5*(1), 113-121.

Kilmann, R. H., & Taylor, V. A contingency approach to laboratory learning: Psychological types versus experiential norms. *Human Relations*, 1974, *27*(9), 891-909.

Kilmann, R. H., & Thomas, K. W. Interpersonal conflict-handling behavior as reflections of Jungian personality dimensions. *Psychological Reports*, 1975, *37*(3), 971-980.

McCaulley, M. H. How individual differences affect health care teams. *Health Team News,* 1975, *1*(8). (Available from the Center for Applications of Psychological Type, Suite A, 2720 N.W. 6th Street, Gainesville, Florida 32601)

Pratt, L. K., Uhl, N. P., & Little, E. R. Evaluation of games as a function of personality type. *Simulation & Games,* September 1980, *11*(3), 336-346.

Rifkind, L. J. An analysis of the effects of personality type upon the risky shift in small group discussions (Doctoral dissertation, Florida State University, 1975). *Dissertation Abstracts International,* 1976, *36*(12), 7734A. (University Microfilms No. 76-13, 830)

Steele, F. I. Personality and the "laboratory style." *Journal of Applied Behavioral Science,* 1968, *4*, 25-45.

Human Information Processing

Agor, W. H. Brain skills development in management training. *Training and Development Journal,* 1983, *37*, 78-83.

Evered, R. D. Organizational activism and its relation to "reality" and mental imagery. *Human Relations,* 1977, *30*(4), 311-334.

McKenney, J. L., & Keen, P. G. How managers' minds work. *Harvard Business Review,* 1974, *52*, 79-90.

Robey, D., & Taggart, W. Measuring managers' minds: The assessment of style in human information processing. *Academy of Management Review,* 1981, *6*(3), 375-383.

Smith, A. W., & Urban, T. F. *Myers-Briggs personality orientations and information processing styles: Implications for management education and development.* Paper presented at the meeting of the National Academy of Management, San Francisco, August 1978.

Taggart, W. M., & Robey, D. Minds and managers: On the dual nature of human information processing and management. *Academy of Management Review,* 1981, *6*(2), 187-195.

Job Satisfaction

French, R. M., & Rezler, A. G. Personality and job satisfaction of medical technologists. *American Journal of Medical Technology,* 1976, *42*(3), 92-103.

Williams, M. R. The relationship between the MBTI and job satisfaction: A preliminary report. *American Journal of Medical Technology,* 1975, *41*(2), 56-60.

Leadership

Beck, J. B. Relationships between personality type and managerial style of leadership personnel in nursing (Doctoral dissertation, University of Florida, 1976). *Dissertation Abstracts International,* 1976, *37*, 4988B. (University Microfilms No. 77-8142).

Dietl, J. A. *A study reflecting the dominant personality style most successful in exemplifying effective situational leadership within a corporate organization.* Unpublished doctoral dissertation, U.S. International University, 1980.

Duch, R. G. *The inservice preparation of Catholic secondary school principals for a leadership role in local staff development.* Unpublished doctoral dissertation, University of Pittsburgh, 1980.

Gryskiewicz, S. S., Vaught, S., & Johanssan, C. B. *Describing the creative leader.* Paper presented at the First National Conference on the Myers-Briggs Type Indicator, Gainesville, Florida, October 1975.

O'Roark, A. M. *Type and leadership.* Paper presented at the First National Conference on the Myers-Briggs Type Indicator, Gainesville, Florida, October 1975.

Schweiger, D. M., and Jago, A. G. Problem-solving styles and participative decision making. *Psychological Reports,* 1982, *50*, 1311-1316.

Wyeth, E. R. Evaluation of the effectiveness of the leadership training program in the area of the deaf at San Fernando Valley State College. *American Annals of the Deaf,* 1965, *110*, 479-482.

Management Information Systems

Barnes, P. H. A study of personality characteristics of selected computer programmers and computer programmer trainees (Doctoral dissertation, Auburn University, 1974). *Dissertation Abstracts International,* 1974, *35,* 1440A. (University Microfilms No. 74-20, 785)

Davis, D. L. *An experimental investigation of the form of information presentation, psychological type of the user, and performance within the context of a management information system.* Unpublished doctoral dissertation, University of Florida, 1980.

Mason, R. O., & Mitroff, I. I. A program for research on management information systems. *Management Science,* 1973, *19*(5), 475-487.

Managerial Problem-Solving Styles

Bouchard, T. J., Jr. Personality, problem solving procedure, and performance in small groups (Doctoral dissertation, University of California, 1966). *Dissertation Abstracts International,* 1967, *27,* 3685B. (University Microfilms No. 67-5007)

Bouchard, T. J., Jr. Personality, problem-solving procedure, and performance in small groups. *Journal of Applied Psychology,* 1969, *53*(1, Pt. 2), 1-29.

Caldwell, B. S., Jr. Task situation and personality characteristics as influences on the consistency of behavior in learning and problem solving tasks (Doctoral dissertation, University of Texas, 1965). *Dissertation Abstracts International,* 1965, *26,* 2047-2048. (University Microfilms No. 65-10, 715)

De Waele, M. Managerial style and the design of decision aids. *Omega: The International Journal of Management Science,* 1978, *6*(1), 5-13.

Ellis, N. D. The relationship between identifiable attributes and decision-making ability of purchasing personnel as measured by the results of a management game (Doctoral dissertation, North Texas State University, 1973). *Dissertation Abstracts International,* 1973, *34,* 1417A-1418A. (University Microfilms No. 73-22, 841)

Hellriegel, D., & Slocum, J. W. Managerial problem-solving styles. *Business Horizons,* 1975, *18*(6), 29-37.

Hellriegel, D., & Slocum, J. W., Jr. Preferred organizational designs and problem-solving styles: Interesting comparisons. *Human Systems Management,* 1980, *1,* 151-158.

Hellriegel, D., Slocum, J. W., Jr., & Woodman, R. W. Managerial problem-solving styles. *Organizational Behavior* (3rd ed.). St. Paul, MN: West, 1983.

Henderson, J., & Nutt, P. The influence of decision style on decision-making behavior. *Management Science,* 1980, *26*(4), 371-386.

Hoy, F., & Vaught, B. C. The relationship between problem-solving styles and problem-solving skills among entrepreneurs. *Research in Psychological Type,* 1981, *4,* 38-45.

Keen, P. G. The implications of cognitive style for individual decision making (Doctoral dissertation, Harvard University, 1973). *Dissertation Abstracts International,* 1974, *34,* 5238B. (University Microfilms No. 74-09036)

Kerin, R. A., & Slocum, J. W., Jr. Decision-making style and acquisition of information: Further exploration of the use of the Myers-Briggs Type Indicator. *Psychological Reports,* 1981, *49,* 132-134.

Mitroff, I. I., & Kilmann, R. H. Stories managers tell: A new tool for organizational problem-solving. *Management Review,* 1975, *64*(7), 18-28.

Steckroth, R., Slocum, J., & Sims, H. Organizational roles, cognitive roles and problem-solving styles. *Journal of Experimental Learning and Simulation,* 1980, *2,* 77-87.

Vasarhelyi, M. A. *Man-machine planning systems: A behavioral examination of interactive decision-making.* Unpublished doctoral dissertation, University of California at Los Angeles, 1973.

Wade, P. F. *Some factors affecting problem-solving effectiveness in business: A study of management consultants.* Unpublished doctoral dissertation, McGill University, 1981.

Management Training/Staff Development

Duch, R. G. *The inservice preparation of Catholic secondary school principals for a leadership role in local staff development.* Unpublished doctoral dissertation, University of Pittsburgh, 1980.

Holt, D. A. *Use of MBTI in management training.* Paper presented at the First National Conference on the Myers-Briggs Type Indicator, Gainesville, Florida, October 1975.

Wyeth, E. R. Evaluation of the effectiveness of the leadership training program in the area of the deaf at San Fernando Valley State College. *American Annals of the Deaf,* 1965, *110,* 479-482.

Motivation

Gantz, B. S., Erickson, C., & Stephenson, R. W. Measuring the motivation to manage in a research and development population. *Proceedings of the 79th Annual Convention of the American Psychological Association,* 1971, *6*(1), 129-130. (Abstract)

Organization Development

Collins, J. A. Individual personality and organizational climate (Doctoral dissertation, Claremont Graduate School, 1965). *Dissertation Abstracts International,* 1966, *27,* 623A. (University Microfilms No. 66-3361)

Mink, O. G., Schultz, J. M., & Mink, B. P. *Developing and managing open organizations.* Austin, TX: Learning Concepts, 1979.

Slocum, J. W., Jr. Does cognitive style affect diagnosis and intervention strategies of change agents? *Group & Organization Studies,* 1978, *3*(2), 199-210.

Organizational Evaluation

Hoy, F., & Hellriegel, D. The Kilmann and Herden model of organizational effectiveness criteria: An empirical test. *Academy of Management Journal,* 1982, *25*(2), 308-322.

Kilmann, R. H., & Herden, R. P. Towards a systemic methodology for evaluating the impact of interventions on organizational effectiveness. *Academy of Management Review,* July 1976, 87-98.

Kilmann, R. H., & Mitroff, I. I. Qualitative versus quantitative analysis for management science: Different forms for different psychological types. *Interfaces,* 1976, *6*(2), 17-27.

School and College Administration

Cohen, S. R. Using the Myers-Briggs Type Indicator with teachers, supervisors, administrators and students: A program review. *Research in Psychological Type,* 1981, *3,* 42-47.

Duch, R. G. *The inservice preparation of Catholic secondary school principals for a leadership role in local staff development.* Unpublished doctoral dissertation, University of Pittsburgh, 1980.

Fobinash, R. J. A study of principals' personalities and their differences in judging the prime competencies required to perform the tasks of the secondary school principalships (Doctoral dissertation, University of Utah, 1976). *Dissertation Abstracts International,* 1976, *37,* 1325A. (University Microfilms No. 76-20, 746)

Frederick, A. H. Self actualization and personality type: A comparative study of doctoral majors in educational administration and the helping relations (Doctoral dissertation, The

University of Alabama, 1974). *Dissertation Abstracts International,* 1975, *35,* 7055A. (University Microfilms No. 75-9896)

Grant, W. H., & Foy, J. E. Career patterns of student personnel administrators. *National Association of Student Personnel Administrators Journal,* 1972, *10*(2), 106-113.

Jensen, D. C. An analysis of administrative functions and their relationship to personality preferences of selected Wisconsin school superintendents (Doctoral dissertation, Loyola University of Chicago, 1977). *Dissertation Abstracts International,* 1977, *37,* 6872A. (University Microfilms No. 77-10, 726)

Kellerman, J. S. *Changes in management/personality styles of department chairpersons: A case study at Valencia Community College.* Unpublished doctoral dissertation, Nova University, 1975. (ERIC Document Reproduction Service No. ED 129 393)

Plaxton, R. P. *Personality of the principal and school organizational climate.* Unpublished master's thesis, University of Alberta, 1965.

Schroeder, C. S. Designing ideal staff environments through milieu management. *Journal of College Student Personnel,* 1979, *19,* 129-135.

Stone, A. G. An investigation into personality relationships between principals and teachers (Doctoral dissertation, University of Utah, 1974). *Dissertation Abstracts International,* 1974, *35,* 2613A. (University Microfilms No. 74-22, 688)

Von Fange, E. A. *Implications for school administration of the personality structure of educational personnel.* Unpublished doctoral dissertation, University of Alberta, 1961.

Von Fange, E. A. Principals and personality. *The Canadian Administrator,* 1962, *11*(4), 1-2.

Wright, J. A. The relationship of rated administrator and teacher effectiveness to personality as measured by the Myers-Briggs personality type indicator (Doctoral dissertation, Claremont Graduate School, 1966). *Dissertation Abstracts International,* 1967, *28,* 981A. (University Microfilms No. 67-10, 765)

Strategic Management

Evered, R. D. Conceptualizing the future: Implications for strategic management in a turbulent environment (Doctoral dissertation, University of California, 1973). *Dissertation Abstracts International,* 1973, *34,* 3625A-3626A. (University Microfilms No. 73-32, 663)

Mitroff, I. I., Barabba, V. P., & Kilmann, R. H. The application of behavioral and philosophical technologies to strategic planning: A case study of a large federal agency. *Management Science,* 1977, *24*(1), 44-58.

Stress Management

Cooley, E. J., & Keesey, J. C. Moderator variables in life stress and illness relationship. *Journal of Human Stress,* 1981, *7*(3), 35-40.

John A. Sample is the executive director of Professional Development Specialists, Inc., a Tallahassee, Florida, consulting and training firm that specializes in management and organization development. Mr. Sample formerly was an assistant professor and director of the Master of Science in Management Program for the Graduate School, Biscayne College, Miami, Florida. His teaching interests include cultural and behavioral factors in organizations, human resource management, adult learning and development, and management and organization development.

INTRODUCTION TO THE
PROFESSIONAL DEVELOPMENT SECTION

This is the first Professional Development section to appear in an *Annual*. The purpose of this section is to bring together a variety of materials that will aid in the personal, professional development of practitioners in the field of human resource development. The section will include surveys of how the field is progressing and where it might be going; discussions of stresses and dilemmas encountered by professionals in their daily work; new techniques and technologies; new perspectives, outlooks, and theoretical developments; and overviews of specific content areas.

This section will include articles that HRD professionals can bring to the attention of their management colleagues or present in a training session. Such articles can be useful in supporting a position or in further explaining an intricate or subtle point. These articles also might be useful to help "sell" HRD to line managers who prefer to learn by reading or who need some background information to support their emerging understanding.

The new Professional Development section also includes the type of content that formerly appeared in the Lecturettes and Resources sections. Some lecturettes now will be incorporated into related structured experiences or instruments. Those that appear alone will include more background and theory for the HRD professional as well as information on when and where such a lecturette would be appropriate. Resource pieces will alert the reader to additional readings, educational programs, materials, groups, or other sources of further professional development in a wide variety of subject areas related to applied behavioral science, management, and training and development.

The fourteen articles that appear in this first Professional Development section cover a range of topics and concerns. The initial piece is an attempt by the editors, based on their experiences in the field of human resource development, to review the current status and future directions of that emerging field. This is followed by an article by Pareek and Rao on the critical importance of line managers in the human resource development process. The third piece, by Lewis, cogently argues that organization development requires a management perspective—one that is often neglected.

Warren Bennis, one of the seminal figures in HRD, offers an observation on why it is so difficult to apply behavioral science theory and knowledge in organizations. One of our international colleagues, Mastenbroek, provides us with an incisive analysis of the importance of power in organizational relationships. Thomas follows with a practical guide to using a variety of needs-assessment procedures in assessing HRD needs in an organization. Goodstein and Cooke then offer an introduction to and overview of organization development, a primer on this important part of HRD.

Following this are conceptual articles that focus on specific processes rather than on the total sytem. Zobrist and Enggist offer a way of including sociotechnical systems thinking in the consulting process. Sashkin provides a guide to participative management, including an analysis of what forms participative management can take, the known consequences of participative management, and how to install such programs. Ackerman offers a provocative piece on the new role of the manager in facilitating transformation and managing the flow state in the organization. Sample identifies the implications of the expectancy theory of motivation for HRD professionals. Rasmussen provides a new view of interpersonal feedback and some of its problems.

McCormick offers a resource guide for additional information and training in neuro-linguistic programming (NLP) as well as a review of the research in this new field. Finally, Pfeiffer provides a hard-nosed look at the responsibilities of consultants in helping managers to deal effectively with marginal employees.

The HRD professional who is able to absorb and apply the content of this Professional Development section will be well prepared to deal with the job demands of today and many of those of the foreseeable future. One of the roles of HRD professionals is to try to "stretch" participants in HRD programs. It seems only fitting that we, the professionals, should do the same thing to ourselves.

HUMAN RESOURCE DEVELOPMENT: CURRENT STATUS AND FUTURE DIRECTIONS

Leonard D. Goodstein and J. William Pfeiffer

There have been few periods in time when there have been more interest and excitement in the "people" dimension of organizations, in the field of human resources. Three books in this field have been at the top of the *New York Times* nonfiction best-seller list for almost a year: *In Search of Excellence* (Peters & Waterman, 1982), *Megatrends* (Naisbitt, 1982), and *The One Minute Manager* (Blanchard & Johnson, 1982). Organizations are buying these books in case lots to distribute to their management teams. Operating concepts are being challenged and corporate cultures are being changed as applications of the lessons from these books are attempted in a variety of organizations.

Perhaps the most significant reason for the increased interest in human resources has been the growing awareness that many American organizations are not winning the competitive game. The figures on the decline of American productivity in the past three decades are too well known to require repetition here, as is the success of Japanese business on an international basis. This success has been attributed to the devotion and dedication of the Japanese workers. In contrast, the indifference and apathy of American workers has led to a sharp decline in the quality and marketability of American products. The contrast between American and Japanese productivity and success has produced a crisis in American business. This crisis has been analyzed and discussed extensively, and the concern is not limited to such business publications as the *Wall Street Journal, Forbes, Fortune,* or *Business Week.* There is increasing agreement that the solution to this problem is to be found in better utilization of America's human resources. Such utilization would require a better understanding of (and more emphasis on) human resource management. The Sunday newspaper's *Parade Magazine* of July 10th, 1983, identified human resource management as one of three or four "hot" occupations of the coming decade, with a need for talented people who would assume considerable organizational responsibility (and salaries to match). However, these people will be functioning in an organizational environment that is different from that of the past. This "new breed" of managers will be exercising its power in a broader-based, productivity-oriented environment.

THE EVOLUTION OF HUMAN RESOURCE MANAGEMENT

Three rather different and traditionally separate organizational components previously have been concerned with the management of the organization's human resources: (a) *personnel administration*—the administrative and maintenance function (record keeping, recruitment, compensation, etc.); (b) *industrial relations*—the function of dealing with unions (collective bargaining, union-management grievances, etc.); and (c) *human relations*—the function of dealing with people and organizational relationships (training, career development, organization development, etc.). Although the structure of these three components varies from organization to organization and from industry to industry, their separateness and, all too often, their competitiveness within the organization are historical fact. It is now clear that there is a strong shift toward integration of these three components into a single, integrated human resource management function.

There are several reasons for this change. First is the growing awareness that we must develop, conserve, and optimize the human resources in organizations if we are to reverse the trend toward declining productivity. There also is increased awareness that a piecemeal, catch-as-catch-can approach simply will not produce the increases in effectiveness that are required.

As Michael Beer, professor of management at the Harvard Graduate School of Business, pointed out in a speech at the Annual Convention of the American Society for Personnel Administration in May of 1983, there is a world-wide shift toward an "ideology of communitarism." By this Beer means a greater concern with the whole as more than the sum of its parts. In contrast with the traditional ideology, which supports individualism, property rights, and the marketplace as the regulator, the new ideology is concerned with the community and its well-being, not just with the well-being of individuals. It is concerned with the rights of those who are managed as well as with the rights of managers. Communitarism also recognizes that the marketplace as the ultimate control system simply does not work as was once expected. There also are more stakeholders in the organizational matrix, including the community and the government, in the form of regulations. These regulations focus on the consequences of decisions (and how these decisions fit together into a pattern, with a pattern of consequences). Beer believes that changes are taking place in our view of human resources that reflect this fundamental shift. Marilyn Ferguson (1980) chronicles this "construct shift" in her book, *Aquarian Conspiracy:* "There is a transformation of organizational values taking place, one generated from within organizations" (p. 143).

Changes in the Human Resource Function

The traditional human resource function was dominated by either the labor relations or personnel staff, depending on the nature of the business. There was little attempt to coordinate efforts into a total, integrated system. This fractionation of the HRD function typically has led to inappropriate competition for limited resources by the rival factions, turning human resource development into a lose-lose game in the eyes of senior management.

Another serious problem has been the failure to see training in a systemic way. Consider the following all-too-typical example: Management asks the training staff to design a program that will increase the communication skills of the first-line supervisors so that the turnover of production workers will be reduced. The training staff obligingly performs, and all first-line supervisors obediently complete the latest and best supervisory-skills training program. A year later, top management discovers that there has been no change in turnover and blames the training director.

Only a courageous and skillful training director would respond that the program probably *did* work, that the supervisors did acquire the desired skills as a result of attending the program. But there may be neither incentives nor rewards in the system for *practicing* the skills. All too often, neither the performance expectations nor the compensation program is adjusted to support the use of new skills or new ways of doing things. Obviously, a nonintegrated human resource system is a nonfunctional system. The human resource management staff must be concerned with the system-wide aspects of human resource utilization in the organization, with the "fit" between personnel policies and practices and between them and the organization, just as engineering or finance must be concerned on this integrative, global level with how policies about machinery or money are integrated.

The Term "Human Resource Management"

The evolution of the term "human resource management" is the most significant sign of the transformational development of the field. Its rapid adoption will facilitate the necessary integration of those piecemeal practices that have heretofore limited the impact of the field.

Acknowledgment of the critical importance of *managing* human resources will dramatically and significantly change the role of the human resource professional in organizations. Although training and development undoubtedly will continue to be part of their function, human resource personnel will be recognized as an integral part of the top-management team, with increased status and power to influence the direction of the organization.

With this shift in title and emphasis, human resource management will be able to influence organizations in profound ways, including the focusing of management's attention on the necessity for a shift in the locus of organizational control. There already has been a shift in top-down control toward more worker participation, especially in production facilities in which quality circles have been installed successfully. There also has been a shift toward focusing more on the importance of intrinsic satisfaction in work rather than on traditional rewards (which have only the effect of reducing dissatisfaction rather than producing satisfaction). There also is increased emphasis on opening up the system more to workers—to sharing more information about what is happening in the organization and why certain decisions have been made—and on encouraging workers to speak out about their concerns. These trends will be accentuated and accelerated with the changing stature of the human resource manager, and other changes also will occur.

HUMAN RESOURCES ACCOUNTING

One of the most basic changes occurring in organizations is the increased recognition that employees are part of the assets of the organization. George Odiorne, professor of management at the University of Massachusetts and the developer of management by objectives (MBO), proposed in his presentation at the HRD '83 Conference that the worth of an organization's human resources can never be included in the organization's profit-and-loss statement but, rather, should be included in the organization's balance sheet. This kind of human resources accounting leads to a very different attitude about human resources on the part of top management.

There is a flow of people into, through, and out of any organization. This flow involves recruitment, placement, performance appraisal, career development, human resource planning, and outplacement. There is a real cost to this human resource flow. As more and more organizations begin to understand the asset value of their human resources, there is a stronger tendency to regard these as fixed rather than variable costs of doing business. One role of human resource management will be to collect data on which such accounting decisions can be based and to share these data regularly with the rest of the management group.

Human resource personnel traditionally have been concerned with human relations issues. With their changing role, they will be concerned with some new and different aspects of work life, such as increasing the competency of the work force (especially the competencies that lead to organizational effectiveness), work-force motivation (especially in the area of productivity), and the commitment of people to the organization and its goals. For example, one of the effects of the recent recession has been a forced emphasis on enhancing productivity for organizational survival. Some of the nonproductive members of the work force—the deadwood—have been eliminated, resulting in leaner, more efficient organizations. Trade unions have made wage and benefit concessions and, more importantly, have altered restrictive work practices that have hindered productivity in the past. Managing productivity-enhancing programs must be perceived as part of the expanded role of the human resource practitioner.

ORGANIZATIONAL CULTURE AND THE PLANNING PROCESS

One concern of the new human resource manager is examining and understanding the corporate culture. This interest, in part, comes from the understanding that organizational excellence—a goal to which many organizations aspire—requires a different set of organizational values than those that traditionally have been found in American organizations. Peters and Waterman (1982), in their book, *In Search of Excellence*, identify two core values that distinguish America's sixty-two best-run companies. These organizations believe in the importance of delivering superior quality and service and they genuinely value the people in the organization as individuals. If such values are to drive and motivate organizations, they must be central to the organization's strategic plan and to the planning process.

When organizations begin to examine their values (especially values such as these) as part of the strategic-planning process, there are at least two immediate consequences. One is that human resource considerations become much more important than they were before; the second is that the planning process becomes much more psychological than it was before, with value clarification, conflict management, and striving for consensus becoming key issues. This means that human resource personnel come to the planning table as stakeholders as well as facilitators of the process. This dual role, despite the best of intentions, inevitably leads to a conflict of interest. Thus, one person should not simultaneously attempt to represent HRD interests at the planning table and also facilitate the process. It is far better to have two different people involved in the strategic-planning process—the organization's human resource manager and an external consultant who has no vested interest in the outcome of the deliberations and can, therefore, facilitate the process more objectively.

As a stakeholder, the human resource manager has the responsibility to link human resource planning to general strategic planning. To do this, the human resource manager must understand the nature of strategic planning and also believe in it to the degree that he or she can champion the process. If anything, the human resource manager must understand that strategic planning is the human process through which senior management clarifies what it intends for the organization to accomplish and what its goals are, with special emphasis on nonfinancial goals. The process by which such a set of decisions is made requires an impressive level of problem-solving skills. Human resource managers must be clear on their roles in this process. The human resources necessary for the achievement of goals must be identified, and the gap between present and future human resource requirements must be carefully identified. The success of the organization's basic strategy depends on how effectively its two most precious resources, people and money, are utilized.

Most strategic-planning decisions have clear impacts on human resources (e.g., the number of people needed, the type of people, the training that is needed by these people, and whether the organizational culture supports the required activities). It is critical that the human resource manager both surface such issues and be able to assist other senior managers in exploring the issues and in answering questions raised by each consideration. This invariably requires moderate to high levels of expertise in areas outside the human resource field, including an understanding of finances, of legal constraints, of the competitive marketplace, of the long-term trends in the industry, of the market potentials for the organization's goods or services, and of what is new in the organization's area of endeavor. Although the focus of the human resource manager's concern should be the utilization of human resources, such managers also must be able to hold their own in the general give-and-take and conceptual elements of strategic-planning discussions.

THE BLURRING OF BOUNDARIES

A consequence of these changes in the field of human resource management is that there will be a blurring of the lines between human resource managers and all other managers, including line managers. This is the key to the enhanced role of the manager who has primary responsibility for human resources. As long as human resource professionals are seen as different from the rest of the management cadre—as not sharing the same commitment to the ongoing success of the organization, to the "bottom line"—their potential is restricted. They must be committed to and *perceived* as being committed to the bottom line in both a short- and long-term perspective.

Some interesting data to support this argument are supplied by a research report from the A.T. Kearney organization (1983), a Chicago management-consulting group. The report contrasts the human resource function in sixteen highly productive businesses in eleven industries with twenty-four less-productive organizations in the same industries, using financial data to define the two groups. The key difference is that in the productive organizations, the human resource function also is likely to implement business strategies and is involved in making business decisions. The human resource groups in the productive organizations also are more likely to use their current resources and programs to solve important company problems. New human resource programs are added in these companies only to give the organization a competitive edge, either in productivity or in attracting or retaining personnel. At the leading companies, the human resource groups are twice as likely to be proactive in their programming, while in the less-productive organizations, the human resource personnel are reactive, primarily to line requests. Most importantly, in the leading companies, human resource staffs are three times as likely to share responsibility for developing and administering programs such as succession planning and incentive compensation with line managers. It seems obvious that in highly productive companies, the human resource function operates more as a line organization and less as a traditional staff organization. The distinction between the human resource function and other organizational components is becoming less clear.

One such blurring of the distinction between the human resource function and line management already seems to be operational. More and more human resource staffs are insisting that line managers play an active role in the design and delivery of training. The rationale for this is that only the line managers can reinforce the behavioral changes produced by training. The role of the HRD professional is becoming one of developing or purchasing training materials, training the manager-trainer, scheduling and arranging the training, and assisting the manager in conducting the training. This increasingly more common arrangement provides a solution to the problem of lack of managerial commitment to reinforce the training. If the manager actually presents the training, there will be more commitment to requiring the training skills to be exercised in the work place.

Although this arrangement may seem unusual, or even uncomfortable, for a period of time, the benefits to the human resource function should be readily apparent. The human resource professional has more time and energy to do the work of human resource management, of conducting training audits, of designing worthwhile programs, and of participating in the planning process. Most importantly, he or she can engage in the critically important work of being an equal partner with other managers in running the organization—a responsibility that was neglected when human resource professionals were too busy actually presenting all the training in the organization (and emphasizing their staff rather than line functions).

CHARACTERISTICS OF THE NEW HUMAN RESOURCE PROFESSIONAL

Several characteristics will be necessary for the new type of human resource manager. Perhaps the most important one is an attitude of "tough love" in contrast to one of unconditional positive regard. Tough love reflects the attitude that regard for others is best demonstrated by a high set of standards rather than acceptance of any level of performance. If I genuinely care for you and about you, then I expect, even demand, that you achieve as much as you are capable of achieving. To accept less than that from you demeans both you and me and further suggests that my concern for you is not as profound as I have suggested. Tough love is a new form of accountable humanism; it now seems to be preferred over unconditional acceptance. The competent human resource professional holds other people to a set of high performance standards, recognizing that such expectations provide different kinds of self-fulfilling prophecies than do expectations that allow for unsatisfactory or marginal performance.

There are other important characteristics of the new type of human resource manager. These include concern for the organization, its strategies, and its customers or clients, as well as for its human resource problems. If we take seriously the conclusions of Peters and Waterman (1982) in *In Search of Excellence*, there are two characteristics of excellent organizations: they are committed to quality of product and service and they value their employees as people. The latter has always been the concern of the human resource professional. The former, however, has not been perceived as an equal concern. It is only when there is a true commitment to both criteria on the part of human resource professionals that they will begin to assume the role that is rightfully theirs.

In today's competitive business climate, organizations need to increase their productivity through better utilization of their human resources. Human resource managers will become equal members of the management team when their behaviors reflect a clear awareness of this concern.

REFERENCES

A.T. Kearney, Inc. *Managing the human resources for strategic results.* Chicago: Author, 1983.

Beer, M. *Managing human resources.* Speech presented at the Annual Convention of the American Society for Personnel Administration, New York, May 1983.

Blanchard, K., & Johnson, S. *The one minute manager.* New York: William Morrow, 1982.

Ferguson, M. *Aquarian conspiracy: Personal and social transformation in the 1980's.* Los Angeles: J.P. Tarcher, 1980.

Naisbitt, J. *Megatrends: Ten new directions transforming our lives.* New York: Warner, 1982.

Odiorne, G. *Managing a human resource portfolio.* Speech presented at the HRD '83 Conference, San Francisco, March 1983.

Peters, T.J., & Waterman, R.H., Jr. *In search of excellence: Lessons from America's best-run companies.* New York: Harper & Row, 1982.

Leonard D. Goodstein, Ph.D., is the chairman of the board, University Associates, Inc., San Diego, California. He specializes in organizational behavior, consultation skills, and organization development and team building with executive groups. Dr. Goodstein is a diplomate in clinical psychology of the American Board of Professional Psychology and formerly was the chairman of the Department of Psychology at Arizona State University. He is the co-editor of the 1982, 1983, and 1984 Annuals.

J. William Pfeiffer, Ph.D., J.D., is the president of University Associates, Inc., San Diego, California. He consults internationally with a variety of organizations and has a special interest in working with boards of directors/trustees to enhance their legal accountability and organizational effectiveness. He also specializes in the management of change, strategic planning, organization development, leadership/management development, and the training of trainers. Dr. Pfeiffer is the co-editor of the Annuals (1972-1984), the Handbooks of Structured Experiences for Human Relations Training (Volumes I-IX), and the Reference Guide to Handbooks and Annuals.

LINE MANAGERS AND
HUMAN RESOURCE DEVELOPMENT

Udai Pareek and T. Venkateswara Rao

Many organizations are adopting human resource development (HRD) systems and practices. Human resource development has the following objectives:

1. To provide a comprehensive framework and methods for the development of human resources in an organization;
2. To generate systematic information about human resources for purposes of manpower planning, placement, succession planning, and the like;
3. To increase the capabilities of an organization to recruit, retain, and motivate talented employees;
4. To create a climate that enables every employee to discover, develop, and use his or her capabilities to a fuller extent, in order to further both individual and organizational goals.

The following components of HRD help in achieving its objectives:

1. *Performance Appraisal* includes identification of key performance areas, target setting, assessment of behavioral dimensions, and self-assessment. In an open appraisal system, all information is available to the appraisee. Performance analysis focuses on helping the appraisee to understand job-related issues concerning his or her behavior.
2. *Potential Appraisal* involves identification of critical functions and qualities required to perform these functions for each role in the organization, measurement of these critical attributes, periodic assessment of employees for potential to perform higher-level roles, and promotion policies.
3. *Career Planning and Development Systems* usually include identification of career opportunities within the organization, plans for organizational growth, promotion policies, feedback and counseling, job rotation, identification of career paths, and managing of problem employees.
4. *Feedback and Counseling Subsystems* are sequels to performance appraisal, potential appraisal, and career development.
5. *Training* is usually concerned with assessment of training needs and policies, dissemination of information about training opportunities, organization of internal training programs, and evaluation and follow up.
6. *Reinforcement* (usually called reward systems) helps in reinforcing desirable values, attitudes, behaviors, and collaboration in an organization.
7. *Organization Development and Research* subsystems aim at maintaining and monitoring organizational health; assisting problem departments; helping interested units and departments in self-renewal, conflict management, and creation of strong teams; and establishing processes that promote enabling capabilities in the organization. Research also helps in analyzing information generated by the HRD subsystems.

8. *Management Information* systems maintain and update information about skills, capabilities, biographical data, performance appraisals, potential appraisals, and training.

These various subsystems are interrelated (Pareek & Rao, 1981). For example, performance appraisal provides inputs for training, research and OD, data storage, and feedback and counseling. When all these subsystems operate simultaneously and in concert, the organization may be said to have integrated HRD.

Three emphases are involved in the concept of HRD. First, persons working in organizations are regarded as valuable resources, implying that there is a need to invest time and effort in their development. Secondly, they are *human* resources, which means that they cannot be treated as one treats material resources. Thirdly, HRD does not merely focus on employees as individuals, but also on other human units and processes in the organization. These include the roles or jobs in the organization, dyadic units (each consisting of an employee and his or her boss), the various teams in which people work, interteam groups, and the total organization.

Personal development would imply the following: (a) helping the person's self-management by the development of skills and the setting of realistic goals; (b) monitoring growth and development; and (c) facilitating advancement or promotion. The main emphasis in the job or role area is on producing pride, so that the individual feels worthwhile. For the dyadic group (the employee and the supervisor), the main focus is on the development of trust and mutuality. The emphasis of HRD for the various teams (task groups, committees, departments, etc.) is on developing collaboration and problem-solving capability both in the members and in the teams. The main emphasis in interteam development is on cooperation among various groups and teams. For the organization, the main emphasis is on viability and self-renewal.

THE HRD MATRIX

We have briefly mentioned six different units in the organization concerned with HRD. There are five main components of HRD: training, appraisal (both performance appraisal and potential appraisal, including performance review and counseling), organization development (including research and system development), rewards, and career planning. We thus have a matrix consisting of six foci of HRD and five components of HRD. The six foci of HRD are interrelated. The effectiveness of one contributes to the effectiveness of the others. The following matrices (Tables 1 and 2) illustrate the relationships between these six foci of HRD and the five functions or components of HRD.

We shall now use the matrix concept to discuss the respective roles of line management and the HRD specialist.

THE ROLE OF LINE MANAGERS

Line managers have an important role to play in ensuring the realization of HRD objectives. While the top management should make available the resources required for investment in human resources and the HRD department should provide instruments and systems that can be used by the organization, it is ultimately the line managers who translate these into action. This requires realization on the part of the line managers that they have the *responsibility to develop* and utilize their employees.

Development can be defined as the acquisition of new capabilities. These capabilities may help in performing existing tasks better or faster or in performing new tasks. They may be cognitive abilities or skills. They may deal with managerial functions or technical functions or behavior.

Table 1. HRD Matrix: HRD Responsibility

HRD Components

Foci of HRD	Training	Appraisal	OD	Reinforcement	Career Growth
Person	Establish system for training-needs survey and follow up.	Design systems, implementation, and follow up; provide reinforcement.	Develop person-oriented interventions.	Reward attributes.	Develop potential-appraisal system.
Role	Establish job training and follow up.	Prepare KPAs and CAs.	Provide role interventions, job enrichment, and work redesign.	Reward responsibility.	Provide role growth through motivation; review role content.
Dyad	Provide training in counseling.	Appraise counseling and trust.	Develop team-building interventions.	Reward employee development.	Provide counseling.
Team	Do strategy planning; provide team training.	Provide team appraisal.	Develop team-building interventions.	Develop system for team rewards.	Emphasize leadership role.
Interteam	Do strategy planning.	Provide for inter-group work.	Establish collaboration.	Develop system for interteam rewards.	Develop system of rotation among departments.
Organization	Provide training on goals, organizational values, philosophy, etc.	Emphasize role of institutional values.	Provide survey feedback; disseminate information on experiments.	Develop intrinsic rewards.	Provide career counseling for people who have achieved maximum growth in organization.

Table 2. HRD Matrix: Line Management Responsibility

HRD Components

Foci of HRD	Training	Appraisal	OD	Reinforcement	Career Growth
Person	Request training; help in implementation.	Set goals; do performance analyses.	Create conducive climate.	Provide intrinsic rewards.	Set career goals; suggest career-growth plans.
Role	Provide role analysis.	Set objectives for KPAs; provide feedback on new KPAs.	Provide more responsibility.	Provide intrinsic rewards.	Provide support and help.
Dyad	Counsel; provide feedback to HRD.	Counsel employees; provide feedback to HRD on problems and achievements.	Create conducive climate.	Encourage interaction.	Provide counseling.
Team	Identify needs.	Counsel teams.	Reinforce; request interventions.	Reward cooperation.	Encourage interdepartmental experiences.
Organization	Volunteer as a trainer.	Establish linkage between goals and values.	Implement plans; request surveys.	Reward institutional contributions.	Counsel and help.

Development of employees requires certain conditions:

1. The employee should perceive that acquiring new capabilities helps in fulfilling his or her psychological needs.
2. The employee should be aware of the capabilities he or she needs to develop.
3. The employee should perceive opportunities for acquiring such capabilities.
4. The employee should have the means to assess his or her own rate of growth.
5. The employee should enjoy the process of growth itself.

A line manager plays an important role in creating these conditions for subordinates. Quite often, managers have the impression that the HRD department ensures that these conditions are met; however, the HRD department can only provide the instruments or mechanisms for use by the line managers.

The HRD department and line managers play complementary roles. Each supplements (and supports) what the other does in relation to the development of employees. This relationship can be summarized as follows:

TRAINING RESPONSIBILITIES

Line Manager	HRD Department
1. Analyzes each employee's role and lists detailed functions to be performed, outlining managerial, technical, and behavioral capabilities required.	1. Designs systems to identify training needs.
2. Identifies training needs of each employee in terms of relevant functions and communicates these to HRD department.	2. Collects information about training needs from line managers. 3. Keeps up to date on trends in training. 4. Collects information about available training programs.
3. Encourages employees; provides opportunities to take responsibility and initiative and to learn on the job.	5. Disseminates information about training opportunities to line managers.
4. Provides continuous coaching and helps employees to develop problem-solving skills.	6. Analyzes training needs and plans in-house training.
5. Sponsors subordinates for training with HRD department.	7. Manages training production (functions and facilities).
6. Obtains feedback from subordinates about capabilities acquired during training; discusses opportunities for trying out what they have learned; provides such opportunities.	
7. Institutes group discussions, etc., to help subordinates learn to work as a team.	

PERFORMANCE APPRAISAL

Line Manager	HRD Department
As Appraisor:	1. Designs appraisal systems and modifies them periodically to meet company needs and managers' requirements.
1. Identifies and clarifies key performance areas (KPAs) for each subordinate.	2. Provides orientation training for managers about the performance-appraisal system.
2. Helps subordinates set challenging goals.	3. Monitors appraisal and review discussions, return of forms, and appraisal trends.
3. Identifies support needed by subordinates and makes it available.	

Line Manager	HRD Department
4. Helps subordinates experience success.	4. Provides feedback on trends to managers.
5. Helps subordinates recognize strengths and weaknesses through periodic feedback.	5. Develops procedures for reward administration.
6. Holds regularly scheduled appraisal and performance counseling discussions.	6. Helps managers with appraisals and counseling.
7. Understands difficulties experienced by subordinates in performing their functions and provides necessary support.	7. Conducts periodic surveys on the quality of appraisals, counseling, etc.
8. Generates climate of mutuality, openness, and trust to encourage identification and use of subordinates' capabilities.	8. Analyzes performance data for different units and provides feedback concerning inhibiting factors and facilitating factors.

As Appraisee:

1. Sets challenging goals for self.
2. Reflects on own strengths, weaknesses, and overall performance.
3. Identifies problems hindering performance and communicates these to own supervisor.

ORGANIZATION DEVELOPMENT

Line Manager	HRD Department
1. Identifies subsystems that need OD efforts and notifies HRD department or top management.	1. Identifies subsystems that may need OD.
2. Responds frankly to organizational-diagnosis surveys.	2. Identifies managers who can be trained as process specialists.
3. Participates actively in discussions arranged by process specialists.	3. Conducts periodic organizational-diagnosis surveys.
4. Prepares realistic action plans for OD interventions and implements them.	4. Plans and conducts OD interventions and monitors follow up.

REINFORCEMENT

Line Manager	HRD Department
1. Acknowledges the contributions of subordinates.	1. Conducts job-enrichment programs.
2. Assigns challenging functions and tasks.	2. Monitors and recommends new employee-reward systems.
3. Rewards teamwork and collaboration.	3. Develops systems for providing intrinsic rewards.
4. Encourages interaction between subordinates and boss.	4. Assists managers in decisions relating to rewards.

CAREER DEVELOPMENT

Line Manager	HRD Department
1. Identifies career opportunities in the organization for each subordinate and assesses capabilities to be acquired.	1. Prepares career paths for different roles in the organization.
2. Helps subordinates assess their own capabilities in relation to possible career paths.	2. Prepares a directory of functions and capabilities required to perform them and makes it available to managers.

Line Manager	HRD Department
3. Gives feedback to subordinates about their potential.	3. Develops and monitors career-counseling services for employees.
4. Encourages subordinates to develop potential and provides opportunities.	4. Develops potential-appraisal system.
	5. Develops policies and mechanisms for job rotation and monitors these.
	6. Makes projections about manpower requirements and makes these available to line managers for career counseling.
	7. Assists those who have reached a saturation level in the organization with future career planning.
	8. Identifies qualities required for higher-level managerial jobs and incorporates into appraisal systems and development work.
	9. Arranges training programs for managers.

This discussion makes it clear that human resource development is the joint responsibility of line managers and HRD personnel. While the HRD departments can design and provide instruments for use by line managers, the line managers have the responsibility for using these instruments (and a variety of other mechanisms) to develop their subordinates. If the line managers do not make demands on the HRD department and do not take follow-up action, HRD efforts in an organization are not likely to succeed. The participation of line managers in HRD efforts also increases the managers' competence to deal with many human problems in other areas of their work.

REFERENCE

Pareek, U., & Rao, T.V. *Designing and managing human resource systems.* New Delhi: Oxford & IBH, 1981.

Udai Pareek, Ph.D., holds the Larsen & Toubro Chair in Organizational Behavior at the Indian Institute of Management, Ahmedabad, India. Currently on leave, he is serving as US-AID provincial human-resource-system development consultant to the Government of Indonesia. His specialties are organization development, human resource development, and organizational design. The author of a number of books, instruments, and papers, Dr. Pareek is on the editorial board of several professional journals.

T. Venkateswara Rao, Ph.D., is the Larsen & Toubro Professor of Human Resource Development at Xavier Labour Relations Institute, Jamshedpur, India. His specialties include human resource development, entrepreneurship, organizational behavior, performance appraisal, and public systems management. He has authored or co-authored several books and is a consultant in human resource development to several organizations in India and other Asian countries.

OD WITH A MANAGEMENT PERSPECTIVE

John C. Lewis

In the past few years, concern has been expressed about the future of organization development (OD). Introspective articles (Burke & Goodstein, 1980; Lundberg, 1981) and conferences have criticized OD for being too limited in scope, for using simplistic models, for being conceptually naive, for working with only some areas (too low) in the organization, and for rarely impacting on the bottom line. The self-doubt is expressed: Is OD relevant? Does it meet the needs of client systems or is it focused on what practitioners feel is important? Will it survive as a profession?

Kegan (1981) suggests that OD will not survive as an independent field and that OD consultants should meld their skills with those of traditionally recognized areas such as finance, personnel, law, or manufacturing. This article proposes, however, that combining OD skills with a total systems view of the client's business/service would provide OD consultants with a more relevant perspective, enabling them to deal with issues of concern to management and to have greater influence in bringing OD values to the attention of management.

Most definitions of OD agree that it involves planned change, is long range, involves the total organization or a coherent part, uses behavioral science concepts, and is a process aimed at improving the client system. However, articles, presentations, and discussions with consultants indicate that much OD does *not* fit these definitions. OD consultants have tended to intervene primarily in team building (Spier, Sashkin, Jones, & Goodstein, 1980); in the processes of problem solving, decision making, action planning, goal setting, and communicating; in interpersonal relations; and in the quality of work life. All this is extremely important, but is it what organizations need most? Consultants must also be able to move beyond intragroup dynamics (Harris, 1980) to all elements of management, into areas such as organizational culture, strategic planning, and organizational design. OD consultants must be able to utilize the concepts and theories of OD in the organizational world of the *manager*.

MANAGEMENT'S ORGANIZATIONAL WORLD

Managers engage in all of their management tasks at various times and with varying degrees of consistency, timeliness, understanding, and intensity. They seldom articulate the complexity, interrelationship, and interdependence of the elements of those tasks. Consultants often find it difficult to describe to managers what is going on in the client system in a way that is comprehensive yet understandable in their frame of reference. Existing consulting and organizational models differ among themselves; the critical element of results is lacking in most, and they do not present a logical, sequential flow of actions that reflect managerial thinking. Furthermore, the models reflect the perspective of the behavioral scientist; as Tichy and Nisberg (1976) point out, the consultant then approaches the task from this perspective. What is needed is a model that reflects the context of *management* and demonstrates how OD technology can be applied to all aspects of managing an organization. The model presented here enables OD practitioners to perceive the manager's point of view, to communicate in the manager's language, and to explain what OD can do in terms that make sense to managers. The Management's Organizational World model (Figure 1) depicts the management team being guided by the overall purpose of the organization, supported by organizational foundations, fed

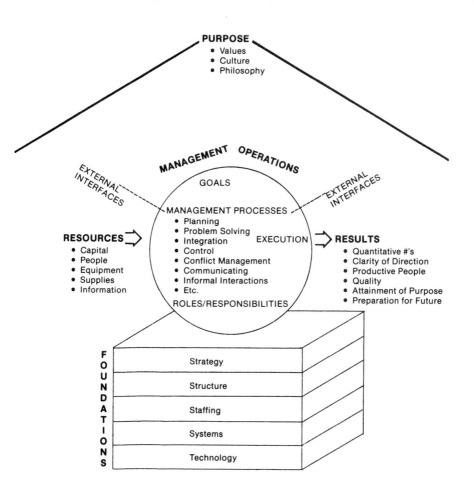

Figure 1. Management's Organizational World Model

by critical resources, interacting within its own sphere of operations, interfacing with its environment, and producing specific results.

Organizational Purpose

A statement of organizational purpose should be comprehensive, addressing the issues: What business are we in? What customers do we serve? Why does this organization exist? What about this organization is different from others in its field? This statement not only specifies the ultimate aims of the organization, it also directs the formulation of strategy and promotes a sense of shared expectations.

The consultant must examine the organization's stated purpose, its values and culture—both existing and desired—and its *management philosophy*. There is growing evidence that organizations with shared values and a strong culture are more successful. To be effective, the purpose, values, and management philosophy must be clearly stated, communicated, and understood throughout the organization. The OD consultant can assist management with values clarification, with an understanding of organizational culture and how to develop it, and with the formulation of a management philosophy that accurately reflects management's behavioral expectations. Deal and Kennedy (1982) and Peters and Waterman (1982) provide fertile starting points for working in this area.

Organizational Foundations

In order for the management team to operate effectively, the foundations of strategy, structure, staffing, systems, and technology must be supportive and congruent. If the foundations are not stable and supportive of the organization's purpose and desired results, actions taken to improve conditions within the operating sphere of management will be of short-term benefit, at best. In addition to the need for the foundations to support the overall purpose and desired results, they must also fit with and support one another. Considerable attention must be paid to the process of developing each of the foundation elements.

Ability to contribute in these areas is not based on technical or functional knowledge but, rather, on the ability to help with the decision-making process; with developing alternatives; with opening up new, creative ways of thinking; and with energizing activity. Consultants can be extremely valuable in sensing and diagnosis and in exploring the impact and the implications of change on the other elements of the model and on various parts of the organization (Harris, 1980). Specific areas for consultant consideration are elaborated in Table 1.

Resources

The major question about resources is whether they are adequate for the strategy of the organization. Does the organization have the necessary capital, people, equipment, supplies, and information to do what it wants to do? The OD consultant can have an impact in planning for and allocating resources. The process of allocation must reinforce the organization's foundations, must consider its desired results, and should be flexible enough to permit redirection of resources as conditions change. The availability of resources will affect management operations and must not be ignored in consulting efforts.

Management Operations

The sphere of management operations is where OD consultants have traditionally focused their energies in consulting to management. This is where most of the work of management happens, where actions are visible, and where results are seen most readily. For most consultants, it is where the excitement and energy are and, therefore, it is more fun and more rewarding to concentrate on these elements. The five elements in the sphere of management operations are: goals, roles/responsibilities, external interfaces, management processes, and execution.

Goals follow directly from the organization's long-range strategy, the technology, and the resources available. Each subordinate organization translates the overall strategy into shorter-range, measurable objectives. Challenging but achievable goals, collaboratively developed by those responsible for their execution, build commitment and motivation toward their accomplishment. Individual goals must be supportive of organizational goals and, at the same time, satisfy individual needs.

Table 1. Considerations in Examining Organizational Foundations

FOUNDATIONS	ISSUES FOR CONSULTANT CONSIDERATION
STRATEGY	Is there long-range direction for the product, technology, and customers? Is the strategy supportive of the organization's purpose? What is the basis of assumptions; how is testing and tracking to be done? OD can help with processes, assumptions, creativity, and open-systems planning.
STRUCTURE	Does the structure support management's philosophy and strategy? How well does the structure support centralization vs. decentralization, the span of control, differentiation of functions, and integration of activities? Does the structure take into consideration both present work and future growth? OD can help with decisions and planning, readiness for change, transition processes, coordination, and flexibility.
STAFFING	Is the personnel strategy supportive of the business strategy? Does the selection process fit the management philosophy and plans for future growth and change? Is there a balance of skills and sufficiency, for both the present and the future? Is there career planning and development? Are there appropriate procedures for performance appraisal and promotions? OD can help in human resource planning, establishing processes, management and career development, and assessment.
SYSTEMS	Do the systems fit with the philosophy, strategy, and structure? Are there adequate financial, personnel, logistic, and management information systems? Are there regular, formal information flows? Are there established policies, procedures, and meetings? Do the systems facilitate operations and provide helpful mechanisms? Are systems flexible and adaptable to change? OD can help in systems establishment, fit, implementation, change processes, communication, and meetings.
TECHNOLOGY	Does the technology fit the philosophy? Is it adequate for the strategy? Does the technology include automation, robotics, computer-aided manufacturing (CAM), or computer-aided design (CAD)? What are the effects of the technology on the work force? OD can help in assessment of impact, integration of processes, sociotechnical systems, and transition management.

Probably the most common contributor to poor teamwork or difficult intergroup relations in organizations is unclear or conflicting *roles and responsibilities*. Organizations often do not make the necessary effort to determine who should do what and with whom. This often results in various groups operating with different sets of assumptions and expectations. Failure to delegate the responsibility and authority that are necessary to permit people to adequately perform their jobs is another common problem in this area.

An extremely critical, but frequently neglected, function of management is dealing with the external environment or *external interfaces*. This model emphasizes the necessity for proactive and interactive relationships between the organization and the external agencies on which it depends or that can have major impact on it. Most internal changes are precipitated by shifts in external factors (Burke & Goodstein, 1980). Changes in the environment continually must be factored into an organization's strategy and may even impact its purpose.

At the core of the managerial world are *management processes*—day-in and day-out planning, organizing, directing, problem solving, decision making, communicating, and conflict management. It is this element of management that the consultant should examine first when results are not achieved as desired.

As much attention should be paid to the flow of work, task configurations, and relationships of management teams as is paid to these areas on the production floor. The best competitive strategies and new product plans can be wasted if management does not execute them effectively. Successful *execution* is enhanced by good project-management techniques, efficient work flows and procedures between functional management groupings, adequate and timely information and feedback, and good leadership. The consultant should be attuned to how the desired organizational values, culture, and management philosophy are manifested in the actual management style of the organization. Table 2 is a sample of some specific considerations for examining management operations.

Results

The element of *results* is missing in most OD models, but everything else is of little interest to managers if they are not achieving the results that are important to them. For most managers "results" means "numbers"—sales, profits, moves per day, and return on investment. Little attention is paid to other important outputs of management.

Because *quantitative* results—movements, yields, new designs, bookings, costs, margins, etc.—will be of greatest concern to most clients, any discussion of results should probably begin at that point. Are the desired results clearly identified and tied directly to the goals that have been set by the organization? Are they being achieved?

Beside quantitative results, there are five other critical results of the management process. The first is *clarity of direction*. Is it clear what the organization is trying to accomplish and how? Do people know and understand it? The next output of effective management is *productive people*. Are people committed and motivated; do they feel satisfaction in the way they are treated and in what they are doing? Next comes the question of *quality*. Does the product or service of the organization meet the specifications of management and the customer? How is quality defined and measured, and what is the attitude of the whole organization toward quality? Another important result of management is the *attainment of the organization's purpose*. Is the organization doing what it set out to do and in a manner that meets its avowed values and philosophy? Finally, a result that is often ignored is *preparation for the future*. Is what is being done today helping to prepare for the future or will it undermine future plans? Are today's decisions and changes made with the future in mind? OD consultants can help management to develop a more complete picture of what the results of its work should be and can support management in determining how to measure results, in defining "good" results, and in deciding what needs to be improved. An examination of results should be the starting point of almost any OD activity with managers, in order to identify the goals of the change strategy.

USES OF THE MODEL

The Management's Organizational World model puts the content of management work into a perspective that is workable for both the client and the OD consultant. To that content, consultants add processes and interventions. It is essential, therefore, that existing process

Table 2. Considerations in Examining Management Operations

MANAGEMENT OPERATIONS	ISSUES FOR CONSULTANT CONSIDERATION
GOALS	Do goals support the organization's purpose and strategy? Are they mutually developed and challenging but achievable? Are they specific and measurable in time and results? Are goals understood throughout the organization? OD can help in goal-setting processes, MBO, integration, and review.
ROLES/ RESPONSIBILITIES	Are roles and responsibilities delineated and understood? Do roles and responsibilities fit with the organization's strategy, structure, resources, and desired management style? Do people have sufficient responsibility and authority to perform their jobs? Is there monitoring and correction of overlapping, conflicting, or unassigned responsibilities? OD can help in role clarification, role analyses, responsibility charting, job redesign, and intergroup meetings.
EXTERNAL INTERFACES	Is the organizational environment monitored for opportunities, threats, and changes? Is there a proactive response to pressures from owners, unions, competitors, consumers, government agencies, etc.? Are there interactive relations with pertinent external groups? Are there established procedures and mechanisms for coping with change? OD can help in intergroup activities, responsibility charting, organizational mirroring, open-systems planning, and understanding boundary politics.
MANAGEMENT PROCESSES	Is there anticipatory, iterative, and collaborative planning? Is there effective, timely problem solving? Do managers engage in participation and delegation? Is there trust, openness, and synergism in the management team? How does information flow (up, down, laterally)? Is information timely, complete, filtered, etc.? What are the integration procedures and mechanisms? Is there transition management? OD can help in management-team development, process consultation, survey feedback, conflict resolution, and communication processes.
EXECUTION	Does management work reflect the desired culture, values, and management philosophy of the organization? What are the management and leadership styles? Are there established systems for project management, tracking, reviews, and correction? Is there cross-functional support? How effective are controls, performance measures, accountability systems, and feedback mechanisms? Are there quality-improvement programs? Are there regular rewards for effective performance toward goals? OD can help with sensing and diagnosis, culture and values analysis, improvement of management styles, project management, control systems, reward procedures, and quality-improvement programs.

models be used in a manner that is complementary with the model of Management's Organizational World. The multiplicity of interventions that could be appropriate for each of the model's elements clearly elicits employment of the full range of OD theories, models, tools, and skills.

The model can be used with important subordinate organizations as well as for the total organization, with minor variations. For a subordinate unit such as a divisional profit center, the parent organization will certainly have impact on, and some control over, the foundations (particularly systems) and resources. The division's purpose and management philosophy must be studied within the context of the parent organization. External interfaces for a division include most of those of the larger organization as well as those activities within the company that are external to the division but provide input or support to it or receive output from it.

For Briefing Managers

Most OD consultants have difficulty explaining OD to clients. The Management's Organizational World model is an effective way to describe managerial elements, possible areas of concern, and types of interventions that might be appropriate for various issues. It is valuable in describing the organization from an OD perspective while focusing on the totality of management activity. The model also can be useful in helping managers to recognize the connections between the various elements of the organization and the need for fit between these elements. In addition to the relationships between organizational groups and activities, between systems, and between processes, there are the management relationships. A change in strategy, for example, may have implications for structure, staffing, systems, technology, resources, goals, and roles/responsibilities, as well as external interfaces. Organizational interventions are inherently complex and require a means to display that complexity without oversimplifying or overgeneralizing.

As a Diagnostic Tool

The model can be used to assess the health of the management group or to assess a specific problem of unknown cause. It can be entered at any point and tracked in any direction. For many projects, it may not be necessary to examine all elements of the model. For example, a unit manager in an electronics corporation requested OD assistance because his production output was not satisfactory and he wanted to do something "to improve the effectiveness of the production people." Management's Organizational World was used as a diagnostic tool, beginning with results in an effort to clarify the problem of unsatisfactory output. This analysis revealed that there was a lack of clarity of direction. Backing up in the model to examine management execution revealed problems with management style, project-management procedures, and feedback mechanisms. Had the consultant not been using a comprehensive diagnostic process, the assessment might have been stopped at this point and corrective action taken. However, in continuing back through the model, the consultant uncovered problems within management processes in planning, information flow, interface, and integration procedures. These were aggravated by unclear roles and responsibilities between units. An examination of the reasons for the unclear roles revealed that basic structural defects were causing most of the other problems and symptoms. It was clear that until the structural issues were resolved, all other remedies would be short lived. The change strategy, therefore, followed the reverse route of the diagnostic process, beginning with structural changes, then clarification of roles, improvement of managerial processes, and so on.

This overview of one use of the model exemplifies the systemic nature of most organizational problems and the need for OD consultants to apply a broader focus (Spier,

Sashkin, Jones, & Goodstein, 1980) to all aspects of organizational relationships. If the practice of OD is to survive, it must be perceived by management as contributing to the effectiveness of the organization. Thus, rather than providing help with "people" problems, it must be perceived as providing solutions to management problems involving people; rather than helping to improve morale and working relationships, it must be perceived as helping to improve organizational effectiveness. By understanding and examining all aspects of the organization that affect management operations, the OD consultant can contribute to the enhanced perception—and the enhanced effectiveness—of the field of organization development.

REFERENCES

Burke, W. W., & Goodstein, L. D. Organization development today: A retrospective applied to the present and the future. In W. W. Burke & L. D. Goodstein (Eds.), *Trends and issues in OD: Current theory and practice*. San Diego, CA: University Associates, 1980.

Deal, T. E., & Kennedy, A. A. *Corporate cultures: The rites and rituals of corporate life*. Reading, MA: Addison-Wesley, 1982.

Harris, R. T. Toward a technology of macrosystem interventions. In W. W. Burke & L. D. Goodstein (Eds.), *Trends and issues in OD: Current theory and practice*. San Diego, CA: University Associates, 1980.

Kegan, D. L. Organization development: Casual careers in a precarious profession. *OE Communique*, 1981, 5(4), 70-71.

Lundberg, C. C. What's wrong with OD? In E. J. Pavlock (Ed.), *Organization development: Managing transitions*. Washington, DC: American Society for Training and Development, 1982.

Peters, T. J., & Waterman, R. H. *In search of excellence: Lessons from America's best-run companies*. New York: Harper & Row, 1982.

Spier, M. S., Sashkin, M., Jones, J. E., & Goodstein, L. D. Predictions and projections for the decade: Trends and issues in organization development. In W. W. Burke & L. D. Goodstein (Eds.), *Trends and issues in OD: Current theory and practice*. San Diego, CA: University Associates, 1980.

Tichy, N. M., & Nisberg, J. N. Change agent bias: What they view determines what they do. *Group & Organization Studies*, 1976, 1(3), 286-301.

John C. Lewis is a senior organization development consultant with Signetics Corporation, Sunnyvale, California; is the president of Lewis and Pike Associates, San Jose, California; and is a lecturer in organization development at the University of California Berkeley Extension. He also has nearly twenty years of management experience. Mr. Lewis' primary focus is consulting to upper management, with emphasis on organizational culture, management-team development, start-up and reorganization, strategic planning, and interorganizational activities.

ORGANIZATIONAL USE OF THE
BEHAVIORAL SCIENCES: THE IMPROBABLE TASK

Warren Bennis

Few people would argue with the statement that we are living in the most satisfying and most unsettling period in the history of the human species. We must question whether what we know today will be valid tomorrow. The nonutilization of knowledge and the lack of communication among different groups in our society become less tolerable as we find ourselves unable to rely on tradition and more dependent on knowledge and adaptability. Individuals with important contributions must be aware of the ways in which they can make their contributions useful for society.

Nowhere is the gap between knowledge and implementation more glaring than in the behavioral sciences. The literature indicates reliable and significant applications for social policy, yet theories proliferate while actual practice lags behind.

Kurt Lewin was preoccupied with the link between theory and practice, the abstract and the concrete. He wrote: "The research worker can achieve this only if, as a result of a constant intense tension, he can keep both theory and reality fully within his field of vision" (1948). Alfred North Whitehead also commented on the problem: "In this modern world, the celibacy of the medieval learned class has been replaced by a celibacy of the intellect which is divorced from the concrete contemplation of complete facts" (1947).

This complex problem of how to translate knowledge into action generally seems to be avoided or dismissed as a mystery. This article will attempt to answer three questions concerning the usability of knowledge. Question one, "What's so?," will deal with applying knowledge to organizations. Question two is "So what?" Two short, state-of-the-art cases on the uses of knowledge to improve organizational behavior will lead to a better understanding of the implications of current practice. Finally, the answer to the third question, "Now what?," will be an attempt to advance a theory of practice.

WHAT'S SO?

Knowledge Utilization

Lester F. Ward was one of the earliest social scientists in America to proclaim that "modern men" must extend scientific approaches to the planning of changes in the patterns of their behaviors and relationships. Aware that we were utilizing our intelligence to induce changes in the nonhuman environment, he foresaw a major role for the emerging social sciences in extending a similar planning approach to the management of human affairs:

> Man's destiny is in his own hands. Any law that he can comprehend he can control. He cannot increase or diminish the powers of nature, but he can direct them. . . . He can make it his servant and appropriate to his own use all the mighty forces of the universe. . . . *Human institutions are not exempt from this all-pervading spirit of improvement.* (Commager, 1950)[1]

Adapted and used with permission from *Handbook of Organizational Behavior*, Jay Lorsch (Ed.), Prentice-Hall, 1985 (in press).
[1]From *The American Mind* by Henry S. Commager. New Haven, CT: Yale University Press, 1950.

Ward's proclamation seemed foolish if not sacrilegious to many of his contemporaries. William Graham Sumner, a sociologist, emphasized both the folly and sacrilege of prophecies such as Ward's:

> If we can acquire a science of society based on observation of phenomena and study of forces, we may hope to gain some ground slowly toward the elimination of old errors and the re-establishment of a sound and natural social order. Whatever we gain that way will be by growth, never in the world by any reconstruction of society on the plan of some enthusiastic social architect. The latter is only repeating the old error again, and postponing all our chances of real improvement. Society needs first of all to be free from these meddlers—that is, to be let alone. Here we are, then, once more back at the old doctrine, *laissez-faire.* . . . Mind your own business. It is nothing but the doctrine of liberty. (Commager, 1950)[2]

Today, laissez-faire has been widely abandoned as a principle of social management, and human interventions designed to shape and modify the institutionalized behaviors of people are commonplace. Helping professions have proliferated, and organization development is as firmly established as social work. The reason for these professions is to induce changes in the future behaviors and relationships of their various client populations. This is most apparent in the newer professions such as psychiatry, social work, nursing, counseling, management, and consultation. But older professions such as medicine, law, teaching, and the clergy also have been pressed to become agencies of social change rather than of social conservation.

Behavioral scientists have been drawn into consultation, training, and applied research. Helping professionals, managers, and policy makers in various fields increasingly seek the services of behavioral scientists to anticipate more accurately the consequences of change and to plan to control these consequences. But attempts to apply knowledge in planning and controlling organizational change tend to be fragmented by change agents in specialized and largely noncommunicating professions and hampered by lack of collaboration among policy makers and action planners in various institutional settings.

One can observe a split even within applied behavioral science; some view the application of organizational sciences as either meaningless or as coercion. David Bakan, for example, views the historical relations between the social sciences and the military as encouraging a "positivistic science, on the one hand, and a hierarchy-obedience-force military orientation, on the other" that "keeps [the social sciences] from properly serving in the solution of political, social, and economic problems, thus exacerbating the world crisis and increasing the likelihood of war" (1982).

On the other side of the dichotomy are McKelvey and Aldrich (1983)[3], who write:

> Organizational science. . . is much less visible on the applied front. The National Academy of Sciences, a body formed to offer advice to the Federal government, does not include organizational scientists. No Presidents' council of organizational scientists exists, and organizational scientists do not frequent the halls of Congress. At UCLA, 100 teams of MBA students act as consultants to Los Angeles organizations each year and find numerous opportunities to apply their knowledge of their accounting and finance, marketing, industrial and labor relations, and operations research, but almost never find ways to apply ideas or findings from organizational science.

Kenneth D. Benne (1976) clarifies and elaborates this ambivalence. His typology dichotomizes the cognitive worlds of behavioral scientists and of social practitioners and action leaders. He argues that effective collaboration requires recognition and affirmation of epistemological differences on both sides of the social divide, not denial of differences on the ground that both are of good will or polarization as "theoretical" and "practical" approaches.

---

[2]From *The American Mind* by Henry S. Commager. New Haven, CT: Yale University Press, 1950.

[3]Reprinted by permission of the authors from "Population, Natural Selection, and Applied Organizational Science," *Administrative Science Quarterly*, 1983, 28.

Table 1. From K.D. Benne, 1976[4]

The Cognitive World of Behavioral Scientists	The Cognitive World of Social Practitioners and Action Leaders
1. People and human systems are not of interest as particular cases but as instances to confirm or disconfirm generalizations about people and human systems. Knowledge is organized around verbally (and/or mathematically) articulated generalizations.	1. People and human systems are clients or constituents. The concern is with particular cases, situations, and practical difficulties in order to help, improve, or change these. Knowledge is organized around kinds of cases, situations, and difficulties and effective ways of diagnosing and handling them.
2. The occasion for inquiry is some gap or discrepancy in a theory or conceptual scheme. "Success" in inquiry is measured by attainment of more warrantable statements of variable relationships that fill the gap and/or obviate the discrepancy.	2. The occasion for inquiry is some difficulty in practice, some discrepancy between intended results and the observed consequences of actions or excessive psychic and/or financial costs of established ways of working. "Success" in inquiry is measured by attainment of ways of making and/or doing that are more effective in fitting means to ends and/or in reducing costs of operation.
3. Scientists try in the course of their research to reduce or eliminate the influence of extraneous values (other than "truth" value) from the processes of collecting data and determining and stating the meaning of the data within the research context. Knowledge is relatively independent of the uses to which it may be put.	3. Practitioners and action leaders try to find and interpret data that enable them to serve the values to which they are committed: productivity, health, learning (growth), and—in more political contexts—the power, freedom, and welfare of their clients or constituents. Knowledge is consciously related to specific uses.
4. Scientists set up their research to reduce the number of variables at work in the situations they study, by controlling the effect of other variables. Experimental results take the form of statements about the relationships of abstracted and quantified variables.	4. Practitioners and action leaders work in field settings where multiple and interacting variables are at work. Their understanding of situations tends to be holistic and qualitative, though they may use quantitative methods in arriving at their "estimate of the situation." They do not attend to all the variables involved in the full understanding of a situation but rather to variables that are thought to be influential and accessible to their manipulation in handling the situation in the service of their chosen values.
5. Time, in the form of pressing decisions, does not influence their judgments and choices directly. They can reserve judgment, waiting for the accumulated weight of evidence. A longer time perspective operates in their judgments of what needs to be done now and later. Their statements of what they know are more qualified, less impregnated with their own hunches and insights as to what incomplete evidence means for purposes of action.	5. Time presses practitioners to decide and act; judgments cannot wait. They must judge in order to meet deadlines, whether the evidential basis for judgment is "complete" or not. They must depend on their own hunches and insights in attributing meaning to incomplete or contradictory evidence, so their knowledge is impregnated with these hunches and values. It is more personal, more dependent on their ability to read a situation than the more impersonal knowledge that the scientist professes and communicates.

[4]From K.D. Benne, "Educational Field Experience as the Negotiation of Different Cognitive Worlds." In W. Bennis, K.D. Benne, & R. Chin, *The Planning of Change* (3rd ed.). New York: Holt, Rinehart and Winston, 1976. Used by permission of Holt, Rinehart and Winston (CBS).

Over the past two decades, a substantial literature has demonstrated that these cognitive polarities can be transcended and has included examples of successful utilization of knowledge of organizational behavior. Although the literature is abundant, the findings are inconclusive. Beyer and Trice (1982) argue that one of the problems is that the literature is innocent of convincing empirical data. "In the hundreds of sources we pursued, we did not find a single thorough review of the empirical literature on utilization." They point out that, for the most part, the literature on knowledge utilization has focused on the deficiencies of research, but they believe that the problem stems primarily from characteristics of organizations. They focus on the organizational processes that facilitate or deflect the utilization of organizational knowledge and point out most of the variables connected with effective utilization. They fall short in ignoring two other fundamentals: the quality/characteristics of the research and the nature of the relationship between researcher and client system. Glaser and Davis (1976), have prepared a table that summarizes four of the most widely used models (see Table 2).

The other three elements in knowlege utilization that require formal elaboration are: (a) practitioner/researcher (or change agent/client) relationships; (b) resistances to change; and (c) stages/phases of organizational knowledge utilization.

Producer/User, Researcher/Practitioner, Change Agent/Client Relationships

Mohrman, Cummings, and Lawler (1982) argue that "useful information cannot be produced *for* organizations, but must be generated *with* them.... If organizational research is to be useful, researchers and organizational members must become partners in the research effort. Such research should be action oriented, jointly controlled, and involve relevant stakeholders from both researcher and user committees. Attention must be directed at the transactional contexts of the research." That about sums it up.

The principle of *with*, not *for* can be summarized with the following seven "rules":

1. The research focus must reflect the interests and concerns of the client system.
2. The practitioners should be involved in all phases of research.
3. The research team should include members of the client system—the more influential (within the client system), the better.
4. Frequent and honest communication between researchers and practitioners reduces the likelihood of resistance.
5. Early and continuous clarification of expectations between researchers and practitioners must be engaged in.
6. The consultant should be able to withdraw from the relationship, if necessary, to permit independence.
7. Provision should be made for evaluation.

These requirements are easier said than done. The outcome of any successful knowledge-utilization activity appears to hinge on that—on how well the giver and receiver of help understand and participate in that relationship. Over twenty years ago, for the first edition of *The Planning of Change*, I wrote:

> A number of features distinguish the "deliberate and collaborative relationship": (a) a joint effort that involves mutual determination of goals; (b) a "spirit of inquiry"—a reliance on determinations based on data publicly shared; (c) an existential relationship growing out of the "here-and-now" situation; (d) a voluntary relationship between change-agent and client with either party free to terminate the relationship after joint consultation; (e) a power distribution in which the client and change-agent have equal or almost equal opportunities to influence the other; and (f) an emphasis on methodological rather than content learnings. (Bennis, Benne, & Chin, 1984)

The basis for this emphasis on collaboration, which virtually every scholar/writer/practitioner has since extolled, was not only the important ethical considerations but, more important, the pragmatic considerations. The only way to get any client to adopt new

Table 2. Factors Influencing the Likelihood of Adoption or Adaption of a Seemingly Promising Innovation by an Organization: Integrated Findings[5]

H. Davis (8 Factors)	E.M. Glaser (20 Factors)	G. Zaltman et al. (Condensation of 19 Factors)	R. Havelock et al. (10 Factors)
Ability to carry out the change	Capability and resources	Financial and social costs	Structuring Capacity
Values or self-expectancy	Compatibility	Compatibility Publicness vs. privateness Impact on interpersonal relations	Homophily Empathy
Idea or information about the qualities of the innovation	Credibility Ease in understanding and installation Observability Trialability Divisibility Reversibility	Communicability Divisibility Reversibility Complexity of concept or implementation Susceptibility to successive modifications Scientific status Point of origin Terminality	Openness
Circumstances which prevail at the time	Willingness to entertain challenge A climate of trust Structural reorganization		Proximity
Timing or readiness for consideration of the idea	Sensitivity to context factors Early involvement of potential users Suitable timing		Linkage Synergy
Obligation, or felt need to deal with a particular problem	Relevance Widespread felt need to correct undesirable conditions Shared interest in solving recognized problems	Degree of commitment	Energy
Resistance or inhibiting factors	Skill in working through resistances	Risk or uncertainty of various kinds Number of gatekeepers or approval channels	
Yield, or perceived prospect of payoff for adoption	Relative advantage An incentive system	Efficiency of innovation Perceived relative advantage Gateway to other innovations	Reward

[5]From E.M. Glaser & H.R. Davis (Eds.), *Putting Knowledge to Use: A Distillation of the Literature Regarding Knowledge Transfer and Change.* Los Angeles: Human Interaction Research Institute and National Institute of Mental Health, 1976. Used by permission of the author and Human Interaction Research Institute.

knowledge is by providing enough positive support so that the opposing forces in the client's situation can be re-equilibrated on a new and desirable level. This means making the client (as well as the change agent) aware of the relevant data necessary to diagnose the situation. The source of much of these data is in the client system itself, if the client can make it publicly available. Without *trust*, generated in and by collaboration, the change agent and client must work with limited and occasionally distorted data.

The process of developing a collaborative relationship between client and change agent can provide a crucible for understanding the problems the client faces in his or its work and life environments. Thus, the collaborative relationship can provide a cognitive support as well as a basis for examples of other possible problems.

In reality, it is difficult to find a purely collaborative relationship; the best to be hoped for is a commitment to work toward it. Nevertheless, collaboration is a necessary condition of the successful use of organizational behavior knowledge—not only because it generates the necessary trust and facilitates the collection and interpretation of data but also because the positive aspects of the relationship are necessary in order to overcome many of the fears of and resistance to change in the client system.

Perhaps the best summary of factors that affect resistance was compiled by Zaltman, Duncan, and Holbek (1973)[6]:

1. Among the possible determinants of resistance are: (a) the need for stability; (b) the use of foreign jargon; (c) impact on existing social relationships; (d) personal threat; (e) local pride; (f) felt needs; and (g) economic factors.

2. Structural factors affecting resistance include: (a) stratification; (b) division of labor; and (c) hierarchical and status differentials.

3. Individual resistance factors include: (a) perception; (b) motivation; (c) attitude; (d) legitimization; (e) accompaniments of trial; (f) results of evaluation; (g) actual adoption or rejection; and (h) manner of dissonance resolution.

It is important to remember that most persons and client systems are in a "quasi-stationary equilibrium" with some forces driving them toward change and others resisting. To reduce the resistance creates forward movement with less tension than if an effort is made only to override. However, one must not overlook the importance of the social role of the defenders who try to preserve the valuable elements of the old in the face of a tumult of change (Klein, 1966).

SO WHAT?

The examination of two case studies may help to clarify much that has been written about the application of knowledge in organizational settings.

Project Camelot

A spectacular case of failure is Project Camelot, an action-research study, as described by its task title, of "methods for predicting social change and internal war potential." Camelot was to take three to four years and to cost approximately six million dollars. The research areas were those in which there was considered to exist a high potential for internal revolution: the starting point was Latin America, and proposed future research areas included several countries in Europe, Asia, and Africa. In the first of four phases, it was proposed to examine existing data on internal war, and it was during this period that the project was interrupted.

---

[6]From G. Zaltman, R. Duncan, & J. Holbek, *Innovations and Organizations*. New York: John Wiley, 1973. Copyright © 1973, John Wiley & Sons, Inc. Used by permission of the publisher.

The beginning of the end occurred when an invitation to many American and foreign social scientists to a four-week planning conference stated the objectives of the study and the identity of its sponsor, the U.S. Army.

One of the recipients was a Norwegian sociologist teaching in Chile at UNESCO's Latin American Faculty of Social Science, whose area of research is conflict and conflict resolution in underdeveloped countries. "He could not accept the role of the U.S. Army as a sponsoring agent in a study of counterinsurgency. He could not accept the notion of the Army as an agency of national development; he saw the Army as not managing conflict but even promoting conflict" (Bennis, 1970, p. 2).

In April, 1965, an assistant professor of anthropology at the University of Pittsburgh made a trip to Chile on other academic business. He offered to speak to his friends in the Chilean academic community about Camelot, and the Camelot authorities accepted the offer. Although Chile was not intended to be one of the countries in which research would be done, it was hoped that Chilean social scientists would participate. He met with the vice-chancellor of the University of Chile and discussed the study without identifying the sponsor or which social scientists were involved. At a second meeting, confronted with a copy of the invitation, he stated that he knew nothing of the sponsorship and that he had been misinformed and would protest to Washington. The issue soon became known to the Chilean press and members of the Chilean Senate. The time was dramatically inopportune; it was shortly after the United States' intervention in the Dominican Republic.

Some American sources report a different course of events: the professor was neither given the opportunity to explain who the sponsor was nor to discuss the study. According to Camelot authorities, the "brouhaha" was from Communist-inspired attempts to make "a mountain out of a molehill." Whatever the cause, the effect was that, throughout Latin America, people of all political opinions were aroused.

The U.S. Congress also questioned the disparity that gave the Defense Department much greater funding for research than the State Department had. State expressed concern that this kind of research might have a damaging effect on foreign affairs. The State Department was accused in some circles of deliberately leaking the crisis to the press to emphasize the question of appropriate sponsorship by the military of foreign affairs and social science research.

Academicians, concerned for the future of social science research, protested censorship and questioned the ability of the State Department to evaluate research.

The Exxon Effort

What appears to be an OD success story started at the Baton Rouge refinery of Esso (now Exxon), when some key management personnel suggested that "sensitivity training"—experience-based learning—could help to open up communication and develop trust within the organization (Rush, 1973).

In 1956, the company asked behavioral scientists about the action-research method of using sensitivity training for managers. At that time, sensitivity training ("T-groups," "laboratory training," or "encounter groups") was a relatively new development in the business community. A highly placed and influential corporate executive had been through a "lab" and was receptive to the idea for management development. He specified that participation in the training should be the option of each operating plant's management, in keeping with Exxon's decentralization policy. After some key executives from several plants had gone through the basic, two-week sessions, they returned enthusiastic about the potential that this kind of training held for what Exxon then called "organizational improvement."

Management at the Baton Rouge refinery decided that sensitivity training was just what was needed to help the organization cope with operational changes then taking place. Automation, union-management problems, manning practices, and personnel reductions were causing major problems. Underlying these problems was a fundamental problem: how to maintain a competitive cost position. If the refinery were to retain its profitability, so management figured, it would have to make changes with as little upheaval as possible.

Beginning in 1957 and continuing into the early Sixties, the refinery had over seven hundred supervisors, managers, and scientists participate in what became known as a "classic, fourteen-day sensitivity-training lab." Exxon had decided to use outside, university-based "trainers," on the premise that it would be far more expensive, not as relevant, and too time consuming if all the managers were shipped out to attend. These training sessions for teams of managers may have been the first examples of "in-house" laboratory training for management. The company was more than satisfied with the results.

Despite that apparent success, sensitivity training began to fade in the early Sixties because management believed that, while it was extremely effective and had high value for the individual manager, it was not designed to accomplish work-related objectives.

It then turned to the Managerial Grid as its main source of OD. The introduction of the Grid at the Baytown, Texas, refinery was an action-research project with normative values: "to validate the concepts and the hypotheses of quantifiable changes in the culture of a functioning organization with multiple internal and external influences (as contrasted with a pure laboratory environment)" (Rush, 1973, p. 61). As such, the project was followed and measured throughout (Blake, Mouton, Barnes, & Breiner, 1964).

About eight hundred managers at all levels participated in the Grid OD experiment. An evaluation study indicated that the organization changed in the direction posited by Grid theory. Exxon continued to use the Managerial Grid, and the program was extended to six hundred unionized workers, one of the first times that this kind of training fell below middle management. After around 1966, no more formal OD activities were employed; according to Rush, group process training is still used but "only on a selective basis...or in special circumstances" (Rush, 1973, p. 61). An internal change agent at Exxon told Rush:

> We were convinced that Grid was appropriate for the Baytown culture at that time, but since we have found we are able effectively to use other techniques of organization improvement, such as rational methods of problem solving and goal setting in a modified managing-by-objectives program." (Rush, 1973, p. 61)

The causes of failure in the Camelot project and the relative success of the Exxon project were identical: sponsorship, clearance, communication, and collaboration.

The Camelot project was sponsored by the American government, indicating an acutely one-sided, pragmatic purpose. Almost all Latin American countries mentioned the *sponsorship* as cause for doubting the credibility of the approach. The Exxon program was sponsored by top management, and the decision to pursue OD was made at local plants with local options. When the union was involved in Baytown, it, too, was consulted and maintained "joint ownership" of the program with management.

The proposed host countries of Camelot apparently did not *understand* the project or its intent. Although statements were made that these parties had been adequately informed, there was great emphasis that *henceforth* no such research would be done in a foreign country without the country's prior knowledge and consent.

The failure to go to the top for *commitment*, as well as to gain the cooperation, *clearance*, opinions, and advice of all parties relevant to the research effort, both subjects and clients, betrays a prevalent naivete. However, the behavioral scientists at Exxon were no better prepared and certainly no better trained than the Camelot social scientists. The latter failed to develop a *collaborative relationship*—the sharing and exchanging of ideas and opinions at all stages of research. Such lack of collaboration is always a disadvantage in a scientific undertaking and can be fatal in research designed to explore sensitive areas or areas in which the researchers hope to influence their subjects.

Those behavioral scientists at Exxon used *sponsorship, clearance, communication,* and *collaboration* in such a manner that the client system internalized (institutionalized) the capacity to make deliberate choices of its own about future training needs and also developed the internal staff to implement them.

The normative goal of OD—using OD as the exemplar of "knowledge utilization in organizations"—is to "humanize" bureaucracy. But values (or normative goals) are not the most important consideration. There is a pragmatic issue at stake as well, for as organizations grow, as they increase their complexity and scope, the problems of leadership, coordination, collaboration, and communication force themselves on our attention. Most knowledge-utilization efforts have to do with maintaining the virtues of bureaucracy—its speed, precision, predictability, and efficiency—while trying to preserve an adaptability to change and a climate of creativity, personal growth, and satisfaction for the work force.

Organizations today operate under uncertain and ill-defined conditions. Institutions also are becoming the focus for a new kind of politics: mobilizing public opinion; working closely with external (especially state, local, and Federal agencies and legislatures) influences; and shifting constituencies. "Managing external relations" no longer can be left exclusively in the hands of the public affairs department. Top leadership and OD practitioners must be involved. These changing characteristics of the organizational environment will become even more pronounced in the years ahead.

NOW WHAT?

OD practitioners cannot dispense their knowledge without human contact; they must be deeply involved with their clients. Neutrality is impossible when profound human changes are at stake. The classical realm of science is at odds with the messy, unwieldy, deeply human findings of the social sciences. In the "pure" sciences, one can "do" science on subjects. In applied behavioral science, one cannot; the subjects must become co-investigators if the research is to have any meaning.

The second factor exacerbating the situation is the strong idealism that most change agents bring to their tasks. Role ambivalence is deepened because there are essentially two strategies for truth gathering. One is the *exoteric* mode—exoteric meaning "knowledge generated for the public interest"—and the other is *esoteric* knowledge—produced for "one's learned colleagues." Exoteric knowledge springs from direct experience of immediate, intimate relationship to the sources of data; esoteric knowledge is consciously more detached, socially disengaged, and remote. Most change agents and OD practitioners are trained esoterically and have to practice exoterically. This is the major source of ambivalence that must be reckoned with, if not resolved.

Recommendations for Knowledge Research

The social sciences will provide no easy solutions in the near future, but they are our best hope, in the long run, for understanding our problems in depth and for providing new means of lessening tensions and improving our common life. (National Academy of Sciences, 1969, p. 17)[7]

There is a fable, carefully nurtured over the centuries by...those who see basic (science) as pure, about the relation between the scientist who acquires information and the problem solver who applies that information... that scientists acquire the knowledge, that this knowledge goes into the public domain, and that when a problem solver needs some knowledge to solve his problem, he extracts it from the public domain, uttering words of gratitude as he does so.... Knowledge needed by the problem solver occurs in some mysterious fashion...so effective that no tampering must be allowed.... The less contact the scientist has with the problems of the problem solver, the more apt he will be to fill the public domain with knowledge of ultimately greatest import to the problem solver. This is the fable, but like all fables, it is a myth. It does not work that way at all. (Garner, 1972)[8]

---

[7]From *The Behavioral Sciences and the Federal Government*. Washington, DC: National Academy of Sciences, 1969.

[8]From W. Garner, "The Acquisition and Application of Knowledge," *American Psychologist*, 1972, 27(10), 941-946.

The preceding quotations bespeak another myth: that, just as the natural sciences lead to technology that will make us all healthier and wealthier, so the social sciences, if applied, can solve our social problems. The intellectual task of developing a valid framework for an applied social (or behavioral) science is only beginning, but the following can serve as guidelines to what can be called *valid* knowledge:

1. An interdisciplinary applied social science that takes into consideration the behavior (including attitudes, feelings, and values) of persons operating within their specific institutional environments.

2. An applied social science capable of accounting for the interrelated levels (person or self, role, group, and macrosystem) within the social-change context.

3. An applied social science that in specific situations can select from among variables those most appropriate to a specific local situation in terms of its values, ethics, and moralities.

4. An applied social science that is pluralistically "real," accepting the premise that groups and organizations as units are as amenable to empirical and analytical treatment as the individual.

5. An applied social science that can take into account "external" social processes of change as well as the interpersonal aspects of the collaborative process.

6. An applied social science that includes propositions susceptible to empirical test, focusing on the dynamics of change.

One must also consider some of the strategies of truth gathering for an applied social science—some methodological considerations. In order to develop usable knowledge, the following values (biases) should be taken into account in all action-research undertakings:

1. Research is a collaborative undertaking and can be enhanced by including members of the client system in the team effort.

2. The image of *organization* stems from a preference for observing process and change rather than order and continuity. It should not be disconcerting to confront contradiction and conflict.

3. The researcher's most productive stance is curiosity and dissatisfaction with current paradigms for understanding organizational life.

4. Findings should be important—not just interesting—and demonstrable in terms of larger social relevance.

5. Research reports should contain a vivid description of the experience of researching. "Values" should be squarely faced in these reports. Reports should present not only the findings but also the questions raised by the research.

Recommendations for Policy

With so many valid ideas missing their mark, with policy makers ignorant of or indifferent—if not antagonistic—to pivotal facts, it is inappropriate, if not dangerous, to focus only on the perils of closer cooperation between the realms of science and action. (Recently, California legislators responsible for drafting new legislation on the control and rehabilitation of drug addicts said that their opinions were largely formed by their friends, druggists, family doctors, and lobbies. They reported being unaware of or antagonistic to the findings of the experts who have produced a prodigious literature on the issue.)

My specific recommendations regarding policy are:

1. *Deepen and broaden mutual understanding between scientists and policy makers.* Especially of each other's systems of values.

2. *Develop the science of science utilization.* What seems to merit attention is research on the utilization of knowledge. Without such research, all data lose some of their potential effectiveness, given the pace at which we are acquiring new knowledge.

3. *The yield of social science must be loud and clear—and useful.* To exercise influence and effect, social scientists must make their achievements visible and communicated well. Worth is often measured by tangible product.

4. *The public must support larger social science efforts.* Research activity accomplishes many purposes aside from the main one of adding to the store of knowledge. Our Federal government, which can grant greater research funds than foundations or universities and which grants billions of dollars for work on weapons systems, still haltingly grants funds on a year-to-year basis for the social sciences.

5. *Social scientists must be social as well as scientific.* Human subjects have intelligence, feelings, hypotheses, and expectations as well as some urges to subvert the experiment (Argyris, 1980). The people with whom the social scientist works—whether they are subjects or clients—must *understand* and must feel *commitment* to the collaboration for mutual benefit. Indeed, this attitude is essential to the scientific ethic. Without trust and commitment to the research task, the data generated are often phony or incomplete.

All this may not be completely within the grasp of the individual social scientist. Rather, it is in the realm of those institutions that educate social scientists. Most social scientists do not receive any formal instruction in one of their primary tasks, teaching, during their graduate education, nor do they receive systematic practice or supervision in the human side of the research enterprise. These must be learned the hard way, through guided experiences.

6. *Social scientists must re-examine and modify their own values.* Social scientists must aim for complete honesty in their research. They must not attempt to conceal the motives or the sponsor of the research, since denouncement is inevitable and can destroy the research. Similarly, sponsors must respect the social scientists and consider their objections honestly and thoroughly, altering the plan of action if criticisms are merited.

We tend to think of applied social scientists as experts, analysts, consultants, designers, and sometimes temporary "help." The myriad of relationships involved can obscure the value that an applied social science provides. At its most impactful and professional level, an applied social science is profoundly important to what is occurring in the world today and is essential to fully realizing the potential that organizations represent for our lives.

REFERENCES

Argyris, C. *Inner contradictions of rigorous research.* New York: Academic Press, 1980.

Bakan, D. The interface between war and the social sciences. *Journal of Humanistic Psychology*, 1982, *22*(1), 5-18.

Bennis, W. The failure and promise of the social sciences. *Technology Review*, September, 1970, pp. 2-7.

Bennis, W., Benne, K. D., & Chin, R. *The planning of change* (4th ed.). New York: Holt, Rinehart and Winston, 1984.

Benne, K. D. Educational field experience as the negotiation of different cognitive worlds. In W. Bennis, K. D. Benne, & R. Chin, *The planning of change* (3rd ed.). New York: Holt, Rinehart and Winston, 1976.

Beyer, J. M., & Trice, H. M. The utilization process: A conceptual framework and synthesis of empirical findings. *Administrative Science Quarterly*, 1982, *27*, 591-622.

Blake, R. R., Mouton, J. S., Barnes, L. B., & Greiner, L. E. Breakthrough in organization development. *Harvard Business Review*, December 1964, LXV.

Commager, H. S. *The American mind.* New Haven, CT: Yale University Press, 1950.

Garner, W. The acquisition and application of knowledge. *American Psychologist*, 1972, *27*(10), 941-946.

Glaser, E. M., & Davis, H. R. (Eds.). *Putting knowledge to use: A distillation of the literature regarding knowledge transfer and change.* Los Angeles: Human Interaction Research Institute & National Institute of Mental Health, 1976.

Klein, D. C. Some notes on the dynamics of resistance to change. In W. Bennis, K. D. Benne, & R. Chin, *The planning of change* (2nd ed.). New York: Holt, Rinehart and Winston, 1966.

Lewin, K. *Resolving social conflicts.* New York: Harper & Row, 1948.

McKelvey, W., & Aldrich, H. Population, natural selection, and applied organizational science. *Administrative Science Quarterly*, 1983, *28*.

Mohrman, S. A., Cummings, T. G., & Lawler, E. E. *Creating useful research with organizations: Relationship and process issues.* Paper delivered at conference held at the University of Pittsburgh, School of Business Administration, Fall, 1982.

National Academy of Sciences. *The behavioral sciences and the federal government.* Washington, DC: Author, 1969.

Rush, H. M. F. *Organization development.* New York: The Conference Board, 1973.

Whitehead, A. N. *Science and the modern world.* New York: Mentor Books, 1947.

Zaltman, G., Duncan, R., & Holbek, J. *Innovations and organizations.* New York: John Wiley, 1973.

Warren Bennis, Ph.D., *is the Joseph DeBell Distinguished Professor of Management and Organization at the University of Southern California's Graduate School of Business Administration, Los Angeles, California. His specialties are leadership and power in organized settings and organizational change. Dr. Bennis has received the Distinguished Service Award of the American Board of Professional Psychology and the Perry Rohrer Award for contributions to the practice of organizational consulting. His two new books on leadership are now in press.*

ORGANIZATION DEVELOPMENT AND POWER

Willem F.G. Mastenbroek

This article presents a theoretical approach to organizational interventions that combines traditional organization development (OD) strategies with one that also involves power, conflict, and competition for scarce resources. Four types of intraorganizational relationships are explored: (a) instrumental; (b) socioemotional; (c) power; and (d) negotiating. These four types of relationships reflect a view of organizations as networks of interdependent units. Each of these types of relationships produces problems and frictions within the organization. For each type of relationship and its ensuing problems, specific consultant-intervention tactics are recommended, each of which should be a part of an overall intervention strategy. The major element of this strategy is the "political" orientation of the consultant as he or she attempts to develop a coalition strong enough to implement a set of solutions in the client organization.

ORGANIZATIONS AS NETWORKS

Organizations are networks of units (individuals, groups, departments, etc.). Units are dependent on one another, but they also have their own interests. One could call each network a coalition of various interests. Units are bound to one another by relationships. Relationships between units are characterized by the dilemma of autonomy versus mutual dependence. This requires those concerned to find a balance between cooperative and competitive behavior.

The way in which one manages mutual relationships involves strategic behavior. Problems and frictions arise between units and can become chronic. These problems and frictions often are the reasons why OD consultants or human resource development (HRD) experts are called into the organization. Various relationships call for different types of strategic behavior and create various problems—problems that require specific interventions. Schematically:

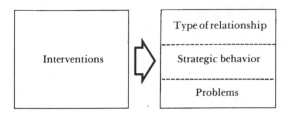

FOUR TYPES OF RELATIONSHIPS

There are four primary aspects of the relationships between organizational units:

1. *Instrumental relationships.* People in organizations are regarded as means of production for one another. They use one another's accomplishments to help to achieve their own work goals.

2. *Socioemotional relationships.* People within organizations are emotionally involved with one another. This involvement may be strongly individual oriented in the form of

sympathy or antagonism. It also can be group oriented in the form of positive or negative social identity.

3. *Negotiating relationships.* People in organizations must share many scarce resources with one another, and, in order to get one's share, one is dependent on others when decisions about resource allocations are made.

4. *Power relationships.* People in organizations determine, to some extent, the behavior of others; usually, people attempt to increase their own opportunities and to fortify their positions in relation to others.

Each type of relationship involves three dynamics for the OD or HRD practitioner: (a) which strategies are involved; (b) what problems and frictions are to be expected; and (c) what interventions can be applied.

Instrumental Relationships

Instrumental relationships always have received considerable attention in organizations. These concern the way in which work and tasks are organized. Division of labor and specialization make workers more or less dependent on one another. One can no longer produce without delegating work to an ever-increasing number of other people. In general, people tend to use *rational strategies* when managing this sort of relationship, e.g., collecting information, determining the criteria a solution must meet, or comparing alternative solutions. Preferably, quantitative information and methods are used. The approach is primarily rational, and a reasonably satisfying solution that permits work to continue is often sufficient. In Simon's (1957) terms, "satisfying" is often the objective, rather than "maximizing." In any case, personal interaction is of a different nature than when power relationships or scarce resources are in question. As March and Simon (1958) put it, the difference is between "bargaining" and "politics," on the one hand, and "problem solving" and "persuasion" on the other.

Problems in instrumental relationships are goal and task oriented. Problems are seen as "logical" rather than "political," and those concerned direct their behavior accordingly (Shull, Delbecq, & Cummings, 1970; Thompson, 1964; Thompson & Tuden, 1959). The problems can assume numerous forms: insufficient consensus about priorities, mutual misunderstandings, use of "different languages," lack of communication skills, awkward procedures for dealing with problems, insufficient mutual exchange, obscure task assignments, poor coordinating structure, and so on.

Suitable *interventions* are of a rational, problem-solving nature, such as soliciting substantive advice from an expert. One can also deal with a transfer of insights and methods that facilitates seeking a solution in the areas of objectives and means, task division, and coordination (Kepner & Tregoe, 1965; Maier, 1963). Furthermore, consultants can be procedure oriented and recommend a systematic problem-solving model (Drucker, 1963). They can play a significant role in the various steps contained in such a model, e.g., collecting information, formulating problems, and developing alternative solutions. Depending on the type of problem, consultants also can use more specific procedures, for example: strength/weakness analysis, Beckhard's (1969) confrontation meeting, the job-expectation technique, and the role-analysis technique (French & Bell, 1978; Huse, 1975).

Socioemotional Relationships

The human relations movement, with its attention on the informal organization, has focused attention on the socioemotional aspect of relationships. People in organizations affiliate themselves with one another on the basis of personal sympathies, similar norms and values, and mutual objectives. These emotionally loaded ties can engender a very strong "we" feeling. The informal groups that arise are often more meaningful to people than the more formal work relationships. The *strategies* that people use in these situations are clearly different from rational behavior. In a certain sense, they are even so *irrational* that the term strategy is no longer applicable. This is the area in which people pay attention to their "feelings." In this area, there are greater chances for spontaneity, openness, and personal concern.

Problems arise in this area when personal or collective identity is challenged. Such problems are highly emotionally charged. They concern one's self-image, the prejudices related to this self-image, and questions of acceptance and trust. Feelings of affiliation and identification with certain groups, institutions, and symbols are questioned. Problems also can be related to how one manages personal relationships—how people approach and react to one another. This can produce strong negative feelings of suspicion and stereotyping.

After World War II, with the rise of laboratory training and organization development, socioemotional relationships were considered central to organization development. Feedback sessions, sensitivity training, and encounter groups became frequently used interventions (Beckhard, 1969; Bradford, Gibb, & Benne, 1964; Lippitt, Watson, & Westley, 1958; Miles, 1975; Schein & Bennis, 1965). More recently, however, enthusiasm for an *intervention* strategy exclusively oriented toward socioemotional relationships has waned (Bradford, 1974).

The two previously discussed groups of interventions are sometimes applied in combination. Usually, the accent is on the socioemotional side of relationships. Later, the focus is on the instrumental aspect: how can we increase organizational effectiveness? Examples of such intervention strategies are: Blake and Mouton's confrontation meeting, Grid OD, and organizational mirroring (French & Bell, 1978; Huse, 1975). Both types of relationships, instrumental and socioemotional, play a central role in theories of leadership styles. The distinction between task orientation and socioemotional orientation is maintained in most variations. It is repeatedly emphasized that both aspects require separate attention and different kinds of behavior. Dealing with problems in these two sorts of relationships is probably the best developed of the OD strategies.

Negotiating Relationships

People in organizations also are bound together by having to share material resources such as space, salaries, budgets, personnel, and other facilities. In this regard, everyone is dependent on everyone else within the organization.

To the extent that resources are allotted on the basis of hierarchical decisions or clear criteria, these problems can be dealt with either as part of the power relationship or as instrumental issues. If this is not the case, then there is room for negotiation. Those concerned must meet to discuss a fair allocation of resources. Negotiating relationships can be characterized as follows:

1. Clear-cut interests of persons or units are at issue, and these interests conflict with those of others.
2. Mutual dependence is also involved. (This is especially true in organizations in which a workable relationship between units must be maintained.)
3. There is a certain balance of power. (A "certain" balance because the parties need not be in equilibrium, but the more "out of balance" a party is, the less chance there is to effectively apply negotiation as a strategic behavior.)

The characteristics of negotiation as strategic behavior and the various problems related to it are discussed elsewhere (Mastenbroek, 1980). The most evident problems are:

1. Impasses are normal.
2. The appearance of all sorts of negotiating styles, such as open versus closed and hard versus relenting, is accompanied by resulting emotional consequences.

3. Supporters may not be satisfied with anything but "winning."

4. Harder, more bitter negotiating, i.e., an escalation toward more aggressive behavior, may develop.

Interventions that can be applied to negotiation situations are:

1. Instead of striving for a solution based on extensive research, develop a provisional proposal, using it as a step toward compromise.

2. View impasses and crisis situations as natural—and sometimes even constructive—and use them as such.

3. Rather than defending one's own point of view or carefully prepared solution, encourage the parties to formulate the conditions on which they would be able to agree.

4. Make constructive use of deadlines.

5. Be sensitive to the constituency; cooperate in "selling" the results.

6. Function as discussion leader/chairman in negotiations.

7. Limit the parties' opportunities to extend their arguments, directing the conversation to concrete proposals and conditions.

8. Actively take the role of mediator, knowing that one party can sometimes make concessions to a third party more easily than to the opponent.

9. Make regular use of adjournments.

10. If negotiations are stalemated, ensure that the parties explore the consequences of *not* reaching agreement.

Developing the negotiating skills of members of the organization can be a significant contribution. It is an alternative to the sometimes forced attempt to have people "cooperate." Lack of openness and trust does not have to lead to unhealthy human relationships or a destructive atmosphere. Destructive tendencies can be avoided through negotiation. Mutual respect remains possible. Negotiation can even have a challenging, motivating effect. To deal with a negotiation situation, a consultant must be able to use a different style than if he or she were handling socioemotional problems or trying to establish a proper decision-making process.

Table 1 offers a summary of the situations discussed thus far.

Power Relationships

Mulder (1977, p. 15) defines the exercise of power as: "determining, to a certain degree, the behavior of others or giving direction to the behavior of others." Power can be seen as a type of relationship or as an aspect of all human relationships. Formal position within a hierarchy or an arsenal of means of persuasion alone do not determine power relationships. Such things as expertise, credibility, and informal contacts also play a role. People within organizations usually have a very finely developed understanding of power relationships. They recognize that they are more or less dependent on those with more power and act on that basis.

The maintenance or strengthening of one's own strategic position in terms of these power positions is the motive for much behavior. Competing individuals and groups within organizations attempt to improve or safeguard their positions in relation to one another. One does this as an individual, sometimes by identifying with a given professional group or functional branch of the organization. One also can try to gain power by monopolizing and manipulating expertise of substantive interest to the organization. One attempts to gain additional power by reorganization that allows one to achieve a more central position. The strategies used can be more specifically identified from case to case. Pettigrew, for instance, (1973, p. 150) lists some of the strategies used by specialists within organizations to secure their power vis a vis others. These usually are very cautious strategies—political maneuvers or power plays—concealed behavior aimed at maintaining and building status and prestige within the organization and consolidating and expanding one's power position. Because it is also necessary to work together, the "power game" has a subtle and seldom articulated character. In itself, it is also a power strategy because a blatant move to strengthen one's power can undermine that very power.

Table 1. Three Types of Organizational Relationships

Types of Relationships	Problems	Strategies	Consultant Interventions
Instrumental	Decision-making problems; difficulties in defining and coordinating.	Rational/technical approaches: problem analysis, more efficient meeting and decision-making behavior, improved planning, clear division of tasks.	Teaching techniques of problem analysis and decision making; introducing better coordination and planning procedures.
Socioemotional	Lack of trust and acceptance; personal irritations; stereotyping.	Expression of "irrational" feelings and irritations; talking out matters, putting oneself in others' shoes.	Training in open communication; discussing irritations and stereotyping.
Negotiating	Continuing impasses; increasing pressure; escalation toward "fighting."	Recognizing opposition; give-and-take instead of proving; exploring disadvantages of no compromise; keeping constituency at a distance.	Proposing compromise; training in negotiating techniques; chairing negotiations.

Limitations of space prevent an adequate exposition of the frequently recurring power networks, such as equal-to-equal, higher-to-lower, and higher-to-middle-to-lower, which have been discussed elsewhere (Mastenbroek, 1982). But the specific interventions appropriate to resolve power-relationship problems are presented in Table 2, where they are contrasted with the appropriate strategies for the three other types of relationships. The important thing to recognize about the power-based interventions in Table 2 is that they require a strong advocacy position on the part of the consultant and are not usually regarded as traditional OD interventions.

THE ONE-ON-THREE MODEL

The four types of relationships are not equal. The power relationships usually are much more important than the other three in organizational life. Power relationships determine behavior to a large extent. Much power behavior is termed "political," although it is often disguised. In effect, power relations recondition the other three aspects of interunit relations. The concern of OD practitioners with socioemotional and, to a lesser extent, instrumental problems often presupposes a certain balance of power and a highly developed interdependence between units. Such a balance, however, may not be present.

The one-on-three model of interunit relations is as follows:

	Instrumental aspect
Power aspect	Socioemotional aspect
	Negotiating aspect

Table 2. Intervention Strategies for Four Types of Relationships

Power Relationships	Negotiating Relationships	Instrumental Relationships	Socioemotional Relationships
Clarify the dynamics of power relationships, e.g., by simulation or analysis.	Develop negotiating procedures with the parties: agenda, strategies to be pursued.	Teach techniques of problem analysis and decision making.	Train people in expressing emotions and irritations.
Apply own power as expert or outsider.	Train in negotiating techniques.	Train people to meet efficiently.	Develop mutual trust and acceptance in teams (e.g., interpersonal process consultation).
Press for influence from higher authority.	Assist parties in specifying conditions under which they can accept a suggested solution.	Introduce better coordination and planning procedures.	As third party, set rules and procedures for managing personal conflicts.
Use structural measures such as developing power centers by reorganization.	Chair the negotiations.	Create clearer division of tasks.	As third party, reduce distrust and irritation between departments (e.g., confrontation meeting).
Forge a dominant coalition.	Clarify common interests.	Use management by objectives.	Reinforce unit's identity (through greater autonomy, "house style").
Integrate units to modify existing power.	Develop a compromise.	Assist in formulating policy and setting objectives.	
Organize lower levels of the organization.	Assist in selling the compromise to the constituency.	Interface management by introducing project groups or searching for and resolving barriers in the units' working relationships.	
Balance organizational units in size and power.			
Remove middle level or give it more authority.			
Separate units in space.			

This theory of intervention covers more problem areas than does traditional organization development. What is still lacking is an *intervention strategy*, that is, a model in which individual interventions can be integrated into a total intervention program. Three basic steps in this strategy are:

1. Identification of the problem (by surveying the different perspectives of the problem);
2. Development of a dominant coalition;
3. Solution of the problem with the help of the one-on-three model.

An important point of this strategy is that in order to realize and implement a solution, consultants need a *dominant coalition*. They must take the political structure of the organization into account when trying to find a formula that will bring about such a decisive combination. When such a coalition does not exist, a principal role of the consultant is to develop such a coalition. The consultant must enter the political arena of the organization and use his or her power to develop adequate support to make certain that the interventions will produce the change in the power relationships. This would be a clear case of "fighting fire with fire." This overall strategy is a very different one from the more external stance taken in traditional OD interventions. Here the consultants use their power to realign the power relationships within the organization in order to help the organization to reach its desired level of effectiveness.

REFERENCES

Beckhard, R. *Organization development: Strategies and models.* Reading, MA: Addison Wesley, 1969.

Bradford, L. P. *National Training Laboratories: Its history 1947-1970.* Bethel, ME: National Training Laboratories, 1974.

Bradford, L. P., Gibb, J. R., & Benne, K. D. (Eds.), *T-group theory and laboratory method: Innovation in re-education.* New York: John Wiley, 1964.

Drucker, P. F. *Managing for results.* San Francisco: Jossey-Bass, 1963.

French, W. L., & Bell, C. H. *Organization development.* Englewood Cliffs, NJ: Prentice Hall, 1978.

Kepner, C. H., & Tregoe, B. B. *The rational manager: A systematic approach to problem solving and decision making.* New York: McGraw-Hill, 1965.

Huse, E. F. *Organization development and change.* St. Paul, MN: West, 1975.

Lippitt, R., Watson, J., & Westley, B. *The dynamics of planned change.* New York: Harcourt Brace Jovanovich, 1958.

Maier, N. R. F. *Problem-solving discussions and conferences.* New York: McGraw-Hill, 1963.

March, J. G., & Simon, H. A. *Organizations.* New York: John Wiley, 1958.

Mastenbroek, W. F. G. Negotiating: A conceptual model. *Group & Organization Studies,* 1980, 5(3), 324-339.

Mastenbroek, W. F. G. *Conflict hantering en organisatie-ontwikkeling (Conflict regulation and organization development).* Alphen aan den Rijn, The Netherlands: Samsom, 1982.

Miles, N. G. *Werken met groepen [Working with groups].* Alphen aan den Rijn, The Netherlands: Samsom, 1975.

Mulder, M. *Omgaan met macht [Dealing with power].* Amsterdam: Agon Elsevier, 1977.

Pettigrew, A. M. *The politics of organizational decision-making.* London: Tavistock, 1973.

Schein, E. H., & Bennis, W. *Personal and organizational change through group methods.* New York: John Wiley, 1965.

Shull, F. A., Delbecq, A. L., & Cummings, L. L. *Organizational decision making.* New York: McGraw-Hill, 1970.

Simon, H. A. *Models of man.* New York: John Wiley, 1957.

Thompson, J. D. Decision making, the firm and the market. In W. W. Cooper, H. J. Leavitt, & M. W. Shelly (Eds.), *New perspectives in organizational research.* New York: John Wiley, 1964.

Thompson, J. D., & Tuden, A. Strategies, structures and processes of organizational decision. In J. D. Thompson, P. B. Hammond, R. W. Hawkes, B. H. Junker, & A. Tuden (Eds.), *Comparative studies in administration.* Pittsburgh, PA: Pittsburgh University Press, 1959.

Willem F.G. Mastenbroek, Ph.D., is the managing partner of the Organisatie Adviesgroep Nederland (Holland Consulting Group) in Amsterdam and also is an assistant professor in organizational consultancy in the Department of Social Psychology at the Free University of Amsterdam. Dr. Mastenbroek is an organizational consultant and trainer, with particular emphasis on reorganization, management development, and conflict management. He has developed training programs in the areas of conflict management, negotiation skills, and dealing with power and influence.

NEEDS ASSESSMENT: AVOIDING THE "HAMMER" APPROACH

Joe Thomas

In the hands of a skilled craftsman, a hammer has an almost infinite number of uses. However, a carpenter would not attempt to build a house with only one or two types of hammer. Similarly, the needs diagnosis is an essential tool for a program builder. Unfortunately, many program designers have one or two favorite needs-assessment tools that are applied to many situations, regardless of fit. Just as the hammer can be used by a skilled craftsman to force a square peg into a round hole, an assessment technique can be forced to fit a given situation.

A recent literature review (Moore & Dutton, 1978) concluded that needs assessments are not being performed appropriately. They tend to be performed on a periodic, program-oriented, "crisis management" basis, with little attempt to coordinate the assessment with other organizational activities. Blake and Mouton (1980) have stated that "responding to felt needs rather than real needs might be the number one problem facing HRD professionals today" (p. 107). Felt needs for which programs are often designed include the need for better communication, better leadership, better time management, and more effective decision making. Improvement often is needed in these areas. Because people do not argue against these needs, the standard procedure frequently is to develop a program. Like the square peg fitting into the round hole, the program may not quite fit the real needs of the situation.

Individuals who conduct needs assessment often tend to reduce the scope of their assessment by looking only at a limited number of sources of information and by using only one or two favorite techniques for collecting and analyzing the data. In a typical assessment program, the program designer meets with the department manager and they determine that the supervisors seem to be having trouble explaining the new cost-control system to their subordinates. They agree that it looks like a communication problem and that a communication program would probably be useful.

This scenario may be oversimplified, but it does illustrate three common pitfalls in diagnosing program needs. First, the source of information about the need for a program is limited—in this case, the source is the department head and program planner's *perception* of the problem. Other sources of information could have been explored. Second, the interview was the only technique that was used to diagnose the problem. Again, other techniques such as questionnaires, observation, and critical incidents may have been more appropriate. Finally, the decision was made by only the two individuals. Other means of data analysis obviously could have been helpful.

This article will identify a variety of diagnostic tools for assessing training and development needs. For each technique, issues regarding its use will be discussed and references to further information will be provided. These techniques will then be developed into a model that will help to integrate the various sources of information, techniques of data collection, and methods of analysis for the program designer.

SOURCES OF INFORMATION

A needs assessment is conducted to determine the extent of a specific organizational problem and to design a program to resolve that specific concern. The first step of the program designer is to try to acquire an understanding of the problem. This understanding usually is achieved by collecting information. Individuals, groups, public sources, and organizational records all are potential sources of information, as shown in Table 1.

Table 1. Sources of Data

Individuals	Internal sources External sources
Groups	Committees Constituents
Public Sources	Government publications Trade associations Indexes Business services Public statements
Organizational Records	Company reports Performance records Task analyses

Individuals

Information gathered from people on an individual basis can provide very useful data. If the individuals selected have regular contact with the problem area, they are likely to have a deeper understanding of the problem. Depending on the type of program to be designed, knowledgeable individuals could include persons within the organization or external to it.

Internal sources of data might include the people on whom the program will focus or their superiors, subordinates, and/or peers. These individuals frequently can provide good anecdotal evidence that can be used to diagnose weaknesses. The same examples then can be used later to add substance and relevance to the program.

In the scenario previously described, when the program designer interviewed the *supervisors*, she found that they could not explain the new system to their employees because it had not been clearly explained to them. In this case, meeting with the people on whom the training was to focus revealed that they did not need general communication training, but merely a better explanation of the system they would be using. The person who was then called on to explain the accounting system was able to focus on the supervisors' questions and to provide appropriate examples. The supervisors were then able to explain the system to their subordinates.

Consultants also are frequently used as *external* sources of information. Although consultants can be very helpful, research by Tichy (1975, 1978) and Slocum (1978) shows that consultants may have limited perspectives about how to approach a problem. Like many people, they use certain activities and techniques in most situations. If the information desired is in one of "their areas," the consultants can provide a wealth of information. Otherwise, their perceptions may be biased or misleading. Consultants also may tend to diagnose the problem to fit their areas of expertise, even though it may be only marginally related to the true problem.

Care must be taken to assure that the information obtained from individuals is representative. If only a few individuals have direct involvement with a particular problem, they may be hesitant to share their knowledge for fear that the information may be detrimental to them in the long run. Using only a few sources of information may also limit a statistical analysis of the data. Finally, the "expert" status of the information source may restrict the range of alternatives considered in designing the program. When an "expert" states an opinion on something, many people are reluctant to challenge that viewpoint. The impact of these issues depends on the nature of the data sought.

Groups

Groups also can provide valuable information for a program planner because they represent a variety of viewpoints about a particular concern. A sample of group members can provide measures of the frequency or importance of issues. Committees and constituents are groups that are commonly used to generate data.

A *committee* with members from diverse backgrounds can give the program planner numerous perspectives regarding the problem under consideration. An ad hoc group with the explicit purpose of assisting in program design can provide information during the planning phases of the program and can help to anticipate and resolve problems during the implementation stages.

In developing a vocational training program, for example, individuals with relevant experience could advise on program development, provide input about what the students should be capable of doing on completion of the program, and help to determine what training is actually feasible within the setting. This temporary committee could meet periodically during the early phases of the program to provide assistance in solving problems of implementation. Frequently, members of the temporary committee later serve as members of a permanent advisory committee that helps to keep the program relevant to its initial goals or provides guidance concerning modification of the program.

Standing committees formed to accomplish a specific function also can provide information for program design. In the performance of their regular duties, members of these committees frequently perceive areas that could benefit from training and development activities or difficulties that could arise as a result of planned changes. For example, if a business were considering secretarial training programs to introduce word-processing skills, valuable input could be obtained from a standing committee on computer usage. This committee also might be able to identify future training needs in other areas of computer usage.

Constituency groups also can provide useful data about the performance of an organization (Bartee & Cheyunski, 1977). These groups include providers of resources and services, developers of technology, and consumers of goods and services produced. It is common to think of these groups as outside the organization; however, departments and groups within an organization may provide resources and services to, or utilize outputs of, the group being studied. Their perception of the group is likely to be different from that of the group's members.

For example, the trimming department of a diecasting facility was unable to meet the production standards established by the engineering department. Although piece-rate incentives had been established for employees who exceeded a set level of production, employees rarely were able to meet the level needed to qualify for the production bonus. The production manager believed that employees in the trimming department needed training to make them more efficient. However, the trimming employees blamed the workers in the casting department for producing defective components that required excessive trimming and slowed production. Interviews with members of the constituency group, the casting department, indicated that the parts did conform to existing tolerances. The problem was that as the dies became more worn, the components produced needed more trimming. However, replacing the dies in the casting department would cost the members of that group time and thereby reduce their production bonuses. So, as long as the parts met specifications, they were going to produce with worn dies. Meeting with constituency groups in this case enabled management to see that the problem was not defective parts, but a combination of excessive tolerances and the current production bonus system.

Public Sources

A vast amount of information relevant to solving business and economic problems is readily available to the diagnostician. Such information can be useful in identifying problems, industry trends, and potential solutions. Much of this information is free or comes with a subscription to a publication, which is quite reasonable compared to the expense of collecting the data. Common sources of information include government publications, trade publications, indexes, business guides and services, and speeches. Goeldner and Dirks (1976) provide a comprehensive review of sources of business facts.

Government publications are available from many agencies at the Federal, state, and local levels. The *Monthly Catalog of United States Government Publications* provides a comprehensive list of publications issued by various Federal agencies. Other data are available through the Bureau of the Census, U.S. Department of Commerce. Probably the most difficult aspect of obtaining government data is finding out which agencies publish the relevant information.

Trade associations provide much basic data about the operating characteristics of their members. The *Encyclopedia of Associations* and the *National Trade and Professional Associations of the United States* provide a variety of information about the thousands of trade and professional associations operating in the United States.

Some *periodicals* also publish special reports about particular industries. For example, *Business Week* publishes an annual survey of the liquor industry every February or March.

Indexes can provide references to authors, subjects, and titles of books, pamphlets, periodicals, and other documents. Many indexes are available in public libraries.

Business guides and services provide information about particular industries or companies. *Moody's Industrial Manual* provides information about principal officers, products, business history, and properties. Standard and Poor's provides *Industry Surveys* (annual surveys of each industry), *The Outlook* (weekly stock-market letters), and *Stock Guide* (investment data concerning many common and preferred stocks).

Speeches made at professional meetings, seminars, commencements, and other public events also can provide insight into industry trends, problems, and challenges.

This brief review of sources of published information is not comprehensive; a variety of information is publicly available. Such information is especially useful to a consultant who is not familiar with a particular industry. Reviewing published data provides a means for determining how common certain problems are to the industry and how other firms within the industry have resolved such problems. Such information also can familiarize the consultant with the specific terminology of the industry.

Organizational Records

Internal company records are often underutilized in diagnosing problems within the organization. Much information that has been collected for other purposes is available and useful for problem diagnosis, but other groups in the organization may not realize that it exists. One indirect benefit of using a committee to collect information is that the various committee members may be familiar with different company records. These records might include company reports, performance records, and task analyses.

Company reports are compiled from a number of sources and vary widely in their usefulness for diagnostic work. They are useful in developing a broader understanding of the company, its operations, and its personnel. For example, annual reports provide statements of organizational goals and information about the firm's product line(s). Annual reports also usually provide information about officers, customers, and geographical locations. The recognition of interrelationships between locations and/or individuals is especially important when changes in one aspect of an organization impact others. Other typical company reports relate to personnel practices, marketing efforts, financial conditions, and operating techniques and changes.

Similarly, *performance records* can be useful in problem diagnosis. They can provide information about individual, departmental, or organizational performance. They may be able to show the development of trends. They also may be useful in pinpointing when a particular problem or behavior began, which could be helpful in establishing causes of existing problems. For example, one organization noticed a decline in productivity in a particular department. The review of performance records showed that the decline had been occurring for almost two years, although it had only recently become critical. Further examination of company records showed that the decline had started about six weeks after the appointment of a new head of the department. This discovery helped to shift the focus of the training program from one of improving workers' productive skills to one of improving working relationships between the employees and the department head.

Task analyses that identify specific attributes of a job also can be useful in designing training and development programs. The analysis should provide a description of the skills and abilities needed by job incumbents as well as the actual work, working conditions, and other relevant information. If the people being hired to perform the task do not meet the necessary requirements, a program to develop the needed skills and abilities is indicated.

Task analyses also can be used to compare the actual performance of the task to the way it is supposed to be done. This can be especially useful in diagnosing problems that result from unclear instructions and role ambiguity or from differences between written job descriptions and the actual tasks being performed.

DATA-COLLECTION TECHNIQUES

The next problem faced by the diagnostician is to determine how to collect the needed data from the various sources available. Many methods can be used. Some of them require the involvement of individuals or groups. Others such as observation and review of existing data require less direct involvement. Table 2 is a partial listing of techniques for collecting information. For more complete discussions of data-collection techniques, refer to Bouchard (1976) and Nadler (1977).

Table 2. Data-Collection Techniques

Individually Oriented Methods	Interviews Questionnaires Tests
Group-Oriented Methods	Sensing interviews Committees Delphi technique Nominal-group technique Brainstorming
Observation	Systematic observation Complete observation Participant observation
Review of Existing Data	Sensitivity Originality

Individually Oriented Methods

Most data-collection techniques involve either the people who are to be trained or individuals who have frequent contact with the prospective trainees. These techniques include questionnaires, interviews, and tests (see Table 2). Each method has unique features that influence its appropriateness.

One of the most commonly used methods for gathering data is the *interview*. Frequently, the person doing the needs assessment meets with the potential trainee and the trainee's supervisor or subordinates and asks questions that are designed to identify the training needs. Such interviews often are conducted informally; usually, the people to be interviewed are not given enough notice of or details about the meeting to prepare themselves adequately.

In one instance, the author was interviewing employees of an airplane manufacturer in an effort to establish causes of excessive employee turnover. Subjects were selected at random and asked to report to the interviewing room at a specified time. Just before receiving the notice to report for the interview, one worker had argued with her boss about her job performance. She came to the interview expecting to be fired. It took most of the time allocated for the interview to convince the worker that the purpose of the interview was not to hear her side of the argument.

An unprepared interviewee usually can offer only opinions, unsubstantiated by "hard" data. Obviously, such information also may be superficial. This problem is more severe if the interviewee is relatively unfamiliar with the subject or the interviewer is not highly skilled in interviewing. The interviewer must know how to ask probing questions to get at the real problems.

A second problem associated with interviews is determining whom to interview. If unfavorable information about someone is introduced, there is always the fear that the source of the information will be revealed to that person. Unless an atmosphere of trust is developed with the interviewee, the information shared may be slanted, particularly if the subject is the interviewee's supervisor or another supervisor. A trusting relationship can take time to develop. Some people never will "open up" to an interviewer, and many people will tell the interviewer only what they think the interviewer wants to hear. Information acquired under such circumstances should be evaluated carefully and compared with data acquired from other sources.

The *questionnaire* or survey is another commonly used method of collecting data from large groups of people, although many factors can bias this data (Bouchard, 1976). Any questionnaire or instrument should be checked for its ability to measure what is desired (validity) and the consistency, over time, of the ratings obtained (reliability). Questions should not be phrased so that the answers received are biased. Closed-ended questions limit the responses an individual can make. For example, if the choices on the instrument form are limited to "team development," "MBO," and "performance appraisal," but the respondent actually feels that the answer should be "a lack of organizational direction," it is unlikely that the respondent will write in "lack of direction" even if a space is left for "other."

Another way that bias is introduced is in the use of questionnaires is through leading questions. Such questions indicate to the respondent how he or she is expected to answer (Bartee & Cheyunski, 1977). If asked whether assistance in improving leadership abilities would be useful, who would say no? This does not, however, mean that leadership training is actually the most crucial training need.

Tests also can be used to assess the skills, abilities, or perspectives of an individual for diagnostic purposes. Tests are probably the least used of the techniques for assessing individuals, although they may be quite appropriate. It is worthwhile for a program designer to have an understanding of how accomplished the class is before starting the program. Many programs repeat too much information that is already known or assume too much prior knowledge. Tests are a convenient way to assess the entry-level abilities of the class members in order to customize the program to meet the needs of the individuals involved.

One of the major disadvantages of tests is that they frequently are perceived as threatening, and people become quite defensive about their scores. The purpose of the test, i.e., to identify needs for developmental purposes, should be stated explicitly if the test is to serve as a motivational tool.

Group-Oriented Methods

In contrast to individually oriented methods of data collection, group-oriented methods allow people to receive assistance from other group members to support their viewpoints. Such techniques also allow members to "piggyback" on other persons' ideas, generating expanded information. However, they also can limit opinions that do not represent the majority viewpoint. This limitation can be an advantage or a disadvantage, depending on whether the researcher wants a variety of ideas or ideas common to the majority of group members. The most commonly used techniques for collecting data from groups are sensing interviews, committees, the Delphi technique, the nominal-group technique, and brainstorming.

Sensing interviews are often used to ascertain the concerns, issues, needs, and resources of people within an organization (Huse, 1980). Various individuals from different groups in the organization are selected to share their views with the data collector. Members' reactions to different program alternatives can be explored or issues that are of greatest concern to the group can be examined. The resulting information can be analyzed to determine common themes, and programs can then be designed around the themes identified.

Sensing interviews may be preferable to individual interviews in terms of time utilization and group support of ideas, but they do have potential weaknesses. First, as with most data-collection methods, the respondents must feel that their answers will be used in the intended manner. Trust of the leader and the other group members is a prerequisite to an honest, open discussion. Second, people who were not invited to be members of the group may feel that they were excluded deliberately; thus, they may feel threatened. An explanation of the purpose of the sensing interview (or continued use of the technique) should be given to alleviate (or confirm) the fears of such people.

Committees may be ad hoc or permanent advisory groups whose purpose is to provide input and guidance in program design. Alternatively, functional committees—such as a safety committee or a planning board—may provide insight into particular problems. Often, committee members can see skill deficiencies, attitudinal barriers, or other factors that hinder performance. Because of their expertise, they also may be able to specify the type of employee development that would be most useful in overcoming the problems.

Another useful method of gathering data from a group of people is the *Delphi technique* (Bunning, 1979; Dalkey, 1969). This process is especially useful if it is necessary to obtain information from individuals in a variety of locations. Generally, the process starts with the selection of a panel of individuals who are knowledgeable about a particular area of concern. These individuals are requested to identify the major aspects of a specified issue. These issues are then integrated into a questionnaire that is sent back to the panel of experts, who are asked to indicate the extent of the problem. The responses are summarized and returned to the panel members with another questionnaire; this time the experts are asked to complete the questionnaire and to explain their rationale for deviating from the mean group response on each question. The process reveals both the group members' opinions and reasons for differences of opinion.

The *nominal-group technique (NGT)* (Delbecq, Van de Ven, & Gustafson, 1975; Ford, 1975) is somewhat similar to the Delphi technique. The major difference between the two methods is that in the NGT, the panel members meet as a group to discuss the various issues, rather than operating independently as in the Delphi method. The individuals participating in an NGT exercise are given a subject or theme and asked to write their thoughts about the topic on a sheet of paper. The next step is to proceed around the group, asking each member to share one thought or idea with the group, in turn. These ideas are recorded without discussion until all ideas are shared and recorded.

The major advantages of the NGT are that it assures that every group member contributes to the generation of ideas and that multiple facets of ideas are surfaced. It also helps to gain commitment from the participants because they have had equal opportunities to contribute and to evaluate ideas.

Brainstorming (Pfeiffer & Jones, 1974) is similar to the NGT. In this approach, ideas are voiced as they occur and are recorded without discussion of their merit. This allows participants to build on other members' ideas. Quantity of ideas is the first concern of brainstorming. After numerous ideas are generated and no new ideas are forthcoming, the discussion turns to the feasibility of the ideas. The major advantage of this approach is that "piggybacking" of ideas can occur. The technique does not assure that all members will participate.

Observation

A third group of techniques used to collect data (and also to verify data collected by other methods) is observation (Bouchard, 1976). The techniques range from observing a sample of behavior to some form of "undercover" observation by a concealed observer. The advantage of observation is that behavior is more natural and people are not required to provide the information directly. They continue to function as they would normally. Ideally, this would decrease the intervention impact caused by the data-collection process. Still, observation is likely to have *some* impact on behavior. Subjects being observed may "perform" for the observer and thus bias the data.

Systematic observation techniques frequently require a sampling of the desired behavior. For example, a task being performed could be observed on a random basis. After a series of observations, a pattern of activities would evolve, showing how time was spent and what problems were encountered. If the observation revealed that much time was spent in giving instructions, it might be deemed worthwhile to design a program to facilitate the communication of instructions. This might involve a training program on communication skills or the development of written instructions to reduce the need for verbal ones.

Complete observation occurs when the observer openly uses a camera, audio recorder, videotape, or other technique to record relevant behavior. This method can yield massive amounts of information. It also can require large expenditures of time and money.

The complete-observation technique can be used within a training program to record participant behavior during an activity. The primary purpose of such a recording would be to allow the trainer to discuss relevant issues with the trainees without interrupting the dynamics of the original session. However, it also would allow the trainers to analyze the session later, in order to improve the design of the training program. This type of observation also can be useful in analyzing meetings and other group events.

In a final method of observation, the observer is also a *participant*. This may require the diagnostician to actually perform a task in order to learn what is involved in doing the work. Participation gives the data collector added credibility as well as relevant examples.

In another version of participant observation, the observer *surreptitiously* becomes a member of the group. Ideally, this method reduces the bias caused when the subjects realize that they are being observed. However, because the observer is intervening in the group's activities, his or her actions can bias the results. A potentially more serious issue is one of ethics and credibility (Friedlander & Brown, 1974). How would employees respond to data gathered by such means? Would they trust a leader who used such techniques to gather data? This method would be especially counterproductive if the program based on the data were to require openness and trust among the participants.

Review of Existing Data

A review of existing data is useful in gathering information because the information is collected after the action, so there is no danger of biasing the behavior. An example of this technique is a review of critical incidents or performance evaluations to determine employee strengths and weaknesses. It may be possible to trace a number of incidents to common causes and, thus, to identify potential problem areas.

Although a variety of data are available in most organizations, there do not seem to be well-established techniques for collecting such data. Information collected is often in the form of case studies, which may be used to demonstrate a point during a program, indicate needs for program development, or verify the results of information acquired through other means. The keys to the use of this data-collection technique seem to be *sensitivity* and *originality*. One must be very sensitive to the type, quality, and initial purpose of the information that is being reviewed. Creativity or originality in interpreting and analyzing the data can lead to new insights. Historical data also can be used to supplement and confirm data collected from other sources and by other means.

DATA ANALYSIS

After the sources of needed information are identified and the data are collected, it is necessary to analyze and interpret the data. The procedures that are frequently used include some form of gap analysis, scaling methods, weighting formulas, and consensus. These procedures can be used to analyze data collected by a variety of techniques, and more than one procedure can be used to analyze a group of data. These techniques are listed in Table 3.

Table 3. Methods of Data Analysis

Gap Analysis	
Scaling Methods:	Rating scales Rankings Nominal-group technique
Weighting Formulas	
Consensus:	Voting Compromise

Gap Analysis

A fairly easy method of analyzing data is examining the gap between where the organization "is" on a particular issue and "where it should be" or "where it would like to be." The differences between actual and desired states indicate potential areas for program development. A difference between 50 percent turnover for a particular firm versus a 10 percent average turnover for the industry would signal a potential problem. Once such differences are identified, it is necessary to attach priorities to the gaps to guide program development.

Scaling Methods

Scaling methods such as measurements on a continuum or rankings can be used to establish the relative significance of issues.

Scales are frequently used to show the importance or magnitude of various issues to the person completing the scale. The most frequently used is the Likert scale, on which the respondent indicates agreement on a continuum ranging from "strongly agree" to "strongly disagree." Other frequently used measurements include ranges of importance or desirability. A variation of this technique is to ask the respondent to mark a scale to indicate where the organization is and where it should be on particular issues. This helps to identify major gaps between the current and desired status of the organization.

Various data also can be *rank ordered* in terms of their importance, desirability, frequency, etc. Individual rankings then can be combined to establish the relative value that the group places on each issue.

In the *nominal-group technique*, discussed earlier, the participants in a group rank the items identified in the group discussion in order of importance. The responses of all participants are then compiled, and the results are reported to the group. The group ranking then can be used to establish priorities for discussion, training, or other program design.

Weighting Formulas

One of the problems in using scales is that no mechanism is provided to indicate the relative differences in the importance of the scales. Weighting formulas allow the respondents or diagnostician to attach more value to one scale than another. A common weighting method is to ask the respondent to indicate how *important* a particular attribute (skill, attitude, need) is, how *frequently* the attribute is encountered, or how *deficient* the subject feels in terms of the attribute. A recent study (Thomas & Sireno, 1980) asked managers to indicate how important a particular competency was for their subordinates, how frequently the subordinates needed the competency, and how well prepared the subordinates were in that competency. These three responses were then combined to determine the need for a program to develop the competency. This study also identified substantially different priorities for job competencies among industries—again supporting the need to customize training programs rather than interpreting the training needs to fit the existing program.

Consensus

One of the most commonly used methods of reaching agreement is consensus (a majority or all members agree on an issue, a ranking, or a next step). This is not to be confused with voting, compromising, or "horse trading." Although the latter are often easy methods for decision making, they may not include a careful weighing of all the relevant information.

If a committee uses a nonquantitative method to collect information, a *vote* of the committee often is used to determine the implications of the data collected. However, one or two persons or issues frequently dominate the discussion, or individuals with high status, such as experts or superiors, often voice their views on the subject. Unless there is information that clearly contradicts these high-powered views, the subsequent vote and recommended actions will likely follow along.

If there are a number of strong feelings about an issue, a common solution is a *compromise*. This often results in a nonthreatening, suboptimum recommendation that is acceptable to all but will do little to solve the problem. In fact, a compromise program could worsen the problem by raising the expectations of participants. Then, if the expected results are not achieved, the program, its sponsor, and its planner look bad.

A DIAGNOSTIC PROCESS MODEL

The preceding discussion has identified three important dimensions associated with the performance of an organizational needs diagnosis. To develop an organizational improvement program, the program designer should consider the possible sources of data, how the data will be collected, and how the data will be analyzed. Figure 1 shows a representation of a diagnostic model based on these three dimensions.

This model can be used to demonstrate several points. First, it provides a systematic framework for thinking about needs assessment. It shows various sources of data and techniques for collecting and analyzing the data. Second, the model shows the interactive nature of data sources, collection, and analysis methods. The three dimensions of needs assessment indicate an ongoing, systematic process. The accuracy of the needs assessment will be improved if all three elements of the diagnostic process are considered simultaneously.

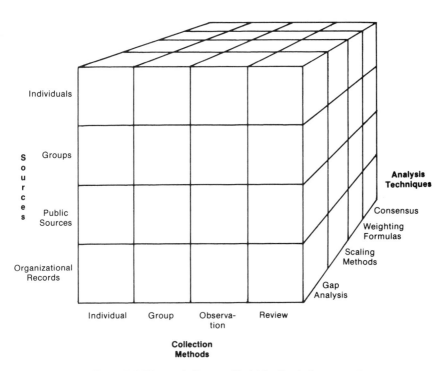

Figure 1. A Diagnostic Process Model for Needs Assessment

Just as the carpenter needs a variety of tools to build a structure, the program builder needs a variety of tools to diagnose program needs. Although it is possible to design a program based on an interview with an employee or a few supervisors, a wider perspective is helpful in assessing the needs that the program should attempt to meet. In general, the more sources of information, techniques of data collection, and methods of data analysis that can be used to diagnose a problem, the better the understanding one has of the problem. The better one's understanding is of the problem, the less likely one is to try to hammer a square program into a round problem.

REFERENCES

Bartee, E.M., & Cheyunski, F. A methodology for process-oriented organizational diagnosis. *Journal of Applied Behavioral Science*, 1977, *13*, 53-68.

Blake, R., & Mouton, J.S. HRD controversy: A la Blake & Mouton. *Training and Development Journal*, 1980, *34*(5), 106-108.

Bouchard, T.J. Field research methods: Interviewing, questionnaires, participant observation, systematic observation, unobtrusive measures. In M.D. Dunnette (Ed.), *Handbook of industrial and organizational psychology*. Chicago: Rand McNally, 1976.

Bunning, R.L. The Delphi technique: A projection tool for serious inquiry. In J.E. Jones & J.W. Pfeiffer (Eds.), *The 1979 annual handbook for group facilitators*. San Diego, CA: University Associates, 1979.

Dalkey, N.C. The Delphi method: An experimental study of group opinion. Rand Corporation Memorandum (RM 5888-PR), 1969.

Delbecq, A.L., Van de Ven, A.H., & Gustafson, D.H. *Group techniques for program planning*. Glenview, IL: Scott, Foresman, 1975.

Ford, D.L., Jr. Nominal group technique: An applied group problem-solving activity. In J.E. Jones & J.W. Pfeiffer (Eds.), *The 1975 annual handbook for group facilitators*. San Diego, CA: University Associates, 1975.

Friedlander, F., & Brown, L.D. Organization development. *Annual Review of Psychology*, 1974, *25*, 313-341.

Goeldner, C.R., & Dirks, L.M. Business facts: Where to find them. *MSU Business Topics*, 1976, *24*(3), 23-36.

Huse, E.F. *Organization development and change*. St. Paul, MN: West, 1980.

Moore, M.L., & Dutton, P. Training needs analysis: Review and critique. *Academy of Management Review*, 1978, *3*, 532-545.

Nadler, D.A. *Feedback and organization development: Using data-based methods*. Reading, MA: Addison-Wesley, 1977.

Pfeiffer, J.W., & Jones, J.E. Brainstorming: A problem solving activity. In J.W. Pfeiffer & J.E. Jones (Eds.), *A handbook of structured experiences for human relations training* (Vol. III). San Diego, CA: University Associates, 1974.

Slocum, J.W. Does cognitive style affect diagnosis and intervention strategies of change agents? *Group & Organization Studies*, 1978, *3*, 199-210.

Thomas, J.G., & Sireno, P.J. Assessing management competency needs. *Training and Development Journal*, 1980, *34*(9), 47-51.

Tichy, N.M. Demise, absorption, or renewal for the future of organization development. In W.W. Burke (Ed.), *The cutting edge: Current theory and practice in organization development*. San Diego, CA: University Associates, 1978.

Tichy, N.M. How different types of change agents diagnose organizations. *Human Relations*, 1975, *28*, 771-799.

Joe Thomas, Ph.D., is an assistant professor of business administration at Northeast Missouri State University in Kirksville, Missouri. His primary interests are in organizational behavior, strategic planning, and needs assessment in organization development, and he has published articles on these topics in several professional journals.

AN ORGANIZATION DEVELOPMENT (OD) PRIMER

Leonard D. Goodstein and Phyliss Cooke

Organizations, like individuals and families, frequently find themselves in need of professional help. Sometimes they need content experts—persons who can propose solutions to specific technical problems, such as how to determine an appropriate product mix or how to establish a foreign subsidiary. There are numerous technical experts available to help organizations with such problems.

Often, however, an organizational problem is not easily identified. Symptoms such as low productivity, tardiness, and high employee turnover indicate organizational distress. Organization development (OD) consultants look beyond symptoms in order to gain understanding of the problem(s) reflected in the symptoms. Organization development consultants help the client organization to diagnose and modify the circumstances that have led to the presenting complaints.

DEFINING ORGANIZATION DEVELOPMENT

> Organization development is an educational process by which human resources are continuously identified, allocated, and expanded in ways that make these resources more available to the organization and, therefore, improve the organization's problem-solving capabilities. (Sherwood, 1972, p. 153)

Organization development typically:

- is a long-range effort to introduce planned change;
- is based on a diagnosis that is shared by the members of an organization;
- involves the entire organization or a coherent system or part thereof;
- has the goal of increasing organizational effectiveness and enhancing organizational choice and self-renewal;
- utilizes various strategies to intervene into the ongoing activities of the organization in order to facilitate learning and to make choices about alternative ways to proceed.

The most general objective of organization development is to create self-renewing, self-correcting systems of people who learn to organize themselves in a variety of ways according to the nature of their tasks and who continue to expand the choices available to members of the organization as it copes with the changing demands of a changing environment.

While organization development typically is characterized as a *result* of planned change efforts, it is important to remember that organizations also develop as a natural consequence of day-to-day interactions. Thus, organization development really refers to both the natural, emergent dynamics and to the change that results from consciously set goals and planned interventions. The task of the OD consultant is to be helpful in the process of establishing desired change and in helping the client system to develop the skills needed to stay on top of the natural forces for change that are inherent in the system and in the environment.

Although OD activities focus on people and groups and the changed relations among them, the target of OD efforts is the organization. The long-term success of any OD effort is dependent

---

Adapted by permission from P. A. Keller and L. G. Ritt (Eds.), *Innovations in Clinical Practice: A Source Book* (Vol. 2). Sarasota, FL: Professional Resource Exchange, 1983.

on the development of collaborative attitudes and interdependent behaviors within the system, but OD is not simply human relations training. OD efforts are designed to *guide* the human resources within the organization in understanding and managing its growth and direction.

Most OD consultants would prefer to work with healthy organizations, aiming toward fuller actualization or growth of the organization, but finding them is rare. Just as most individuals seeking professional help are experiencing some pain or discomfort, most organizations seeking OD are in some kind of trouble—and are just as willing to terminate the relationship after initial pain reduction, rather than move to increased health. Thus, although much of the OD literature suggests that OD intends to focus on positive growth or development, experience suggests that OD in practice has a more ameliorative quality, focusing on short-term solutions to immediate problems. Most OD consultants would prefer it to be otherwise.

Regardless of whether the focus is on short-term problems or long-term growth, the organization development consultant operates on the assumption that the organization, not the individuals in the organization, is the client. The consultant responds to immediate problems such as low morale, requests for team building, or the need for a performance-appraisal system with a general systems approach. Such an approach guides the OD practitioner or "change agent" in attempting to assess, diagnose, and prescribe for a given system (Burke, 1982).

MODELS OF ORGANIZATION DEVELOPMENT

The behavioral sciences offer a variety of principles and concepts with which we can understand and describe the functioning of organizations. Consultants can use these principles and concepts to evaluate the effectiveness of organizations in reaching their goals and the satisfaction of members of the organization with their lives in that system. These two concerns are primary foci of organization development.

Many conceptual models, primarily based on open-systems theory, depict organizations as systems of interacting elements and identify both the explicit and implicit structures of organizational life. For example, Weisbord (1976, 1978) views organizations in terms of a "Six-Box Model" in which *leadership* is necessary to ensure that balance is achieved between and among the five other boxes, which include: (a) the *purpose* of the organization, which must be clearly articulated; (b) the *structure* through which the work that is necessary to achieve the organization's purpose is done (such work must be optimal); (c) the *rewards* for doing the work, which must be appropriate and sufficient; (d) the *helpful mechanisms* needed to adequately coordinate work, which must be available and operating; and (e) the *relationships* among people and groups, which must be managed appropriately to ensure high levels of satisfaction and productivity (see Figure 1).

A more complete model is offered by Jones (1981) in his "Organizational Universe Model." Typical organizational values, including respect and dignity in the treatment of people, cooperation, functional openness, interdependence, authenticity, and profitability, are placed at the core of a set of concentric circles. The next ring, *goals*, considers how the values are articulated or operationalized. For example, if one of the values is respect for people, courtesy in all interpersonal interactions might be the operationalized goal. When people are treated discourteously, it can be assumed either that the value of respect is not authentic or that the relationship between courteous behavior and respect is not clear to members of the organization or not explicit enough to guide their behavior. (See Figure 2.)

The OD consultant must consider not only the organization's purpose and philosophy (values) and its aims (goals) but also how these goals will be implemented (the structure of the organization). Several structural elements must be reviewed by the consultant in order to adequately assess the functioning of an organization. These include the formal organizational chart, the informal social structure of the system (how things *really* work in the organization's informal structure), the degree of overlap between the two, and how well these structures are working.

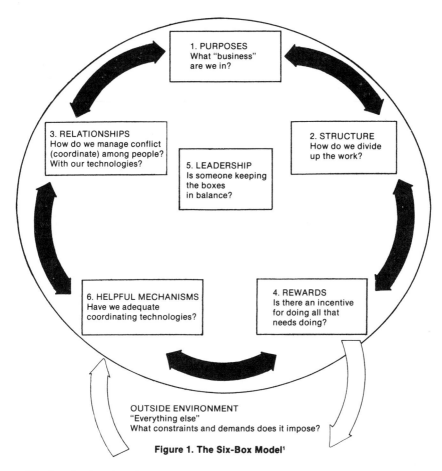

Figure 1. The Six-Box Model[1]

The functioning of the formal and informal structural systems in a variety of areas should be examined. These include:

1. Accountability—the formal system for evaluating individuals who work in the system as well as the individual latitude exercised and the interpretations made of this dimension of organizational life;

[1]From Marvin Weisbord, Organizational Diagnosis: Six Places to Look for Trouble with or Without a Theory. *Group & Organization Studies*, 1976, *1*(4), 430. Used with permission.

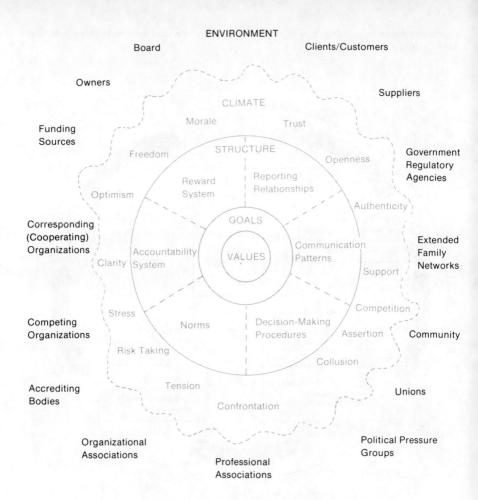

Figure 2. The Organizational Universe Model[2]

2. Rewards—the tangible and intangible rewards given by the organization for work performed and the impact of these rewards on the quantity and quality of work performed;

3. Reporting relationships—the designated lines of authority along with the demonstrated power to influence the behavior of others in a desired direction;

4. Decision-making procedures—the processes through which problems are identified and solved (who, when, where, in what manner), along with the individual preferences that guide the formal procedures followed;

[2]From John E. Jones, The Organizational Universe. In J.E. Jones & J.W. Pfeiffer (Eds.), *The 1981 Annual Handbook for Group Facilitators.* San Diego, CA: University Associates, 1981.

5. Communication patterns—the formal and informal systems through which organizational information is disseminated and meanings are transferred within the organization; and

6. Norms—the formal and informal rules of conduct, dress, and speech, as well as the observable behavior in these areas.

Organizational climate, the next ring of the model, is a by-product of the interaction of the values guiding the organization, its goals, the structural elements of the system, and the "goodness of fit" between these internal elements and the external environment in which the organization goes about its work. Some organizational climates feel "healthy" and others feel "unhealthy." These climate indices are primarily symptomatic and offer little understanding of the real causes of problems, even though they may be of concern to the client. Little significant change can occur from addressing climate problems alone; their *causes* are to be found closer to the center of the organizational universe.

ORGANIZATIONAL ASSESSMENT AND DIAGNOSIS

A valid organizational diagnosis includes a description of the root causes of the organization's malaise. For example, the organization's reward structure may not fit its articulated value of achievement and accomplishment, or constant bickering between various groups may be hidden by a norm of smothering conflict. Such analyses—when supported by clear behavioral data— help both the consultant and the client to understand both the cause of the problem and what can be done to remedy the situation.

Data Collection

Several methods of data collection can be used by the OD consultant. The first is direct observation, including unobtrusive measures. Such observation begins when the consultant enters the waiting room of the client organization. How is the room decorated? How easily is entry gained? What is the attitude of the receptionist to the visitor? How are the offices arranged? The answers to these and similar questions are all data, although much additional observational data will be collected as the consultant moves through other areas of the client system. Additional data will either support or disconfirm the initial impression.

The second way to collect data is to analyze written records such as reports, interoffice memoranda, newsletters, appointment records, attendance at staff meetings, report distribution lists, and so on. Such data provide clues about patterns of communication and influence and the differences between the formal and informal organizational structures.

The most general source of data, however, is the diagnostic interview. Who is interviewed and the content of the interview will be determined largely by the organizational model used by the consultant. The open-systems model, explicit in both the Six-Box and Organizational Universe models, focuses on values, goals, and the supporting structures that articulate these central concerns. These models lead the consultant to examine the social psychology of the organization, how the various subsystems are bound together, and how effectively they operate. Weisbord (1978) has developed a semistructured interview schedule to guide the consultant in applying his or her diagnostic model to actual organizational life.

A final type of data collection utilizes a variety of paper-and-pencil inventories to tap such dimensions as morale, attitudes, and job satisfaction. This category includes well-standardized instruments such as the Survey of Organizations (SOO) (Bowers & Franklin, 1977; Hausser, Pecorella, & Wissler, 1977), a host of semistandardized instruments such as the Organizational Ideology Scale (Harrison, 1972), and those that are specially created for work with the individual client by the consultant. The pros and cons of using such instruments are virtually the same as those involved in using such instruments with individuals (Pfeiffer, Heslin, & Jones, 1976), including the critical question of how to share the data collected. Survey-guided feedback, one of the strategies of organizational change to be discussed in this article, relies almost entirely on the feedback and analysis of such data with groups of individuals within the organization.

Some consultants prefer to use direct observation and interviews, while others rely more on formal assessment procedures. The model of organizational life used by the consultant and his or her views about organizational health certainly will affect the process of data collection.

STRATEGIES FOR ORGANIZATIONAL CHANGE

Once the client and the consultant agree on the diagnosis of the organization's current difficulties, attention can be paid to remedies. Among the intervention strategies typically used by OD consultants are training, coaching (individualized training), techno-structural changes in the organization, role negotiation, formal (survey) feedback, sensitivity training with organizational members, team building, and process consultation. Although it is beyond the scope of this article to review each of these procedures in detail, a brief description of each is appropriate.

Training—especially training in communication skills, interpersonal relationships, management and supervisory practices, and performance appraisal—can dramatically change the functioning of an organization. This is particularly true if the training programs relate to the basic problems identified in the diagnosis and involve most of the relevant members of the organization. Of course, training programs must have acceptance and impact if they are to be successful.

Coaching involves having the consultant spend a good bit of time with one or more key members of the organization (typically top managers), observing and reviewing their behavior and providing feedback to them about what has been observed. This strategy is particularly useful if the persons being coached have been identified as critical elements of the basic problem. For example, if the president of the corporation espouses the value of collaboration but makes snap, independent decisions on a regular basis, the consultant would identify this behavior when it occurs and offer feedback on the discrepancy. Such confrontation is expected to lead to change, just as it does in counseling or therapy.

Technostructural interventions attempt to simultaneously change the way in which work is accomplished (the technology of work) and who does the work (the structure of the organization). To attempt to do either separately is to deny the close, natural interdependence of these two aspects of work. For example, in a typical production facility, quality control is functionally separate from the production line, which creates an adversary relationship between the two units. The management of quality standards is not a production responsibility, but is assigned to others. One strategy often adopted by the production staff is to find ways to *hide* production defects from the quality-control staff, rather than to correct the cause of the defects. One possible resolution of the problem is to reorganize the production system so that a single, integrated system is responsible for production, including quality control. But such a change in the technology of production all too often fails because the change neglects structural issues, particularly the issues of territory, status, and interprofessional disputes. Only when both the structural and technological issues are addressed simultaneously can *effective* organizational change occur.

In technostructural change, *role negotiation* is a critical substrategy. The consultant attempts to help the various people to determine what they agree to do on the job and what they are willing to agree to allow others to do. The overlaps and the gaps then can be identified and treated as problems to be solved rather than as dust to be swept under the rug.

Formal (survey) feedback involves collecting responses to questionnaires from all members of the organization, collating the data from the responses, and making the data available to the organization. Such data make the members' concerns explicit; this forces the organization to acknowledge the issues raised. The major problem, of course, is for the consultant to help the organization—particularly the work groups—to analyze the data, accept the validity or lack thereof, and plan action steps to remedy the problems identified.

Team building, and sensitivity training as one vehicle for doing team building, involve a simultaneous examination of the attitudes and skills of a work group (team) needed for the accomplishment of a task and the amount of cohesion and involvement of the members of the team (Goodstein, Cooke, & Goodstein, 1983). Teams have tasks to accomplish and they need both to be committed to their tasks and to have the skills needed to accomplish their work. Skills such as agenda building, identifying and utilizing resources, and decision making too often are taken for granted in the creation of work teams and the assignment of tasks. Members of work teams also will differ in their *attitudes* about group work and in their *skills* in working in groups. In team building, the consultant must assess the attitudes and skills of the various team members for both the task and maintenance functions and then assist the members to clarify their attitudes and acquire the necessary skills.

In *sensitivity training*, an unstructured group setting, the members of the work group are encouraged to explore their interpersonal relationships, especially those that have interfered with effective collaboration. The clinical skills of the consultant in such an intervention need to be exceptionally high. Issues raised in work-group sensitivity training do not "go away" when the session is over.

The unique OD consultation intervention, however, is *process consultation* (Burke & Goodstein, 1980). The term process consultation was first introduced by Schein (1969). Process consultation involves the examination of *how* things are done in an organization rather than *what* is done; the process consultant examines the patterns of communication, how such patterns were developed, what the patterns show about the distribution of power, and how these differ from the espoused values and goals of the organization.

The OD consultant uses process-consultation techniques in conjunction with other techniques. For example, while observing a staff meeting or helping a group try to understand its survey data, the consultant might ask why no one ever seems to respond directly to questions asked by a particular member or might inquire why certain issues always seem to be so low on the agenda that they are never addressed. In this way, the consultant attempts to expose the questions concerning values and goals that have previously been identified as core problems. The role of the consultant here is to be counternormative, to ask why the emperor is wearing no clothes and, perhaps, also to ask why the group has chosen not to comment on it.

THE ROLE OF THE OD CONSULTANT

Because the field of OD is still relatively undefined, atheoretical, and new at applying the behavioral sciences, there are few constraints on the individual OD consultant. Check lists for monitoring one's own interventions can be developed. Once the consultant develops a clear understanding of his or her own values, models, preferred modes of organizational functioning, expectations about how people in organizations should interact, and so on, it becomes easier to ask value-based questions of the client. These questions include: What is an organization? What purpose(s) should organizations serve? For whom? How should organizations balance their needs with the individual needs of their members? How does one understand the process of change on an organizational level? On a societal level? Because the personal answers by the consultant to these questions guide all phases of his or her work, clarity and commitment to one's answers are key aspects of OD consulting. And, because there are no easy or widely accepted answers, formulating one's own answers is a slow, developmental process.

Because the client system must generate the data necessary for a diagnosis and also accept the consultant's diagnosis based on those data, the typical clinical model of expertise and distance rarely works. Even more importantly, the client system must accept full responsibility for implementing the changes necessary to reach its desired state. Organization development cannot occur if the organization does not undertake the task of improving its own functioning. Thus, the most functional relationship between consultant and client is one of collaboration and support, in which the responsibility for both accepting and implementing any change is the client's. Consultants cannot prescribe new behaviors to their clients and be certain that the client will accept and implement the prescriptions. Only when the client "buys" the diagnosis and prescription is there hope of change.

Despite the widely held view that a collaborative style works best, many consultants take a more directive style. This is typically a top-down approach in which what is to be done, to what standard, by whom, when, and in what manner is decided by the consultant. Although many consultants who operate from an "expert" orientation utilize this directive style, they are not necessarily the same. For example, a consultant operating from an expert orientation might still use a consultative approach in which the final decision rests with the client. His or her role would be to offer the client the best judgment about the potential consequences of various courses of action, but leave the choice to the client. Furthermore, it would be expected that the client system would use its human resources to make the decision; such decisions are most likely to produce commitment from those involved in them.

Still another style is the facilitative one, in which all decision-making authority is turned back to the client system and the consultant avoids even the expert orientation. The consultant's focus is on identifying the key linking pins of the client system. Whatever information is necessary to make the decision can be found by those persons. The primary role of the consultant is to facilitate communication between the functioning units within the system. The efficacy of this approach is determined by the readiness of the system to participate in the change effort and the problem-solving skills of the members. Obviously, this facilitative style is most useful when the energy of the organization for change is high and the skills of organizational members are well developed. Stepsis (1977) provides a fuller discussion of these several consulting styles.

Internal and External Consultants

There are two major ways in which OD consultants work: as internal consultants—full-time regular employees of the organization to which they provide help—and external consultants—outside specialists who provide help on an irregular basis, either per diem or on retainer. One fascinating aspect of OD consultation lies in the unique relationship that exists between internal and external change agents who collaborate to bring about an OD effort. *Internal* consultants, who are sometimes called trainers, personnel administrators, employee-relations specialists, or program analysts, have a different and fuller understanding of the organization. They know levels of nuance and shades of meaning that no outsider can comprehend. On the other hand, the external consultant brings a fresh approach, a naivete about organizational issues that enables him or her to ask questions that would not occur to the internal consultant.

The external consultant also should be more willing to take risks, to ask embarrassing questions, or to point out collusion. The risk of losing a consultancy is qualitatively and quantitatively different from the risk of losing one's job. The courage inherent in being "outside" the system stems from both lack of awareness of specific risks and willingness to accept risks in general. The subtle chemistry of cooperation between insider and outsider makes such relationships uniquely profitable for the organization.

In any event, the ultimate goal of the external consultant is to work himself or herself out of a job. As the internal resources of the client system—including the internal change agents—develop necessary skills, including the perspective brought by the external consultant, to set and achieve organizational goals, the reliance and dependence on external resources must be diminished.

REFERENCES

Bowers, D. G., & Franklin, J. L. *Survey-guided development I: Data-based organizational change.* San Diego, CA: University Associates, 1977.

Burke, W. W. *Organization development: Principles and practices.* Boston: Little, Brown, 1982.

Burke, W. W., & Goodstein, L. D. Organization development today: A retrospective applied to the present and the future. In W. W. Burke & L. D. Goodstein (Eds.), *Trends and issues in OD: Current theory and practice.* San Diego, CA: University Associates, 1980.

Goodstein, L. D., Cooke, P., & Goodstein, J. T. The team orientation and behavior inventory (TOBI). In L. D. Goodstein & J. W. Pfeiffer (Eds.), *The 1983 annual for facilitators, trainers, and consultants.* San Diego, CA: University Associates, 1983.

Harrison, R. Understanding your organization's character. *Harvard Business Review,* 1972, *50,* 119-128.

Hausser, D. L., Pecorella, P. A., & Wissler, A. L. *Survey-guided development II: A manual for consultants.* San Diego, CA: University Associates, 1977.

Jones, J. E. The organizational universe. In J. E. Jones & J. W. Pfeiffer (Eds.), *The 1981 annual handbook for group facilitators.* San Diego, CA: University Associates, 1981.

Pfeiffer, J. W., Heslin, R., & Jones, J. E. *Instrumentation in human relations training* (2nd ed.). San Diego, CA: University Associates, 1976.

Schein, E. H. *Process consultation: Its role in organization development.* Reading, MA: Addison-Wesley, 1969.

Sherwood, J. J. An introduction to organization development. In J. W. Pfeiffer & J. E. Jones (Eds.), *The 1972 annual handbook for group facilitators.* San Diego, CA: University Associates, 1972.

Stepsis, J. A. Structure as an integrative concept in management theory and practice. In J. E. Jones & J. W. Pfeiffer (Eds.), *The 1977 annual handbook for group facilitators.* San Diego, CA: University Associates, 1977.

Weisbord, M. R. *Organizational diagnosis: A workbook of theory and practice.* Reading, MA: Addison-Wesley, 1978.

Weisbord, M. R. Organizational diagnosis: Six places to look for trouble with or without a theory. *Group & Organization Studies,* 1976, *1*(4), 430-447.

Leonard D. Goodstein, Ph.D., *is the chairman of the board, University Associates, Inc., San Diego, California. He specializes in organizational behavior, consultation skills, and organization development and team building with executive groups. Dr. Goodstein is a diplomate in clinical psychology of the American Board of Professional Psychology and formerly was the chairman of the Department of Psychology at Arizona State University. He is the co-editor of the 1982, 1983, and 1984* Annuals.

Phyliss Cooke, Ph.D., *is the director of professional services and dean of the Master's in Human Resource Development program at University Associates, Inc., San Diego, California. She specializes in the design of training programs, leadership development, women in management, assertiveness training, and facilitation training. Dr. Cooke formerly served as director of the Cleveland Institute for Rational Living, as a psychologist for the Cleveland Board of Education, and as a therapist in private practice.*

SOCIOTECHNICAL SYSTEMS THINKING IN MANAGEMENT CONSULTING: A HOLISTIC CONCEPT FOR ORGANIZATION DEVELOPMENT

Arthur Zobrist and Robert E. Enggist

BACKGROUND: THE DEVELOPMENT OF SOCIOTECHNICAL SYSTEMS THEORY

Norbert Wiener (1948) gave, with his classic treatise "Cybernetics: Or Control and Communication in the Animal and the Machine," the first impulse to an emerging science. Systems theory was to become one of the most significant contributions to an array of varied disciplines. In the German literature, the work of Ulrich (1968) and his view of the firm as a "productive social system" greatly contributed to open systems theory and practice.

In Great Britain, the Tavistock Institute of Human Relations contributed significantly to practical applications. Based on an early recognition of the importance of systems theory, Eric Trist and his colleagues developed a framework for viewing the business organization as an open, sociotechnical system, rather than as a closed, social organization, insulated from its environment. Trist, Higgin, Murray, and Pollock (1963), Rice (1963), Emery (1969) and other scholars quickly realized in their studies of industrial firms that imbalances in the social system are difficult to remove as long as "social structures" hinge on the requirements of technological systems. They contended that every attempt to improve one system (technological) without regard to its counterpart (social), or vice versa, will lead to suboptimal results. Only the simultaneous monitoring and control of their mutual dependencies will bring about optimal and lasting results.

The members of the Tavistock Group also realized the interdependencies between the business enterprise and its environment. They argued against the treatment of a business as a closed system. Likewise, they considered isolated analysis of the social structures to be dysfunctional in introducing change and warned that it could distort the explanation of phenomena.

In the United States, open systems theory gained acceptance primarily through the work of Ludwig van Bertalanffy (1968). Churchman (1968) and Ackoff (1974) introduced holistic and interactive approaches to the planning and management of societal systems.

Criticism of the sociotechnical approach comes predominantly from production-oriented studies. It is undoubtedly true that the approach did lead to such innovations as the humanization of the work place, projects of democratization, and the creation of autonomous work groups. Unfortunately, there are few examples of organizations in which change processes were investigated from a "holistic" perspective.

The approach originally developed at the Tavistock Institute especially influenced the European advocates of organization development, but recently has begun to impact American social science (Pasmore & Sherwood, 1978).

Harold Leavitt (1964) published the first simple, but very useful, model of a sociotechnical system (Figure 1). Leavitt did not mention the Tavistock Institute in his work and drew few direct conclusions from the general systems-theory framework. In particular, he viewed his model as a closed system.

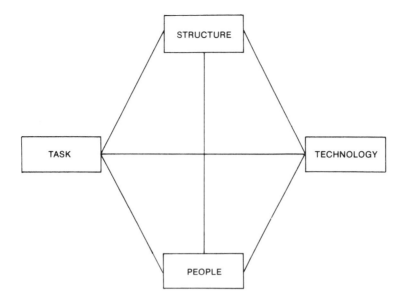

TASK: The purpose of the organization in terms of production of goods and services, including all further subtasks necessary for the accomplishment of the primary task

PEOPLE: Those who participate in the system

TECHNOLOGY: All the technical instruments and procedures for task fulfillment

STRUCTURE: All issues of communication, hierarchy, and work process

Figure 1. Leavitt's Model of a Sociotechnical System[1]

In an organization, these four variables (task, people, technology, and structure) form an interdependent system. A change in one variable always has an impact on the others. To effect organizational change, different approaches can be chosen, based on (a) the structural determinants, (b) the technological determinants, or (c) the social determinants. The structural and technological determinants of change affect the solution of existing, visible problems, often even if new difficulties are created as a result. The social determinant is essentially manipulative and affects resistance to technically, structurally, and economically "necessary" decisions.

Although the human relations movement tried to make people the focus of OD, twenty years after Leavitt's article the structural and technological elements still dominate in organizational change. The attempts of the social sciences to make these adaptations bearable for people are miniscule compared to holistically developing and changing organizations as systems.

Harold Bridger (1977), a colleague of Emery, Rice, and Trist, established with his pentagram (Figure 2) a linkage to Leavitt's model.

[1]From H.J. Leavitt, "Applied Organizational Change in Industry: Structural, Technical, and Human Approaches." In W.W. Cooper (Ed.), *New Perspectives in Organization Research*. New York: John Wiley, 1964. Used by permission of William W. Cooper.

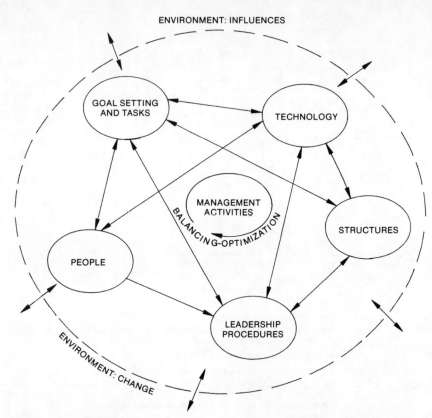

ENVIRONMENT: INFLUENCES

GOAL SETTING AND TASKS

TECHNOLOGY

MANAGEMENT ACTIVITIES

BALANCING-OPTIMIZATION

STRUCTURES

PEOPLE

LEADERSHIP PROCEDURES

ENVIRONMENT: CHANGE

ENVIRONMENT: The organization as a system in a continuous exchange with a turbulently changing environment

PEOPLE: Values, claims, attitudes, education, group and peer ties, leadership behavior, power relationships, and dependencies

GOAL SETTING AND TASKS: The primary purpose and task of the organization in terms of delivering goods and services at a profit

TECHNOLOGY: Administrative resources and procedures, accounting, information systems, marketing, sales, advertising, investment goods, production, etc.

STRUCTURES: Division of labor, hierarchy, communication and leadership structures, organizational structure, etc.

MANAGEMENT ACTIVITIES: Selection, evaluation, and promotion systems, wage and salary systems, control and monitoring systems

LEADERSHIP PROCEDURES: Balancing and design processes that are required to run the entire system

Figure 2. Bridger's Pentagram Describing a Sociotechnical System[2]

---

[2]Harold Bridger, "The Value of the Organization's Own Systems in Coping with Stress." *Proceedings of the International Committee on Occupational Mental Health Congress*, New York, 1977.

R.L. Ackoff (1981) recently described the dynamic and dialectic nature of organizational problem solving: "A technocratic culture runs the risk of getting the right solutions to the wrong problems. A humanistic culture runs the risk of getting the wrong solutions to the right problems" (p. 62).

The true challenge and potential of sociotechnical systems thinking is in a continuous, adaptive learning process.

SOCIOTECHNICAL SYSTEMS THINKING AS AN OD CONCEPT

In the course of development of systems theory, there has been dialectic tension. Taylor's (1947) techno-economic postulate carried an exclusive emphasis on efficiency and economy of the system. Man's needs did not count. With the human relations movement, the pendulum swung to the other side, which created the danger of an exaggeration of the human element. Modern sociotechnical systems thinking in organization development is a synthesis. On the one hand, the approach attempts to overcome the formal reasoning of the traditional organizational technocrats and the biased posture of Taylor's management-science approach. On the other hand, rather than focusing only on organizational psychology, the new synthesis is a conceptualization of the interdependencies within the whole system and its relationship to the environment.

Although specific perspectives and competencies are developed by various branches within the social sciences, no one approach forms the basis for analysis or strategy selection in change theory. Effective consulting activities utilize and build on *interdisciplinary* thinking.

The concept of organizations as purposeful systems that can be understood only in terms of their relationship to the environment has gained wide acceptance among scholars as well as practitioners of management. Most thinkers realize that businesses today face the ever-increasing demands of a hectic and dynamic environment.

Each organization exists because of and with its past, present, and future. It makes little sense to consider only the present without an understanding of the organization and its history, as well as a projection of scenarios for its future. The sociotechnical systems approach is not a new form of organization development. It is an attempt to provide a framework that can lead to a holistic understanding of organizations, permitting a more effective use of well-known OD techniques.

If we view Bridger's pentagram not only as an internal process between elements and their relation to the environment but also in a longitudinal perspective, the framework becomes multidimensional. The Bridger model has three critical dimensions: its purpose (to diagnose exchanges between and within its systems and its environment); its performance (in terms of breakdowns and disturbances); and its structure (systems and subsystems).

The Diagnosis

We are accustomed to looking for deviations and their causes within *elements* (e.g., the social structure) of a system or subsystem (e.g., production control), rather than in the *interaction* between elements or subsystems, or in exchanges between systems and the environment. We also often forget that development includes the factor of time—the evolution from the past to the present and to a future state. A diagnosis for an intervention strategy is sound only if all the following aspects are considered.

1. The system itself:
   a. the parts (elements), with their specific values, human resources, tasks, structures, technology, leadership, and instruments;
   b. the subsystems (divisions, departments, functions);

c. the dynamic processes between subsystems and elements.
2. The system in its relation to the environment:
   a. the requirements of the environment imposed on the system, existing conditions, possibilities, and constraints;
   b. the mode by which the system recognizes and takes advantage of these possibilities (opportunities);
   c. the system production that flows back to the environment as output or performance.
3. The time component (longitudinal):
   a. past, present, and future developments in the environment;
   b. necessary past, present, and future reactions of the system to environmental influences.

Breakdowns and Disturbances

Insufficient performance of a system can be caused by outside factors such as failure to adapt to the environment or higher ranking metasystems, but it also can be caused or influenced by:

1. Deficiencies within an element of the system itself;
2. Problems in the relationship between one element and another and the resulting tensions;
3. Mutation of one element without simultaneous adjustment for the impact on other elements.

In order for the system to regain a state of balance, it is necessary to discover the key deviations and their causes.

Systems and Subsystems

Every organization can be divided into subsystems, i.e., organizational units. The pentagram (Figure 2) depicting the entire organization also applies to the individual subsystems. Thus, the overall system functions as a "system-internal environment" to the subsystems. The difference between a traditional view of organizations and a sociotechnical perspective is shown in Figure 3.

Summary

The main points of the preceding discussion are:

1. Organizations as sociotechnical systems can only be understood *holistically*.
2. Elements and subsystems are interdependent.
3. Changes in one element or subsystem always influence other elements or subsystems.
4. Exclusive focus on one element or subsystem without simultaneous attention to other subsystems leads to suboptimal results and new disturbances.
5. The past, present, and future stages of the organization must be considered.
6. Organizations are open systems and, as such, are viable only in mutual interaction with and adaptation to the changing environment.

CONSIDERATIONS IN APPLYING THE SOCIOTECHNICAL SYSTEMS APPROACH TO ORGANIZATION DEVELOPMENT

The Institute for Organizational Psychology espouses the following analytical procedure as a first step in introducing organizations to OD.

Purpose

1. To understand the strengths and weaknesses of the enterprise from a holistic, organizational perspective.
2. To recognize sensitive areas.
3. To learn to apply the holistic perspective as an instrument.

Procedure

1. Represent and explain Bridger's pentagram (this usually takes no more than ten minutes).
2. Have the participants picture their organization through the framework of the pentagram. Define specific elements such as goals, tasks, technology, leadership processes and procedures, structures, and people, as well as the essential environmental influences that affect the activities and performance potential of the organization. Generally, this step will take approximately one hour. Figure 4 is a questionnaire that can be used to ascertain the most important points.
3. Identify the actual problems, strengths/weaknesses, and sensitive areas. These usually result from the daily interactions among the various organizational elements. This generally takes about one hour. For this purpose, another questionnaire is presented in Figure 5. The most important results of the discussion can be recorded on this form.
4. Share the most important discoveries in a plenary session (about fifteen minutes).

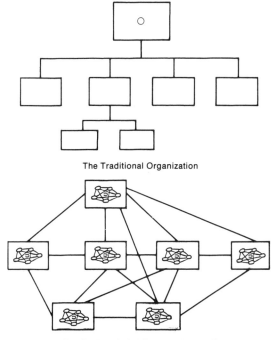

The Traditional Organization

The Sociotechnical Systems Approach

Figure 3. A Comparison of Traditional and Sociotechnical Views of Organizations

ENVIRONMENT

1. What are the most important aspects of and changes in the environment?
2. Where do we see the effects of these factors on the work and on management?
3. What are the key characteristics of the particular business environment?

GOALS/TASKS

1. What are the essential goals of the enterprise?
2. What are the main tasks and what characterizes them?
3. What questions, issues, or problems result from this task profile?
4. What are the major problems that the organization experiences in setting goals/objectives and in establishing tasks?

STRUCTURES

1. What different structures exist within the organization?
2. What are the characteristics of the individual structures?
3. What are the consistencies, overlapping areas, and inconsistencies among the structures?
4. What strengths and weaknesses, and what kind of supports, problems, or conflicts result from these structures?

LEADERSHIP PROCEDURES

1. What key leadership procedures and processes are implemented in the organization?
2. Are these procedures coordinated and focused?
3. What are the deficiencies and advantages of the individual procedures?
4. Is there a need for more leadership procedures or processes?

PEOPLE

1. What are the primary characteristics of the employees (education and training, etc.)?
2. What attitudes, behaviors, and values do the workers bring to the job?
3. What similarities and differences exist among various employee groups?
4. Is it possible to characterize the human climate? Are there any typical traits that distinguish the organization from its competitors?

TECHNOLOGIES

1. What are the essential resources, procedures, methods, and technologies that determine the work processes?
2. What are the characteristics of the production and service processes?
3. What kind of changes are foreseen for the next several years?

Figure 4. Questions for Identifying Elements of the Pentagram

PRACTICAL IMPLICATIONS FOR MANAGEMENT CONSULTING IN ORGANIZATION DEVELOPMENT

Although organization development is often a problem-solving activity, it also should be viewed in its essentially literal sense, as a purposefully conceptualized activity for the development of an organization. It is not enough to avoid uncontrolled developments and changes. The consciously planned development of organizations facilitates the accomplishment of a useful and constructive contribution to society, mindful of the present as well as the future.

Organization development professionals who are exposed to sociotechnical systems thinking as a planning and decision-making tool quickly realize the *strategic* orientation of the approach. To use Ackoff's (1981) terminology, they become "interactivists," that is, they begin to perceive planning as the design of a *desirable* future and the invention of ways to bring it about, rather than accepting the future that appears to confront them.

ENVIRONMENT

1. What are the major factors in the organization's environment that influence the work?
2. What characteristic environmental problems arise?
3. In which elements of the system are the interactions with the environment most visible?
4. What is the organization's greatest strength vis-a-vis the environment (competitive advantage, labor market, productivity, etc.)?
5. What is the organization's most obvious weakness?

GOALS/TASKS

1. What factors within the system most influence goal attainment (positively/negatively)?
2. Which elements of the system are most affected by changes in goals and tasks?
3. Are the rest of the elements coordinated with respect to the goals/objectives and tasks?
4. Where are the strengths and weaknesses in the interactions among elements?
5. What are the sensitive points that repeatedly cause frictions, problems, or conflicts?

STRUCTURES

1. Are the existing structures useful for the attainment of the goals and tasks?
2. How do people adapt to or cope with these structures?
3. Are the structures supportive of the needs and capabilities of the leadership (management) and the work force?
4. Do the structures encourage cooperation and collaboration?
5. Do the structures facilitate a rational use of resources and technologies?
6. What major strengths/weaknesses result from the structures interacting with other elements in the system?

LEADERSHIP PROCEDURES

1. Are the existing leadership procedures and processes focused on the specific goals/objectives and tasks?
2. Do these procedures fit the organization's specific social and technical realities (technologies, other procedures, composition of work force, etc.)?
3. Are managers sufficiently trained in using the procedures (e.g., performance evaluation)?
4. What influences and changes from the outside are expected? What re-examination of the present procedures might these changes entail?
5. What are the most significant strengths and weaknesses in the leadership procedures and their application?

PEOPLE

1. What is the basic attitude of various employee groups toward the organization?
2. What are the effects of these attitudes on performance and teamwork?
3. How do managers and their subordinates adapt to the existing structures?
4. Do the employees feel that the structures, technologies, and procedures serve as an incentive to full involvement (motivational effectiveness)?
5. Where are the biggest obstacles, problem areas, and sources of conflict?

TECHNOLOGIES

1. How do changes in procedures and support systems affect people and structures in the organization?
2. Do changes produce resistance?
3. When technological changes occur, are the structures and processes adapted or modified accordingly?
4. Is there a timely attempt to prepare people for technological and organizational changes, e.g., through personnel management, training, or participatory decision making?
5. What and where are the most important strengths and weaknesses between technology (including processes and procedures) and the other elements of the system?

Figure 5. Questions for Identifying Interactions Among the Elements of the System

If we are convinced that sociotechnical systems thinking represents an appropriate basis for our strategies, an array of implications for practical work results.

Requirements for Consultants

Organization development is not a model or a closed-system discipline, but a series of pragmatic strategies to help organizations perform tasks. This requires a holistic approach—the inclusion of all elements of the sociotechnical system in analytical efforts. The OD professional must be ready for a critical dialog that is based in reality yet open to continuous adaptive learning.

This ambitious goal can be achieved only if OD consultants prepare themselves as follows:

1. Determine the basic structure of the organization.
2. Develop a well-grounded, general knowledge of all the elements of the system to be worked on.
3. Develop specific knowledge, skills, and experience in dealing with organizational structures and leadership systems.
4. Develop know-how and sensitivity in dealing with the change processes in a turbulent, dynamic environment.
5. Acquire expertise in the social and behavioral sciences, along with the capability to merge that knowledge base with the contributions of experts from other disciplines.

The OD consultant must measure his or her competence in the field in terms of the *requirements of the sociotechnical system.* In order to conceptualize intervention and interaction strategies with a social-science focal point, the consultant must be acquainted with the influences and dependencies of all processes. Only then is he or she likely to be successful in avoiding the following mistakes:

1. Creating new problems while attempting to solve others.
2. Enhancing, rather than reducing, the bias of those with whom he or she engages in debate and conversation.
3. Looking for problems in areas in which the consultant feels competent instead of where they actually exist.
4. Developing patent remedies and marketing them, rather than facing the challenges of a continuous learning process and living with the uncertainty such growth entails.

Teamwork Between the Consultant and the Client

It is a great temptation for the consultant to make executive decisions for the client, but this serves neither well. The consultant must develop a collaborative decision-making process in which both parties have their own responsibilities and rights. From the perspective of sociotechnical systems thinking, one can derive a number of positive consequences from such cooperation.

Shared Values and Positions

The client and consultant initially must clarify their positions and values with each other. A fruitful cooperation is not possible if the two parties have divergent views of basic issues. If there is no consensus capable of standing the load, the consultant is better off rejecting the contract.

Collaboration and Responsibility

The collaborative approach between consultant and client has been described many times in the literature (Argyris, 1970; Vansina, 1976). From the sociotechnical point of view, because of the complexity of the tasks in question, combining all available resources of the client with those of the consultant becomes a must. There is far more involved than the withholding of information or constraint of the information base. The issue is one of becoming convinced that only mutual acceptance and support will generate true problem solving.

The responsibility for fundamental decisions that affect the system and its changes always rests with the client. The consultant assumes responsibility for professional competence and for his or her readiness to determine with the client a basis for recommendations.

Mitigating and Facilitating Conditions for Development and Change

It would be a mistake to assign to the consultant all the responsibility for the success of sociotechnical systems approaches. The most essential prerequisite appears to be the readiness—oriented to past, present, and future—to continually wrestle with reality and to refrain from attempting to project Utopia onto reality.

In order to be able to solve concrete problems arising from an ineffective interplay among the elements in a sociotechnical system—or between the system and the environment—one must define the premises that are amenable to analysis. According to a study by von Clare Graves (quoted from Mitchell, 1977), stress is indispensable for change and development. A primary task of the consultant is to help the client learn how to cope with stress and its uncertainties.

Three prerequisites must exist for this to be possible:

1. Dissatisfaction with the present state (i.e., stress) as a motivational basis for change;
2. Energy and courage as positive forces to initiate the development of a proactive and reactive mode;
3. A conscious and insightful motive that is based in reality, to achieve concrete, planned changes.

When one of these three conditions is lacking, there is little chance for development or for solving existing problems. The necessary diagnostic work to examine the existence or absence of these conditions is an important part of the start-up of an OD project. It requires expertise, well-established diagnostic instruments, and the development of a workable relationship between the client and the consultant.

Principles for the Establishment and Maintenance of the Client-Consultant Relationship

The consultant should avoid building client dependencies or permanent relations that are not warranted by the tasks and problems to be solved. Each party also must be at liberty to end the partnership if certain basic conditions are not fulfilled. Finally, there must be continuous joint evaluation and step-by-step decision making regarding the project when new aspects or consequences emerge or when interim goals have been accomplished.

CONCLUSION

The sociotechnical systems approach offers the best opportunity to analyze the problems of today's organizations and to develop workable solutions. The social sciences can make a contribution in this area, leading away from an overly organized, technocratic, work environment toward a more meaningful world in which the applied sciences and institutions exist for man and society and not vice versa.

REFERENCES

Ackoff, R.L. *Redesigning the future.* New York: John Wiley, 1974.
Ackoff, R.L. *Creating the corporate future.* New York: John Wiley, 1981.

Argyris, C. *Intervention theory and method.* Reading, MA: Addison-Wesley, 1970.

von Bertalanffy, L. *General systems theory: Foundations, development, applications.* New York: George Braziller, 1968.

Bridger, H. The value of the organization's own systems in coping with stress. In A. McLean, G. Black, & M. Colligan (Eds.), *Reducing organizational stress. Proceedings of the International Committee on Occupational Mental Health Congress,* New York Hospital-Cornell Medical Center, May 10-12, 1977.

Churchman, C.W. *The systems approach.* New York: Delacorte Press, 1968.

Emery, F.E., & Trist, E.L. Sociotechnical systems. In F.E. Emery (Ed.), *Systems thinking: Selected readings.* London: Penguin Books, 1969.

Leavitt, H.J. Applied organizational change in industry: Structural, technical, and human approaches. In W.W. Cooper (Ed.), *New perspectives in organization research.* New York: John Wiley, 1964.

Mitchell, A. *The effects of stress on individuals and society.* Menlo Park, CA: Stanford Research Institute, 1977.

Pasmore, W.A., & Sherwood, J.J. *Sociotechnical systems: A source book.* San Diego, CA: University Associates, 1978.

Rice, A.K. *The enterprise and its environment.* London: Tavistock, 1963.

Taylor, F.W. *Scientific management.* New York: Harper & Row, 1947.

Trist, E.L., Higgin, G.W., Murray, H., & Pollock, A.B. *Organizational choice.* London: Tavistock, 1963.

Ulrich, H. *Die unternehmung als produktives soziales system.* Bern & Stuttgart: Verlag Paul Haupt, 1968.

Vansina, L.S. Beyond organization development. In P. Warr (Ed.), *Personal goals and work design.* New York: John Wiley, 1976.

Wiener, N. *Cybernetics: Or control and communication in the animal and the machine.* Cambridge, MA: MIT Press, 1961.

Arthur Zobrist, Dipl. Psych., *is the director of the Institut fur Organisationspsychologie und Managemententwicklung (Institute for Organizational Psychology and Management Development) in Lucerne, Switzerland. He is a consultant to institutions and business organizations in Switzerland and other European countries, with a special focus on helping firms and institutions to adapt both organization and management to the requirements of a turbulent environment.*

Robert E. Enggist, Ph.D., *is a management consultant and heads Rob Enggist Associates, Princeton Junction, New Jersey. He also is a professor in management on the Faculty of Business at Fordham University, New York City. He specializes in operations management, socioengineering, organizational behavior, and strategic management. He currently is involved in management training and curriculum design for engineers and other professionals in transportation.*

A GUIDE TO PARTICIPATIVE MANAGEMENT

Marshall Sashkin

Participative management recently has become popular as an element of the effort to revitalize American business. In reviewing one new book on management-labor cooperation, Lohr (1983) said, "The next big fad in business management is on the horizon. It carries the fancy title of 'participative management'. . . ." Lohr concluded, however, that the authors (Simmons & Mares, 1983) had in fact demonstrated that "employee participation has worked to raise productivity in many cases."

Participative management is not new. There is evidence to show that it was used by "advanced" Roman plantation owners about two thousand years ago (Sashkin, 1982). For the past fifty years or so, research evidence has steadily accumulated regarding the positive effects of participative management on performance, productivity, and employee satisfaction. Still, the level of application of participative management in American organizations has been less than impressive.

A major reason why American managers do not implement participative management as much as one might expect is simply because they do not know how to apply it in their organizations. In order to facilitate such application, the discussion that follows will address three major questions:

1. What is participative management?
2. What are the effects of participative management?
3. How does participative management work?

WHAT IS PARTICIPATIVE MANAGEMENT?

Participative management traditionally has been treated as a single, undifferentiated approach. However, if we are to talk sensibly about participative management, we must first understand the major participative approaches and how they are used. In general, participative management involves workers in the planning and control of their own work activities, but there are important differences in the various types of work planning and control in which subordinates can participate. At least four major varieties of participation can be identified: participation in setting goals; participation in making decisions; participation in solving problems; and participation in developing and implementing change.

Participation in Setting Goals

In this form of participation, workers, as individuals or in groups, are involved with their supervisors in determining, to some degree, the goals that they will attempt to reach with respect to work performance and output. Research in both laboratory and organizational settings has conclusively demonstrated the power of participation in goal setting (Latham & Yukl, 1975; Locke, Shaw, Saari, & Latham, 1981). More than 90 percent of the research on goal setting confirms this.

Participation in Making Decisions

Participation of subordinates in decision making may range from consultation, through having some influence on the outcome, all the way to actually having responsibility for the decision. When workers are directly involved in generating the decision alternatives, participation in decision making may seem to overlap with participation in problem solving. Strictly speaking, decision making is limited to the examination and evaluation of alternatives that already have been developed. Research indicates that in a wide variety of situations, participation in decision making has positive benefits (Lowin, 1968).

Participation in Solving Problems

This type of participation is clearly more difficult than the previous two forms. It requires subordinates to analyze information and develop new ideas on the basis of that information. Research, however, suggests that obtaining positive benefits from participation in problem solving depends more on the training received by the supervisors and employees than on the innate mental abilities of the individuals (Maier, 1963).

Participation in Developing and Implementing Change

This form of participation is the most difficult and complex of all. It goes beyond participation in problem solving because it requires managers and employees to participate in generating, analyzing, and interpreting organizational data in order to develop specific, innovative solutions to organizational problems. This type of participation is regarded by most organization development practitioners as a critical aspect of successful OD (Huse, 1980).

Three Different Approaches

In addition to the four types of participation, there are also different ways to use participative approaches. Participative management can be applied (a) with respect to *individual* subordinates, (b) in the context of the *superior-subordinate* relationship, or (c) in a *group* context. Although the second method, superior-subordinate participation, is probably the most common, each of the three approaches seems feasible in different circumstances. It is likely that under some organizational conditions it would be appropriate for individuals to set their own goals, make their own decisions, solve their own problems, or develop and carry out changes relevant to their own work. On the other hand, such individual-centered participation clearly would not be appropriate when several workers depend a great deal on one another in the normal conduct of their work activities. For people who spend most of their time working together as a group, the group method of participation obviously makes the most sense.

In order to have a basis for choosing which of the twelve combinations of participation types and approaches to use, a manager must understand the dynamics of participative management and what impacts the combinations can have on workers. A foundation for that understanding is provided by the many research studies on participative management.

WHAT ARE THE EFFECTS OF PARTICIPATIVE MANAGEMENT?

The Hawthorne Studies

A series of research studies conducted from the mid-1920s through the mid-1930s at AT&T's Western Electric Hawthorne plant has come to be recognized as a landmark in participative-management research (Roethlisberger & Dickson, 1939). The results of these studies have been analyzed and reanalyzed, attacked and defended, for over forty years (Carey, 1967; Landesberger, 1958; Shepard, 1971). What was so controversial was not the research findings but their philosophical interpretations. Disguising their wrangling as scholarly debate and criticism, people argued about the worth, importance, and accuracy of the participative-management approach that developed as a result of these studies.

During the studies, work conditions at the Hawthorne plant were analyzed to determine how human work capacities varied with changes in the physical environment such as lighting, heat, noise, ventilation, and so on. A special test area was set up. Workers and supervisors were selected to participate in the study, in which work behavior was measured as physical conditions varied. At first, the results seemed perfectly reasonable. When lighting levels were increased, for example, production also increased. A number of such correlations were found under different conditions. However, when the level of light was later decreased, production *continued* to increase until the workers were producing more than ever, under conditions equivalent to bright moonlight! At this point the engineers gave up, unable to explain what was happening. A new research team from Harvard was brought in, headed by Fritz Roethlisberger, who worked with the company's personnel-department liaison. W.J. Dickson. The character of the experiments changed; instead of investigating physical work conditions, the researchers began to study social relationships on the job. The researchers attributed the performance and productivity improvements to the involvement and participation of the workers in the management of their own job activities.

In later years, other scholars looked at the Hawthorne reports and asserted that the conclusions derived by the Hawthorne researchers were misleading. It became generally accepted that the results obtained by the Hawthorne researchers were due primarily to the special treatment given to the workers. That is, because the workers saw themselves as part of a special experiment and because they received special treatment, they worked especially hard to please the researchers, even when working conditions were quite poor. This situation—workers doing especially well because of special treatment—is commonly called "the Hawthorne effect."

Even if the primary factor in the Hawthorne studies was simply special attention, such special attention is now one small element in the participative-management approach. Roethlisberger (1950) said:

> People like to feel important and have their work recognized as important.... . They like to work in an atmosphere of approval. They like to be praised rather than blamed.... . They like to feel independent in their relations to their supervisors.... . They like to be consulted about and participate in actions that will personally affect them.

A variety of factors other than special attention probably also had some impact in the Hawthorne case. For example, the supervisor had been selected because of his reputation as one of the best in the plant. The workers—who also had been carefully chosen—probably worked hard to satisfy him, even when working conditions were poor. Furthermore, the workers were given special privileges: they actually participated in work decisions that were meaningful to them and they formed a cohesive work team (Katz & Kahn, 1966). Finally, social experiments are subject to a pervasive effect known as the "self-fulfilling prophecy." When one sets out to create a productive work group, one is more likely to succeed just because of having stated the goal and letting people know what is expected of them. For example, when teachers are told that certain students are "bright" and that certain others are "dull," the so-called bright students (chosen at random) score better on objective tests. This is partly because the teachers pay more attention to the "bright" students and give them better instruction, but it is also because the teachers subtly (and sometimes not so subtly) communicate their expectations to the students. The "bright" students do better, then, because they know that they are expected to.

The Hawthorne workers were specially selected and were subject to special attention, good supervision, participative-management practices, and self-fulfilling prophecy. All of these factors may have affected the results of the study, but over the years the Hawthorne studies have been most associated with the term "human relations," not with "participative management."

The attempted applications were based essentially on the issue of special attention. It was hoped that if workers were treated with special care, they would perform at higher levels and be more productive. The findings concerning the benefits of worker participation and the use of a cohesive work group for such participation were all but ignored by American managers, while the simplistic conclusion that performance and productivity could be dramatically improved if managers were to pay more special attention to their subordinates was widely accepted by American managers. These were not recommendations made by the Hawthorne researchers.

One reason why supposedly sophisticated managers accepted these oversimplified conclusions is that they were presented as the result of scientific research. Americans of the 1940s and 1950s had experienced the effects on society of the automobile, air transportation, the telephone, radio, and television. Why, then, should they question the validity of social-science research—especially when research on management and organizations had proved to be useful in identifying the most efficient ways to approach specific tasks by means of time and motion analyses?

Another factor that influenced managers was the tempting simplicity of the solution. All a manager had to do was show concern and attention to subordinates and treat them "properly," and they would respond by increasing their productivity. The theory and practice sounded simple and straightforward; the manager did not need to learn new skills or make any substantial changes with respect to the way the job was organized or in terms of involving subordinates in decisions, goal setting, problem solving, or change. For a minimal investment of effort, the manager was promised, in effect, a "free lunch."

The Backlash

Of course, managers soon discovered that the positive effects of special attention are shortlived. Despite the fact that participative management had not received a trial—let alone a fair trial—a substantial backlash developed against it. The situation is illustrated by two articles that appeared in the *Harvard Business Review* in the late 1950s. In one piece, titled "What Price Human Relations?," Malcolm McNair (1957) argued that managers should not have expected the simple human relations approach to have positive benefits on productivity, because these benefits would require a tremendous and unrealistic investment on the part of managers, amounting to abrogating much of their authority. McNair suggested that managers return to their traditional, controlling roles and forget the false promises of the human relations approach. Because most managers had never abandoned their original approach, McNair simply offered an easy rationalization for dropping the special-attention effort. Soon thereafter, Robert N. McMurry (1958), a well-known management consultant, was even more direct in arguing "The Case for Benevolent Autocracy."

Over the next decade, human relations became institutionalized in business management curricula and ignored in managerial practice. However, various dedicated researchers who had strong commitments to action applications in organizations continued to study the elements of participative management first identified in the Hawthorne studies. These studies eventually coalesced to form the basis of a theory of participative management.

Participation in Setting Goals: Research Results

The vast proportion of studies on worker participation in goal setting have yielded positive results, demonstrating conclusively that goal setting has a positive outcome in terms of performance. This is true for individuals who set their own goals, for a supervisor and subordinate who set goals together, and for groups that set goals. Whichever method is used, goal setting seems to help people gain greater control over their work activities by identifying the specific aims of those activities. More than any other behavioral science innovation, goal setting has been proved to reap positive rewards in organizations (Locke et al., 1981).

Participation in Decision Making: Research Results

Conceptually, the distinction between problem solving and decision making is clear. Decision making involves selecting from among a range of reasonably well-defined alternatives. Problem solving, however, requires that the alternatives be generated first and a selection made. Thus, at least in theory, problem solving involves considerably more effort—and skill—than does decision making.

A classic organizational experiment involving worker participation in decision making was conducted more than twenty-five years ago by two researchers at the University of Michigan, Nancy Morse and Everett Reimer (1956). The experiment was conducted in a large department in the home office of an insurance company and involved primarily clerical employees. About thirty-three supervisors and more than two hundred nonsupervisory employees were divided into four similar divisions of roughly equal size. In two of the divisions, a program was instituted for increasing decision-making responsibility at lower levels. Clerical workers were given responsibility for many small decisions that previously had been the prerogative of supervisors. For example, workers made decisions about when to take breaks, how to handle cases of tardiness, and how to deal with questions of work methods or work processes. Although many decisions were made by individuals, work groups were also involved. Questionnaire results several months later showed that workers clearly did perceive the nature of these changes.

In the other two divisions, changes in decision-making practices also were instituted. These changes were the exact opposite of the changes made in the first two divisions. Employees became less involved in decision making than ever before; all decisions were made at the departmental level, and employees had no influence whatsoever over them. Again, there was little doubt that employees perceived these changes.

The experiment ended after one year. Many of the results were just as expected. It was, for example, expected that workers in the participative divisions would increase in "self-actualization," measured in terms of job challenge, opportunity for personal growth, and opportunity to try new ideas. It was expected that the scores of workers in the hierarchical-control departments would decrease on these measures, and that is exactly what happened. Similarly, supervisory relationships were much better at the end of the year in the participative divisions but had dramatically worsened in the hierarchical-control divisions.

When workers were asked how they felt about the two programs, the results again were as expected: workers in the participative program liked it very much and wanted it to continue, while workers in the hierarchical-control division were happy to see the program end. It was also expected that measures of job satisfaction would reflect the same differences. While the job satisfaction of workers in the hierarchical-control divisions did drop substantially over the year of the experiment, the job satisfaction of workers in the participative-decision-making divisions did not increase much at all.

The researchers were surprised, however, when they observed that productivity, measured in terms of the number of clerks needed to complete a given amount of work, had increased in *all four* divisions. This meant that although there were fewer clerks in each division, the same amount of work was being completed as had been done previously by more people.

What seemed to have happened was that in the participative-decision-making divisions, the increase in productivity was real; some workers had been transferred to other divisions, while others who left the company had not been replaced. In the hierarchical-control divisions, however, the productivity was increased by assigning fewer workers to handle the same volume of work and simply ordering them to work harder. In fact, of twenty-three workers who left the company complaining of work pressures during the time of the experiment, nineteen were from the hierarchical-control divisions.

Whether the productivity increases could have been maintained indefinitely in both the participative and hierarchical-control divisions must remain a matter of speculation. It does seem likely that if the workers had had more control over their work flow, productivity would have been still further enhanced in the participative-decision-making divisions. Equally clear is the fact that a powerful management was able to pressure workers into increasing their work output. In the years since this experiment, a great deal of research has suggested that the strategy used to increase productivity in the hierarchical-control division does have serious, long-run costs for the company as well as for employees (Franklin, 1975; Likert & Seashore, 1963).

The Morse and Reimer study involved both individual and group participation in decision making. More recent work by Jay Hall (1971) has demonstrated the benefit of group participation in decision making, with respect to a decision task having a single correct solution. Hall showed that when the group followed a structured discussion process that provided for full discussion and participation on the part of all group members, groups performed substantially better than without such a discussion procedure. Much earlier, Norman Maier (1963) demonstrated similar results in terms of improved decisions when a structured discussion procedure was used. Hall's work strongly supports this type of participative management; however, it also sounds a warning: the effective use of the consensus decision-making process requires training and skill on the part of all group members. In fact, training is critical to the effective application of any of the four types of participative management discussed in this article.

Participation in Problem Solving: Research Results

Although individuals may be given problems to solve or may work on problems with their supervisors, most of the research on participation in problem solving involves groups. Much of the work on participative problem solving in groups is attributable to Norman R.F. Maier, who spent more than thirty years studying participative group problem solving and training managers in how to use this participative approach (Maier, 1950, 1967, 1970).

Maier defined two critical questions that can be posed with respect to a problem situation to determine whether group participation in problem solving is desirable. The first question is "Will acceptance or rejection of the solution to the problem by any of the workers involved in carrying out the solution make a difference in how well it is carried out?" When worker acceptance is not an issue, there is no real need to involve workers participatively in solving the problem. When acceptance is an issue, it is important to provide workers with some means of influence or control over the solution that is chosen. This results in workers' commitment to and acceptance of the solution.

The second question is "Is the quality of the solution of concern to management?" When quality is of little concern but worker acceptance is important, a group problem-solving discussion is both appropriate and simple. If the group leader and members have some basic skills in group problem solving, the group should have no trouble reaching consensus. If quality is important but acceptance is not, it is appropriate for a manager to solve the problem alone, without group involvement. However, in their model of problem solving and decision making, Vroom and Yetton (1973) point out that in such cases a manager may sometimes wish to involve subordinates participatively on a one-to-one basis. This kind of employee participation can be appropriate, according to Vroom and Yetton, if the manager needs additional information in order to develop a good solution.

Finally, when both worker acceptance and the quality of the solution are important, Maier suggests that participative group problem solving is appropriate, but difficult. In such cases, the leader must facilitate and integrate the discussion while taking into account both the needs of the employees and the requirements of management. Although leading such discussions is not easy and does require skill, Maier and his associates have demonstrated repeatedly and conclusively that managers can learn such skills. Skill in two activities is crucial: (a) posing the problem and (b) encouraging participants to share information (Maier & Sashkin, 1971).

Participation in decision making or goal setting provides workers with increased control over situations and over their own work activities, which in turn can lead to the workers'

University Associates

acceptance of and commitment to a course of action. Participation in problem solving can have the same effects, but often has some additional benefits. First, workers involved in participative problem solving are engaging in a new aspect of work—an aspect that adds substantial *meaning* to the work itself. Second, problem solving is, of necessity, *a complete task activity*, involving gathering information, interpreting that information, developing alternatives, weighing and selecting a specific solution from among the alternatives, and developing implementation strategies. This form of participation not only adds meaning to the work but also represents a complete cycle of work activities in which the employees are involved *from the beginning to final completion*. In this manner, participation in problem solving can have a positive impact on worker satisfaction, since one basis for satisfaction is the *successful completion of meaningful tasks*. Thus, participation in problem solving goes beyond the simpler forms discussed earlier.

Participation in Change: Research Results

The crucial importance of employee participation in planning and carrying out organizational changes is so widely recognized by behavioral scientists that it is hard to comprehend why managers so often attempt to institute such changes unilaterally, with little or no employee participation. This state of affairs is particularly puzzling when one considers the fact that most managers are well aware of the phenomenon of workers' resistance to change.

In fact, examination of research studies conducted in the 1940s on participation in change reveals that one important reason for attempting to involve workers in developing change was to manipulate them into accepting changes that management wanted. This kind of situation is evident in Kurt Lewin's (1958) studies on change in housewives' food-preparation habits during World War II, when the government was trying to encourage the use of foods traditionally considered undesirable, such as sweetbreads. Through group discussion, housewives were manipulated into "solving" the problem of unavailable meats by agreeing to change their food buying and preparation habits to make use of available but less desirable food products. Similarly, in a classic industrial study, the early phases of which were conducted under Lewin's supervision, his colleagues Lester Coch and John R.P. French (1948) successfully manipulated workers into identifying and agreeing to the exact changes that management had wanted prior to the involvement of the workers.

Perhaps the greatest value of these early studies was to demonstrate the tremendous power of group participation for making change work. The firm that Coch and French worked for continued and expanded participative management until, by the 1960s, it was absolutely real, not merely a manipulative sham. By that time, all forms of participative management had spread throughout the organization.

The work of Floyd Mann at the University of Michigan's Institute for Social Research probably serves as a better illustration of participation in change. In his capacity as consultant, Mann conducted a survey at Detroit Edison in 1948. At that point, the survey was not part of a formal experiment. However, positive experiences with the methods he devised for reporting data back to both management and employees laid the groundwork for more extensive research. The 1948 survey was conducted throughout the entire organization and included all employees. Mann wanted to report the results of this survey in a way that would best lead to acceptance by the employees. Eventually, the employees would use the data gained from the results to solve problems and make changes. Mann's approach was to present the results by means of "an interlocking chain of conferences." These conferences began with a report to the president and top executives of the company, followed by similar reports to successively lower-level groups of managers, all the way down to supervisors and first-line workers. Managers and their immediate subordinates were provided with summaries of their own survey data. These data were the basis for group discussions in which problems were identified and changes recommended.

The formal experiment was based on the first survey as well as two subsequent surveys conducted in 1950 and 1952. The 1950 effort surveyed more than eight hundred employees in eight accounting departments. Data comparing the results with those of the 1948 survey were provided to the departments.

In four departments, the researchers helped to conduct a series of feedback meetings. These meetings focused on supervisors and their immediate subordinate groups and were carried out in much the same manner as the organizational feedback done in 1948. Nothing was done in two other departments. This allowed the researchers to establish a "control group"—a yardstick to determine whether changes were the result of feedback efforts or normal evolution over a period of time. (Managerial changes in the two remaining departments made it impossible to draw any conclusions; these were dropped from consideration.)

A third survey, conducted in the six departments in 1952, revealed extensive and significant changes in a positive direction for the experimental feedback departments, as compared with the departments in which no survey feedback was carried out. The survey-feedback program was associated with large improvements in employees' attitudes about their work, their supervisors, their careers, and their work groups' effectiveness. Furthermore, employees in the survey-feedback departments reported that their supervisors got along better with department members than did the supervisors in departments in which no action was taken.

In the experimental survey-feedback departments, supervisors held more meetings, and these meetings were judged to be more effective than meetings in the other two departments. Finally, Mann reported the greatest change in those departments in which the members were all extensively involved in the survey-feedback experiment. The greater the degree of involvement, the greater the positive change (Mann, 1957).

Although Mann's study vividly demonstrated the strong positive results of participation in change, it must be noted that Mann's results were attained partly because of prior, extensive, training efforts for managers and workers in the organization in the techniques of small-group participative problem solving. The extreme importance of this kind of background training has been demonstrated in a wide variety of research studies by Mann's colleagues at the University of Michigan (Bowers & Franklin, 1977; Franklin, Wissler, & Spencer, 1977; Hausser, Pecorella, & Wissler, 1977).

By now it should be clear that the four approaches to participative management are not independent of one another. Rather, each progressively more complex approach seems to depend on the concepts and skills developed in the simpler approaches. Thus, effective use of participation in change seems to require understanding and mastery of participation in problem solving, decision making, and goal setting. Similarly, productive use of participation in problem solving is based on the skills and knowledge needed to apply participation in decision making and goal setting.

A study by Bragg and Andrews (1973) provides a good example of this. Thirty-two hospital laundry workers were involved in planning and carrying out changes. As the project proceeded, the laundry workers also participated in decision making. Although goal setting does not seem to have been involved, participation in problem solving and decision making were clearly part of the participation in change approach and led to increased productivity, improved attitudes, and decreased absenteeism and turnover.

The Special Importance of Groups

The two more complex types of participative management—participation in change and participation in problem solving—are consistently associated with *group* methods of operation. This is not simply coincidence; there are several good reasons why groups are most commonly used to implement participation in problem solving and change.

First, groups have the potential to develop more good ideas than the same number of individuals working independently. The simplest way to get ideas from a group is through the widely known "brainstorming" procedure.

Second, group methods provide a tool for dealing with the complexity of the problems and issues involved in creating organizational change. In organizations today, especially those that rely on the applications of advanced technologies, people in groups are more dependent on one another than ever before. Such interdependencies become especially important in dealing with problems and with the planning and implementation of change. Under such circumstances, the need for coordination is greater, but it is impossible to coordinate effectively simply by using the "standard" methods—written reports, the chain of command, or informal contacts between managers. The sociologist James Thompson (1967) has suggested that in these cases there is a need for coordination by "mutual adjustment." That is, the effective coordination required to solve complex problems and to successfully plan and carry out changes can be accomplished only through direct feedback among the parties involved.

The third reason is that the involvement of individuals in face-to-face group discussions develops social support for decisions, solutions, or changes. This was the primary discovery of the research studies conducted by Kurt Lewin (1947) and his group. Lewin discovered the tremendous effect that group norms—shared beliefs about how people ought to behave— actually have on the behavior of individual group members. This is especially true for behaviors that are overt and easily observed and norms that are openly and explicitly stated and recognized by all group members. Coch and French observed, in their early study on participation in change, that resistance to change was more easily overcome when all workers were involved in the discussion than when only representatives of the workers were allowed to take part. Mann also found that when more workers were more involved in the survey-feedback discussions, and when more discussions were held, the change effects were strongest.

Perhaps this factor of involvement is so important for effecting change simply because of the basic human need for social interaction. Most of us are so used to spending a large portion of our time with other people and take social interaction so much for granted that we tend to forget what social creatures we really are.

A factor that bears careful consideration, then, is the common isolation of workers while doing their work. For many workers, especially those at low levels, there is little opportunity to obtain the social satisfaction that can come through doing a job with other people. Participation in group tasks such as problem solving or developing changes may fulfill these needs. In any case, group-based norms are extremely important; they play a part in determining what we see, how we interpret what we see, and how we behave in response to these perceptions and interpretations.

In summary, the use of *groups* to implement participation in problem solving and change will greatly strengthen the results and impact of such participation and may even be a requirement for the effective use of participative methods for problem solving and change.

HOW DOES PARTICIPATIVE MANAGEMENT WORK?

The Industrial Revolution of the Nineteenth Century changed our work lives as well as our private lives. Unfortunately, the changes in work were not very desirable. Workers lost most of the control they previously had over their work activities. Work became fragmented into tiny, meaningless, repetitive bits, and workers became socially isolated rather than members of a work unit. Each of these three major changes in the nature of work acts in direct opposition to a basic human work need. Effectively implemented participative management can reverse these changes and can result in improved performance, productivity, and worker satisfaction.

Powerlessness

Early sociologists observed how the development of the industrial organization contributed to the creation of a new class of relatively powerless workers. It was not until the 1950s, however, that behavioral scientists began to explore seriously the implications of such powerlessness. Chris Argyris (1957, 1973), in particular, argued—and over the next decade successfully demonstrated—that as people mature, a basic human need for autonomy and control of one's own behavior emerges as part of the natural process of development. Argyris showed how modern organizations actively frustrate this need. The Harvard psychologist David McClelland (1975), whose work reflects the same conclusions, identified the need for power as one of the most significant motivational factors in organizations.

The participative-management approaches of goal setting and decision making increase workers' autonomy and sense of control over their jobs. Although participation in goal setting and decision making will not magically and totally remedy workers' feelings of powerlessness—which have been fostered by organizations over the past hundred years—sound evidence indicates that participative-management approaches involving goal setting and decision making do increase workers' feelings of power and control (Tannenbaum, 1967).

Meaninglessness

One of the most profound treatments of the meaninglessness of work as a consequence of industrialization is found in the writings of Emile Durkheim (1893/1947), a French sociologist whose major work was done at the turn of the century. Earlier, it had been observed how decisions and problems became the province of the supervisor, leaving the worker powerless and contributing to feelings of meaninglessness. When Durkheim worked and wrote, the Industrial Revolution had had its major impact on society. Durkheim noted the increasing fractionation of work itself, partly through application of the scientific-management approach developed by Frederick W. Taylor (1911). Furthermore, the efforts of time-and-motion-study engineers such as Frank Gilbreth (1911) made the loss of meaning through less involvement in decisions and problems appear to be a relatively minor issue. The fractionation of jobs into minute sets of activities that were repeated over and over, unendingly, was an absolute guarantee of meaninglessness, carried to the ultimate.

The fact that meaningless work is psychologically distressing hardly needs proof. However, such work is not merely unpleasant but is overtly harmful. The very structure of the human brain seems to press individuals to achieve a sense of completion or closure with respect to perceptions, tasks, and activities (Zeigarnik, 1927). McClelland's (1976) research on motivation in organizations and society has demonstrated the widespread importance of the need for achievement, which is only possible through the accomplishment of complete, "whole" tasks.

It is not surprising, then, that the problem of meaningless work is alleviated when workers engage participatively in solving problems and creating changes. Literally hundreds of research studies by Maier and his associates clearly demonstrate that workers involved participatively in group problem solving find this activity meaningful and interesting and become more satisfied with the work situation. Mann reached the same conclusions in his experiments on the use of group participation in creating changes. In the thirty years since Mann's research study, similar findings have been obtained over and over again.

However, normal day-to-day work activities may be just as meaningless as ever. One approach to this persistent problem is to make the work itself more meaningful, either by "enriching" the job through methods such as those pioneered by Frederick Herzberg (1968) or by redesigning the job so that it contains the elements identified by Hackman and Oldham (1980) as characteristic of work that has meaning and over which workers can exercise control. Another approach, developed by Rensis Likert (1961, 1967) and his associates, is to maximize the use of participative methods so that participation—in all four forms—is to the greatest extent possible the central focus of work activities. In fact, Likert specifically labels the system of management and organization that he advocates as "participative."

Although research has clearly demonstrated the positive effects of participation in problem solving and change in terms of making work more meaningful, these effects are likely to be ameliorative rather than real cures. That is, the negative effects of meaningless work will be reduced temporarily but, unless the work itself is redesigned so as to provide more workers with the opportunity to accomplish a complete task, or unless management practices are extensively refocused to emphasize worker participation, the relief will be only temporary.

Isolation

Various sociologists have observed and commented on the social isolation of workers imposed by modern industrial organizations. Indeed, Durkheim suggested that it was the combination of social isolation and meaningless work that led to such feelings of alienation as to provoke suicide. However, it was Elton Mayo, a multifaceted man perhaps best thought of as a social philosopher, whose work was most directed toward resolving the social isolation of workers. In a sense, this brings us full circle, for it was Mayo who was the primary off-site advisor at Harvard to the Hawthorne researchers.

Mayo was particularly opposed to the scientific management advocated by Frederick Taylor. In fact, Mayo's philosophy was, in part, shaped as a response to Taylor. In 1919 Mayo wrote:

As a system Taylorism effects much in the way of economy of labor; its chief defect is that workmen are not asked to collaborate in effecting such economies. . . No social system can be considered satisfactory which deprives the great majority of mankind of every vestige of autonomy.

Obviously, Mayo was well aware of the factors of powerlessness and meaninglessness. At the time he helped to plan and interpret the Hawthorne studies, Mayo's primary focus was on the work group. Mayo felt that through reduced isolation, workers could be better integrated into the social mainstream, making for a less "pathological" society and one with fewer social problems. This is why the Hawthorne studies focus so much on work-group interactions and the development of cohesive work teams.

The previous discussion of the special importance of groups indicates that Mayo was on the right track. Furthermore, studies of motivation by McClelland (1955) identified the need for affiliation. It can therefore be argued that worker isolation is best remedied through participative management using group methods. Mayo's error was his neglect of the factor of management. In the Hawthorne studies, the prescription was simply to allow small groups of workers maximum freedom in controlling their own work. It was expected that within these groups the workers would establish their own patterns of coordination. Then, by recognizing and supporting such informal organization, management would gain the support and cooperation of workers, leading to greater productivity and at the same time eliminating worker isolation. Although one can argue that this is exactly what happened in some of the Hawthorne experiments, it is quite clear that in other experiments conducted at the Hawthorne plant the reverse was true. Workers did indeed form cohesive groups with informal patterns of coordination and strong norms. However, these norms were, in some cases, opposed to management and to increased productivity. For example, in the bank-wiring room, where men wired the terminals on which telephone-switchboard circuits were installed, the workers had established clear norms as to what constituted a fair day's work. From the viewpoint of managers, however, the standard applied by the workers constituted restriction of production. The unrealistic laissez-faire managerial approach that seems to have been idealized by Mayo and his associates is probably one reason why managers rejected the group-participation recommendations of the Hawthorne studies.

Other Effects of Participative Management

In their large-scale study of how management affects the performance of scientists and engineers in organizations, Donald Pelz and Frank Andrews (1978) identified some additional effects of the participative methods discussed here. They found that the increased autonomy that was given to scientists and engineers provided them with a sense of security. They also found that participation in working on difficult problems not only provided quite meaningful tasks, but also provided high levels of challenge. When scientists and engineers were involved in decision making and in problem solving, they experienced strong feelings of autonomy (which produced feelings of security) and perceived their work assignments as being difficult and highly meaningful (which led to feelings of challenge), all at the same time. Pelz and Andrews found that when both security and challenge were present, scientific performance in terms of innovation and the successful accomplishment of research tasks was heightened. Thus, the direct effects of participation—increased control and autonomy and meaningful work—may have some additional indirect effects for scientific workers—increased security and challenge—which can lead to increased scientific performance.

HOW PARTICIPATION WORKS: A MODEL

The model shown in Figure 1 summarizes how participation works. The two simpler types of participation, participation in goal setting and in decision making, provide workers with an increased amount of control or autonomy. These benefits, in turn, led to acceptance and commitment with respect to goals and decisions. Such acceptance and commitment have one ultimate outcome: increased performance and productivity. Heightened autonomy also leads to increased feelings of security for scientific workers, one of the two conditions needed for effective scientific performance.

The two more complex types of participation, participation in problem solving and in planning and carrying out changes, have the primary effect of providing meaningful "whole" tasks. These types of participation, however, also result in increased degrees of control and autonomy for workers and, therefore, promote the same chain of indirect effects as do the two simpler forms of participation. Thus, the effects of the two simpler types of participation are reinforced when the more complex forms are also used. Having meaningful tasks that can provide a sense of accomplishment and completion leads to feelings of satisfaction, which then have a long-range impact on performance and productivity. Being given meaningful tasks may also result in feelings of challenge for scientific workers, thereby providing the second of the two crucial conditions necessary for high scientific performance.

The simple chains of events shown in Figure 1 reflect research evidence. It would be foolish, however, to assume that such cause-and-effect relationships are automatic or guaranteed. For one thing, the various effects shown in Figure 1 can occur only if effective management, as well as participation, is provided. As has been discussed, this was the greatest failing of the Hawthorne research.

CONCLUSION

After fifty years of formal research—and thousands of years of experience—there is no doubt that participative management is effective in terms of performance, productivity, and employee satisfaction. It is also clear, however, that effective outcomes depend on careful design, planning, and implementation. Organizational factors such as the nature of the technology, the social-psychological "climate," typical patterns of leadership, and the design of jobs must be taken into account, and significant changes may be required for participative management to succeed. Kanter (1982) has noted that "failures" of participative management are often due to the same error that the Hawthorne researchers made: too much emphasis on participation and too little on management.

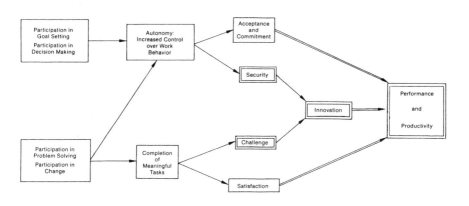

Figure 1. A Model of How Participative Management Works

The Question of Choice

In one sense, the application of participative management is a matter of choice or preference. Some recent reviews of research on participative management are basically flawed by the authors' attempts to determine just how effective participative management is in comparison with other approaches (e.g., see Locke, 1982, or Locke & Schweiger, 1979). As Lowin (1968) long ago noted, participative management "is a complex phenomenon beyond proof or disproof" (p. 63). Although organizational factors are changing such that participative management is more likely to succeed (Sashkin, 1982), it is still possible to design and manage nonparticipative organizations with good results in terms of productivity and profit, at least in the short run. Why, then, should managers bother with participative management?

One answer is that doing so is more efficient, as well as more productive, in the long run. Another reason is based on ethical considerations. More and more research evidence shows that when the three basic human work needs are not met, the result is physical (as well as psychological) damage to workers (Sashkin, 1983). Various studies have demonstrated that repetitive, meaningless work, work that cannot be controlled by the worker, and work that is performed in social isolation is associated with physiological measures related to coronary heart disease (Cox, 1980; Jenkins, 1971; Johansson, 1975; O'Hanlon, 1978). Other researchers have shown that job dissatisfaction is related to physical illness (Jenkins, 1971; Sales & House, 1971). In a fifteen-year longitudinal study, Palmore and Jeffers (1971) found that the best predictor of longevity was job satisfaction, and that it was a better predictor than physicians' judgments of workers' overall physical health!

Perhaps most interesting are the results from several studies that directly examined the effects of worker nonparticipation. They show that high participation was related to increased feelings of responsibility, better work relations, more positive attitudes toward work, and higher output (French & Caplan, 1972). Quinn and Shepard (1974) found that nonparticipation was correlated with depression, escapist drinking, and overall poor physical health—findings confirmed in other research studies (Margolis, Kroes, & Quinn, 1974; Singer, 1975).

The Ethical Choice

On the basis of these and other research findings, we can assert that participative management is an ethical imperative, that to fail to use participative management is morally reprehensible. We know that participative management, properly applied, is as—or more—effective in the short run than nonparticipative approaches. It is also clear that, in the long run, participative management is, when properly applied, inevitably more effective than nonparticipative approaches because it develops rather than damages people. Because of the proven harm to employees of nonparticipative approaches and in light of the clear advantages of participative management in "bottom-line" financial terms (as well as in terms of human satisfaction), I argue that failure to use participative management is morally wrong (Sashkin, 1983).

A decade ago, participative management was labeled by Preston and Post (1974) as the "third managerial revolution." Now that we know that participative management works, how it works, and how to make it work, it is a revolution whose time has come.

REFERENCES

Argyris, C. *Personality and organization.* New York: Harper & Row, 1957.

Argyris, C. Personality and organization theory revisited. *Administrative Science Quarterly,* 1973, *18,* 141-167.

Bowers, D. G., & Franklin, J. L. *Survey-guided development I: Data-based organizational change.* San Diego, CA: University Associates, 1977.

Bragg, J., & Andrews, I. Participative decision making: An experimental study in a hospital. *Journal of Applied Behavioral Science,* 1973, *9,* 727-735.

Carey, A. The Hawthorne studies: A radical criticism. *American Sociological Review,* 1967, *32,* 403-416.

Coch, L., & French, J. R. P., Jr. Overcoming resistance to change. *Human Relations,* 1948, *1,* 512-533.

Cox, T. Repetitive work. In C. L. Cooper and R. Payne (Eds.), *Current concerns in occupational stress.* Chichester, England: John Wiley, 1980.

Durkheim, E. *The division of labor in society.* (G. Simpson, trans.). New York: Free Press, 1947. (Originally published, 1893.)

Franklin, J. L. Relations among four social-psychological aspects of organizations. *Administrative Science Quarterly,* 1975, *20,* 422-433.

Franklin, J. L., Wissler, A. L., & Spencer, G. J. *Survey-guided development III: A manual for concepts training.* San Diego, CA: University Associates, 1977.

French, J. R. P., Jr., & Caplan, R. D. Organization stress and individual strain. In A. J. Marrow (Ed.), *The failure of success.* New York: AMACOM, 1972.

Gilbreth, F. B. *Motion study.* New York: Van Nostrand Reinhold, 1911.

Hackman, J. R., & Oldham, G. R. *Work redesign.* Reading, MA: Addison-Wesley, 1980.

Hall, J. Decisions, decisions, decisions. *Psychology Today,* 1971, *5,* 51-54ff.

Hausser, D. L., Pecorella, P. A., & Wissler, A. L. *Survey-guided development II: A manual for consultants.* San Diego, CA: University Associates, 1977.

Herzberg, F. One more time: How do you motivate employees? *Harvard Business Review,* 1968, *46*(1), 53-62.

Huse, E. F. *Organization development and change.* St. Paul, MN: West, 1980.

Jenkins, C. D. Psychologic and social precursors of coronary disease (II). *New England Journal of Medicine,* 1971, *284,* 307-317.

Johansson, G. Psychophysiological stress reactions in the sawmill: A pilot study. In B. Ager (Ed.), *Ergonomics in sawmills and woodworking industries.* Stockholm: National Board of Occupational Safety and Health, 1975.

Kanter, R. M. Dilemmas of managing participation. *Organizational Dynamics,* 1982, *11*(1), 5-27.

Katz, D., & Kahn, R. L. *The social psychology of organizations.* New York: John Wiley, 1966.

Landesberger, H. J. *Hawthorne revisited.* Ithaca, NY: Cornell University Press, 1958.

Latham, G. P., & Yukl, G. A. A review of research on the application of goal setting in organizations. *Academy of Management Journal,* 1975, *18,* 824-845.

Lewin, K. Frontiers in group dynamics. *Human Relations,* 1947, *1,* 5-42.

Lewin, K. Group decision and social change. In E. E. Maccoby, T. M. Newcomb, & E. L. Hartley (Eds.), *Readings in social psychology* (3rd ed.). New York: Holt, Rinehart and Winston, 1958.

Likert, R. *New patterns of management.* New York: McGraw-Hill, 1961.

Likert, R. *The human organization.* New York: McGraw-Hill, 1967.

Likert, R., & Seashore, S. E. Making cost control work. *Harvard Business Review,* 1963, *41*(6), 96-108.

Locke, E. A. Employee motivation: A discussion. *Journal of Contemporary Business,* 1982, *11*(2), 71-81.

Locke, E. A., & Schweiger, D. M. Participation in decision making: One more look. In B. M. Staw & L. L. Cummings (Eds.), *Research on organizational behavior* (Vol. 1). Greenwich, CT: JAI Press, 1979.

Locke, E. A., Shaw, K. N., Saari, L. M., & Latham, G. P. Goal setting and task performance: 1969-1980. *Psychological Bulletin*, 1981, *90*, 125-152.

Lohr, S. New social contracts. *The New York Times Book Review*, March 6, 1983, 12, 29.

Lowin, A. Participative decision making: A model, literature critique, and prescriptions for research. *Organizational Behavior and Human Performance*, 1968, *3*, 68-106.

Mann, F. C. Studying and creating change: A means to understanding social organization. In C. Arensberg et al. (Eds.), *Research in industrial human relations*. New York: Harper & Row, 1957. (Industrial Relations Research Associates, Publication Number 17.)

Mayo, E. *Democracy and freedom: An essay in social logic*. Melbourne: Macmillan, 1919.

Maier, N. R. F. The quality of group decisions as influenced by the discussion leader. *Human Relations*, 1950, *3*, 155-174.

Maier, N. R. F. *Problem-solving discussions and conferences*. New York: McGraw-Hill, 1963.

Maier, N. R. F. Assets and liabilities in group problem solving: The need for an integrative function. *Psychological Review*, 1967, *74*, 239-249.

Maier, N. R. F. *Problem solving and creativity in individuals and groups*. Monterey, CA: Brooks/Cole, 1970.

Maier, N. R. F., & Sashkin, M. Specific leadership behaviors that promote problem solving. *Personnel Psychology*, 1971, *24*, 35-44.

Margolis, B. L., Kroes, W. H., & Quinn, R. P. Job stress: An unlisted occupational hazard. *Journal of Occupational Medicine*, 1974, *16*, 659-671.

McClelland, D. C. *Studies in motivation*. New York: Appleton-Century-Crofts, 1955.

McClelland, D. C. *The achieving society*. New York: Irvington, 1976.

McClelland, D. C. *Power: The inner experience*. New York: Irvington, 1975.

McMurry, R. N. The case for benevolent autocracy. *Harvard Business Review*, 1958, *36*(1), 82-90.

McNair, M. P. What price human relations? *Harvard Business Review*, 1957, *35*(2), 15-39.

Morse, N. C., & Reimer, E. M. The experimental change of a major organizational variable. *Journal of Abnormal and Social Psychology*, 1956, *52*, 120-129.

O'Hanlon, J. F. *Performance and physiological reactions to monotony in simulated industrial inspection*. Paper presented at the Nineteenth International Congress of Applied Psychology, Munich, August 1978.

Palmore, E. B., & Jeffers, F. (Eds.). *Prediction of life span*. Boston: Heath-Lexington, 1971.

Pelz, D. C., & Andrews, F. M. *Scientists in organizations* (Rev. ed.). Ann Arbor, MI: Institute for Social Research, The University of Michigan, 1978.

Preston, L. E., & Post, J. E. The third managerial revolution. *Academy of Management Journal*, 1974, *17*, 476-486.

Quinn, R. P., & Shepard, L. *The 1972-73 quality of employment survey*. Ann Arbor, MI: Survey Research Center, Institute for Social Research, The University of Michigan, 1974.

Roethlisberger, F. J. *The human equation in employee productivity*. Speech presented to the Personnel Group of the National Retail Dry Goods Association, 1950.

Roethlisberger, F. J., & Dickson, W. J. *Management and the worker*. Cambridge, MA: Harvard University Press, 1939.

Sales, S. M., & House, J. Job dissatisfaction as a possible risk factor in coronary heart disease. *Journal of Chronic Diseases*, 1971, *23*, 861-873.

Sashkin, M. *A manager's guide to participative management*. New York: American Management Associations, 1982.

Sashkin, M. *The ethics of participative management*. Manuscript in preparation, 1983.

Shepard, J. M. On Alex Carey's radical criticism of the Hawthorne studies. *Academy of Management Journal*, 1971, *14*, 23-31.

Simmons, J., & Mares, W. *Working together*. New York: Alfred A. Knopf, 1983.

Singer, J. N. Job strain as a function of job and life stresses. (Doctoral dissertation, Colorado State University, 1975). *Dissertation Abstracts International*, 1975, *36*(6B), 3109B.

Tannenbaum, A. S. (Ed.). *Control in organizations*. New York: McGraw-Hill, 1967.

Taylor, F. W. *Scientific management*. New York: Harper's, 1911.

Thompson, J. D. *Organizations in action*. New York: McGraw-Hill, 1967.

Vroom, V. H., & Yetton, P. W. *Leadership and decision making*. Pittsburgh, PA: University of Pittsburgh Press, 1973.

Zeigarnik, B. [The recollection of completed and uncompleted tasks.] *Psychologische Forschung*, 1927, *9*, 1-85.

Marshall Sashkin, Ph.D., *is a professor of industrial and organizational psychology at the University of Maryland University College. He has conducted training seminars on managerial topics and has published numerous books and professional articles on organizational behavior and change, performance appraisal, leadership, and participative management. Dr. Sashkin's latest UA book, co-edited with William R. Lassey, is* Leadership and Social Change *(Third Edition, Revised and Updated).*

THE TRANSFORMATIONAL MANAGER: FACILITATING THE FLOW STATE

Linda S. Ackerman

Management literature over the past few years has been crowded with concepts and success strategies taken from the Japanese. With the myriad of demands facing American managers today, it is no wonder that they are open to these new ideas. Old practices no longer satisfy today's and tomorrow's challenges. Unfortunately, in many cases the Japanese approaches have added to the frustrations of American managers. The Japanese methods are successful because the Japanese culture supports them. American culture usually does not. The belief system, management approaches, and needs of the Japanese industrial environment are congruent and supportive of one another. Given the painful symptoms in American organizations, it is evident that our ways of thinking, our management practices, and the needs we have are not equally compatible. Japanese approaches are foreign to our way of working and our organizational traditions. In addition, many companies have utilized these new practices as techniques, or "band-aids." Applied to problems that have been developing for decades, they can do very little to help. Thus, they are cast off as failures.

If we are to develop our own approaches to solving organizational problems, we must challenge fundamental assumptions about managing organizations. To do this, we must also confront the traditional image and role of managers. This article will examine a particular way of viewing organizations and will explore the implications of this view for American managers. The constructs presented will introduce a new way of managing that may assist us in our current struggles.

THE TRADITIONAL VIEW OF ORGANIZATIONS

There are numerous traditional models of organizations and, overall, they vary only slightly. Nadler and Tushman (1980) present the organization as made of tangible parts, such as structure, processes, people, tasks, and resources (see Figure 1). Their model also describes some less tangible aspects such as history, values, politics, and leadership. Such models offer us a way to picture the *form* or substance of the organization. This is especially useful in assessing or designing organizations. Models also help to reveal the complexity of organizations—the many variables or parts that contribute to the total system.

Another important feature of most organizational models is that they indicate the relationships or interdependencies that exist *among* the parts. Nadler and Tushman (1980) say that the parts must "fit together" for the organization to work effectively. This has become a fundamental assumption in management thinking.

In theory, then, good managers define what parts are necessary, based on organizational needs; ensure that each part is uniquely essential to the overall strategy; and then see that the parts work well with one another. When carried a bit further, this type of thinking can lead to the

---

A more complete version of this concept is available in the book, *Transforming Work*, edited by John D. Adams, published by Miles River Press, Alexandria, Virginia, 1983.

tendency to "fix" the parts so that they fit in order to maintain or regain the status quo. This is consistent with the belief that good managers are skillful problem solvers. Thus, managers design ways to maintain control over work, schedules, and people's needs in order to keep the parts fitting.

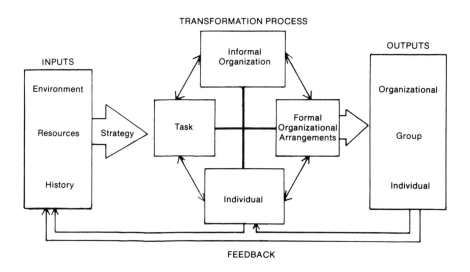

Figure 1. Nadler and Tushman's Organizational Model[1]

The reality, however, is that life in the organization is more dynamic, more complex, and more out of control than the models describe. Naisbitt (1983) states, "The world that once seemed so certain, solid, has changed radically. Now, conflict, confusion and great uncertainty is the norm for sure" (p. 1). If managers believe that their task is to solve problems, meet their numerical goals, and keep things under control, it is no wonder that they are frustrated.

The solution may be for management to pay greater attention to the arrows in the organizational model, rather than just the boxes. More attention paid to the relationships and the frictions between the parts will require less attention to what form the parts take or how to control them. This shifts our attention to daily, or even momentary, awareness of what is happening in the organization, what is assisting the fit, what is blocking the flow, and what is needed in the long range for things to happen the way management would like. The key to viewing organizations in this way is to see them as dynamic—moving, changing, shifting, pushing, pulling—in short, as *energy.*

---

[1]Reprinted, by permission of the publisher, from "A Model for Diagnosing Organizational Behavior" by D.A. Nadler and M.L. Tushman, p. 47, *Organizational Dynamics*, Autumn, 1980, © 1980 by AMACOM, a division of American Management Associations, New York. All rights reserved.

ORGANIZATIONS AS ENERGY

Physicists hypothesize that there really is no such thing as form, only particles that are perpetually moving in unique ways. This is the embodiment of energy. In great quantity, the particles compose atoms, which (also in great quantity) are perceived as form. From this we can evoke the analogy of organizations as energy. Webster defines energy as "the capacity for action or performing work." This is a primary reason why we organize in the first place: to accomplish something. The performance, the action, the work, that is, the *energy*, is the substance of the organization, not the numbers, the machinery, or the organizational chart.

Organizational models then can be viewed in much the same way as what appears to be solid mass. We can use these apparent realities as stepping stones to understanding the nature of what it is we are to manage. Webster defines form as "shape, structure; the orderly method of arrangement; the established method of doing something." It is important to note the finality or control implied by the terms structure, orderly, and established. This is consistent with the assumptions of management that we are questioning: the need to make things fit, to retain or regain the status quo, and to manage the form. "Organization" is a noun; it is static.

The energy model is based on the verb, *to organize*, or the process of organizing. The movement, the act of managing, implies that things are always changing. Managers continually are faced with new data and new challenges. Inevitable forces alter the way things happen. There is very little that does *not* change at some time in the organization. Dealing with the *process* of managing, rather than just the result, is the point of the energy model.

The organization as energy is depicted in Figure 2. Note that it does not depict the *behavior* of energy. At the core of the organization is its *purpose* or reason for being. This purpose gives meaning and direction to the energy and the form of the organization. When fully understood and appreciated throughout the membership of the system, it becomes the central linking force of everything and everyone. Ideally, the core purpose of the organization is the one energy force that touches all people and ties them all together. Everything seeks to contribute to the pursuit of the purpose.

The next ring identifies the *sources* of energy—where it comes from. The third ring describes typical *channels* through which energy flows in the organization. The outer level identifies the *fields* that are created when energy is having a widespread effect in all or large portions of the organization.

The rings of the chart describe the energy inside the organizational boundaries. However, boundaries are merely form; energy flows through and around them as it does with all forms. The world outside the organizational boundaries is also filled with energies that directly impact the functioning of the organization. These energies are called *environmental forces*; they include: social values and culture; the economy; government regulations and politics; competitors; suppliers; the marketplace and customers; technology; and the labor force and unions.

Environmental energy forces enter into and influence the behavior and effectiveness of the organization. Today's managers are experiencing the turbulence that occurs whenever two or more dynamic forces meet. Serious problems occur when these energy forces are misunderstood, ignored, or let loose without guidance.

Sources of Energy

In order to manage energy, we need to know where it comes from. A primary source of energy is the myriad of competing forces that exist in the organization. Energy results from the tension that is generated by the pushes and pulls of two or more opposing sides. Tension in this case need not be perceived as negative but, rather, as a description of the force set up. The pull can be felt as the desire or need for movement in one direction or another. Usually, neither side is better; there is a fundamental and natural reciprocity between them, which is why they continue to exist. At any time, one side will be more attractive or powerful than the other. At another time, as circumstances shift, the opposing side will gain strength. Ingalls (1979) describes a term used by Carl Jung, enantiodromia, which is the tendency of all things to turn into their opposites over time.

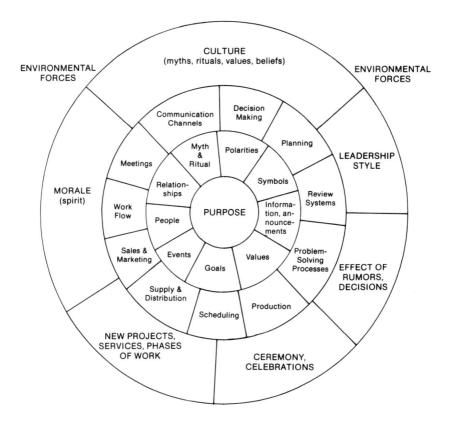

The context for managing energy is found in the purpose of the organization, which is the central linking force in the model. The next ring cites SOURCES of energy; the third, CHANNELS of energy; and the fourth ring, energy FIELDS. The organization also is influenced by ENVIRONMENTAL energy forces.

Figure 2. The Organization as Energy

Ingalls also describes a series of polarities that underlie human energy, such as control versus creativity and ambiguity versus certainty. Organizational polarities include long-term versus short-term needs, quantity versus quality, and line versus staff. Another polarity is the tendency to believe that one should manage form rather than energy. The emphasis on energy does not negate the form; energy surrounds the form and plays off it. The desire is to create a balanced view of the two.

Polarities are only one source of energy. The building and evolving of human relationships as well as functional relationships generate energy as well. Boss-subordinate, peer, job-related, and social relationships all create and use energy in the organization. When a relationship between two people is particularly strained, everyone uses up energy talking, worrying, and strategizing about it. When relationships between people or departments are smooth, everything seems to flow. The health of relationships can greatly add to or drain organizational energy. When a great deal of activity or feeling occurs in the organization, it is always because of some source of energy. These include: key figures in the organization, important events, announcements, values, myths or stories, ritual acts or ceremonies, symbols such as logos or mementos, rewards, goals, and information and language. In addition, the effects of these sources of energy can change over time. Tracking whether these sources are helpful or hindering is part of management's responsibility in this model of the organization. Ingalls (1979) describes a matrix between action and consciousness. For this perspective to be useful, we must become *conscious* of the energy and understand how it can guide our actions. We also must be able to translate our conscious aims into action.

Channels of Energy

The energy that exists within the organization can scatter widely, build or die naturally, or be *channeled* through the forms existing in the system. This is where effective management counts. For instance, energy flows through the communication networks in the organization during all decision-making, planning, review, and problem-solving processes. All meetings have the potential to move energy or block it, depending on their outcomes. Work flow, scheduling, and supply and distribution systems each channel energy when working effectively. Sales, marketing, and production lines move energy as they carry out their roles in the organization. Energy flows, whether by plan or not.

Energy also can be blocked by delays, confusion, inefficiency, bureaucracy, battles, inhibitions, and breakdowns. Over time, tradition can become a hindrance to energy flow. Policies and cumbersome procedures can get in the way, even if they were initially created to assist. People's attitudes and beliefs, negative emotional states, fear, and distrust can act as obstacles to the energy flow. The "grapevine" can set off resistance in the organization because of the potential for rumors to carry negative energy. One key to managing effectively is to keep channels of information and communication open and to ensure that the flow of energy, in the form of information and indications, is as clean and accurate as possible.

Energy Fields

In situations in which a feeling is widespread, an energy field is created, almost like a blanket of mist that envelops the organization. All who are within the energy field experience the same mood—the effect of the field. Organizational morale is an example of such an energy field. Energy fields can occur spontaneously within minutes or grow over a long period of time. Some energy fields disappear or change radically very quickly; others last a very long time or never disappear at all. Energy fields are generated by things such as:

1. Specific events: changes in leadership, acquisitions of new businesses or products, divestitures, start-ups, ceremonies, celebrations, and so on.
2. Information: announcements, policies, rumors, and key decisions.
3. Leadership style and philosophy: e.g., authoritarian, inspirational, humanistic, maverick, entrepreneurial, or participative.
4. Culture: values, norms, myths, rituals, feelings, beliefs, rewards, and traditions.

Lasting and profound energy fields, such as organizational culture, are great challenges to managers in times of change. The patterns they create become hypnotic and habitual. The density of the field tends to blind people to anything but the field. In order to change anything, we must first "face up" to where we are and then begin to create new options that are more appropriate to our desired outcomes. Understanding how energy and energy fields work provides a tool with which to assist the change process.

A CONTINUUM OF MANAGEMENT STYLES

There are times when it is necessary to alter an organization's fields, channels, and key sources of energy. This requires the ability to free up the energy in order to transform it. Three management styles can help or hinder this process in varying degrees. The ideal manager for the model is a true agent of change, facilitating the release and channeling of energy, that is, *managing in the flow state.* The manager on the opposite end of the continuum is one who works against the system, constraining or blocking the natural flow, that is, *managing in the fear state.* Somewhere between these two is the manager who is effective at working in the traditional model, the organization of form. This person works the system from the point of view of results, decisions, and structures. This is the *solid-state manager.* Table 1 describes the orientation of each of these three styles. A manager can alter his or her style at any time. A manager who is feeling threatened is likely to move toward the fear state. One who feels powerful or effective is likely to move toward the flow state.

Table 1. Continuum of Management Styles

Fear-State Management	Solid-State Management	Flow-State Management
Works against the system	Works with the structures of the system; tries to ensure that they "fit"	Works with the energy flow in the system; works for harmony; alters structures to free up energy
Win/lose mentality; destructive competition	Win/win when possible; competition within reason is useful	Winning and losing is not important; doing what is necessary is
Self-oriented	Department, function oriented	Total-system oriented
Strategically creates obstacles, barriers	Rearranges obstacles; moves around numbers and structures	Removes, dissolves obstacles; changes the structure to respond to energy needs
Slave to time; frenetic	Tries to manage time; still crisis oriented	Respects imposed time-tables and uses sense of "right timing" for events
Preoccupied with payoffs, rewards, image	Concerned with rewards; respects and responds to external influencers; image is important	Motivated from within; sees rewards as tools; image is an illusion
Overly controlling; with-holds information, responsibility	Controls using formal systems, policies, rules; shares information as necessary; delegates when appropriate	Lets the flow of energy guide behavior; uses information to unblock the flow and indirectly "control"/guide events; encourages others to take responsibility

Table 1. (Continued)

Fear-State Management	Solid-State Management	Flow-State Management
Gives lip service to results that serve own needs	Results and outcome oriented; MBO	Oriented to process; results are only temporary realities
Distracted, scattered, anxious, confused, depressed, sick	Pulled in many directions; concerned; seeks information for understanding; works regardless of mental state	Clearly focused; attentive without concern; clarity and foresight; active, healthy
Uncertain of own limits; closed to feedback on performance	Accepts responsibility without knowledge of own limits; aims to please; accepts feedback when given	Clear about own limits and those of others; seeks feedback from own performance as well as from others
Intimidated by tradition	Respects, preserves tradition	Respects purpose of tradition, alters it when necessary
Cannot see polarities; sees only one way	Sees polarities; fights for right answers; resists shifts	Allows polarities to emerge, shift as necessary; embraces both sides as legitimate
Work has little meaning; totally ignorant of the organization's purpose	Meaning is in results, numbers, profit; organization's purpose is perceived as a number	Meaning is in the pursuit of the organization's purpose, its viability, and the process of making a contribution to the larger social environment as well as people's lives; purpose is used to connect everyone together
Believes in complete scarcity of resources, rewards; must fight for them	Resources and rewards are finite and must be distributed in logical, standardized ways	Believes in abundance of resources and rewards; knows how to create them from existing or new sources
Mistakes are suicidal	Mistakes are inevitable, but to be avoided; move on quickly if they occur	Mistakes provide the most valuable source of learning; they are welcome if they occur; it is important to understand them
Focuses on controlling others	Focuses on using others to carry out tasks	Focuses on empowering others
Attachment to own position; power hungry; holds on to authority irrespective of position	Looks after own position; seeks opportunities for power; exercises authority over others consistent with position	Not attached to self, power, authority; can move in and out of these conditions with ease
Erratic mental processes and behavior	Left-brain, analytical orientation; traditionally male behavior	Right and left brain balanced for synergy; androgynous in behavior and orientation

MANAGING IN THE FLOW STATE

There is little question that an expanded perspective is required of our executives and leaders. Quinn (1980) refers to this new image as "the guiding executive," one who sees change as ongoing and who understands how to work with many variables in order for things to proceed and flow smoothly in the organization.

The concept of flow can be traced back to the Eastern philosophy of the Tao, which encourages harmony with the natural order of things, the way the universe is meant to unfold. It states that there is a natural sequence to life; that change, like a flowing river, is perpetual; and that we can, at best, facilitate the flow by removing obstacles from its way. Applied to management thinking, to be in a flow state implies seeing the large picture—understanding, objectively, the most appropriate changes or shifts that must occur and assisting these changes with the least amount of cost or disruption to the people and outputs of the organization. Being in the flow state means working in harmony with others and looking after the good of the whole, not just the favored parts of the system. Csikszentmihalyi (1975) describes it as "the holistic sensation that people feel with total involvement." Siu (1980) describes the ability in this state "to act from an instantaneous apprehension of the totality." This requires a broad perspective of what is going on and a sensitivity to, or intuition about, what is needed. It means balancing the factual data in each situation with one's hunches about how to act. As mentioned in Table 1, this balance can be seen in managers who effectively use the functions of both brain hemispheres— the left being analytical and structured, the right being intuitive and creative. It is the synergy between the two that enables the flow to occur.

Values That Support the Flow State

Certain values are espoused by flow-state managers. They see themselves as being in service to the larger purpose of the company. They strive for the fulfillment of as well as for the potential of the individuals who contribute to it. They have patience and trust in people's intentions to work for common goals without sacrificing their personal identity. Work to them is meaningful, and they feel enriched from their effort and time spent on behalf of the organization. They believe that there are numerous opportunities in which to demonstrate competence and effectiveness.

Flow-state managers encourage the best effort from everyone and value a work environment that supports learning, exploration, and creativity. In their efforts to ensure harmony among the parts of the organization, they also promote opportunities for group synergy and group recognition. They understand that their values must be shared in order to have a positive impact.

Many of the values of the flow-state manager are illustrated by the life of Gandhi. Gandhi was deeply guided by his inner purpose, his belief in equality and justice, peace, and patience. Having no resources or form with which to manage his cause, he became a master at managing energy. He used himself and other public figures as models and sources, created a widespread energy field on behalf of his vision, and opened new channels for action in the British government and the Indian and Muslim states. He trusted that the flow of events eventually would realize his vision. Of course, such a person must also be aware of the potential risks involved and the personal sacrifices that may be required.

The "flow state" describes the perspective from which this new type of manager operates; because of this person's ability to facilitate profound changes and achievements in the organization, he or she may also be referred to as the "transformational" manager—one who transforms energy.

The Fear-State Manager

In most traditional organizations, people strive to advance their own causes, compete for scarce resources, and are rewarded solely for how well they control results. In and of themselves, each of these acts may be a positive condition if it serves the collective purpose of the organization rather than a few individuals. The individual, self-centered focus drains the potential performance of the system. This self-centered focus is the accompaniment of fear and defensiveness. Fear-state managers have a win-lose attitude, play political games, and grasp and control information, assignments, meetings, and other events to serve themselves before all others.

People who act out of fear perceive threat in the forces around them. They assume that there are not enough resources or rewards to go around. Such people believe that they have no choice but to try to win, assuming that others must, thereby, lose. These people typically hear and see everything in the organization with the question "How can this hurt me?" in their minds. It is nearly impossible to have a clear sense of how to proceed appropriately when one is in this state of mind. The physiological reactions to fear shut down our ability to respond freely and be open to new input. The fear state drives people to withhold and protect information and power and to demonstrate blind allegiance to tradition for fear of losing ground.

Under normal conditions, this state can be observed in individuals who lose their tempers frequently, become workaholics, have difficulty delegating responsibility, are reluctant to let go of a lost debate or unpopular decision, or frequently blame others for negative conditions. These symptoms then breed greater strain and fear in others. The fear state is highly contagious in organizations and the costs are appalling: from wasted energy and low morale to out-and-out conflict between people or organizational units.

The Solid-State Manager

The solid-state managerial style is familiar; it reflects the traditional attitudes of business in the Western hemisphere. Solid-state managers are skillful at managing the traditional structures in the organization: the charts, policies, schedules, numbers, and "head counts." A variety of familiar management styles fall into this category: the authoritarian, the organizer, and the administrator. Some of the more people-oriented managers also are within this range. The common factor is that they manage the components—the form of the organization—and do not see or emphasize the relationships, dynamics, and processes as well. They function largely from a left-brain orientation, influenced by external forces such as goals, deadlines, and policies, and are unaware of or afraid to trust their instincts about trends, patterns, and energy flow. They respond to rewards and punishments, visibility, political expectations, and traditions. They plan according to available, quantifiable facts and are truly the "good soldiers" of management.

Solid-state managers frequently are successful in what they attempt to do. However, more and more of these managers are faced with the dilemma described at the beginning of this article. Their best strategies somehow are not working. Because of their tendency to preserve tradition (perhaps for fear of rocking the boat), solid-state managers do not actively question the way things are done. They are more apt to resist change than to initiate it. It is rare that they will take the time to truly appreciate and learn from mistakes (or successes, for that matter). Conflicts are seen as inevitable, but to be avoided; if they arise, they are to be controlled or diffused in order to regain the status quo. Solid-state managers are skilled in analysis and measurement, sometimes to a fault. Their dependence on "figuring" and "proving" can deprive them of more creative, intuitive responses to challenges. Unfortunately for many of them, we are no longer living in a time of stability and certainty. Pressures, polarities, and ambiguity are a large part of reality. Status-quo thinking alone cannot satisfy these complex demands. There is a need for a new vision of management.

How the Flow State Works

The flow-state, or transformational, manager's perspectives are influenced by several unique attitudes, and these, in turn, deeply influence his or her decisions and behaviors.

An Abundance of Opportunities

To begin with, the flow-state manager feels that the organization offers an abundance of opportunity to those who seek it. The "one big chance" mentality is an illusion; there is no scarcity of options and potentials. Believing in abundance releases energy and excitement. If now is not the time, another chance will emerge or, better, a new opportunity as yet unforeseen will surface. By staying fresh and aware, one actively participates in the opportunities of the day.

Learning Is Essential

To sustain this openness, the flow-state manager values calculated risks and continual learning. People must have the freedom to explore and make mistakes. Without testing limits, it is difficult to know whether or not one is on or off course, moving too fast or too slowly. Faith in the process includes believing that the process will indicate how to self-correct or how to reorganize in order to keep moving—much like water seeking new channels to keep flowing. Each event, positive or negative, provides more information about where one has been and where one needs to go next.

Structures Are Necessary and Changeable

The flow-state manager recognizes that certain structures are necessary and useful. For instance, job descriptions provide clarity as well as reasonable boundaries between functions. For this manager, however, such boundaries are like walls: although they are useful for defining what is inside them, they inevitably close out some things as well. As part of his or her continuing task to facilitate the process, this manager realizes that role boundaries may need to be changed to reflect changes in circumstances or people. This is true for all structures in the organization. They are vehicles to facilitate the flow—easily created, easily removed. This has major implications for how one organizes, develops plans, and uses policies and rules.

Using Common Purpose as a Bond Between People

Given the uncertainty in organizations, most people require some form of security or stability to perform effectively. This security comes from two major sources: shared acceptance of the purpose and future goals of the organization and the sense of togetherness or community that is created by collective effort. The flow-state manager encourages people to feel connected and attuned to one another. At all levels of the organization, this sense of community can enhance people's motivation to work together effectively, especially during periods of uncertainty or change.

Attending to All Stakeholders

Because the tides can shift at any time, it is important to heed and value all constituents or stakeholders of the organization. Siu (1980) warns of the dangers of taking constituents lightly. As appropriate, some form of recognition and attention to all interested parties is wise. To accomplish this, the flow-state manager may ask for input or feedback, may test a new idea, may praise a point of view, or may reward some contribution as a way of keeping life in the relationship with each of the stakeholder groups. All doors are kept open, and all parties are actively involved.

There Is Meaning in All Events

At times, events and circumstances may change radically in the organization, disrupting people and plans. A shift in leadership or direction may cause pressure or conflict. The flow-state manager respects such transitions whether or not he or she agrees with them, because each change in the organization serves some purpose in the long run.

Seeing the Big Picture that Surrounds Polarities

The flow-state manager is open to conflicts, differences, and polarities. The solid-state manager usually can see two sides of an issue or conflict and perceives one as correct. Unique to the flow-state manager, however, is the ability to view an issue from all angles, as if from above. This allows a more complete and objective perspective from which to make decisions. It enables the manager to rise above the conflict without labeling any position as "right" or "wrong," thus keeping all options open. The flow-state manager realizes that all forces are cyclical in nature and that each will have its turn in time.

A formal decision-making system based on this principle is described by Ackoff (1979). One task force is established to thoroughly investigate why a major decision should be made (the advocacy position). A second task force is also formally created to study why the same decision should *not* be made. The deciding body can then maintain a clear view of the large picture while having both sides thoroughly and legitimately reviewed.

Nonattachment to Self, Action, and Power

The flow-state manager knows that one must always be ready to respond according to the emerging need: to act or to stop an action, to give up a position of power or to step into one; to take on leadership or to demonstrate followership. This requires letting go of one's ego attachments to favored positions; such attachments quickly become constraints. This approach increases freedom, self-direction, and choice, allowing the manager to select the actions that are most appropriate at the time.

Focus on Empowering Others

"Freedom from self" allows one to consider the needs of others. The flow-state manager seeks opportunities for others to make a contribution. He or she attempts to facilitate higher levels of performance, to empower others to act on their best intuition and skills. Through delegation, giving away responsibility and authority, and demonstrating trust, a manager can unlock a tremendous amount of motivation and excitement. Becoming an advocate for what others (including subordinates) want to do is a key strategy for unblocking human energy in the organization and transforming it.

Flow-State Strategies

In accordance with flow-state principles, anything that helps to facilitate the unfolding of events in the organization is considered a valuable approach. A few strategies are particularly useful in this regard.

Managing Ambiguity

Given the high degree of ambiguity in organizational life, managers need to be able to cope with uncertainty. Most people, however, want information, clear choices, and advantages and disadvantages spelled out. They want reinforcement or reassurance from others before they are willing to act. Flow-state managers are aware of these natural tendencies and work to generate as much clarity and understanding as possible. Quinn (1980) writes of managers who strive to amplify people's understanding of different alternatives and their seeking of clear criteria for making decisions. This takes time and care. Others also will grow more comfortable with new directions if given an appropriate period for adjustment and an opportunity to sample a new approach.

According to Pascale (1978), a basic skill in managing in an uncertain environment is knowing the distinction between having enough data to *decide* and having enough data to *proceed*. It takes courage to proceed; the flow-state manager knows that further action will reveal even more data.

The key strategies in managing in ambiguous circumstances are as follows:

1. Pursue as much clarity and understanding as possible.
2. Establish criteria to test the decision.
3. Create lead time for more information to surface and to facilitate people's levels of comfort.
4. Take slow or partial steps that do not risk the entire project; send out test balloons and watch for prevailing winds.
5. Encourage people to voice their concerns and frustrations with the unknown and reinforce the climate for learning.

Sense of Timing

In uncertain situations, knowing when to act is a skill; timing is an important element in the success or failure of many endeavors. The transformational, flow-oriented manager knows how to order events on a linear timetable, providing the logical sequence so necessary to planning and implementing complex changes. This person also knows how to sense the energy, readiness, and momentum in the organization for implementing critical changes; when to act; and when not to act. This manager also senses people's need for direction and their openness to change.

Building Readiness: The Use of Critical Mass

Building readiness is a key component of the flow-state perspective. Nuclear physics offers us the term "critical mass"—the point at which the momentum necessary for action to occur is reached. Until this happens, the flow-state manager engages in building awareness, understanding, and support for the desired outcome. Critical mass in an organization can be described as the necessary number of "ready" people—a momentum or energy field from which the effort can proceed on its own without continual support.

The flow-state manager identifies people throughout the organization who are best suited to advocate a desired change. He or she invites their support and describes the collective effort that is required for the change to occur. They then use their skills, reputations, influence, and resources to attract others to the effort. When the number of people who advocate the move, with their combined energy and intention, outweigh those who resist or have not committed themselves, a critical mass is reached and the effort proceeds.

It must be emphasized that this is a strategically proactive move for the transformational manager. The approach is active rather than responsive. This form of influence grows from a manager's intuitive sense of what is needed to facilitate the flow and is congruent with the larger picture as well. Maintaining this ability requires that the manager keep his or her awareness of the organization finely tuned.

Nurturing the Inner Flow State

An organization functions effectively when its purpose is clear, its members work together in pursuit of the purpose, and the energy flows smoothly. This picture of organizational health is a collective reflection of the health of members of the organization. An inner flow state in every person directly affects that person's level of performance and ability to be in synchronization with the flow of the larger organization.

The flow-state manager is keenly aware of his or her inner state and balances and cares for four core aspects of the person: the mind, the body, the heart (emotions), and the spirit. As in the organization, these components are interlinked. Peak performance is the outcome of all four working in support of one another. The mind-body-heart-spirit model is applicable at the organizational level as well. The flow-state manager looks after the mental functioning (decision making, planning, and problem solving, for example); the physical ability (operations, structure, and use of resources); the emotions (morale, creativity, and culture); and the spirit (meaningful work, alignment of the parts, and sharing of a common purpose) of the organization. The balance of these aspects directly affects the health of the organization and the degree to which its energy can flow naturally.

Assessing the Situation

The characteristics described in this article can be exemplified by several questions that the flow-state manager might ask to assess any situation in the organization.

1. How does this situation fit the larger purpose of the organization?
2. What is needed to have this situation turn out ideally for everyone involved? What opportunity is here? What is at stake?
3. What circumstances and events have led up to this point? How does this historical perspective influence the way in which we might proceed or the outcome desired? What polarities exist? What is the existing energy field?
4. What do we have going in our favor (people, resources, motivation, timing, etc.)? What real or potential obstacles stand in our way?
5. What in our direct control can be easily created or removed to assist this effort? What channels can be opened? What structures are needed?
6. What requires indirect influence, longer lead time, or special consideration? How might these things happen?
7. Who is essential to the critical mass? How can these people be reached and involved to help open channels and build a positive energy field?
8. What assumptions are we making about our desired outcomes or the needs/opportunities facing us? Are these consistent with other people's views?
9. What is my interest in this? What is in this for others? How can I be an advocate for them or empower them?
10. What is the best timing for events to occur? What is an appropriate sequence?
11. Should we be proactive or is it best for us to let things unfold for now?
12. How visible should we be? Should the total effort move ahead at once or should we proceed one piece at a time or in phases?
13. What other pressures might emerge (e.g., resistance, loss of resources, change of leadership, etc.)?
14. What can we learn from this experience? What is meaningful about it?
15. As I look at the overall picture, what hunches or feelings do I have about how to proceed?

The information from these questions shapes a strategy for action. From each action, new learnings and data emerge to help shape ensuing strategies. Flow-state managers ask such questions on an ongoing basis while keeping the underlying principle in mind: What is the best way to proceed to serve the highest purpose for all involved? At times they may choose to do nothing but watch and support.

IMPLICATIONS OF MANAGING IN THE FLOW STATE AND THE USE OF ORGANIZATIONAL ENERGY

The concepts presented here describe an ideal state. This model is created to help to explain an expanded view of the dynamics of managing. Whether it is possible or practical in today's organization bears further exploration and discussion.

How Would Organizations Be Different Under this Frame of Reference?

The implications of applying the flow-state concept in our existing organizations include the need for attention to the following:

1. A new terminology to discuss energy and flow operationally. Awareness of the shift from talking about nouns (forms and results) to speaking in terms of verbs and gerunds (processes). Descriptions of reality that use action terms to define the energy flow better.

2. New organizational forms and systems that are responsive to the energy flow rather than obstacles to it. Such new forms must be self-organizing, self-correcting, and adaptable.

3. Greater focus on the purpose of the organization and monitoring to ensure that it continues to fit the demands of the larger environment and that all members of the organization are aware of it and understand it.

4. Assessment of the existing sources, channels, and fields of energy to ascertain what helps the organization to adapt to greater complexity and what hinders it. Examination of pervasive cultural factors to see whether they block the self-responsibility, creativity, and adaptability that are necessary for change to occur.

5. Understanding of organizational members' beliefs about the organization's future, its management style, responsibility, and change. This awareness can indicate the need for new perspectives and actions. What beliefs would support desired changes?

6. Understanding of the model of energy as an organization moves through its natural life cycle. Assessment of which management strategies are appropriate to the current growth rate and phase of the organization.

Assuming that It Is Desirable, How Does One Implement Change in Organizational Forms and Management Styles?

Organizations must determine whether their existing energy channels can be opened up or new ones created. The experience of energy flowing freely is a great motivator to continue the process. Each manager can be asked to reflect on the way he or she views the organization (as form, as processes, etc.) and where he or she sits on the continuum of management styles. Key sources of energy (people, events, etc.) can be identified, along with ways to use them best to serve the larger purpose of the organization. A strategy can be developed for building a critical mass of supporters within the targeted system. It is necessary to identify whom to invite initially, how to use these people, and how to spread the awareness.

It is also necessary to study carefully the impact of the potential changes on existing structures and managers. What specifically would need to be changed? Who would assist the effort? What forms of resistance might be encountered? What sacrifices must be made, compared to what gains? What would be the cost in dollars, time, resources, emotion? From this information, an approach can be developed in which changes are sequenced and paced appropriately. Care must be taken not to push the existing system beyond its limits to absorb and respond to changes.

There is also a need to explore how computers and other technology can be utilized to enhance information and energy flow.

Finally, managers must be taught the principles of the flow state. Learning experiences, language, and feedback mechanisms must be developed that reflect the state itself.

Life in the Organization in the Flow State

The objectives of the flow-state model are to have organizational members care about one another, work collaboratively across functions, conduct debates about problems and possible solutions, and then follow up responsibly, no matter what the outcome. The model predicts higher motivation, constructive tension, more trust and patience, a more satisfying quality of work life, pride in performance, and a deeper alignment with the purpose of the organization.

The flow state is a process, not an end result. It is a state of being, not a place to go. Managing in the flow state is an attitude, not an absolute. A great deal of personal commitment and integrity are necessary to maintain the flow-state frame of mind. As a way of viewing the world, it is an inspiration for behavior. Whatever aids the natural unfolding of events *is* the flow state. The value felt will match the situation at hand; the possibilities are limitless.

With the increasing complexity and need for change in today's organizations, it would seem that anything that would make life in the organization run more smoothly would be welcomed. Executives cannot fight or ignore the challenges, nor can they hope to apply "band-aids" to organizational wounds. Some shift in perspective is essential before we can experience relief. That shift is internal to us, to our attitudes and beliefs. Fear *can* be transformed. Form and energy can work in harmony. No matter what we actually do, things will continue to unfold. Managers can assist that unfolding, if only by not blocking the way. We can consider ourselves successful if. . .

> When [the effective leader] is finished
> with his work, the people say,
> "It happened naturally."
>
> Lao Tse
> (Quoted in M. Maccoby, 1981, p. 11)

REFERENCES

Ackoff, R. *Management seminar proceedings*, Sun Company, Inc., Radnor, PA, Fall 1979.

Csikszentmihalyi, M. *Beyond boredom and anxiety*. San Francisco: Jossey-Bass, 1975.

Ingalls, J. D. *Human energy*. San Diego, CA: Learning Concepts, 1979.

Maccoby, M. Quotation from Lao Tse. *The leader: A new face for American management*. New York: Simon & Schuster, 1981.

Nadler, D. A., & Tushman, M. L. A model for organizational diagnosis. *Organizational Dynamics*, Autumn, 1980, p. 47.

Naisbitt, J. *Trend Letter*. 1983, *2*(4), 1.

Pascale, R. T. Zen and the art of management. *Harvard Business Review*, March-April, 1978, p. 156.

Quinn, J. B. Managing strategic change. *Sloan Management Review*, 1980, *21*(4), 7, 5.

Siu, R. G. H. *The Master Manager*. Chichester, England: John Wiley, 1980.

Linda S. Ackerman *is the president of Linda S. Ackerman, Inc., Washington, D.C. She specializes in managing complex change, organizational effectiveness, and organizational transformation. Ms. Ackerman is a founding member of the Center for Excellence in Organizations in Washington, D.C. She previously served as manager of human resources planning and development for the Sun Petroleum Products Company, Philadelphia, Pennsylvania.*

THE EXPECTANCY THEORY OF MOTIVATION: IMPLICATIONS FOR TRAINING AND DEVELOPMENT

John A. Sample

Human resource development (HRD) practitioners have long considered motivation theory in the design of learning programs for employees and managers. Although the "content" theories of Maslow and Herzberg have been used widely over the years, the newer "process" theories (expectancy, equity, path-goal) are now receiving more attention. Instructional design for training and development should incorporate the "process" theories of motivation, which suggest that motivation is a combined function of an individual's perception that effort will lead to performance and of the desirability of the outcomes that could result from such performance. In this approach, people are presumed to be practical, reasoning beings who have anticipations and expectations about their future in an organization. According to Casio (1982):

> Individuals make conscious choices among outcomes according to their estimated probabilities of occurrence and the personal values attached to them. . . . The individual seeks first to determine "what's in it for me, and is it important to me?". . . . It is the anticipation of reward that energizes behavior and the perceived value of various outcomes that gives behavior its direction. (p. 283)

Designers and coordinators of HRD systems should ask themselves: "Why should our employees and managers sacrifice valuable work time to attend training and development programs? Of what future utility to them is the effort to learn and the desire to perform at higher levels? Does the future utility include more money, promotion, more autonomy, job satisfaction, or some other intrinsic or extrinsic reward?" These questions are important in considering motivation from the perspective of "expectancy-valence" theory, which links effort (e.g., completing a training program) to performance on the job (a first-level outcome), which then becomes instrumental in the employee's receiving a promotion, raise, or other valued reward (a second-level outcome). Campbell, Dunnette, and Weick (1970) cite support for the utility of the expectancy model in training and development. They stress that an individual's anticipation or expectancy about how well he or she will absorb the program content will greatly influence the person's motivation and attitudes in the learning situation. The clearer the link between training and development, the individual's performance, and valued rewards and outcomes, the more positive will be the employee's attitude and motivation to seek out and complete a learning activity.

Expectancy theory also can help to explain attendance and dropout patterns. When an adult "perceives that his or her expectations of gaining specific benefits from participation are unlikely to be realized, he or she will probably drop out" (Darkenwald, 1982, p. 286).

THE EXPECTANCY MODEL

Connolly (1976) states that "expectancy type models have become firmly established as the dominant paradigm for research on work related motivation" (p. 37). Depending on the source one quotes, as few as thirty and as many as fifty empirical studies have been conducted in business and industry (Campbell & Pritchard, 1976; Connolly, 1976; Kopelman & Thompson, 1976). The theoretical foundations of the expectancy-valence theory of motivation were laid by Tolman (1932) and have been developed in business and industry by Vroom (1964) and Lawler (1975) and in educational settings by Mowday (1978) and Miskel, DeFrain, and Wilcox (1980). Cross (1981) cites extensively the work by Rubenson, a Swedish educator, who investigated the competing forces that motivate adults to participate in continuing education.

Basic Elements of Expectancy

The basic variables in this theory are expectancies, outcomes, instrumentalities, and valences; they are interrelated as shown in Figure 1.

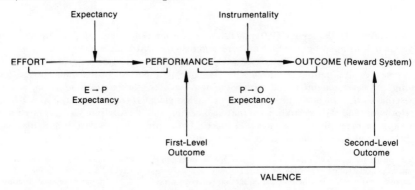

Figure 1. Key Variables in Expectancy-Valence Theory

Expectancy

Vroom (1964) defines expectancy as the perceived relationship between a given degree of effort and a given level of performance—a first-level outcome. For example, attending a management development program (effort) may lead to increased productivity on the job (performance). An expectancy can be expressed as a subjective probability ranging from 0.00 to 1.00. Lawler (1975) has taken the generalized notion of expectancy and divided it into two specific types: effort → performance and performance → outcome. An E → P expectancy reflects a belief that effort will lead to a desired level of performance. The closer the "perceived" relationship between effort and resulting job performance, the greater the E → P expectancy. A belief that performance will lead to a particular outcome (a promotion or raise) is a P → O expectancy. E → P and P → O are the expectancy variables.

Outcomes

Outcomes are the consequences of one's behavior and, in this context, they refer to the reward system. Rewards may be intrinsic (recognition, commendation, autonomy, etc.) or extrinsic (raise, promotion, or transfer to valued assignment).

Instrumentality

Whereas expectancy relates to first-level outcomes (performance), instrumentality relates first-level outcomes to second-level outcomes (the reward system). Instrumentality deals with the question "To what extent does the actuality of a first-level outcome become instrumental in obtaining second-level outcomes?" Employees tend to see beyond immediate performance outcomes (meeting goals and objectives) and begin to assess consequences in terms of desired secondary results (raise, promotion, etc.).

Valence

Valence is the fourth major component in the expectancy-valence equation. It can be defined as the perceived value that employees place on first- and second-level outcomes. Valences have theoretical values of from +1.00 to -1.00. Employees may desire to join a particular work group (group membership = first-level outcome) because they believe that joining will enhance their status in the organization (second-level outcome). An outcome has a valence of zero when the employee is indifferent to its attainment. Valence is expressed as a negative value if employees strongly want to avoid the outcome (being fired, demoted, or subject to chastisement).

THE EXPECTANCY MODEL APPLIED TO TRAINING AND DEVELOPMENT

The importance of the interrelationships of the key variables is indicated in Figure 2.

KEY VARIABLES

Examples	$\frac{\text{Effort} \rightarrow \text{Performance}}{\text{E} \rightarrow \text{P expectancy}}$	x	$\frac{\text{Performance} \rightarrow \text{Outcome}}{\text{P} \rightarrow \text{O expectancy}}$	x	VALENCE	=	Motivational Force
1	Expectancy that increased effort through management development will increase performance/productivity.		Expectancy that increased performance/productivity will lead to a promotion and/or merit increase.		High positive valence		
	(E → P = 0.90)	x	(P → O = 1.00)	x	(0.90)	=	0.81
2	Same as above		Expectancy that increased productivity will not lead to promotion and/or merit raise.		Same as above		
	(E → P = 0.90)	x	(P → O = 0.10)	x	(0.90)	=	0.081

Figure 2. Two Examples of Expectancy Variables

Suppose that a manager in example 1 places a high value on management development and believes that effort to increase knowledge, develop new skills, and adopt new attitudes is a worthwhile endeavor. Suppose further that this manager believes that management development efforts will lead to increased performance. In this example, the manager has a hypothetical E → P expectancy of 0.90. If this same manager believes that increased performance will lead to promotion, raise, or other valued outcome, the manager could have a high P → O expectancy of 1.00. If the manager truly values increased performance (a first-level outcome) and a promotion or some other valued reward (a second-level outcome), he or she could be described as placing a high valence of 0.90 on these two outcomes.

At this point, it would be reasonable to state that the manager has a high motivational force to perform because of the multiplicative outcome (0.90 x 1.00 x 0.90 = 0.81). If skills and abilities are high and the role descriptions clear (i.e., job/task description), the manager could expect to realize job success (Steers & Porter, 1975).

In example 2, if the probabilities for the variables remain constant except that the manager does *not* expect performance to lead to a desired outcome (P → O expectancy of 0.10), a computation of the motivational force (0.90 x 0.10 x 0.90 = 0.081) indicates little desire to perform.

Implications for Training and Development

Several implications of expectancy theory are of interest to training and development practitioners. A useful framework for applying the theory is suggested by Steers (1981).

Clarify Effort → Performance Expectancies

Determinants of E → P expectancies are varied and interrelated. The setting of explicit and moderately difficult but potentially achievable goals and performance standards should clarify for the employees precisely what is expected of them (Casio, 1982; Hackman & Suttle, 1977). Ambiguous job design and task descriptions can lead to what Steers (1981) refers to as "wasted efforts while employees search for answers." Personality factors also are key determinants. According to Lawler (1975), employees with low self-esteem are susceptible to low E → P expectancies. Motivating them is difficult because of their predisposition to believe that they cannot perform well. Conversely, employees with high self-esteem will have more realistic expectancies and will respond more predictably and realistically to their environment. The situation becomes problematic when an employee, who believes that he or she is performing well, will not believe that extra effort (such as voluntary participation in training and development) will improve performance. Coaching and supervision can be extremely helpful in clarifying goal expectations and bolstering the self-esteem of employees.

Training and development are critically important if the employee is to focus effort on job-related performance. Without appropriate goal setting and learning activities (both on the job and in the training setting), many employees cannot be expected to link effort to performance. Employees who are denied access to relevant training and development experiences may become discouraged. Casio (1982) states:

> The implications...for training and development are obvious: Explicit goal setting (a cognitive activity) by the *individual* trainee should lead to enhanced commitment to the training (motivation), greater effort, and more efficient learning. (p. 284)

Clarify Performance → Outcome Expectancies

A critical responsibility of the supervisor is to facilitate the link between actual performance and the reward system. Employees need to believe that effort will lead to performance and that performance will lead to rewards desired by the employees. Supervisors may have to work with higher management to "recast the reward and promotion (career) systems so that rewards and promotions more closely reflect performance" (Hackman & Suttle, 1977). The performance-appraisal system becomes an important key in linking performance to a desired reward. Management by objectives (MBO) and behaviorally anchored rating scales (BARS) are useful appraisal methods that link performance to the reward system (Baird, Beatty, & Schneider, 1982).

These implications for training and development apply primarily to supervisory and management development programs. In such programs, the power of intrinsic rewards (praise, positive feedback) also should be covered in depth, and the participation ethic in work-related decisions should be emphasized (Hackman & Suttle, 1977).

Selection and Placement

Most HRD practitioners would agree that scarce budget resources should be spent on selection rather than on training and development, since the former can be less expensive than the latter.

Often it is necessary to integrate selection and training/development functions. However, "training and development are not necessarily the *only* alternatives available for enhancing the person/job/organization match, and it is narrow-minded to view them as a panacea for all organizational ills" (Casio, 1982). Job placement is critical for employees who desire opportunities to perform, thereby increasing the probabilities that their performance will become instrumental in achieving valued rewards. The selection, training, and development of highly motivated employees for dead-end performance opportunities will stifle effort → performance → outcome expectancies.

CONCLUSION

In the past, training and development practitioners have approached the motivational aspects of organizational life through the need and content theories of Maslow and Herzberg. This article introduces an important process theory: expectancy-valence theory. The basic principles are simple and sound: Employees look to the future when assessing present effort and performance on the job, especially when the reward system is contingent on performance.

REFERENCES

Baird, L. S., Beatty, R. W., & Schneider, C. E. *The performance appraisal sourcebook.* Amherst, MA: Human Resources Development Press, 1982.

Campbell, J. P., Dunnette, M. D., & Weick, K. E., Jr. *Managerial behavior, performance and effectiveness.* New York: McGraw-Hill, 1970.

Campbell, J. P., & Pritchard, R. D. Motivation theory in industrial and organizational psychology. In M. Dunnette (Ed.), *Handbook of industrial and organizational psychology.* Chicago: Rand McNally, 1976.

Casio, W. F. *Applied psychology in personnel management.* Reston, VA: Reston Publishing, 1982.

Connolly, T. Some conceptual and methodological issues in expectancy models of work performance motivation. *Academy of Management Review,* 1976, *1*(4), 37-47.

Cross, K. P. *Adults as learners.* San Francisco, CA: Jossey-Bass, 1981.

Darkenwald, G. G. Keep your ADA. In C. Klevins (Ed.), *Materials and methods in adult and continuing education.* Los Angeles, CA: Klevins Publications, 1982.

Hackman, J. R., & Suttle, J. L. *Improving life at work.* Santa Monica, CA: Goodyear, 1977.

Kopelman, R. E., & Thompson, P. H. Boundary conditions for expectancy theory predictions of work motivation and job performance. *Academy of Management Journal,* 1976, *19*(2), 237-258.

Lawler, E. Expectancy theory. In R. Steers and L. Porter (Eds.), *Motivation and work behavior.* New York, McGraw-Hill, 1975.

Miskel, C., DeFrain, J. A., & Wilcox, K. A. A test of expectancy work motivation theory in educational organizations. *Educational Administration Quarterly,* 1980, *16*(1), 70-92.

Mowday, R. T. The exercise of upward influence in organizations. *Administrative Science Quarterly,* 1978, *23*(1), 137-156.

Steers, R. M. *Introduction to organizational behavior.* Santa Monica, CA: Goodyear, 1981.

Steers, R. M., & Porter, L. W. *Motivation and work behavior.* New York: McGraw-Hill, 1975.

Tolman, E. C. *Purposive behavior in animals and men.* New York: Appelton-Century-Crofts, 1932.

Vroom, V. H. *Work and motivation.* New York: John Wiley, 1964.

John A. Sample is the executive director of Professional Development Specialists, Inc., a Tallahassee, Florida, consulting and training firm that specializes in management and organization development. Mr. Sample formerly was an assistant professor and director of the Master of Science in Management Program for the Graduate School, Biscayne College, Miami, Florida. His teaching interests include cultural and behavioral factors in organizations, human resource management, adult learning and development, and management and organization development.

INTERPERSONAL FEEDBACK: PROBLEMS AND RECONCEPTUALIZATION

Raymond V. Rasmussen

In the field of cybernetics, the term "feedback" is used to describe an essential component of self-regulating devices (Ruben, 1972). A thermostat is a familiar example. In human relations, "feedback" has been used to refer to a process of information gathering and correction—one person feeding back his perceptions of another person so that the second person can make his social or work behavior more effective.

A number of writers have said that giving and receiving feedback is one of the most important processes in group dynamics (Devine, 1976; DiBerardinis, 1978; Hanson, 1973; Lundgren & Schaeffer, 1976). Schein and Bennis (1965) have stated that practically all human learning is based on obtaining information about performance (feedback) and then determining how far the performance deviates from a desired goal. According to them, feedback shakes up or "unfreezes" people by creating a perceived threat to their self-concepts. The unfreezing process elicits a need for change. Support for this notion comes from a review of the T-group literature by Campbell and Dunnette (1968), who found that the reception of negative feedback stimulates a group member to alter his or her level of self-satisfaction and to try new behaviors.

Feedback is also a widely prescribed strategy in the management literature (Hackman & Oldham, 1976; Luthans & Kreitner, 1975; Tosi & Carroll, 1970). The utility of interpersonal feedback in the organization has been explained by several writers. For example, Myers and Myers (1973) state that in order to be effective in an organization, people need to know how their behavior impacts others. Solomon (1977) has stated:

> Feedback...can help an individual become more effective in his interpersonal relations, on-the-job behavior, and task accomplishment. If a person's behavior is not having desirable or intended effects, he can change it. Without feedback, the impact of his behavior on others may never be fully or accurately known. (p. 185)

Although feedback has many potential benefits, it also seems clear that it does not always work in practice. Pfeiffer and Jones (1972) have stated that unrestricted, untethered truth can create high levels of anxiety and cause persons to become less able to accomplish their goals; Solomon (1977) suggests that feedback can lead to long-term reprisals; Lundgren and Schaeffer (1976) found that negative feedback was often rejected by the recipient; and Gibb (1961) found that the ways in which messages typically are delivered in interpersonal situations tend to evoke defensiveness.

There are problems in transmitting as well as in receiving feedback. For example, substantial evidence shows that people try to avoid transmitting unpleasant messages (Blumberg, 1972; Fitts & Ravdin, 1953; Oken, 1961; Tesser & Rosen, 1975) and that if they cannot avoid giving feedback, people tend to distort it or make it more positive (Fisher, 1979; Tesser, Rosen, & Tesser, 1971).

A good deal of the literature on feedback is prescriptive in nature and not empirically validated (Argyris, 1962; Egan, 1975; Gibb, 1961; Hanson, 1975; Kurtz & Jones, 1973; Mill, 1976; Morris & Sashkin, 1976; Pfeiffer & Jones, 1972; Solomon, 1977). It suggests that there are certain rules for delivering feedback that will make the feedback more effective. The majority of these prescriptions concern the accuracy, focus, timing, objectivity, and validation of the transmission, that is, ensuring that the recipient receives the correct message. Keltner (1973) stresses:

> For any change to occur not only is feedback essential, but the synonymous meaning of the message must be shared by the generator and the receiver. (p. 97)

It seems likely, however, that accuracy of transmission is not the major cause of problems with the feedback process. Several writers have acknowledged that feedback can hurt people and lead to defensiveness and reprisals *despite skillful delivery* (Porter, 1974; Solomon, 1977). A second, largely unaddressed, problem with the feedback process has to do with the *willingness* of the recipient to utilize the feedback. Until this problem is resolved, feedback may remain underutilized and problematic in human systems. Therefore, this paper will now address the problem of willingness.

FEEDBACK AS PART OF A CHANGE PROCESS

Most of the literature views feedback as an input to help direct behavioral change (Budd, 1972; Hanson, 1975; Mill, 1976). However, the implication that change is necessary or desired evokes feelings about being controlled. According to Gibb (1961), a continual bombardment of persuasive messages from politicians, educators, special causes, advertising, religion, medical experts, and industrial relations and guidance counselors has resulted in cynical and paranoidal responses to messages that contain an element of control. Gibb also states that change messages convey implicit, esteem-reducing information that evokes defensive reactions.

> Implicit in all attempts to alter another person is the assumption by the change agent that the person to be altered is inadequate. That the speaker secretly views the listener as ignorant, unable to make his own decisions, uninformed, immature, unwise, or possessed of wrong or inadequate attitudes is a subconscious perception which gives the latter a valid base for defensive reactions. (p. 143)

Such resistance to change messages is not a new phenomenon; according to McGinnes and Ferster (1971):

> Ever since Machiavelli, and perhaps before, there has been a fear of control and manipulation of one person's behavior for the benefit of another. (p. 432)

The perspective of the behavioralist school also sheds light on why feedback may be a problematic process. According to the behavioralists, society primarily uses aversive or punishment-oriented control techniques (Luthans & Kreitner, 1975; Skinner, 1953). Thus, negative feelings that are associated with being controlled by aversive methods have become associated with any attempt to control behavior, even if the attempt is intended to be helpful.

POSITIVE AND NEGATIVE FEEDBACK

A second reason why change-oriented feedback may cause problems concerns the *focus* of the feedback. Although some writers emphasize that both positive and negative feedback can be given in a group context (Luthi, 1978; Solomon, 1977), the Schein and Bennis (1965) learning model clearly emphasizes that it is negative feedback that is disconfirming and causes unfreezing and the need for change to occur.

The emphasis on feeding back any negative information is strongly opposed by the behavioralists (Gambril, 1977; Luthans & Kreitner, 1975), who believe that the best way to create behavioral change is to focus on positive or desired behaviors and ignore undesirable behaviors. In their view, negative feedback probably constitutes a punishing experience for most people and can lead to detrimental side effects (e.g., anxiety, reduced performance, defensiveness, reprisal).

The counseling literature takes a similar view. Berenson and Mitchell (1969) have distinguished five major types of confrontation, including "strength" confrontation, focused on the confrontee's resources, and "weakness" confrontation, focused on the confrontee's pathology or liabilities. Their research indicates that effective helpers use strength confrontations more frequently and weakness confrontations less frequently than ineffective helpers.

FEEDBACK AND VALUES

The difficulties of the feedback process can be understood further by considering the issue of values. A person who sets a thermostat decides on a "good" temperature. The thermostat does not care. However, in human systems, there often is more than one definition of the desirable state. A discussion and clarification not only of behaviors but also of conflicting *values* often is required. If, for example, there is consensus among group members that it is good to be assertive and members of the group provide feedback about certain behaviors of an unassertive member, the information could help the receiver to become more assertive. If, however, the values of those providing the feedback are not accepted as correct, the feedback may indicate a need to examine the system as a whole. It may be that the "unassertive" individual's values are of a higher order than those of the other members of the group. It also may be that the person who initiated the feedback could benefit from examining his or her reactions to "unassertive" persons.

HELPING OR CONFLICT MANAGEMENT?

Another difficulty in the feedback process has to do with whether feedback is perceived as part of a helping or conflict-management process. In most group situations, the people sending feedback probably see themselves in helping roles whereas, in reality, their position may be better described as being in conflict with the other persons. That is, if one person experiences a drive to send feedback to another person, it usually is because he feels that there is something bothersome or wrong with the other person's behavior. It is probably for these reasons that Rogers (1970) prefers to use the term "confrontation" for encounter situations in which people give one another feedback and why Egan's (1970) definition of confrontation is so similar to what others have called feedback:

> Confrontation takes place when one person, either deliberately or inadvertently, does something that causes or directs another person to reflect upon, examine, question, or change some aspect of his behavior. (p. 295)

When conflict-oriented feedback is sent in the guise of a helping gesture, there is a problem for both sender and receiver. The sender-helper is certain that the problem rests with the other and that the solution is for the other to change. Thus, he fails to examine his own values and behavior. The problem is compounded because the would-be helper is frustrated when the recipient-helpee indicates an unwillingness to accept the information and to change her behavior.

On the other side, although the receiver may feel grateful because of the attention or intention to help, she probably also feels hurt and resentful because she senses that she is being criticized and that a behavior that is comfortable for her is being attacked.

A skilled helper should be able to distinguish between conflict and helping feedback. According to Egan (1975), conflictual feedback stems from a discrepancy between the sender's values and the values and behaviors of the recipient. Helping feedback is based on the discrepancies between the *recipient's* values and behaviors. People who attempt to give feedback in either group or organizational contexts are unlikely to be operating at this level of sophistication. In fact, they simply accept the trainer's implicit suggestion that feedback is "helpful" and, thus, think of themselves as helpers.

In summary, little attention has been paid to the willingness of the recipient of feedback to change his or her behavior. Unwillingness may stem from several factors: whether the recipient perceives the feedback as control, whether the feedback is positive or negative, whether the feedback is based on the sender's or receiver's values, and whether the feedback is described as "help" when it would better be described as "conflict."

RECOMMENDATIONS

If the points made in this article are accepted, prescriptions that have been suggested elsewhere for making the feedback process more effective can be expanded and, in some cases, should be modified.

First, people giving feedback should be able to distinguish between conflict-based feedback and helping-oriented feedback. If the feedback is conflict-based, a conflict-resolution process should be utilized. The feedback then merely would be the start of an examination by both the initiator and the recipient to examine the behavior in question with respect to their different value systems. The resolution could entail a change of attitude or behavior on the part of either the initiator or the recipient or both. Although accuracy of transmission is important, it is *less* important than the recognition that the situation is conflictual. Gordon's (1970) system of Parent Effectiveness Training, Gibb's (1961) Problem Orientation, and Harris' (1969) Transactional Analysis model are all examples of conflict-management processes based on these premises.

Second, some behaviors that would be appropriate in a helping situation would be inappropriate in a conflict situation. For example, consensual validation by others in a conflict situation would be likely to be thought of as interference and could hinder the resolution of the conflict.

Third, in either a conflict or a helping situation, an effort to reinforce desired behaviors and ignore undesirable behaviors would probably be more effective than describing, and thus implicitly criticizing, undesirable behaviors.

Fourth, in *any* feedback situation, it should be acknowledged that the feedback is likely to evoke negative affect and feelings of resistance. The message that feedback is growthful and therefore something that one should gracefully accept denies the reality of the situation and compounds the problem by placing the recipient in a double bind.

Fifth, in a conflict-based situation, the sender of the feedback may well use the urge to send feedback as the beginning of a self-examination that may lead to a change in his or her own attitudes or behavior. This person then may or may not choose to send the feedback.

In summary, problems with the use of feedback in human systems stem from two sources: the difficulty in transmitting messages accurately and the degree of willingness of the recipient to use the transmitted information. The literature deals primarily with techniques for transmission and largely ignores the issue of willingness of receipt. The suggestions in this article for modifying and adding to the prescriptions for users of the feedback process provide an area for further exploration of the use of feedback in group and organizational settings.

REFERENCES

Argyris, C. *Interpersonal competence and organizational effectiveness.* Homewood, IL: Dorsey Press, 1962.

Berenson, B. G., & Mitchell, K. *Confrontation in counseling and life.* Unpublished manuscript, American International College, Springfield, MA, 1969.

Blumberg, H. H. Communication of interpersonal evaluations. *Journal of Personality and Social Psychology*, 1972, *23*, 157-162.

Budd, R. W. Encounter groups: An approach to human communication. In R. W. Budd & B. D. Ruben (Eds.), *Approaches to human communication.* Rochelle Park, NJ: Hayden, 1972.

Campbell, J. D., & Dunnette, M. D. Effectiveness of T-group experience in managerial training and development. *Psychological Bulletin*, 1968, *70*, 73-104.

Devine, D. A. Interpersonal feedback as consensual validation of constructs. In J. W. Pfeiffer & J. E. Jones (Eds.), *The 1976 annual handbook for group facilitators.* San Diego, CA: University Associates, 1976.

DiBerardinis, J. P. The effects of videotape feedback on group and self-satisfaction. *Group & Organization Studies*, 1978, *3*(1), 108-114.

Egan, G. *Encounter: Group process for interpersonal growth.* Monterey, CA: Brooks/Cole, 1970.

Egan, G. *The skilled helper.* Monterey, CA: Brooks/Cole, 1975.

Fisher, C. D. Transmission of positive and negative feedback to subordinates: A laboratory investigation. *Journal of Applied Psychology,* 1979, *64*(5), 533-540.

Fitts, W. T., & Ravdin, I. S. What Philadelphia physicians tell their patients with cancer. *Journal of the American Medical Association,* 1953, *153,* 901-908.

Gambril, E. D. *Behavior modification: Handbook of assessment, intervention, and evaluation.* San Francisco: Jossey-Bass, 1977.

Gibb, J. R. Defensive communication. *Journal of Communication,* 1961, *11*(3), 141-148.

Gordon, T. *Parent effectiveness training.* New York: Wyden, 1970.

Hackman, J. R., & Oldham, G. R. Motivation through the design of work: Test of a theory. *Organization Behavior and Human Performance,* 1976, *16,* 250-279.

Hanson, P. C. The johari window: A model for soliciting and giving feedback. In J. E. Jones & J. W. Pfeiffer (Eds.), *The 1973 annual handbook for group facilitators.* San Diego, CA: University Associates, 1973.

Hanson, P. G. Giving feedback: An interpersonal skill. In J. E. Jones & J. W. Pfeiffer (Eds.), *The 1975 annual handbook for group facilitators.* San Diego, CA: University Associates, 1975.

Harris, T. *I'm ok, you're ok.* New York: Harper & Row, 1969.

Keltner, J. W. *Elements of interpersonal communication.* Belmont, CA: Wadsworth, 1973.

Kurtz, R. R., & Jones, J. E. Confrontation: Types, conditions, and outcomes. In J. E. Jones & J. W. Pfeiffer (Eds.), *The 1973 annual handbook for group facilitators.* San Diego, CA: University Associates, 1973.

Lundgren, D. C., & Schaeffer, C. Feedback processes in sensitivity training groups. *Human Relations,* 1976, *29*(8), 763-782.

Luthans, F., & Kreitner, R. *Organization behavior modification.* Glenview, IL: Scott, Foresman, 1975.

Luthi, J. R. Cards: Personal feedback. In J. W. Pfeiffer & J. E. Jones (Eds.), *The 1978 annual handbook for group facilitators.* San Diego, CA: University Associates, 1978.

McGinnes, E., & Ferster, C. *The reinforcement of social behavior.* Boston, MA: Houghton-Mifflin, 1971.

Mill, C. R. Feedback: The art of giving and receiving help. In L. Porter & C. R. Mill (Eds.), *Reading book for human relations training.* Washington, DC: NTL Institute for Applied Behavioral Science, 1976.

Morris, W. C., & Sashkin, M. Feedback: Helping others learn to share information. *Organization behavior in action.* St. Paul, MN: West, 1976.

Myers, G. E., & Myers, M. T. *The dynamics of human communication: A laboratory approach.* New York: McGraw-Hill, 1973.

Oken, D. What to tell cancer patients. *Journal of the American Medical Association,* 1961, *175,* 1120-1128.

Pfeiffer, J. W., & Jones, J. E. Openness, collusion, and feedback. In J. W. Pfeiffer & J. E. Jones (Eds.), *The 1972 annual handbook for group facilitators.* San Diego, CA: University Associates, 1972.

Porter, L. A longer look at feedback: Skill building for senders and receivers. *Social Change,* 1974, *4*(3), 122-124.

Rogers, C. R. *Encounter groups.* New York: Harper & Row, 1970.

Ruben, B. D. General system theory: An approach to human communication. In R. W. Budd & B. D. Ruben (Eds.), *Approaches to human communication.* Rochelle Park, NJ: Hayden, 1972.

Schein, E. H., & Bennis, W. G. *Personal and organizational change through group methods: The laboratory approach.* New York: John Wiley, 1965.

Skinner, B. F. *Science and human behavior.* New York: Macmillan, 1953.

Solomon, L. N. Team development: A training approach. In J. E. Jones & J. W. Pfeiffer (Eds.), *The 1977 annual handbook for group facilitators.* San Diego, CA: University Associates, 1977.

Tesser, A., & Rosen, S. The reluctance to transmit bad news. In L. Berkowitz (Ed.), *Advances in experimental social psychology* (Vol. 8). New York: Academic Press, 1975.

Tesser, A., Rosen, S., & Tesser, M. On the reluctance to communicate undesirable messages: A field study. *Psychological Reports,* 1971, *29,* 651-654.

Tosi, H. L., & Carroll, S. Management by objectives. *Personnel Administration,* 1970, *33,* 44-48.

Raymond V. Rasmussen, Ph.D., is an associate professor of organizational behavior on the Faculty of Business at the University of Alberta in Edmonton, Canada. He specializes in training and organization development and is a founding member of The Training and Development Associates of Alberta. Dr. Rasmussen also writes and does research in the areas of teaching and small-group behavior.

NEUROLINGUISTIC PROGRAMMING: A RESOURCE GUIDE AND REVIEW OF THE RESEARCH

Donald William McCormick

"I can detect radar," claims Richard Bandler, a co-founder of neurolinguistic programming (NLP), the highly popular new intervention method in the field of human behavior. Another founder, John Grinder, claims that he can cure a phobia in ten minutes and can teach an amateur chess player to play chess like Karpov. People who use neurolinguistic programming extol its effectiveness in such areas as therapy, organization development, training, education, sales, negotiation, and hypnosis. They claim that NLP can improve abilities. As Ager (1980) puts it, "The ostensible results [are]. . . better spellers, winning verdicts, bigger sales commissions, more efficient employees, fuller love affairs, and many other good things."

Neurolinguistic programming is being used by an increasing number of professionals in a wide variety of contexts. It has been used in the Pentagon. It is taught internationally, and a book by Bandler, Grinder, and Satir (1976) has been translated into Dutch, Swedish, and German. This author used NLP while doing OD in the Carter White House. Don Novello, who portrays Father Guido Sarducci on television, even makes jokes about "neurolinguini."

Even among people who know that NLP exists, the majority are not aware of the empirical research studies on NLP. Some of these are supportive and some are damning; many are critical for those who use or are considering using NLP in their practice; and a few, although not critical, are quite interesting. For example, it recently has been shown that some people *can* hear radar (Kendig, 1982).

This article is *not* an introduction to NLP; several good ones already exist (see Goleman, 1979, or Laborde, 1982a). Rather, this article will provide a bibliography of NLP resources—books and their reviews, articles, tapes, software, and NLP institutes—and will summarize and draw some conclusions from the disparate and sometimes conflicting research on NLP.

RESOURCE GUIDE

BOOKS ON NLP AND THEIR REVIEWS

Two of the better-known reviewers are John Weakland, a communications theorist from the Palo Alto group, and Jacqui Schiff, a TA therapist. Kitty LaPerriere (1979)[1] offers a good criticism of Cameron-Bandler's (1978) book that actually applies to NLP as a whole:

> [This book] touches on the increasing preoccupation of family therapists with rapid, specific, nonproblematic behavior change and an equating of such change with the totality of the therapeutic experience. If there are conflicts, values, concerns, and dilemmas encountered in the process of therapy that do not lend themselves to an easy a priori decision by the therapist as to what should be fixed and how it should be fixed, that part of the process is not touched, not by Cameron-Bandler any more than by many family therapy schools. (p. 493)

---

[1]From "They Lived Happily Ever After," a review by K. LaPerriere in *Family Process*, 1979, Volume 18, p. 493. Used with permission.

Bandler, R., & Grinder, J. *The structure of magic I: A book about language and therapy.* Palo Alto, CA: Science & Behavior Books, 1975.

Reviews

Bricklin, B., & Bricklin, P. M. *Journal of Learning Disabilities,* 1977, *10,* 61.
Buckalew, M. W. *ETC.,* December 1976, p. 461.
Kadis, L. *Family Process,* 1976, *15,* 265-266.
Schiff, J. L. *Transactional Analysis Journal,* 1978, *8,* 44.
St. Clair, R. N. *Bulletin of the Menninger Clinic,* 1977, *41,* 405.

Bandler, R., & Grinder, J. *Patterns of the hypnotic techniques of Milton H. Erickson, M.D.* (Vol. 1). Cupertino, CA: Meta Publications, 1975.

Reviews

Bustya, C. *International Journal of Clinical and Experimental Hypnosis,* 1978, *26,* 351.
Weakland, J. H. *The American Journal of Clinical Hypnosis,* 1976, *19,* 129.

Bandler, R., & Grinder, J. *Frogs into princes.* Moab, UT: Real People Press, 1979.

Review

Gladfelter, J. *International Journal of Group Psychotherapy,* 1980, *30,* 373.

Bandler, R., & Grinder, J. *Trance-formations: Neuro-linguistic programming and the structure of hypnosis.* Moab, UT: Real People Press, 1981.

Bandler, R., Grinder, J., & Satir, V. *Changing with families.* Palo Alto, CA: Science & Behavior Books, 1976.

Review

Gordon, E. L. *Family Process,* 1977, *16,* 525-526.

Cameron-Bandler, L. *They lived happily ever after: A book about achieving happy endings in coupling.* Cupertino, CA: Meta Publications, 1978.

Reviews

Barth, J. C. *Journal of Marital and Family Therapy,* July 1980, p. 360.
LaPerriere, K. *Family Process,* 1979, *18,* 493.

Chong, D. K. *Auto-hypnotic pain control: The Milton model.* New York: Carlton Press, 1979.

Dilts, R. *Applications of neuro-linguistic programming: A practical guide to communication, learning, and change.* Cupertino, CA: Meta Publications, 1983.

Dilts, R. *Roots of neuro-linguistic programming: A reference guide to the technology of NLP.* Cupertino, CA: Meta Publications, 1983.

Dilts, R. B., Grinder, J., Bandler, R., DeLozier, J., & Cameron-Bandler, L. *Neuro-linguistic programming I.* Cupertino, CA: Meta Publications, 1979.

Gordon, D. *Therapeutic metaphors: Helping others through the looking glass.* Cupertino, CA: Meta Publications, 1978.

Review

Ackerman, B. L. *Journal of Marital and Family Therapy*, January 1980, p. 95.

Gordon, D., & Meyers-Anderson, M. *Phoenix: Therapeutic patterns of Milton H. Erickson.* Cupertino, CA: Meta Publications, 1982.

Grinder, J., & Bandler, R. *Reframing: NLP and the transformation of meaning.* Moab, UT: Real People Press, 1982.

Grinder, J., & Bandler, R. *The structure of magic II.* Palo Alto, CA: Science & Behavior Books, 1976.

Reviews

Barth, J. C. *Journal of Marital and Family Therapy*, January 1980, pp. 95-96.

Edwards, D. G. *Clinical Social Work Journal*, 1978, *6*, 251-252.

Kadis, L. B. *Family Process*, 1977, *16*, 133-135.

Shedletsky, L. J. *Quarterly Journal of Speech*, December 1979, pp. 454-455.

Grinder, J., Bandler, R., & DeLozier, J. *Patterns of hypnotic techniques of Milton H. Erickson* (Vol. 2). Cupertino, CA: Meta Publications, 1977.

Gunn, S. L. *Leisure counseling using NLP.* Stillwater, OK: International Society of Leisure Therapies, 1981.

Jacobson, S. *Meta-cation: Prescriptions for some ailing educational processes.* Cupertino, CA: Meta Publications, 1983.

Lankton, S. R. *Practical magic: The clinical applications of neuro-linguistic programming.* Cupertino, CA: Meta Publications, 1979.

Review

Eliasoph, E. *Journal of Group Psychotherapy, Psychodrama and Sociometry*, 1981, *34*, 148-151.

McMaster, M., & Grinder, J. *Precision: A new approach to communication (high quality information processing for business).* Los Angeles: Precision, 1980.

Richardson, J., & Margoulis, J. *The magic of rapport.* San Francisco: Harbor, 1981.

ARTICLES ON NLP

Laborde and Dillman's article on manipulation is worth reading, as is the column by Edwin Newman, the well-known commentator. He makes fun of the jargon that some NLP practitioners use.

A new, quarterly NLP newsletter called *The VAK* (for Visual, Kinesthetic, and Auditory) is available for $30.00 per year. The address is: 1430 Empire Central, Box 15, Dallas, TX 75247.

Ager, S. Manipulation: It's the...: How to get the response you're seeking. *San Jose Mercury and News.* January 8, 1980, p. 1D.

Andreas, C. Research review. *The VAK*, 1982, *1*(3), 1-2.

Andreas, C., & Andreas, S. Neuro-linguistic programming: A new technology for training. *Performance and Instruction Journal*, 1982, *21*(5), 37-39.

Andreas, C., & Andreas, S. NLP: A reply to Steven Schoen. *Psychotherapy Newsletter*, 1983, *1*(2), 19-24.

Anton, J. Mapping the mind with micros. *Electronic Education,* October 1982, p. 11.

Battino, R. The humanistic psychology movement and the teaching of chemistry. *Journal of Chemical Education,* 1983, *60*(3), 224-227.

Baum-Baicker, C., & deTorres, C. Sensory based target strokes. *Transactional Analysis Journal,* 1982, *12,* 195-196.

Burns, F., & Nelson, L. High performance programming: An operations model for a new age. *O E Communique: The Professional Organizational Effectiveness/Development Publication of the U.S. Army,* 1981, (5)2, 27.

Casella, P. Math strategy and spelling strategy for the Apple II. *Info World,* June 28, 1982, pp. 52-53.

Communicating more than meets the eye. *Nation's Business,* 1981, *69*(2), 72.

Cook, J. NLP could change your life. *The Reston Times,* June 10, 1982, p. C1.

Davis, S. L. R., & Davis, D. NLP and marital and family therapy. *Family Therapy Networker,* May-June 1982, p. 19.

Dillon, B. Values and helping school-age children. *Canada's Mental Health,* 1978, *26,* 7.

Dilts, R. *NLP in education.* Scotts Valley, CA: Behavioral Engineering, 1982.

Dilts, R. A. Let NLP work for you. *Real Estate Today,* February 1982, p. 21.

Edwards, S. Listening to the body-talk. *McLeans Magazine,* September 13, 1982, p. 54.

Executive skills: When they listen but do not hear. Research Institute of America, Personal Report for the Executive, December 4, 1979, p. 8.

Ferguson, M. NLP: A science for increasing "beneficial choices." *Brain Mind Bulletin,* June 21, 1982, *7*(11), 1-3.

Goleman, D. People who read people. *Psychology Today,* July 1979, p. 66.

Grinder, J., & McMaster, M. D. Use an "outcome frame" to produce results. *Successful Meetings,* March 1981, p. 99.

Haley, M. C. The eyes have it. *Real Estate Today,* February 1982, p. 24.

Hampton-Turner, C. The linguistics of therapy: Noam Chomsky, Richard Bandler and John Grinder. In C. Hampton-Turner, *Maps of the Mind.* New York: Collier Books, 1981.

Harman, R. L., & O'Neill, C. Neuro-linguistic programming for counselors. *Personnel and Guidance Journal,* March 1981, p. 449.

Hupp, D. Neuro-linguistic programming and unconscious learning. *Pathways,* Fall, 1981. (Available from the NLP Institute of D.C., 380 Maple Avenue West, Vienna, VA 22180.)

Hupp, D., & Singh, T. T. Meta programming and family therapy. *The Family Therapy Networker,* 1982, *6*(6), 28-31.

Hutchinson, M. Is NLP really magic?: An interview with Leslie Cameron-Bandler. *Wisconsin Counselor,* Spring 1982, p. 23.

Laborde, G. Z. Neuro-linguistic programming. *New Realities,* 1982a, *4*(1), 8.

Laborde, G. Z. Don't eat the menu. *New Realities,* 1982b, *4*(4), 14.

Laborde, G. Z., & Dillman, B. The structure of charisma: Playing with power and matches. *New Realities,* 1982, *4*(4), 8.

Lankton, S. R., Lankton, C. H., & Brown, M. Psychological level communication in transactional analysis. *The Transactional Analysis Journal,* 1981, *11,* 287-298.

The learning curve: Are they telling you the truth? *Electrical World,* 1980, *94*(1), 41.

Mace, S. The eyes have it: NLP learning theories inspire spelling program. *InfoWorld*, March 22, 1982, p. 8.

Mace, S. Neuro-linguistic programming breeds software. *InfoWorld*, 1983, *5*(8), p. 15.

Maron, D. Neurolinguistic programming: The answer to change? *Training and Development Journal*, 1979, *33*(10), 68.

Mathes, L. *Rapport: A workbook*. Vienna, VA: NLP of Washington, DC, 1982.

McCoy, R. Innovative system: Results with disabled children astonish educators, parents. *Rocky Mountain News*, May 26, 1981, p. 40.

McMaster, M. D., & Grinder, J. The art of communicating. *Administrative Management*, 1980, *41*, 56.

Moine, D. J., & Herd, J. H. Neuro-linguistic sales programming: The unfair advantage. *Personal Selling Power*, July-August 1983, pp. 6-7.

Morris, F. R., & Morris, D. G. *The meta system*. South Bend, IN: Center for Creative Change, undated.

NLP. *The Boston Globe*, May 4, 1981, p. 25.

Newman, E. Now for a leak in doublespeak. *The Cleveland Plain Dealer*, March 17, 1982, p. 19A. (Reprinted from *The New York Times*)

Oliver, B. Powerful patterns of persuasion. *The Toastmaster*, March 1982, pp. 25-27.

Rule, W. R. Family therapy and the pie metaphor. *Journal of Marital and Family Therapy*, 1983, *9*(1), 101-103.

Schoen, S. NLP: An overview. *Psychotherapy Newsletter*, 1983, *1*(1), 16-25.

Society of Neuro-Linguistic Programming. *Directory of practitioners, master practitioners and trainers, 1982*. Santa Cruz, CA: Not Ltd., 1982.

Stevens, B. Gestalt and neurolinguistic programming. *The Gestalt Journal*, 1978, *1*(2), 89-91.

Stevens, J. O. Neuro-linguistic programming (NLP) and Gestalt. *The Gestalt Journal*, 1978, *1*(2), 83-88.

Stevens, J. O. Neuro-linguistic programming. In R. Herink (Ed.), *The psychotherapy handbook*. New York: New American Library, 1980.

Tape leaves salesman in stitches. *San Francisco Examiner and Chronicle*, April 3, 1983, p. A5.

Taylor, C. L. Reading non-verbal cues: A key to manager-employee rapport? *Los Angeles Business Journal*, September 15, 1980, p. 423-425.

The, L. Self improvement: Beyond productivity. *Personal Computing*, July 1982, p. 89.

Thweatt, W. H. Effective permission-giving and representational systems. *Transactional Analysis Journal*, 1980, *10*(1), 53-55.

Varven, J. The schoolhouse apple. *Softalk*, May 1982, p. 36.

Waters, C. Richard Bandler: Epistemological magician. *Santa Cruz Express*, January 21, 1982, p. 6.

Wood, W. For them, mind, body are part of the same thing. *Santa Cruz Sentinel*, August 28, 1977, p. 25.

Vallance, K. Hypnotic techniques gain acceptance in business world. *The Christian Science Monitor*, October 28, 1982, p. 6.

Zemke, R. Neurolinguistic programming. *Training/HRD*, December 1979, p. 87.

NLP TAPES

Bandler, R., Reese, E., & Vzee, E. *Induction, utilization, & metaphors for change.* (Video books available from Hypnosis Vo-Cal Productions, P.O. Box 533, Indian Rocks Beach, FL 33535.)

Grinder, J. *Negotiation and mediation.* Santa Cruz, CA: Grinder, Delozier & Associates, 1982.

Grinder, J. *Patterns of organization.* Santa Cruz, CA: Grinder, Delozier & Associates, 1982.

Grinder, J., & Segal, M. *Feldenkrais and NLP.* Santa Cruz, CA: Grinder, Delozier & Associates, 1982.

Gunn, S. L. *NLP and the excellence principle.* (Audiovisual cassettes available from Excellence Unlimited, Inc., Route 2, Box 174, Stillwater, OK 74074.)

NLP COMPUTER SOFTWARE

All computer software is available from Behavioral Engineering, 230 Mt. Hermon Road, #207, Scotts Valley, CA 95066.

Communications Skills Packages

Complete NLP Tools, Volume I.
Includes the following (each may be ordered separately): Eyepilot, Eyeskating, Predicates, Predicate Analyzer, Utilization, Installation (Behavior Generator Strategy).

Complete NLP Tools, Volume II.
Strategy Elicitation, Precision Planner, Mind Reader (Calibration) & Anchoring, Creativity Strategy.

Learning Programs and Games

Typing Strategy
Letter Man
Beginning Composition Strategy
Composition Strategy: Your Creative Blockbuster
Math Strategy (see Casella, 1982)
Spelling Strategy

NLP CENTERS

Behavioral Engineering
230 Mount Hermon Road, #207
Scotts Valley, CA 95066
(408) 438-5649

Grinder, Delozier and Associates
197 Helen Street
Santa Cruz, CA 95065
(408) 475-8540

Massachusetts Institute of NLP
P.O. Box 426
Millis, MA 02054
(617) 376-4541

Eastern NLP Institute
P.O. Box 444
Washington Crossing, PA 18977
(215) 860-0911

Grinder, Laborde and Hill
1 World Trade Center, Suite 7967
New York, NY 10048
(212) 938-8957

Midwest Institute of NLP
1513 Miami
South Bend, IN 46613
(219) 232-1405

New York Training Institute for NLP
155 Prince Street
New York, NY 10012
(212) 473-2853

The NLP Center for Advanced Studies
340 Madrone Avenue
Larkspur, CA 94939
(415) 924-2925

NLP Institute of D.C.
380 Maple Avenue West
Vienna, VA 22180
(703) 255-2211

NLP of Southern California
4211 Glenalbyn Drive
Los Angeles, CA 90065
(213) 225-8386

The Society of
Neuro-Linguistic Programming
P.O. Box 981
Santa Cruz, CA 95061
(408) 425-0403

Southeast Center of NLP
4904 Waters Edge Drive, Suite 155
Raleigh, NC 27606
(919) 881-8688

NLP Canada
111 Woodfield Drive
Ottawa, Ontario, CANADA K2G 0A1
(613) 225-1686

NLP of Colorado
Left Hand Canyon, JSR
Boulder, CO 80302
(303) 442-1102

NLP Northwest
300 Vine Street
Seattle, WA 98121
(206) 622-0970

Ontario NLP Institute
48 Beveridge Drive
Don Mills, Ontario, CANADA M3A 1P3
(416) 444-9442

South Central Institute of NLP
P.O. Box 15757
New Orleans, LA 70175
(504) 895-3665

Southern Institute of NLP
P.O. Box 533
Indian Rock Beach, FL 33535
(813) 442-2855

REVIEW OF THE RESEARCH

Representational Systems

According to Grinder and Bandler (1976), people think primarily in terms of either pictures, feelings, or sounds, that is, visually, kinesthetically, or auditorally. These modes of thinking are called "representational systems." Each individual tends to prefer one mode over the others; this mode is called the person's "primary representational system" (PRS). People use certain kinds of predicates (adjectives, adverbs, and verbs) when speaking that indicate their representational systems.

For example, people with a visual PRS use phrases such as "I see what you mean" or "That is very clear," which indicate that the person is visualizing. People with a kinesthetic PRS use phrases such as "in touch with" or "get a grasp of," and people with an auditory PRS may say "I hear you" or "That sounds right." Most people have either a visual, kinesthetic, or auditory PRS.

The implication of this is that if you speak to someone who has a visual PRS using visual predicates, you will have greater rapport with that person because you will be "speaking his or her language." This implication may be important to counselors, managers, facilitators, trainers, and consultants.

Visuals, Kinesthetics, and Auditories

People with visual, kinesthetic, or auditory primary representational systems generally are referred to as "visuals," "kinesthetics," and "auditories."

In order to determine someone's PRS, one counts how many visual, kinesthetic, and auditory predicates the person uses in general speech. "Hear," "sound," "harmonious," "talk," and "purr" are examples of auditory predicates. "Feel," "hug," "touch," "smooth," and "soft" are examples of kinesthetic predicates. "Looks like," "see," "clear," and "picture" are examples of visual predicates. In classifying people by predicates, most researchers have found that the majority of their samples had a kinesthetic PRS: 88 percent of Falzett's (1979) sample, 81 percent of McCormick's (1975), 100 percent of Birholz' (1981), "most" of Johannsen's (1982), 61 percent of Owens' (1977), and 70 percent of Gumm, Walker, and Day's (1982). There seem to be substantially fewer visuals and auditories. Falzett (1981) found that between 1 to 12 percent of his sample were visuals or auditories; McCormick (1975) found that 16 percent were visuals and 3 percent were auditories; Birholz (1981) found no visuals or auditories; Owens (1977) found 39 percent visuals and no auditories; Gumm, Walker, and Day (1982) found 10 percent visuals and 20 percent auditories; and Mattar (1980) reported no auditories while Shaw (1977) reported no visuals.

In the mid-Seventies, Grinder and Bandler often spoke highly of auditories. They found themselves to be auditories, their prize students were often auditories, and they said that many other outstanding thinkers (such as Gregory Bateson) were auditories. Interestingly enough, the research shows some very complimentary correlations with auditory processing. Birholz (1981) found positive correlations between the use of auditory predicates and the California Psychological Inventory measures of well being, socialization, achievement via conformance, and intellectual efficiency. Brengle (1979) found that subjects who preferred auditory imagery reported fewer and less severe symptoms on a set of psychological tests. This supports the idea that auditories are either superior in some ways or are at least valued as such in our culture.

Representational System Tests

Use of predicates is not the only means of determining PRS. Grinder and Bandler (1979) state that not only can you infer that people are thinking visually when they use visual predicates, but you also can discover which representational system a person is thinking in by observing the person's eye movements. For example, you can infer that Joyce is thinking visually if she moves her eyes up and defocuses. Other researchers wondered whether you could determine someone's PRS from a self-report (questionnaire). If all three measures were valid, (predicates, eye movement, self-report), then all should indicate the same PRS for one person. Nine researchers studied combinations of the three methods.

Hernandez (1981) found some, but not a great deal of, agreement between the predicate and eye-movement methods. Falzett (1981) also reported that these two methods did not seem to agree very much. He found that counting predicates usually results in a disproportionate number of kinesthetics. This large proportion of kinesthetics is reported by Johannsen (1982); Birholz (1981); Owens (1977); Gumm, Walker, and Day (1982); and McCormick (1975) as well.

Four researchers used the self-report and predicate methods. Birholz (1981) found no match between self-reports and predicates. Johannsen (1982) found mostly kinesthetics when he used predicates and mostly "mixed sense types" using the *Survey of Mental Imagery*. Ellis (1980) found no significant correlation between self-ratings and predicates (except in auditory ratings and predicates). Pantin (1982) however, found "an extraordinarily powerful correspondence" between PRS determined by predicates and "self-report visual vs. auditory (verbal) imaginal style in activities of daily living."

Three researchers compared all three methods. Cole-Hitchcock (1980) created a written, multiple-choice measure of PRS. It agreed with an eye-movement test in measuring visuals and auditories but not kinesthetics. She found no relationship between the predicate measure and the other two measures.

Owens (1978) found significant agreement between predicates and eye movements. Self-report was found to be the least reliable means of determining PRS. Gumm, Walker, and Day (1982) reanalyzed Owens' data and questioned the statistical significance of the connection between predicates and eye movements. This is not surprising, considering that Gumm, Walker, and Day looked for agreement between *any* two of the three methods of ascertaining PRS and found *none*. They concluded that it is too difficult, and therefore impractical, to assess PRS.

There are other problems with the concept of PRS beyond the apparent inability to establish effective measures of it. What if someone uses the same number of visual and kinesthetic predicates? Often there is little difference in use between the PRS and the secondary representational system. Hammer (1983) says that half the time "the difference in frequency between PRS and the next most frequently used type was less than or equal to five predicates." In one study (McCormick, 1975) this occurred 19 percent of the time. Gumm, Walker, and Day (1982) found this, too. However, Pantin's (1982) research again confounds the situation. All 124 of her subjects had a PRS, and she used a rule that "required a spread of at least 20 percent of the total sensory predicates between the proportion of predicates in the dominant sensory modality and that in the next most frequently used modality." Thus, there are some real difficulties with the concept of PRS, which is so central to much of the early work and research in NLP.

How the PRS Affects the Practitioner in Action

Matching the client's predicates to achieve rapport. One of the key tasks of the practitioner is to gain the trust of the client. Grinder and Bandler (1976) say that using predicates that match the other person's representational system increases rapport and trust. The question is whether the results are worth the effort. There is evidence both pro and con, but there appears to be stronger evidence on the side of matching. Falzett (1979, 1981) found that clients see their counselors as more trustworthy when the counselors match the PRS (as determined by eye movements) of the clients. Frieden (1981) found partial support for the rapport hypothesis. The matching (as opposed to deliberate mismatching) of predicates increased eye contact from the client and, paradoxically, increased head-to-head distance. Even the more traditional counseling literature stresses the importance of building a therapeutic relationship by "speaking the client's language" (Hammer, 1983, p. 173).

There also is research that contradicts the NLP stance, although much of it is not as strong. For example, Rebstock (1980) found that training therapists to match predicates did not increase rapport with the clients they saw, but he is unsure what to conclude from this and admits that the study may have tested his particular training design, not necessarily the effectiveness of matching predicates. Ellickson (1980) had interviewers determine representational systems by eye movements and then match predicates. Men were markedly more at ease when their representational systems were matched, but women were not affected by matching.

Dowd and Pety (1982) played for their subjects two audio tapes of a counselor and a client interacting; the counselor matched predicates on one tape and mismatched on the other. The subjects rated the counselors on both tapes equally on expertise, attractiveness, trustworthiness, and the subjects' willingness to see the counselor. Pantin (1982), in contrast, showed subjects a transcript of a simulated therapy session in which the therapist's predicate use differed from the client's. Pantin found that a person evaluates another more positively if they share the same PRS and that interaction between people in which language preferences are congruent are evaluated more positively than those in which they are incongruent.

Hammer (1982) warns against interpreting too much from this type of study: "Care must be taken, however, in interpreting Dowd and Pety's study as a test of Bandler and Grinder's hypothesis, which would not necessarily predict increased trustworthiness in a subject who observed someone else's predicates being matched" (p. 174). The implication is that it would be a good idea for future researchers to discuss their designs with an NLP trainer or someone who is familiar with the latest NLP technology, in order that they actually will be researching NLP, not just their approximation of what it is.

Paxton (1980) found some of the most interesting disconfirming evidence using three treatments: matching, mismatching, and nonmatching. The nonmatching counselors infrequently used predicates that presuppose a representational system and, when they did, they changed the representational system frequently. Paxton found that it did not matter whether one matched or mismatched the client's PRS, *both* improved the client's perception of the relationship more than did nonmatching.

Green (1979) found that matching predicates did not increase the subjects' trust in the facilitator. She measured trust by self-disclosure (Jourard's *Questionnaire for Measuring Trust Between Subjects and Experimenters*). But Brockman's (1980) study countered by putting self-disclosure in the context of other measures. He found that counselors who matched predicates were perceived as more empathic by the subjects and by judges and were preferred by three to one over those who mismatched. Brockman is so convinced of the efficacy of matching predicates that he recommends that it be included in beginning courses in counseling and human relations. (Brockman used many standard psychological instruments; the only one that failed to show results was Jourard's measure of self-disclosure, the *Willingness-to-Disclose Questionnaire*.)

Hammer (1983) argues against using PRS as a basis for matching predicates. For example, although Joyce may classify Jonathan as kinesthetic, Jonathan may occasionally use auditory and visual predicates. If Joyce responds only with Jonathan's *primary* predicates, there will be mismatching when Jonathan uses auditory and visual predicates. When one examines sentences, phrases, and smaller units of interaction in these experiments, mismatching often occurs in the treatment group and matching occurs in the control group. This counterbalancing effect may be why researchers such as Paxton and Shaw failed to find an effect when they matched their subjects' PRS.

Hammer's counselors continually tracked and matched the predicates last used by their subjects. Hammer's studies show that tracked and matched subjects perceive more empathy from their counselors than do subjects with mismatched predicates. This was also found in an earlier study (Schmedlen, 1981), which found that clients perceive more empathic rapport with a counselor who tracks and matches the client's predicates than they do with a counselor who mismatches.

Thus, matching PRS is not as effective as tracking and matching predicates. The problems associated with the concept of PRS become irrelevant when predicates are tracked and matched.

Matching the client's predicates to increase relaxation. Three researchers have looked at the effects of matching predicates in work that requires relaxation—hypnosis, guided fantasy, and stress training. The results are mixed.

Yapko (1982) found that subjects who heard a hypnotic induction in which the predicates matched their PRS relaxed the most. The subjects who obtained the second greatest degree of relaxation heard an induction that matched their secondary representational system. The subjects who heard an induction that matched their tertiary representational system obtained the third greatest degree of relaxation—overall, a strong connection between matching PRS and hypnotic relaxation.

Kraft (1982), however, found that when he played relaxation tapes to clients, there was no difference in relaxation regardless of whether the tape matched or mismatched the clients' PRS.

Brengle (1979) developed an "Auditory-Visual Imagery Inventory" for his dissertation on representational systems. He provided forty people who held stressful jobs with one session of relaxation training and four systematic desensitization sessions, worded either auditorily or visually. There was no difference in the results of treatment for the matched and unmatched groups.

Matching the client's predicates to increase memory and comprehension. The studies on this topic are more supportive of matching PRS.

On the negative side, Shaw (1977) found that a person does not remember more from a videotaped story if it is told in his or her PRS. But Pantin (1982) found that performance on standard memory tasks "was facilitated when the mode of item presentation was congruent with the subjects' [PRS]."

Mattar (1980) found that visuals and kinesthetics better comprehended questions containing predicates that matched their PRS.

Eye Movement, Cognitive Strategies, and Representational Systems. Many recent NLP models focus on cognitive strategies for learning, motivation, remembering, spelling, decision making, and many other processes. When a neurolinguistic programmer uncovers a strategy, he or she examines the *sequence* of thoughts. For example, in trying to decide how to spell a word, a person may think of how the word sounds and try to determine each letter from the sound.

A neurolinguistic programmer might teach the strategy of *picturing* the word and checking to see if it feels right. This new sequence would be a visual image followed by an internal feeling. Spelling is a relatively trivial example, but strategies for learning, motivation, and decision making can also be improved by using NLP.

According to Grinder and Bandler (1979), eye movements can indicate whether a person is having visual, kinesthetic, or auditory thoughts. For example, a person may move his eyes up and to the right before answering a question. A neurolinguistic programmer would deduce that the person is looking for the answer by making an internal picture. In 1979, Grinder and Bandler said that most right-handed people experience a visual thought when they move their eyes upward, an auditory thought when they move their eyes to either side or down and to the right, and a kinesthetic thought when they move their eyes down and to the left. Most of the research, however, does not seem to support this.

Beale (1981) found that the predominant eye movements in his subjects were in an upward direction, regardless of the stimulus provided. "Richardson found that upward eye movements may be associated with being interviewed by a female" (Hammer, 1983, p. 174). Thomason, Arbuckle, and Cady (1980) also found that most eye movements were upward. They asked subjects questions that required them to either visualize an image, mentally hear a sound, or feel a sensation. These questions apparently did not influence eye movements. Connierae Andreas (1983), a prominent member of the NLP community, found that subjects looked up and to the left more frequently when asked questions relating to visual memory. Andreas found only minimal connections between down-left eye movements and auditory processing. She found no *other* relationships between eye movements and modes of thought.

Cameron-Bandler (Hutchinson, 1982) points out that, in NLP research, the experimenter's voice timbre or eye movements may influence the subject.

Recently, NLP teachers have backed off from saying that a particular eye movement indicates a particular representational system for any large group of people although some maintain that each person has a consistent pattern of his or her own. In an undocumented study, this author asked people questions that demanded that the subjects *remember* sounds, pictures, and feelings and also *construct* internal sounds, pictures, and feelings. I videotaped their eyes, coded the results, and found that individuals did *not* have consistent patterns of their own for accessing visual, kinesthetic, or auditory information. Because such patterns are not evident in laboratory studies, I doubt that they would be evident in face-to-face interactions. Thus, I do not find the model of eye movements to be useful.

NLP as an Analytic Tool

Although one body of NLP research is connected to representational systems, another body of research uses NLP models to examine the differences between well- and poorly functioning human systems. The researchers analyzed families, couples, people under stress, and salespeople.

Macroy (1978) used a high-school yearbook to obtain a sample of families and compared the more satisfied with the less satisfied families. The NLP model used is called the meta-model (Bandler & Grinder, 1975). It states that problems often occur when people's models of their situation are lacking because they delete information, distort information, overgeneralize, or engage in patterns of thinking called "semantic ill formedness." There are three types of semantic ill formedness: (a) claiming that you know what someone else is thinking without having been told, (b) believing that someone *makes* you feel something, and (c) talking in a manner that indicates that you are being excessively judgmental. These are reflected in a person's language. Macroy predicted that the less satisfied families would use more deletion, distortion, generalization, and semantic ill formedness. In fact, he found only that they deleted more.

Wilimek (1979) used representational systems to analyze the differences between high- and low-adjustment couples. Married couples were divided into two groups based on their scores from the *Dyadic Adjustment Scale*. Wilimek counted their predicates as they described satisfying and upsetting experiences and also gave them a test of mental imagery. He found that "married people become more aware of auditory experience when they are upset (particularly low adjustment wives), and less aware of their visual experience. Also, spouses in high adjustment marriages become more aware of their feelings when upset, while individuals in low adjustment marriages do not become more aware of their feelings."

Johannsen (1982) examined the predicates of people who had recently undergone many stressful incidents to see if they were restricted to fewer representational systems and found that they were not.

Don Juan Moine's (1981) dissertation analyzed the linguistic differences between superior and mediocre salespeople, using the categories Grinder and Bandler (1975) developed in their analysis of the hypnotist Milton Erickson. Moine (1982) reported his findings in *Psychology Today*. In short, "Superior sellers use the techniques of the clinical hypnotists, mediocre ones do not" (p. 52).

Hagstrom (1981) used the linguistic categories developed in *The Structure of Magic, Volume I* (Bandler & Grinder, 1975) to chart changes over time in schizophrenics, but did not study NLP per se.

Ellis (1980) compared the predicates used by students studying art, physical education, and music. Art students described themselves as more visual on a self-report and used more visual predicates. Music students did *not* describe themselves as more auditory but they did use more auditory predicates. Physical education students did not describe themselves as more kinesthetic nor did they use more kinesthetic predicates.

Three Questions

A few studies help to answer three questions of concern to the practitioner who is interested in NLP.

The first concerns the meta-model. This model states how people impoverish their models of the world and also presents a series of questions, based on sentence structures, to be used in recovering the information that was deleted, distorted, lost through overgeneralization, or lost through semantic ill formedness. These questions can be used by a counselor, an OD consultant, or any interviewer who is presented with a version of something that he or she finds vague, hard to comprehend, overly abstract, or somehow lacking.

Ligget (1977) trained people in this "well formed in therapy" model. He found that using the model increased a counselor's abilities "to respond to the core concerns as expressed in the clients' statements and to recognize ambiguity in the clients' statements," but the counselor who used the model generated fewer alternatives than did the control-group counselors.

The next question is whether a hypnotist should use the induction and change techniques suggested in *Patterns of the Hypnotic Techniques of Milton H. Erickson, M.D.: Volume I* (Bandler & Grinder, 1975). Many of these techniques utilize the differences between the right and left brains. Carter, Elkins, and Kraft (1982) did not directly test Bandler and Grinder's model but they did review the right/left brain literature and concluded that "Much of the data is supportive of the models presented by Bandler and Grinder (1975). . . ."

The final question is whether NLP can be used to cure phobias. Allen (1982) tested one group of snake phobics who received no treatment, one group that received a single session of massed systematic desensitization, and one group that received the NLP phobia cure. He compares the NLP group to the other groups: "While NLP treatment subjects neither completed more snake approach tasks nor reported less fear while performing these tasks, they *did* report more frequently that they *thought* they were over their fear of snakes" [italics mine].

CONCLUSION

According to the research on NLP: (a) if you judge by predicates, there are more kinesthetics, but the auditories are better off; (b) the three types of tests do not often agree on PRS, but the concept of PRS is unwieldy anyway; (c) tracking and matching predicates is good for establishing rapport; (d) it is unclear whether matching clients' predicates helps them to relax, but it probably helps clients to remember and understand; (e) when people move their eyes upward and to the left, they may be remembering a picture, but most of the early NLP standardized guides to understanding the meaning of eyeball movements are apparently worthless; (f) less-satisfied families delete more, and well-adjusted couples become more aware of feelings when upset; (g) effective salespeople use hypnotic techniques; (h) music and art students are a bit more auditory and visual; (i) the "well formed in therapy" model is good for cutting through ambiguity and getting to core concerns; and, finally, (j) the phobia cure does not really work, but the clients do not seem to know it.

Obviously, little of the research to date has proven the validity or lack of validity of NLP.

A BIBLIOGRAPHY OF RESEARCH ON NLP

Allen, K. L. Neurolinguistic programming procedures in treating snake phobics. (Doctoral dissertation, University of Missouri-Kansas City, 1982). *Dissertation Abstracts International*, 1982, *43*(3), 861B.

Andreas, C. *The relationship of eye movements while information processing to sensory mode.* Unpublished doctoral dissertation, University of Colorado, 1983.

Appel, R. R. Matching of representational systems and interpersonal attraction. (Doctoral dissertation, United States International University, 1983). *Dissertation Abstracts International*, 1983, *43*(9), 3021B.

Beale, R. The testing of a model for the representation of consciousness. (Doctoral dissertation, The Fielding Institute, 1980). *Dissertation Abstracts International*, 1981, *41*(9), 3565B.

Birholz, L. S. Neurolinguistic programming: Testing some basic assumptions. (Doctoral dissertation, The Fielding Institute, 1981). *Dissertation Abstracts International*, 1981, *43*(5), 2042B.

Brengle, E. Q. Preference for sensory modality of mental imagery and its relationship to stress reduction using a systematic desensitization technique. (Doctoral dissertation, Wayne State University, 1979). *Dissertation Abstracts International*, 1979, *40*(4), 1878B.

Brockman, W. P. Empathy revisited: The effect of representational system matching on certain counseling process and outcome variables. (Doctoral dissertation, The College of William and Mary in Virginia, 1980). *Dissertation Abstracts International*, 1981, *41*(8), 3421A.

Carter, B. D., Elkins, G. R., & Kraft, S. P. Hemispheric asymmetry as a model for hypnotic phenomena: A review and analysis. *The American Journal of Clinical Hypnosis*, 1982, *24*, 204-210.

Cole-Hitchcock, S. T. A determination of the extent to which a predominant representational system can be identified through written and verbal communication and eye scanning patterns. (Doctoral dissertation, Baylor University, 1980). *Dissertation Abstracts International*, 1980, *41*(5), 1908B.

Dilts, R. B. Individual baseline EEG patterns and NLP representational systems. In R. B. Dilts, J. Grinder, R. Bandler, J. DeLozier, & L. Cameron-Bandler, *Neuro-linguistic programming* (Volume 1). Cupertino, CA: Meta Publications, 1980.

Dowd, E. T., & Pety, J. Effect of counselor predicate matching on perceived social influence and client satisfaction. *The Journal of Counseling Psychology*, 1982, *29*, 206-209.

Ellickson, J. L. The effect of interviewers responding differentially to subjects' representational systems as indicated by eye movement. (Doctoral dissertation, Michigan State University, 1980). *Dissertation Abstracts International*, 1981, *41*(7), 2754B.

Ellickson, J. L. Representational systems and eye movements in an interview. *Journal of Counseling Psychology*, 1983, *30*, 339-345.

Ellis, J. L. Representation systems: An investigation of sensory predicate use in a self-disclosure interview. (Doctoral dissertation, University of Minnesota, 1980). *Dissertation Abstracts International*, 1981, *41*(11), 4244B.

Falzett, W. C. Matched versus unmatched primary representational systems and their relationship to perceived trustworthiness in a counseling analogue. (Doctoral dissertation, Marquette University, 1979). *Dissertation Abstracts International*, 1980, *41*(1), 105A.

Falzett, W. C. Matched versus unmatched primary representational systems and their relationship to perceived trustworthiness in a counseling analogue. *Journal of Counseling Psychology*, 1981, *28*, 305-308.

Frieden, F. P. Speaking the client's language: The effects of neuro-linguistic programming (predicate matching) on verbal and nonverbal behaviors in psychotherapy—A single case design. (Doctoral dissertation, Virginia Commonwealth University, 1981). *Dissertation Abstracts International*, 1981, *42*(3), 1171B.

Green, M. A. Trust as effected by representational system predicates. (Doctoral dissertation, Ball State University, 1979). *Dissertation Abstracts International*, 1981, *41*(8), 3159B.

Gumm, W. B., Walker, M. K., & Day, H. D. Neurolinguistics [sic] programming: Method or myth? *Journal of Counseling Psychology*, 1982, *29*, 327-330.

Hagstrom, G. Microanalysis of direct confrontation psychotherapy with schizophrenics: Using neurolinguistic programming and Delsarte's system of expression. (Doctoral dissertation, California School of Professional Psychology, 1981). *Dissertation Abstracts International*, 1982, *42*(10), 4192B.

Hammer, A. L. Matching perceptual predicates: Effect on perceived empathy in a counseling analogue. *Journal of Counseling Psychology*, 1983, *30*, 172-179.

Hernandez, V. O. A study of eye movement patterns in the neurolinguistic programming model. (Doctoral dissertation, Ball State University, 1981). *Dissertation Abstracts International*, 1981, *42*(4), 1587B.

Hutchinson, M. Is NLP really magic?: An interview with Leslie Cameron-Bandler. *Wisconsin Counselor*, Spring 1982, p. 23.

Johannsen, C. A. Predicates, mental imagery in discrete sense modes, and levels of stress: The neurolinguistic programming typologies. (Doctoral dissertation, United States International University, 1982). *Dissertation Abstracts International*, 1982, *43*(8), 2709B.

Kendig, F. Listening to radar. *Psychology Today*, 1982, *16*(12), 80.

Kraft, W. A. The effects of primary representational system congruence on relaxation in a neurolinguistic programming model. (Doctoral dissertation, Texas A & M University, 1982). *Dissertation Abstracts International*, 1983, *43*(7), 2372B.

Lange, D. E. A validity study of the construct "most highly valued representational system" in human auditory and visual perceptions. (Doctoral dissertation, Louisiana State University, 1980). *Dissertation Abstracts International*, 1981, *41*(11), 4266B.

Liggett, K. R. The effects of a linguistic training model and counselor conceptual complexity on counseling skills. (Doctoral dissertation, University of Nebraska-Lincoln, 1977). *Dissertation Abstracts International*, 1978, *38*(8), 3853B.

Lucas, B. A. The effectiveness of unimodal vs. bimodal sensory feedback for males and females in a finger temperature training task. (Doctoral dissertation, Kansas State University, 1979). *Dissertation Abstracts International*, 1980, *41*(1), 399B.

Macroy, T. D. Linguistic surface structure in family interaction. (Doctoral dissertation, Utah State University, 1978). *Dissertation Abstracts International*, 1979, *40*(2), 926B.

Mattar, A. T. Primary representational systems as a basis for improved comprehension and communication. (Doctoral dissertation, Utah State University, 1980). *Dissertation Abstracts International*, 1981, *41*(8), 3162B.

McCormick, D. W. *Primary representational systems and Satir coping styles*. Unpublished paper, The University of California at Santa Cruz, 1975.

Moine, D. J. A psycholinguistic study of the patterns of persuasion used by successful salespeople. (Doctoral dissertation, University of Oregon, 1981). *Dissertation Abstracts International*, 1981, *42*(5), 2135B.

Moine, D. J. To trust, perchance to buy. *Psychology Today*, August 1982, pp. 50-54.

Owens, L. F. An investigation of eye movements and representational systems. (Doctoral dissertation, Ball State University, 1977). *Dissertation Abstracts International*, 1978, *38*(10), 4992B.

Pantin, H. M. The relationship between subjects' predominant sensory predicate use, their preferred representational system and self-reported attitudes towards similar versus different therapist-patient dyads. (Doctoral dissertation, University of Miami, 1982). *Dissertation Abstracts International*, 1983, *43*(7), 2350B.

Paxton, L. D. Representational systems and client perception of the counseling relationship. (Doctoral dissertation, Indiana University, 1980). *Dissertation Abstracts International*, 1981, *41*(9), 3888A.

Rebstock, M. E. The effects of training in matching techniques on the development of rapport between client and counselor during initial counseling interviews. (Doctoral dissertation, University of Missouri-Kansas City, 1980). *Dissertation Abstracts International*, 1980, *41*(3), 946A.

Schmedlen, G. W. The impact of sensory modality matching on the establishment of rapport in psychotherapy. (Doctoral dissertation, Kent State University, 1981). *Dissertation Abstracts International*, 1981, *42*(5), 2080B.

Shaw, D. L. Recall as effected by the interaction of presentation representational system and primary representational system. (Doctoral dissertation, Ball State University, 1977). *Dissertation Abstracts International*, 1978, *38*(10), 5931A.

Thomason, T. C., Arbuckle, T., & Cody, D. Test of the eye-movement hypothesis of neurolinguistic programming. *Perceptual and Motor Skills*, 1980, *51*, 230.

Wilimek, J. F. The use of language representational systems by high and low marital adjustment couples. (Doctoral dissertation, The University of Utah, 1979). *Dissertation Abstracts International*, 1980, *40*(7), 3914A.

Yapko, M. D. Neuro-linguistic programming, hypnosis, and interpersonal influence. (Doctoral dissertation, United States International University, 1980). *Dissertation Abstracts International*, 1981, *41*(8), 3204B.

Yapko, M. D. The effect of matching primary representational system predicates on hypnotic relaxation. *The American Journal of Clinical Hypnosis*, 1981, *23*, 169-175.

Donald William McCormick *is an organizational consultant and researcher. He began studying with Grinder and Bandler in 1974 and conducted the first quantitative research on their ideas. He is completing his doctoral dissertation at Case Western Reserve University's Department of Organizational Behavior. Mr. McCormick's major interests are working with political organizations and the connection between personal growth and work. He has consulted and conducted research in a wide variety of organizations, including the Carter White House.*

ENCOURAGING MANAGERS TO DEAL
WITH MARGINAL EMPLOYEES

J. William Pfeiffer

A continual challenge for both internal and external consultants is to assist managers in dealing with the poor performance of subordinates. Issues around incompetence abound in virtually every organization, and employee performance is—or should be—a bottom-line concern in all of them. Internal and external consultants are in a unique position in organizational life and frequently are able to influence the processes by which management decisions regarding hiring, promotion, and termination are made. In this area, we can be especially helpful to our clients— the organizations in which we consult—in helping them to identify and deal with marginal employees. We can assist management in realizing that if the substandard performance of an employee cannot be corrected in a cost-efficient manner, termination of that employee is the most appropriate solution.

Many consultants are surprised at the frequency with which managers voice their concerns about the issue of productivity and performance. One way for consultants to build credibility, then, is to address these concerns and to actively explore the topic and its implications for managers.

A PERFORMANCE-ANALYSIS MODEL

An innovative way of describing the degrees of effectiveness of people in organizations can be extrapolated from the now classic, product-analysis model of the Boston Consulting Group. This two-dimensional model (Figure 1) evaluates products in terms of their market share and their potential for market growth.

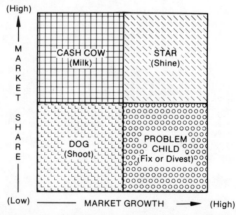

Figure 1. Product-Analysis Model Developed by the Boston Consulting Group

The market-share axis indicates from low to high the amount of the market share commanded by the particular product being analyzed. The market-growth axis indicates the potential for product growth in terms of future sales. A product that is low in both existing market share and potential for market growth is called a "dog," and what one does with an old, ailing dog is put it out of its misery. Products that are low in market growth but high in market share are called "cash cows"; obviously, one milks these. Products that are low in market share but that have growth potential need to be developed; these are the "problem children." If these can be developed efficiently—to have high market share and high market growth—they become "stars." If not, they are divested, dropped. Marketing energy is best put into shining the stars. The analogy is weak in places and it reflects that way that marketing people talk, but it does get the point across.

George Odiorne, the man who popularized management by objectives, has creatively extended the product-analysis model to describe employee performance. The two dimensions in Odiorne's model (Figure 2) are the *performance* of the individual, from low to high, and the *potential* of the individual, from low to high. Odiorne describes people who are low in performance and low in potential as "deadwood." Those who are high in performance but low to moderate in potential are called "workhorses." These are the people who get jobs done in organizations. Those people who are high in potential and relatively low in performance are again called "problem children." Finally, those who are high in both performance and potential are the "stars." The implications of and remedies for these classifications are analogous to those in the marketing model.

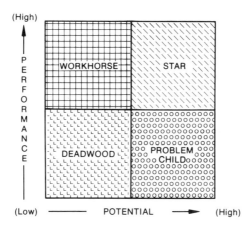

Figure 2. Employee-Performance-Analysis Model Developed by George Odiorne

To take this performance-analysis model a step further, we can substitute the word "productivity" for performance. In the last few years, with the tight economy, organizations have laid off or otherwise divested themselves of a lot of the people who were low in both potential and productivity, the deadwood. Thus, these people probably do not account for one quarter of the employee population, as the matrix model would imply, but for approximately one sixteenth (see Figure 3). In the same vein, the stars probably do not account for a quarter of the working population either—perhaps for one sixteenth of it. The workhorses—the people who keep organizations moving—probably compose almost half the work force. People who are high in potential and low in productivity can be described as either "problem children" or "trainees" in this extension of the model. They number about three sixteenths of the employee population, and different strategies are called for with each of these. Finally, there is a large group of people who are consistently below average in performance and who vary greatly in terms of potential. These are the "marginal" employees. They form approximately one fourth of the employee population.

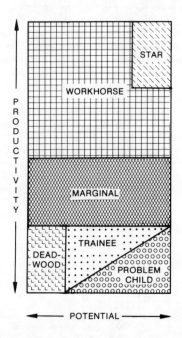

Figure 3. Productivity-Potential Matrix Profile

MANAGERS AND THE MARGINAL EMPLOYEE

A marginal employee may have the proper training, may be committed to the task, and may expend effort at the task, but still may not be able to produce the results that are needed in order for the organization to meet its goals.

For a variety of reasons, managers have tended to be ineffective in dealing with most aspects of substandard performance. Most of the questions brought to the human resource consultant in an organization are related to efforts to bring marginal employees up to standard. Obviously, an inordinate amount of time is spent in trying to "develop" these people, and scarce management resources are expended in the wrong place. This seems peculiar, because if you tell most senior managers that they have made a bad investment with respect to capital outlay, they quickly realize that it is not a good idea to spend good money after bad. If the ship does not float, they scrap the design. But over and over again, consultants find managers at all levels putting time and energy into working with the wrong people—those who do not perform consistently.

A common reason for this ineffective management practice is the "savior syndrome"—the belief of managers that they can make a difference where others have failed. The fallacy in this attitude is believing that the method of approach makes the difference. In most cases, it is doubtful that anything will remedy the situation other than removing the person from the particular job.

Obviously, people are not simply competent or incompetent but are to some degree competent (or incompetent) to do a specific task or array of tasks. Someone who does not perform well in a particular job (array of tasks) may still be capable of doing well in a different job. If the organization has an alternative job available, and if the role match, rather than the individual, is the source of the problem, the solution may be obvious. Unfortunately, however, the situation is not usually so tidy. In most cases, the individual is simply not capable of performing at the level that is required by the job for which he or she was hired.

Another trap into which many managers fall is that of collusion. If people think that they "should" or are expected to do something, they often do it, even against their better judgment. "Developing" employees has become such a value in many organizations that many managers (and trainers) have lost sight of several facts:

1. The people with *potential* are going to provide a return to the organization for its investment in the development effort.

2. It is unfeasible to search continually for the unique blend of insight and ability that *might* be able to make a workhorse out of a marginal employee.

3. Again, some people simply cannot be developed to fit into the jobs that happen to be available in the organization.

In any task, there is an appropriate place to stop. This does not sound like a "nice" thing to say, so people develop the habit of colluding, pretending that everybody has potential if they can just find the right way to tap it.

Another reason why managers do not deal effectively with marginal employees is that most people tend to avoid conflict. It is difficult to terminate an employee, transfer someone to another job, or provide constructive discipline. Furthermore, many managers do not have the skills to feel comfortable in doing these things or to do them effectively. The easiest tactic is to simply ignore the situation and hope that it will take care of itself. In many organizations, marginal employees are given average salary increases and average performance appraisals and are then shuffled from one work group to another.

Obviously, none of these practices is of optimum benefit to the organization, and the realistic probability that the situation will improve in most cases is low to nonexistent.

THE ROLE OF THE CONSULTANT

The most difficult role of the consultant—and yet the most crucial—is to help managers to realize that their job is to benefit the organization, not to "save" people. First of all, managers must be reminded that what benefits the organization is increased productivity. That is the goal of most management and training efforts. Secondly, managers must be helped to examine their past efforts to deal with the people who, for whatever reasons, are simply not capable of producing what is required in the jobs they hold. One tactic is to ask "How many times have you actually been successful?" and, then, "How much time and effort has this required?," "What is the impact of this effort on the other aspects of your job and the other employees in your work unit?," and "Is this really an effective way to utilize your work time and energy?"

When people are allowed to stay in jobs in which they are performing marginally, they know it and, worse, their peers know it. After a while, their peers stop trying to train them, or "cover" for them, or even support them, because these peers have their own jobs to worry about. In the final analysis, it does long-term damage to individuals, to the work group, and to the organization to keep people in marginal roles. Managers need to realize that the humane thing to do is to confront marginality, although it takes some energy to do it, and that it is truly more humane to do this than to let people limp along in jobs that they are not able to do, and that their peers know that they are not able to do, while expecting other people in the organization to either take up the slack or to continue to work at *their* maximum potential despite the obvious discrepancies.

Once managerial behavior has been "unfrozen" in this regard, the consultant can begin to take the manager through a sequence of steps that will help to determine the sources of marginal performance in an organization and what the manager can do about them.

The OD Sequence

It is premature to attempt to deal with issues of individual competence until:

- roles have been adequately clarified
- in the context of an appropriate structure
- to meet obtainable organizational goals.

If what a person is supposed to be doing in an organization is vague or inaccurate, and if the structure in which he or she is supposed to perform tasks is not appropriate to the tasks or to the goals that are to be met, the issue of the person's competence is a symptom rather than a problem. As any professional consultant knows, numerous organizational problems can be solved by adequately defining roles and responsibilities, providing the appropriate structure to accomplish the work, and making sure that the organization's goals are clear and that the work tasks and the structure support and contribute to the achievement of those goals.

If these requirements are met, the issue of individual employee competence is best dealt with through the development of realistic standards of competence for specific jobs, the sharing of information concerning these standards, and consistent action to maintain them. Managers must be clear about what they mean when they describe someone's job performance as "unsatisfactory," "lacking in quality," or "not up to standard."

Assuming that a manager has identified a subordinate who meets the definition provided earlier of a "marginal" employee, it may be helpful to have the manager assess the employee along the dimensions shown in Figure 4.

Name of Employee_____ Name of Manager_____

Circle the appropriate response for each of the following questions:

Competence	Marginally Competent		Competent		Very Competent
1. How well does the individual *currently* accomplish the responsibility of being *task competent* in his/her present job?	1	2	3	4	5

Management Effort	More Than Average Effort		Average Effort		Less Than Average Effort
2. How much management effort does it take to enable the individual to function at his/her most effective level?	1	2	3	4	5

Effect on the System	Negatively		Neither Consistently Positive or Negative		Positively
3. In what way does the individual's behavior (verbal and nonverbal) impact the system?	1	2	3	4	5

Figure 4. Job-Fit Evaluation Form

If the total rating for an individual is below nine points, it is likely that the manager actually is dealing with a marginal employee. There are then several questions that the consultant should ask, and it may take some time and effort for the manager to answer each of them completely.

1. *Does the individual know that he or she is performing marginally?* An incredible number of times, the employee has not been advised of his or her poor performance or of the possible consequences of that level of performance. Many of these people have been transferred from one job to another, some may even have been promoted over the course of time, but it is likely that very few of them actually have been confronted with their performance deficiencies.

The message for the manager is "document it!" An initial interview with the employee may reveal a problem in the employee's private life or a work-related problem that may or may not be amenable to adjustment. Whatever the manager's perception of the cause of the performance deficit, it should be documented in a letter or memorandum to the employee following the interview. Of course, the organization's legal counsel should be consulted if termination is likely to be deemed appropriate, but a few basic guidelines can be offered here. One is that the description of the performance deficit should be behaviorally and quantifiably based. A second is that the employee should be allowed a specific amount of time in which to show improvement in job performance (and may be asked to sign a statement confirming that he or she understands and agrees to this probationary period). It is imperative that the employee be informed of the reasons for the manager's dissatisfaction with his or her work.

2. *How has the manager or organization justified the retention of marginal employees?* In this respect, what are the norms of the organizational culture? It is important to emphasize the negative impact on co-workers when less productive employees are treated the same way as their more productive counterparts. The message that flows through the organizational culture can easily be interpreted as "management really does not *know* who produces" or, even worse, "management really does not *care* if workers produce." The consultant can help managers to realize that confronting substandard productivity has the potential to send a positive message into the system: "Management knows what is happening and it is concerned about productivity."

In addition, although a major focus in most organizations is on the bottom line, the positive- or negative-balance aspect of existing "human resources" simply may never have been perceived as a quantifiable item. Managers can be helped to view human resources just as they view other necessary, perhaps limited, but adjustable aspects of the organizational system.

3. *What is the organization doing to reward productivity and discourage marginal performance?* People in American organizations typically have come to believe that they should be rewarded for *competence*. If a person has the training, education, or experience required to do a job, he or she expects to be rewarded for having achieved that level of expertise. Another expectation is that *commitment* will be rewarded, that is, exhibiting loyalty and dedication, "not making waves," and "fitting in" will result in pay increases and promotions. A third is the expectation of reward for *effort*, for working long, hard hours; coming in early; staying late; and working through the lunch hour or on the weekend. Finally, there is the expectation that *results* will be rewarded. In the traditional organization, people are rewarded for competence, commitment, effort, and results, in some array (see Figure 5).

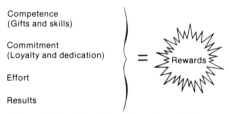

Figure 5. Traditional Employee Expectations

However, experience seems to show that organizations that are excellent in terms of productivity and in terms of growing and nurturing people are organizations in which a primary basis for rewards is positive results—performance (see Figure 6).

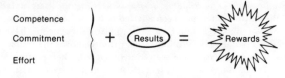

Figure 6. Results-Oriented Reward System

The role of the consultant may be limited here, unless the organization supports a results-oriented approach to employee productivity and rewards. But even at the managerial level, the consultant can help to focus individual efforts to clarify expectations about what level of performance is *expected* and what will generate additional rewards. In many cases, the censure or dismissal of an employee who is widely known to be a substandard producer will send a message throughout the system that incompetence will not be tolerated.

CONCLUSION

As more and more organizations become concerned with productivity and the need to re-examine their utilization of human resources, managers increasingly will be required to justify or deal with the marginal employees for whom they are accountable. Both internal and external human resource consultants will be called on to provide managers with the insights and skills they need to minimize the human and financial drain that is created by people in the organization who are not capable of fulfilling the role requirements of the positions they hold.

J. William Pfeiffer, Ph.D., J.D., is the president of University Associates, Inc., San Diego, California. He consults internationally with a variety of organizations and has a special interest in working with boards of directors/trustees to enhance their legal accountability and organizational effectiveness. He also specializes in the management of change, strategic planning, organization development, leadership/management development, and the training of trainers. Dr. Pfeiffer is the co-editor of the Annuals (1972-1984), the Handbooks of Structured Experiences for Human Relations Training (Volumes I-IX), and the Reference Guide to Handbooks and Annuals.

CONTRIBUTORS

Linda S. Ackerman
President
Linda S. Ackerman, Inc.
3001 Veazey Terrace, N.W.
#813
Washington, D.C. 20008
(202) 364-1147

Warren Bennis, Ph.D.
Joseph DeBell Distinguished Professor of
  Management and Organization
School of Business Administration
Bridge Hall 300A
University of Southern California
Los Angeles, California 90089-1421
(213) 743-8317

Kaaren S. Brown
Assistant Professor
Department of Social Work
King Hall
Eastern Michigan University
Ypsilanti, Michigan 48197
(313) 487-0393

Nadine J. (Hoffman) Carpenter
#3 Merrimack Street, Apt. 1
Concord, New Hampshire 03301
(603) 225-7423

Phyliss Cooke, Ph.D.
Director of Professional Services
  and Dean, MHRD Program
University Associates, Inc.
8517 Production Avenue
San Diego, California 92121
(619) 578-5900

James I. Costigan, Ph.D.
Chairperson
Department of Communication
Fort Hays State University
600 Park Street
Hays, Kansas 67601-4099
(913) 625-5365

Stephen Dakin, Ph.D.
Senior Lecturer
Department of Business Administration
University of Canterbury
Private Bag
Christchurch, New Zealand
  482-009

Dennis M. Dennis, Ph.D., R.N.
Fourth and Pike Building
1424 Fourth Avenue, Suite 903
Seattle, Washington 98101
(206) 628-0083

Patrick E. Doyle
Kingston Campus
St. Lawrence College
Kingston, Ontario, Canada K7L 5A6
(613) 544-5400

Robert E. Enggist, Ph.D.
Rob Enggist Associates
54 Princeton-Hightstown Road
P.O. Box 716
Princeton Junction, New Jersey 08550
(609) 799-6098

David J. Foscue
2910 West Orlando Drive
Pine Bluff, Arkansas 71603
(501) 879-2145

Barbara Schneider Fuhrmann, Ed.D.
Associate Professor
School of Education
Virginia Commonwealth University
1015 West Main Street
Richmond, Virginia 23284
(804) 257-1305

Leonard D. Goodstein, Ph.D.
Chairman of the Board
University Associates, Inc.
8517 Production Avenue
San Diego, California 92121
(619) 578-5900

Ronne Toker Jacobs
President
Ronne Jacobs Associates
401 September Drive
Richmond, Virginia 23229
(804) 741-3388

Joseph J. Lengermann, Ph.D.
Associate Professor
Department of Sociology
University of Maryland
College Park, Maryland 20742
(301) 454-5508

John C. Lewis
President
Lewis and Pike Associates
3250 Hedda Court
San Jose, California 95127
(408) 258-8123

Debera Libkind, Ph.D.
Management Development Specialist
Anheuser-Busch Companies
One Busch Place
St. Louis, Missouri 63118
(314) 577-4226

Donald M. Loppnow
Department Head and Professor
Department of Social Work
King Hall
Eastern Michigan University
Ypsilanti, Michigan 48197
(313) 487-0393

Willem F.G. Mastenbroek, Ph.D.
Managing Partner
Organisatie Adviesgroep Nederland
Singel 399
Amsterdam, 1012 WN, The Netherlands
(020) 224737

Donald William McCormick
Acting Instructor
Department of Organizational Behavior
Case Western Reserve University
Cleveland, Ohio 44106
(216) 368-2128

Michael J. Miller, Ph.D.
Chair and Associate Professor
Department of Supervision
Indiana-Purdue University
2101 Coliseum Boulevard East
Fort Wayne, Indiana 46805
(219) 482-5316

Kenneth L. Murrell, D.B.A.
Associate Professor
Management Department
University of West Florida
Pensacola, Florida 32504
(904) 474-2308

John E. Oliver, Ph.D.
Associate Professor
Department of Management
Valdosta State College
Valdosta, Georgia 31698
(912) 247-3262

Udai Pareek, Ph.D.
c/o Dr. Rolf Lynton
Jl. Wijaya IV/12
Kebayoran, Baru
Jakarta, Indonesia

J. William Pfeiffer, Ph.D., J.D.
President
University Associates, Inc.
8517 Production Avenue
San Diego, California 92121
(619) 578-5900

T. Venkateswara Rao, Ph.D.
Larsen & Toubro Professor of
    Human Resources Development
Xavier Labour Relations Institute
C.H. Area East
P.O. Box 222
Jamshedpur 831 001
Bihar, India

Raymond V. Rasmussen, Ph.D.
Associate Professor of Organizational Behavior
Faculty of Business
The University of Alberta
Edmonton, Alberta, Canada T6G 2G1
(403) 432-2458

Russell Robb
Regional Training Officer
North Canterbury Hospital Board
10 Oxford Terrace
Private Bag
Christchurch, New Zealand

John A. Sample
Executive Director
Professional Development Specialists, Inc.
225 Lexington Road
Tallahassee, Florida 32312
(904) 385-0751

Marshall Sashkin, Ph.D.
Professor of Industrial and
    Organizational Psychology
Graduate Program, University College
University of Maryland
University Boulevard at Adelphi Road
College Park, Maryland 20742
(301) 454-2333

Martha A. Schmeidler
Director of Religious Education
St. Joseph's Parish
215 West 13th Street
Hays, Kansas 67601
(913) 628-2311

Allen J. Schuh, Ph.D.
Professor, Management Sciences
School of Business and Economics
California State University
Hayward, California 94542
 (415) 881-3322

Marc A. Silverman
Director, Organization Consulting Services
Silverman and Associates, Inc.
172 Cushing Street
Providence, Rhode Island 02906
 (401) 272-6490

Donald T. Simpson
104 Tarrytown Road
Rochester, New York 14618
 (716) 244-8556

Elizabeth Solender
Manager of Human Resources
Sun Exploration & Production Company
P.O. Box 2880
Dallas, Texas 75221-2880
 (214) 739-9651

Joe Thomas, Ph.D.
Assistant Professor of
 Business Administration
Northeast Missouri State University
Kirksville, Missouri 63501
 (816) 785-4370

Arthur Zobrist, Dipl. Psych.
Director
Institute for Organizational Psychology
 and Management Development
Geissmattstrasse 34
Lucerne 6004, Switzerland
 (041) 22-88-84